World Wise
Your passport to safer travel

GW00706027

world wise

Your Passport to
SAFER TRAVEL

by Mark Hodson

and The Suzy Lamplugh Trust
The National Charity for Personal Safety

With the World Wise Directory of
information for travellers

Published by Thomas Cook Publishing
PO Box 227
Thorpe Wood
Peterborough
PE3 6PU
United Kingdom

ISBN 1 900341 14 X

Editor: Deborah Parker
Editorial Assistant: Leyla Davies
Text and cover design and illustrations: Amanda Plant
Text typeset in Flareserif, Impact and Arial using QuarkXpress for Windows
Text imagesetting by Fisherprint Ltd, Peterborough
Printed in Great Britain by Fisherprint Ltd, Peterborough

The Publishers acknowledge the assistance of the Youth Exchange Centre of the British Council in the publication of this book.

Supported by the European Commission's Youth for Europe Programme.

The Publishers acknowledge the contribution of The Prince's Trust towards the research upon which this book is based.

Contents

The Prince's Trust
Helping Young People to Succeed

The Prince's Trust aims to help young people to succeed by providing opportunities which they would otherwise not have.

We target those young people who, through disadvantage or lack of opportunity, are failing to reach their full potential. We help them fulfil their ambitions, improve their skills and make a real contribution to their community.

We achieve this through a nation-wide network which delivers practical advice and counselling, support for business start-ups, loans and grants, training, local projects, personal development and support for study outside school. We help both individuals and groups.

Our core target group is young people between the ages of 14 and 25. In some of our programmes, we also address the needs of those who are as young as 11 and up to the age of 30.

To find out how The Prince's Trust can help you, call 0800 842842.

Foreword by HRH The Prince of Wales

ST. JAMES'S PALACE

I was delighted to learn that my Trust has lent its support to the production of this very useful book. Foreign travel is more accessible for young people than it has ever been, which is splendid, but there are hidden dangers for the unprepared that can mean foreign trips end in disaster.

This book will help young travellers gain more from their time abroad. It is a rich source of information, and includes details about the enormously different cultures and lifestyles that thrive in each country in the world. The book also includes an invaluable guide to personal safety. Equipped with this book, the reader will learn much more about the sights and sounds they experience as they go, while travelling wisely and safely.

I would like to thank everyone at The Suzy Lamplugh Trust, Thomas Cook Publishing and all those who assisted in making the whole project a reality. I am pleased that The Prince's Trust, by agreeing to support the research which lies behind it, has been able to play its part in helping young people to travel widely and with a greater sense of security.

Charles

Acknowledgements ─────────────── 8

The Suzy Lamplugh Trust is most grateful to:

The Prince's Trust, for enabling this book to be published by funding the research, and the initial directory, on which the book is based.

The British Council for providing funds to assist the actual publication of this book.

The Foreign and Commonwealth Office, for providing funds to put the Directory on the Internet and for it to be regularly updated.

Oxford Brookes University, for help, support and encouragement.

The Educational Broadcasting Services Trust, for doing so much to get the project off the ground.

Without the help of all these organisations, and indeed of Thomas Cook Publishing, this book would not have come about. We thank you all.

Thomas Cook Publishing would also like to thank the following for the assistance they have given in the compilation of this book:

Charlotte Bendy, MoneyGram; Catherine Berger, Europay; Amanda Catteano, American Express; Samantha Chiles for additional research; Janice Gardner and Kate Garrod, The EBS Trust; Wendy Kochan, MasterCard; Meetali Sachdeva and Tammy Dolling at Thomas Cook Financial Services; Anne Strahan, The Suzy Lamplugh Trust; Prof. Roger Zetter and Simon Horton, Oxford Brookes University.

Introduction

Our eldest daughter Suzy disappeared one sunny summer's day in 1986 during her normal everyday work. She has now been presumed murdered and declared dead. We never cease to miss her and remember her with great joy.

When Suzy rang me on the Friday before that dark Monday when she totally vanished from our lives, she told me with excitement of all the things which she was doing. 'Aren't you overdoing things, darling?' I asked. 'Come on Mum' she said 'life is for living – don't forget that!'

I never have, and I now live with that thought in my heart. Life is for living, but real living needs quality. This means living with the freedom to choose, be ourselves and yet respect and value each other. To be able to do this, we need to live without harassment and fear of danger; to go out and live life to the full and to do so safely.

This is why the mission of The Suzy Lamplugh Trust, set up in the name of our daughter, is to provide practical personal safety for everyone, everywhere, every day. Travelling abroad is such an important part of living life to the full that we felt we ought to explore the risks and possible pitfalls.

We always joked with our children, saying that they and their friends seemed hell-bent on getting their 'BTA' – Been to America/Africa/Australia/Asia – before setting out seriously to earn their living, but since my children explored the world there has been an increase in international travel by young people. Cheaper travel and simple means of transferring money bring more and more exotic destinations within easy reach and make it possible to stay away for longer and longer periods. Effectively planned and prepared for, international travel can be both an education and a challenging experience which opens the mind to both the diversity and common interests shared by countries and peoples across the world.

The vast majority of young people return home safely and with a sense of personal fulfilment and enrichment. However, sometimes things can go wrong: not just the media headline cases but the unreported incidents – theft, health problems, breaches of political or cultural codes for example – or there is a 'fortunate near miss'. These experiences can provoke great anxiety; at worst, they may have severe physical or psychological consequences (for the travellers and their families) which undermine the positive benefits.

It became clear that a major cause of problems has been the misunderstanding or ignorance of the differences between cultures. Social relations, food, dress, body language, hospitality, photography, amongst other factors, all need to be considered if insensitive behaviour, and sometimes potentially dangerous situations, are to be avoided.

The Suzy Lamplugh Trust commissioned a study which is the basis for *World Wise.* We are most grateful to Thomas Cook for publishing this excellent book. Its publication coincides with the creation of a new website by Oxford Brookes University, on behalf of The Suzy Lamplugh Trust. This makes available, on the internet, regularly updated, the directory of advice for over 220 countries at htttp://www.brookes.ac.uk/worldwise.

I have no doubt that while this book does raise awareness about the problems of personal safety, it will also encourage people to travel and will build up confidence in those who have not previously thought that international travel was for them. The book will also, I hope, give some peace of mind for those of us who are left behind!

Diana Lamplugh, OBE
Director, The Suzy Lamplugh Trust

About the authors

Mark Hodson

Mark Hodson has spent a total of 18 months backpacking around Asia and Latin America, and has visited some of the world's most notorious trouble spots from El Salvador and Nicaragua to the Philippines and Northern Pakistan.

He has worked in London, Hong Kong, New York, the Bahamas and Holland (where he lived in a tent and packed flower bulbs). He now writes for the Travel section of The Sunday Times. He is 33 and lives in South London.

The Suzy Lamplugh Trust

The Suzy Lamplugh Trust is the national charity for personal safety, whose mission is to create a safer society and enable everyone to live safer lives.

The Trust encourages people to live life to the full and to travel with confidence – and to do so safely. It provides practical personal safety for everyone, every day, everywhere.

Information about the Trust's resources and training may be obtained from: The Suzy Lamplugh Trust, 14 East Sheen Avenue, London SW14 8AS.

The Suzy Lamplugh Trust is a registered charity, number 802567.

This book has its origins in research conducted on behalf of The Suzy Lamplugh Trust by Oxford Brookes University. This involved interviews with travellers under the age of 25. Many of their experiences are included in this book, through the quotes reproduced in the text.

We would like to thank all those listed below who have contributed to the book through their own words:

Emma Amies
Ady Bungay
Juliet Coombe
Cheryl Cowling
Anna Davies
Brendan Fox
Faith Hagerty
Will Hagerty
Jo Kennedy and Liz Hardy
Diana Lamplugh
Stephanie Miles
Jean-Paul Penrose
Nathan Pope
Victoria Powers
Fiona Pride
Paul Radziwill
Emma Turrell-Clarke

Travel can be a great adventure. The purpose of this book is to encourage people to travel – but in safety.

World Wise – your passport to safer travel has its roots in a report commissioned by The Suzy Lamplugh Trust and researched by Oxford Brookes University. The report related the experiences of young travellers and their thoughts on making themselves safer, especially where they felt they had made mistakes and put themselves in danger. Mark Hodson has based the first section of this book upon this report, as well as drawing on his own extensive travel experiences.

Ideally, you should read this book when you are starting to think about travelling. There is a lot of safety advice and information packed into the first section, so reread it to absorb it all.

This book is pocket-sized and lightweight so that you can carry it around, and use it for reference during your journey.

Your passport to safer travel

- Read through all of the first section well before you start out on your travels.

- Note down any points you need to research further or investigate.

- Use the *More information* chapter, which lists useful contacts, as your starting point for your research

- Then look up any countries in the Directory that you think you might want to travel to.

The Directory

- When you have decided which countries you intend to visit, photocopy these pages and leave them, together with an itinerary, with a member of your family or a friend.

- The Directory is prefaced with an explanation of the symbols and categories used in the country-by-country listing.

- Also explained are health issues and religious observances highlighted in the Directory.

Just before you go...

- Check out updated pages of the Directory on the World Wise website at http://www.brookes.ac.uk/worldwise before you set off.

- The listings in the Directory section were up to date at time of publication, but the information contained within it is liable to change – so browse the website before for the very latest information.

The Suzy Lamplugh Trust offer their own 'PLAN' to help you remain safe, wherever you travel.

Prepare YOURSELF
Plan your journey
Wear sensible clothing
Assess the risks
Leave an itinerary with someone

Avoid PUTTING YOURSELF AT RISK
Your aim is to remain safe
Be wary of strangers
Assess the risks as you venture into new territory

Look CONFIDENT
Be alert and have a sense of purpose
Know where you are going and how to get there
Carry a personal alarm

Never ASSUME
It won't happen to me
They look respectable

Do not ignore your instincts

Your passport to safer travel

Planning your trip

● *Get thinking*

If life was like the movies you would need nothing more than a suitcase, a pair of shades and an open-top sports car. The idea of just hitting the road and leaving behind the monotony of everyday life is enough to get anyone's heart racing. But road movies rarely have happy endings. Think of Thelma and Louise, Easy Rider, Wild at Heart. All those films looked like a whole heap of fun in the first reel but they all ended in disaster.

This doesn't mean you should abandon your dreams of going away. Travel is one of the greatest thrills that life has to offer. Few experiences can compare with the head-spinning, eye-popping excitement of arriving for the first time in a foreign country where every sight, sound, taste and smell is new. It's like sex – you never forget your first time.

Travel is easy but it does involve some element of risk. To abandon everything familiar in your life and place yourself in a totally alien environment can be a daunting, unsettling experience. It can also, if you're not careful, be a dangerous one. That's why you need to have your wits about you, to know something about the country you're visiting, to know something about yourself and to understand how local people see you.

While you are gazing at maps and dreaming about your big trip, your parents and friends may be telling you all the things that might go wrong. In reality, there are two major problems you're most likely to run into – getting sick and being robbed. But neither of these need seriously affect your trip provided you're well prepared, and know what to do if they happen to you. That's one way this book will help – with advice on things like money, insurance and health precautions, and what to do if you get in trouble.

Planning your trip

Getting sick and being robbed are not the only things that can go wrong when you travel – you may breach a cultural code or have a lucky escape. The purpose of this book is to help you avoid these risks, by being well prepared, and knowing what to do if they happen.

● Where, when and who with?

Before you rush out and buy an air ticket or an Inter-Rail pass, think about the kind of trip you want to take. Don't just follow the crowds – consider which parts of the world really interest you. Start browsing through the Internet and reading books, newspapers and magazine articles about the countries you might want to visit. If you're going abroad to work or study, try to learn as much as you can about the area where you'll be staying. If you're interested in art, architecture or food you'll get a lot more out of your trip if you read up on the subject. Don't be just another gormless tourist going from one sight to the next, understanding nothing.

Think whether you want to travel alone, with a group, with a best friend or with a boyfriend or girl-friend. Travelling alone can be a more thrilling experience, giving you maximum exposure to a foreign culture, but it can be more stressful, especially if you get sick or something goes wrong. It will

Planning your trip

also be more expensive if you can't find other travellers to share rooms, taxis and organised tours.

> When I set off around the world most people thought I would be starting a year of loneliness and introspection. All those fears were unfounded. I soon found travelling partners with whom I shared common interests and goals.

In some countries travelling alone is dangerous, particularly if you're a woman. It's a shame, but in many parts of the world a lone female with Western clothes is immediately assumed to be sexually available.

If you travel with a friend you'll probably be safer, but you may have to compromise your own plans. Talk honestly with your intended travel partner about how you each want to spend your time

If you travel on your own, you need to be extra vigilant – there is no one else to look out for you. Careful planning is even more important.

and what you hope to achieve. You might learn that even your best friend has very different ideas about what would make an interesting trip. If you can, go away for a weekend together to see if you would make good travel partners.

If you're looking for an adventurous outdoors trip with minimum danger – and if you're a sociable type – you might consider joining an overland truck tour, travelling across Africa, Asia or South America for up to six months. If you want to contribute to a worthwhile project you could try raising enough sponsorship money to join an environmental expedition where you might be drilling wells in Africa or building orang-utan shelters in Indonesia. You'll find contact numbers for these organisations on pages 96–97.

By doing your own research you'll also learn why there is often a 'wrong' time of year to visit certain countries. For instance, it makes sense to avoid Goa in June and July (the Indian monsoon), and the Caribbean in early September (hurricane season). Don't rely on travel agents or airlines to volunteer this information – check the weather details for each country you intend to visit in the Directory. For the most up-to-date information, visit the

Planning your trip

World Wise website at http://www.brookes.ac.uk/worldwise.

> We arrived by boat at Patras with no Greek money to find the country in the middle of a general strike. All the banks were closed and there were no trains running. If only we had found this out before getting on the boat!

Cultural and political differences can also affect the timing of your trip. Think twice before visiting a strict Muslim country during the month of Ramadan, when restaurants are closed during the day. In politically unstable areas of Asia, Africa and Latin America it's best to avoid general elections when political rallies and demonstrations can quickly turn to riots. The best way to stay in touch is to read a good newspaper.

If you intend to make an extensive overland tour of an undeveloped country invest in a detailed map – it's usually easier to find them at home than once you arrive – and take a good look at the road and rail network to ensure that your plans are not too ambitious. In some parts of the world it might take all day just to cover 50 miles – and that's without punctures and breakdowns. It's a good rule to try not to see and do too much.

Sadly, some parts of the world remain completely off-bounds to travellers because of war, famine or a risk of kidnapping. These include large parts of central Africa, the Indian states of Jammu and Kashmir, Algeria and some remote regions of Indonesia. You shouldn't assume that just because these areas don't appear on the TV news every night that they're safe. They are not.

Use all the resources at your disposal. Borrow guidebooks from your local library, contact tourist boards and embassies, search the Internet and speak to travellers who have recently returned from the countries you intend to visit. You'll also find lots of useful details in the Directory section of this book, including tourist office addresses, hints on currency and transport safety and general information on each country.

For current safety information, use the Foreign Office travel advice service which is updated daily and published on both Ceefax and the Internet. The address is given on page 96.

Planning your trip

● *Buying air tickets*

Before you make a final decision about where and when to go, take a look at how the prices of airline tickets fluctuate throughout the year. You can often save a fortune by delaying the start of your trip by just a few months. For instance, a round-the-world ticket on a popular route such as London-Bombay-Singapore-Bangkok-Sydney-Christchurch-Auckland-Fiji-Los Angeles-London would have cost you £1585 if you had set off in December 1997. But if you had waited until April 1998 to go, the same ticket would have cost just £892, a saving of almost £700.

Find a travel agent or ticketing agent with IATA bonding who specialises in selling the kind of tickets you want. There's no point phoning a bucket shop that sells last-minute charter flights to Spain if you want a discounted multistop ticket to Australia. Nor should you go direct to the airline – the fare will almost certainly be a lot higher. Instead, use the experience and expertise of an agent who knows the parts of the world you're interested in, and how to get the maximum available discounts on those routes.

Don't try to cut too many corners on price. An agent who can sell you the same ticket slightly cheaper than a rival probably has to compromise on service, so if you ring back with an urgent query about your ticket you may find the phone permanently engaged. Similarly, don't always opt for the cheapest fare. If you pay a bit extra to fly on a more reputable airline you're not just paying for a more comfortable flight, you're getting a better safety record, better reliability, more direct routing and less chance of delays. Generally speaking, the bigger airlines suffer fewer long delays because they have the capacity to draft in an alternative aircraft if yours develops a fault.

Many budget travellers make the mistake of buying a cheap ticket to somewhere they don't really want to go, often believing that once they arrive there they can buy another cheap ticket to their intended destination. Nine times out of ten they're disappointed. A flight from, say, Rio to Buenos Aires may be cheaper in London than it is if bought in Rio.

Always buy a two-way ticket that allows you to come home at any time – you may run out of money earlier than you thought. If you don't think you can afford a return ticket, then can you really afford to go?

While travel agents are useful sources of advice on ticketing, they won't be able to tell you which countries you should visit. That's something you need to decide on before you call them. And don't let them persuade you to buy tickets you don't need. Some agents will try to sell you air passes within a country, which may offer, say, 30 days of unlimited flights for, say, £300. These deals may look tempting but to make them worthwhile you'd have to charge about the country spending half your time in airports. You're better off travelling more slowly and getting to know places better.

Finally, you must remember to reconfirm flights as you go, particularly when travelling in developing countries. All tickets carry a warning that you need to reconfirm them within 72 hours of the flight and although this isn't strictly necessary on airlines travelling within Europe, it is vital in other parts of the world. If you don't ring the airline within 72 hours of your departure time, you run the risk of losing your reservation. Any travel agent will be able to do it, but, to be doubly sure, make the call yourself.

● *Gearing up*

If you walk into a specialist travel shop you'll see literally hundreds of items – from crampons to travel washing lines – that manufacturers claim you can't live without. Don't believe a word of it. Unless you plan to climb the northwest face of K2 or sail singlehanded across the Bay of Bengal you can dispense with almost all specialist travel products. Most of the clothes you need will already be in your own wardrobe. If you want to waste your money on a four-season sleeping bag, trekking socks, a pump-action wasp killer and half a dozen tubes of clothes-washing gel, go ahead. But you'll have to carry it all. Never forget the first rule of packing – take half the clothes you think you'll need, and twice the money.

Before I went travelling my friends clubbed together and bought me a good-quality travel pack, the type that zips up into a shoulder bag. It went everywhere with me for two years and is still going strong. I met other travellers with cheap rucksacks that fell apart after a few months.

Rather than buy dozens of small pointless items, invest in a few vital pieces of kit and buy the best you can afford. The most important of these is your backpack. There are dozens of different types of backpacks on the market but in my mind the best option is a 'travel pack', which looks like a big shoulder bag but has one side that zips away to reveal an internal frame that allows it to be worn like a rucksack. This means you can carry a lot of gear on your back in comfort, but you can also look smart when you need to – at immigration checks, police stations or hotel reception desks. Travel packs are easier to lock than conventional rucksacks and they don't tend to get damaged on airport carousels because all the dangling straps and handles that can get caught in machinery are tucked inside the zipped compartment.

Whatever type of pack you decide to buy, make sure it fits you. A good one will have an adjustable frame that can be fitted to your own body shape. The waist strap should sit on your hip bones, not around your waist, and carry most of the weight. Get it right before you leave – don't wait until you're midway through a five-day trek in Thailand or trudging around Athens in mid-August looking for a room.

Don't overpack a rucksack. That's what I did and, even though it was an expensive one, it split within a month.

WHAT TO PACK
ESSENTIALS

money belt ☐

photocopies of all your documents sealed a water-tight bag ☐

padlocks (combination) and small chain (the sort you would use for a bicycle) ☐

Maglite-style torch (doubles as a miniature table lamp) ☐

foam ear plugs, eye shades and inflatable pillow (for long bus journeys and flights) ☐

Swiss Army knife/pen knife (put in your checked bagggage during flights) ☐

string, rubber bands and masking tape ☐

alarm clock (for early starts) ☐

pocket compass ☐

sunblock ☐

sunglasses (with UVP protection) ☐

sun hat or baseball cap ☐

spare passport-size photos of yourself ☐

toilet roll ☐

guidebooks and maps ☐

universal sink plug ☐

first-aid kit (see page 31) ☐

You'll need a daypack (a mini backpack) that's comfortable enough to wear all day long, and bulky enough to hold a guide-book, water bottle, sunglasses, sunblock and camera. It should be lockable and anonymous, so avoid designer labels and garish colours. It should also have two strong shoulder straps so you can wear it on your back with both hands free or swing it round so that it sits on your chest. There are two advan-tages to wearing a daypack on your chest – it helps your balance when you're also carrying a backpack, and it deters pickpockets.

Some travellers wear a bumbag – called a fanny pack in America – to carry cash, a compact camera and other small items. I don't like them because they look like an invitation to thieves and mark you out as a tourist. Some pickpockets don't even bother trying to get their fingers inside them, they just snip the waistband with scissors or slash it with a knife and whisk the whole thing off before you have time to blink. I've seen it happen.

The safest way to carry valuables is in a money belt worn under the front of your trousers, and preferably under a shirt, too. The best ones are made of thin canvas with a zip at the top. Because they're absorbent they can get soaked with sweat in hot weather, so to avoid ruining your cash, cheques and air tickets, put them first in a small sealable plastic folder, like the type you get when buying travellers cheques.

> I imagined it would be a drag having to wear a money belt all the time but I soon got used to it and after a while I would have felt naked without one. Wearing baggy trousers made it a lot more comfortable.

There are dozens of other hidden pockets and wallets on the market, such as neck pouches, invisible pockets and belts with secret zipped compartments, all of which are worth considering. If you're in an area where theft is a very real danger – on some South American bus routes, for instance – you could strap your valuables to one leg with a bandage under long trousers. Some travellers sew $100 bills into the lining of a jacket, which isn't a bad idea so long as you don't lose the jacket or get drenched in a downpour. Others recommend lining your rucksack with chicken wire to deter bag slashers. This isn't a good idea because eventually the wire comes loose and rips your rucksack and your clothes to shreds. I speak from bitter experience on this one. And, yes, I did feel stupid at the time.

You'll need a comfortable pair of walking shoes or boots. It's far better to take one decent pair of shoes rather than two or three shoddy pairs. Wear them in thoroughly before you set off – there are few surer ways of ruining the first couple of weeks of a trip than walking around all day with painful blisters. Don't be tempted to take your favourite trainers as they will make your feet sweat.

When packing clothes, try to stick to lightweight cotton items. Avoid too much black, which absorbs heat, and white, which shows the dirt. In hot climates, lightweight canvas or cotton trousers are a lot more comfortable than jeans. Take at least one jumper or fleece jacket and a set of thermal underwear. If you're going to the tropics this might sound ridiculous but, believe me, you'll need warm clothes, particularly if you spend any time at altitude or in desert areas where nights can be freezing.

Air-conditioned buses are often so cold that you'll wake up in the night shivering.

> **One of the most effective ways to ward off mosquitoes at night is to sleep under a fan in a long-sleeve thermal vest and leggings tucked into socks.**

Pack lots of cotton socks and underwear, which are sometimes hard to buy in undeveloped countries, but not too many T-shirts and pairs of shorts which can be picked up anywhere. T-shirts with naff western logos may be highly prized in some countries so they make good gifts. Make sure you have at least one pair of long trousers (or skirt) and a long-sleeved shirt – you may need it to cover up when visiting temples or churches.

> **Arriving at Windhoek in Namibia before dawn, I was shocked because it was freezing cold. Three hours later we were in the scorching sun in the back of trucks and our hats and sun cream were at the bottom of our rucksacks.**

WHAT TO PACK

CLOTHES

walking shoes or boots ☐

long cotton trousers and/or skirt ☐

T-shirts, shorts, socks, underwear ☐

long-sleeve shirt ☐

sarong (doubles as a towel and beach mat) ☐

thermal vest and leggings ☐

jumper or fleece jacket ☐

flip-flops, leather sandals or sports sandals (for beaches and communal bathrooms) ☐

swimming costume ☐

WASH KIT

toothbrush, toothpaste, soap, shampoo ☐

watertight soap dish ☐

shaving kit (stick soap is lighter and longer-lasting than cans of foam) ☐

washbag (airtight to keep out insects, with a hook for hanging from bathroom doors) ☐

small towel ☐

Try to pack at least one relatively smart outfit (shirt and trousers or a dress) in case you're invited to somebody's house or need to deal with officials. In some remote areas where tourists are a rarity you may even find yourself invited to official functions where muddy boots and a baggy T-shirt wouldn't go down too well. If you can afford it, invest in a pair of specialist travel trousers such as Rohan Globetrotters which are very light, durable, have secret zipped pockets and fold up to the size of a Coke can. They are expensive but well worth it and come in men's and women's sizes. If you've got a

 **WHAT TO PACK**

OPTIONAL ITEMS

camera, film and spare camera battery ☐

shortwave radio (to keep in touch with world news and tune into local stations) ☐

notebook and pens (so you can keep a diary of your travels) ☐

sleep sack (if staying at hostels where linen isn't provided) ☐

small calculator ☐

sewing kit (for repairs to clothes and luggage) ☐

gifts from home (postcards, souvenirs, photographs of your house and family) ☐

rubber door wedge (to stop people entering your room at night) ☐

photo of your travel pack (carry it in your daypack) ☐

pair of combat trousers, leave them at home – in some countries they might get you arrested or mistaken for a paramilitary.

Finally, before setting off try this experiment. Pack everything you plan to take away with you into your rucksack and daypack and put them on, along with your walking shoes and enough layers of clothing to make you feel uncomfortably hot. Now walk for half an hour up and down an unfamiliar crowded street with a map in one hand and a guidebook in the other. Still want to take quite so much stuff? Thought not.

● Who needs guidebooks?

You'd be daft to go abroad without guidebooks (although I have done – in Morocco – and got along just fine) but you'd be equally stupid to treat every word they contain as gospel. Still, that is what some travellers do, particularly in countries like India where almost everybody you meet carries the same guidebook (in this case, the Lonely Planet) and dutifully marches from one recommended guest house to the next, all eating at the same restaurants where – amazingly! – they bump

*There's a lot of useful informa-
tion in the Directory section of
this book. But do also use
guidebooks when planning
your trip – to help you work
out your budget, choose
where to stay that first night,
to find out which areas are safe
to stay in, and to get hints on
local customs, what to tip and
so on.*

into the same people again and
again. I've even met travellers who
refused to stay at perfectly good
hotels because they were not
mentioned in 'the book'. Sad.

> **I got fed up following my
> guidebook so I kept it in
> my rucksack and spent two
> weeks travelling by my own
> wits. It was tricky at times but
> much more rewarding and I
> found places that I would never
> have visited where I saw
> no other Westerners.**

Guidebooks are extremely useful
for picking up general background
information and for orientating
yourself in a new place, but try not
to become dependent on them.
They're not written by gurus or

soothsayers, but ordinary people
who can make mistakes or have
flawed judgment.

Nor are guidebooks always up to
date, particularly in developing
countries where prices change and
restaurants and hotels are continually appearing and disappearing.
By the time some books reach the
shops some of the information
they contain may not be current. If
it's an updated or revised edition,
the author may not have had time
to revisit some remote places
since writing the first edition. On
the other hand, some guidebooks
are published on the Internet, so
they can be updated regularly.

In my experience, some owners of
guesthouses and restaurants recommended in the more popular
guidebooks tend to get lazy
because they know they're guaranteed a steady stream of custom
every day. They may be reluctant
to increase their prices which will
be written in the book, so instead
they allow their standards to drop.
Furniture isn't mended, mattress-
es aren't replaced, the standard of
the food falls and the service
becomes surly rather than welcoming. If you see a newly-opened
rival business down the street that
isn't mentioned in the guidebooks
it may well be smarter and more
friendly, yet empty.

It's possible to dig up vast quantities of travel information on the Internet, though you may have to wade through a lot of irrelevant stuff to find it. And remember, because anybody with access to a newsgroup can post information, you should not believe everything you read.

Once you have decided where you want to go, draw up an itinerary that you can leave with your family or a friend. They may need to contact you.

● *A healthy start*

Make sure you're in good shape before you set off. Start jogging or going to a gym because if you're physically fit you'll have more stamina while travelling and be less likely to fall ill. Ask your doctor for a check-up and make a note of your blood group. If you're a citizen of an EU country and are travelling within the EU get hold of a Form E111, which will guarantee you free or reduced cost emergency medical treatment, available at any post office or freephone 0800 555777.

If you are already taking medication, check with your doctor before you go. Get a letter confirming which drugs you take, giving the generic name in case you need a repeat prescription while you are away. If you have an allergy, ensure you have appropriate medication to counteract the allergy and know how to use it. If you have a medical condition, wear a medic-alert bracelet in case of emergency.

> **I was climbing Tiger Leaping Gorge in China when my mild toothache became so intense that I almost went to a village dentist to have it pulled. In the end I flew to Hong Kong where the extraction cost almost £500. I later found teeth weren't covered on my insurance policy.**

Visit your dentist before you go because you won't want to develop a crippling toothache when you're canoeing up the Amazon or riding a camel across the Sahara. If you plan to travel in undeveloped countries where medical facilities are basic, it's worth investing in a pack of sterile needles and swabs, available from MASTA, the Medical Advisory Service for Travellers Abroad (mail order 0113-239 1707). Boots sells its own version, the Medical Emergency Travellers Kit.

Planning your trip

BASIC FIRST AID KIT

Antiseptic cream ☐

Plasters ☐

Soluble aspirin ☐

Throat lozenges ☐

Anti-diarrhoea tablets ☐

Antihistamine cream ☐

Mosquito repellent ☐

Don't be paranoid about getting sick – the chances of catching a deadly or incurable tropical disease are small. You should see your doctor about two months before travelling to get the various jabs and pills currently on offer. Don't bother with private travel clinics which will give you more or less the same advice but charge a small fortune for it. I found one clinic in London demanding £100 for an armful of jabs that were all available free on the National Health Service.

Most travellers worry about catching malaria and take their daily and weekly tablets with religious adherence. Remember that these pills reduce your chances of catching malaria but they don't make you immune. Malaria is transmitted by mosquitoes and the only sure way to avoid catching the disease is not to get bitten. Mosquito coils, which can be bought almost anywhere, are effective although they're brittle and tend to break when carried in backpacks. Electrical devices that emit a high-pitch note to 'scare off' mosquitoes don't work. If you're planning to get pregnant or already pregnant you might not be able to take malaria tablets – ask your doctor.

Take a good mosquito repellent. I travel with Ultrathon cream, which is used by both the British and US armies and is recommended by Dr Ron Behrens, director of the travel clinic at the Hospital for

Tropical Diseases in London. It contains 33% Deet (the most effective chemical repellent available) which it releases slowly over a 12-hour period, making it particularly effective at night. Look for a similar percentage of Deet (it will be marked on the bottle) if you have to buy repellent abroad. Don't believe people who tell you that malarial mosquitoes only bite at dawn and dusk. Some strains feed from midnight until dawn and those carrying dengue fever can strike at any time during the day.

Because Deet is an unpleasant chemical that dries out your skin and corrodes some types of plastic, some travellers refuse to use it and opt instead for a 'natural' repellent containing an ingredient like citronella or eucalyptus oil. These certainly smell nicer and are more gentle on your skin but there is a problem – they don't work very well.

● *Passports, visas and other boring stuff*

Dig out your passport a least a couple of months before you set off. Check it's valid for at least six months after your intended return date, and that the photograph still

looks like you – if not you can send off a new one to get it changed, but this takes time.

> **I was stopped by an immigration officer who didn't believe that the picture in my passport was of me because my hairstyle had changed. He tried to get me to a pay a bribe but I persuaded him I had no money.**

Find out if you need visas to visit any of the countries on your itinerary (use the Directory section and browse the FCO website) and apply for them in plenty of time, particularly if you need to send your passport away. It's usually possible to apply in person at the relevant embassy and collect your visa the following day.

When applying for a visa, you may have to hand over two or three passport-sized photos of yourself, so take a supply away with you. Most countries ask you to state the purpose of your visit (always write 'tourism'), and your occupation. Don't put 'journalist' or 'photographer' here, because these terms often arouse suspicion and some countries – such as Burma and China – may deny you entry. Anything nondescript such as student, office worker, factory worker or computer operator will do fine. (I once wrote 'goalkeeper' on a visa application form which was stupid because I am 5ft 8in and wear glasses, but I was fortunate enough to get away with it).

You must take out comprehensive travel insurance. It's expensive and tiresome but it could save you a fortune, particularly if you fall ill and need to be taken to the nearest emergency hospital or flown home. Before you run out and buy the cheapest policy check that it offers medical cover of at least £1 million and will cover emergency dental work. The majority of policies do cover watersports and scuba diving, but you will have to pay an extra premium to cover things like skiing and bungee jumping (if that appeals to you). Additional third party insurance is essential if you consider hiring a car in the United States. With insurance, as with most things, you get what you pay for.

Finally, make three sets of photocopies of all your documents, including the back page of your passport, insurance documents, immunisation certificate, visa stamps and air tickets. Keep one set in your luggage, give one to a travelling companion (if you are not travelling solo) and leave the third at home with somebody who can fax it to you in an emergency.

● *Money*

If you plan to travel for more than a couple of weeks you should be thinking not just about how much money to take, but how to keep it safe. Traveller's cheques are secure – provided you keep the receipt separately – and are welcomed almost anywhere in the world, particularly if they're made out in US dollars. Check which denominations you should take by looking in the Directory section of this book. A credit card is useful

because it's easy to conceal and can sometimes be used to get a cash advance in an emergency. Two credit cards are even better, provided you keep them separately so that if one is stolen you'll still have the other. If you're away from home for more than a month you can instruct your bank to pay credit card bills by direct debit. Emergency contact numbers are given for the main credit card companies in the Directory.

> My Switch card was handy in the US, Australia, New Zealand, Singapore and Bangkok where it can be used in any cashpoint with the Cirrus symbol. Take out large amounts each time because there is a flat charge.

If you don't have a credit card, your parents or a close friend may be prepared to let you have a second card on their account, to be used in emergencies only. Unfortunately, credit cards can't be used everywhere. Cheap hotels, hostels, guesthouses, bus companies and even railway ticket offices in some countries don't have the facilities to process the payments. Don't rely on cashpoint cards,

Carrying credit and debit cards and traveller's cheques is more secure than carrying money, but you should always treat cards and cheques as carefully as you would cash.

Keep your traveller's cheque sales receipt separate from the cheques themselves. In North America, traveller's cheques are accepted as readily as cash, but in some parts of Europe (such as some regions of France and Spain) banks are not always authorised to handle foreign currencies.

Memorise your PIN (personal identificaton number) and keep it secret. Verify your daily withdrawal limit before travelling, and test your card before you go. Be observant and cautious when you use an ATM machine. Don't let anyone else see the screen and keyboard, and put your cash away immediately.

Don't let your credit card out of you sight during transactions, and keep all the slips. Report lost and stolen cards and traveller's cheques immediately – use the Directory to find the phone number.

WIRING MONEY ABROAD

One way of getting money in an emergency is to have someone wire you the funds. Sending money abroad this way was once considered expensive and time consuming. However, money wiring services, such as *MoneyGram*℠ and Western Union, specialise in sending money around the world quickly, easily and inexpensively.

HOW *MoneyGram*℠ WORKS

If you run out of money, contact a friend or family member who can help out. They can go to their nearest *MoneyGram*℠ agent (in the UK, most Post Offices and Thomas Cook branches). The sender will need some form of ID, together with the cash they are sending (plus a service fee). The sender can also include a short message to you at no additional charge.

You can collect the money from any *MoneyGram*℠ agent in the world 10 minutes after the sender has completed the transaction, or as soon as the local agency opens. You will usually receive the cash in local currency and there are no extra fees. The sender can enquire where the nearest agent is for you, or you can telephone the local number given in the Directory.

You go to any *MoneyGram*℠ agent with some ID, and collect the cash. If your passport has been lost or stolen, the sender can ask a test question for amounts under $900 as proof of identity – for instance, what is the name of your pet dog? You answer the question correctly and collect the cash.

If you are planning a lengthy trip and want to know that money will be waiting for you later in your journey, or even to receive money on a regular basis, you can ask someone at home to use the *MoneyGram*℠ service to send money to you.

You can collect the cash from any *MoneyGram*℠ location anywhere in the world, as long as you do so within 45 days of the money being sent.

either. Your bank might boast that its cards can be used in ATMs around the world but you're not always likely to see one when you need it. The Directory gives an idea of ATM availability in each country. However, it is no use knowing you can use your card at banks in the capital if you are halfway up a mountain or staying on a remote island.

> At the national airport in Laos my airline would not accept a credit card so I had to get a taxi into town to get a cash advance at a bank then another taxi back to buy a ticket. I should have carried more cash.

I find one of the best ways to top up your money supply as you travel is to carry an American Express card which can be used at any of the company's offices around the world as security against a personal cheque. If you're a cardholder you can either buy travellers cheques or get cash simply by writing a cheque drawn on your current account. All you need to carry is your cheque book and the Amex card which works like a cheque guarantee card.

> In Zimbabwe the banks went on strike for two days and the only way I could get around was by using US dollars cash. Fortunately, I was carrying lots of small notes.

Another way of carrying money safely is Visa Travel Money. This looks just like a credit card. With a VTM card you can obtain local currency from ATMs. You buy a pre-set limit of money, which is electronically 'loaded' onto the card and is used up as you make withdrawals. Buying several cards spreads your total amount, and risk, over a number of cards. The remaining value can be replaced if your card is lost or stolen, and unused amounts are refundable.

Whatever cheques and plastic you carry, it's always important to carry some cash. US dollars in small denominations can be used just about anywhere in the world for tips, taxi fares or some purchases. In the 1980s, New Yorkers started carrying a 'mugger's twenty' – a $20 bill that they would hand over without a fuss if they were robbed in the street. Not a bad idea, but make sure first that your 'attacker' isn't simply an enthusiastic beggar.

Hit the ground running

● *Surviving the flight*

If a bunch of evil scientists were to design a machine to make travellers feel tired, ill, disorientated and bad tempered when they arrive at their destination, then they couldn't do much better than come up with a modern commercial aircraft. Despite the obvious advantages of being able to jet around the world in a matter of a few hours, planes are not comfortable, relaxing or good for your health. Most people disembark after a long-haul flight feeling jet lagged, dehydrated and aching all over.

There are reasons for this. In order to keep fares low, airlines cram in as many passengers as is legally possible. Seats are designed to be lightweight, not comfortable, and cabin air is often stale and infested with airborne infections because constantly renewing it would be too expensive. Cabin crews ply passengers with drink, even though the alcohol will combine with the thin dry air to make them dehydrated on arrival.

If you're flying for more than about eight hours, and crossing several time zones, you can expect to arrive feeling tired and spaced out. That's fine if you're going to be met by a taxi and whisked off to a five-star hotel, but not if you're on your own in a strange city, trying to find your way around and get somewhere to stay.

Here's how to survive a long-haul flight. Take some exercise before boarding, even if that means walking up and down the terminal building. Take warm clothes and a large bottle of mineral water (not sparkling, which expands in your stomach giving you indigestion). When you board set your watch to the time at your destination – this helps beat jet lag by warning your body clock about the changing time zones. Drink lots of water but eat lightly, avoiding coffee, chocolate, red wine and cheese, and try to abstain from all alcohol as this will dehydrate you. Take ear plugs and eye shades to help you sleep. Use moisturiser to stop your skin drying out.

If you experience any aches and pains during the flight, or your legs start to tingle, get up and walk about. If you feel breathless or unwell ask for a canister of oxygen which will alleviate most in-flight

ills and has to be carried on all commercial aircraft under international aviation law. Above all, remember that you're a paying customer and deserve the best available treatment, however surly and superior the cabin crew might appear.

● How airports work

As soon as the wheels of your plane hit the tarmac you need to be on your guard. First, you'll have to deal with the inevitable confusion and bureaucracy in the airport itself. Don't worry. At all airports, wherever they are, the procedure is essentially the same – first you go through immigration, where you'll need to show your passport and visa, then into the baggage hall to collect your checked luggage, then out through

the customs hall where your bag may be searched for illegal contraband.

As a general rule, the bigger the airport the longer all this takes. Countries with strict immigration policies such as the US, the UK and Australia often have the longest queues at immigration for foreign passports holders. Developing countries with a reputation for being inefficient or bureaucratic can be even worse. Ask for a seat near the exit of the aircraft so you can be one of the first passengers off and get straight to the front of the queue.

At the immigration desk you may be asked questions about how long you intend to stay and how much money you're carrying. Often, what they really want to know is whether you plan to work illegally. Be honest about the time you plan to stay, because if you say two weeks instead of two months you may only get a two-week permit stamped into your passport.

Be prepared to prove you have 'sufficient funds' – traveller's cheques and a credit card usually do the trick. You may also need to show an onward or return ticket to satisfy the authorities that you don't intend to stay indefinitely. It always helps to be polite and to dress smartly when dealing with immigration officials. This is serious stuff – if they're not satisfied with your story they can put you on the next flight back home, regardless of whether or not you have a visa.

You may be given an immigration form, which you should fill in before you get to the desk. If it asks you to state where you plan to stay, and you don't have a reservation, copy the name of a hotel from your guidebook. If you have the name and address of a local person, even if it's just a pen-pal or a friend of your family, that may help. Some immigration forms contain seemingly ridiculous questions, such as your mother's maiden name. Whatever you decide to write, don't leave any blanks.

> I bought a one-way ticket from London to Guatemala City but when I turned up at check-in the airline said I needed a return. I had to sign a form saying I would be liable for repatriation costs if I was turned away on arrival. I got away with it, but next time I'd buy a return ticket.

The next challenge is finding the bag you checked in. Luggage has a mysterious habit of disappearing at airports. Occasionally it's stolen but far more often it's lost or sent to another airport with a similar identification code. It isn't unknown for a bag marked TYO (the code for Tokyo) to land up in Toronto (YTO).

If your bag doesn't appear on the carousel don't go directly through customs but report it lost at the baggage handlers desk in the baggage hall. It's a good idea to carry a photo of your pack and to make sure it's clearly labelled both inside and out. Again, don't panic. From the laid-back attitude of the handlers you'll have guessed that luggage is lost dozens of times each day.

Your bag will probably turn up the next day and the handlers will deliver it to your hotel if you give them the address – check first to confirm this. If you don't know where you'll be staying pick a hotel from your guidebook and try to get a room there. Otherwise, phone later with the address. If your bag hasn't turned up after 24 hours check your insurance documents because you may have to report it lost to the police. Because luggage goes astray so often, experienced travellers always carry their valuables, guidebooks and a change of clothes in their carry-on luggage. Better still, travel light and take only hand luggage. The total dimensions of a piece of hand luggage (height times width times depth) is 45 inches. This is no guarantee, but in practice you can get away with more.

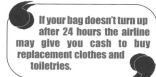

If your bag doesn't turn up after 24 hours the airline may give you cash to buy replacement clothes and toiletries.

The last stage before leaving the airport is customs, which is usually a formality. Most customs officers are looking for large quantities of drugs but on a slow day they may decide to hassle you, particularly if you look like a likely candidate for a shakedown. So it's best not to carry several dozen packets of cigarette papers, or wear a 'Legalise Cannabis' T-shirt.

● Taxi drivers, touts and other pond life

Because all sorts of touts, pickpockets and social misfits hang around airports you need to keep on your toes as you go through customs. In my experience, you're at more risk of being fleeced in your first hour in a country than at any other time. Another good reason not to drink all that free booze on the plane.

If possible, change money inside the airport. You'll usually find branches of the main foreign exchange companies and banks, which will have good rates, long opening hours and – because they're not used by local people – short queues. It may even be possible to change money before you go through customs, which can save a bit more time. Insist on being given your cash in small-denomination notes, plus a few coins for phones and tips. Keep the receipt and count the money meticulously before you leave the counter because it's not completely unknown for bank tellers at airports to take their own unofficial 'commission'.

> At Budapest airport I went to one of the banks and changed $500 into local money. When I counted the cash I found I was short-changed. I told the bank clerk and he just shrugged and gave me another note. He obviously knew what he'd done.

Before leaving the airport building, hide most of your cash in your money belt, leaving enough in your front pocket for bus or taxi fares, drinks, tips and so on. You should already have consulted your guidebook about the best way to get into town. If there is no airport bus you may be able to buy a prepaid taxi voucher at the airport which will save a lot of hassle arguing over a fare. If your plane arrives in the evening or at night it's always worth reserving a hotel room, at least for one night. You may be able to do this, too, in the airport building, although the agent may take a hefty commission.

Most travellers have a horror story about a dodgy taxi driver, particularly those that pick up fares at airports. Some of the cruellest scams are operated at Delhi, where a large number of international flights arrive in the early hours of the morning. Taxi drivers frequently tell new arrivals elaborate lies about riots breaking out across the city, roadblocks going up and shots being fired in the street. They'll offer to take you instead to Agra, the next stop on most travellers' itinerary and some 130 miles away. Some taxi drivers will even tell you the hotel where you have a reservation has just burned down. Of course, he knows another hotel that has vacancies (and will pay him a handsome bribe if he delivers you there). Needless to say, don't listen to a word of it.

> If I'm arriving by air I always ask a local person on the plane how much the taxi fare should be into town. If you get chatting to other travellers you can usually agree to share a cab.

Always try to agree the fare with a taxi driver before setting off. If the cab has a meter, check that it's switched on and working properly, but also ask for an approximate fare. If, when you arrive, the driver demands a lot more, keep calm, stick to your guns and argue your case. Follow your instincts. In some situations you may simply have to hand over the 'correct' fare and walk away, ignoring his protestations. Don't do a runner – if you're in the right tell him where you're staying and say you don't mind if he calls the police (he

won't). This is one reason why you should carry plenty of small notes. It's amazing how many taxi drivers around the world carry no change whatsoever.

I always insist on keeping my pack beside me on the back seat of a taxi. I know it's safe there and I won't be charged any mysterious bag supplement. In some parts of the world where theft is rife, such as South America, you should not get out of a taxi leaving your pack inside. Some travellers have lost all their possessions when they have climbed out and paid the fare and the driver has simply sped away with their bags on the back seat.

On the other hand, there is no need to be rude or aggressive towards taxi drivers, or get stressed out arguing over the equivalent of a few pennies. You would not get into a screaming argument with a cabbie at home so don't do so just because you're abroad. Most taxi drivers are poorly paid and they resort to tricks only out of desperation. If you chat to them and treat them with respect you'll find they can be useful sources of information. Just remember that their advice on where to stay (or where to shop) may not be impartial, and don't tell them too many personal details about yourself. If you're a single woman, for instance, you might want to say you're meeting your husband at the hotel.

> At some airports if you arrive at night there are no buses or taxis and you have to sleep in the airport. I always try to time the flight so I arrive in daylight.

● Arriving by train or bus

Unlike airports, which are usually a long way from the centre of town, train and bus stations tend to be located slap bang in the middle, often in the seediest and most threatening areas. Here, especially, you need to keep a lookout for shady characters, pickpockets and dishonest or unlicensed taxi drivers.

Try not to wander off your train or bus at night with no idea of what to do or where to go next. If you walk around the station looking lost, you may be marking yourself out as a potential victim. Equally, if you start walking down the first street you see with no idea where you are headed, you may find yourself in the middle of a nasty red-light district. Think of the area around King's Cross in London and you'll get the picture.

> I was waiting on a train at Budapest Keleti station when a man started knocking on the window and beckoned me over. At first I ignored him, but as he persisted I opened the window to see what the problem was. I didn't hear his accomplice open the compartment door and take my bag.

Forewarned is forearmed. Study your guidebook before you get there, know exactly where you are, have a plan and stick to it. Try to arrive before dusk so you can feel alert, have your wits about you, and stay sober. Save the celebrations until you've found somewhere safe and comfortable to stay.

● *A shock to the system*

It might sound odd to say that going abroad can be a shocking experience. We've all seen so many movies and TV documentaries during our lifetimes that the world seems such a familiar place. And if you've spent any time in a fast modern city like London, New York or Paris you probably think you've seen it all – drugs, poverty, crime, homelessness. You might even consider yourself unshockable.

But stepping into a foreign culture – particularly a developing country with its many different social problems – can still be a disturbing experience. The noises, the smells, the heat and humidity, the constant attention of beggars and touts can all add to a general sense of bewilderment and frustration, particularly when you don't understand the language.

The symptoms of culture shock are not easy to pin down and they don't always come on straight away. Most travellers feel on a high when they first arrive in a foreign country and it's only a few days or weeks later that they start to get worn down by a combination of the heat and the hassle. If you find yourself becoming impatient and stressed out, losing your temper with people and feeling tired and even a little homesick, you may have just caught a mild dose of culture shock.

Try to recognise the symptoms in yourself. Don't be ashamed of them and don't try simply to tough them out. These feelings are perfectly normal and not a sign of weakness. Coming to terms with them is one of the challenges of travelling. Unlike two-week holidaymakers, who might content themselves with a five-star hotel, a pool and a few palm trees, you're having to deal with total immersion into an alien culture. Look at it this way – if you don't experience some form of culture shock you ain't doing it properly.

The trick is to adapt, not to meet difficulties head on. Try not to judge everything you see by your own values and upbringing. Understand that people aren't trying to make your life unpleasant, that's just the way things happen. In some countries – such as India, China and Morocco – the cultural differences are particularly intense and you'll need to try even harder

Culture shock

Culture shock

to go with the flow. But many people agree that these are the countries where the thrill of travel is at its most potent, where those with open minds can learn humility, understanding and empathy with other people. Travel will broaden your mind – if you let it.

One of the best ways of coping with culture shock is to take a short holiday within your trip. Laze around beside a beach with a good book or splash out a bit of money and stay in a nice hotel. Treat yourself to a burger and a movie. Don't feel guilty about not being a 'real traveller' – whatever that means. After a few days you'll probably find your batteries have been recharged.

If you're visiting a series of countries, you could try starting your trip in a country where English is widely spoken, such as the United States, Australia or South Africa.

You are at your most vulnerable when you arrive in a new place and are tired and disorientated. Keep your wits about you. Try to look alert and confident so that you can be in control of any situation.

Most people who buy round-the-world tickets in London start by flying into Delhi or Bombay and finish their trip in New York when, in fact, it would make much more sense to do it the other way round.

> **In my first few days in Asia I rushed around trying to see everything and wore myself out until I got sick. After that I learned to take it easy, to have a siesta after lunch and just visit the sights that interested me.**

If you are travelling to a hot country you may find yourself frustrated at how long it takes people to perform simple tasks, like changing a travellers cheque or fetching a round of drinks. The reason, of course, is that local people have learned to adapt to the heat, conserving their energy and allowing more time for things to happen. Try to relax and do the same. Avoid setting yourself too many tasks or sightseeing trips, and confine your activities to the cooler times of the day. Try getting up early, taking a nap in the middle of the day and doing chores and shopping trips in the early morning or evening.

● *Language*

In most countries with a significant tourist industry you'll be able to get by speaking English, particularly in hotels, bars and taxis. There are exceptions. Travelling in Latin America is extremely difficult if you don't speak some Spanish (or Portuguese in Brazil), and in some parts of West Africa you won't get by without French. In China only a few young people in the bigger cities speak English and many of these may be reluctant to talk to you in case they 'lose face' by pronouncing words wrongly. This is also true in Japan, where young people can often read English but have poor conversational skills.

But even in countries where English is widely spoken it's worth learning at least a few words of the local language. Making an effort is always appreciated and will help you break down barriers, showing that you're interested in people and not stuffy or arrogant.

> **In a small town in Vietnam I met a man who spoke excellent English, which he had learned from listening to the BBC World Service. He invited me to visit the local school where he taught, which turned out to be one of my most amazing experiences in the country.**

If you learn to count in the local language you might find you can avoid paying 'tourist' prices for everything. But more importantly, speaking the language will allow you to communicate with ordinary people rather than just those who work in the tourist industry – like shopkeepers, waiters and taxi drivers – many of whom are understandably cynical or too busy to chat.

Even in obscure parts of the world where English isn't widely spoken, you'll often come across individuals who speak it, many of whom have remarkable stories to tell. Some may introduce themselves if you look like you have a sympathetic ear but others may be happy to sit around and eavesdrop on your conversation. For this reason you should be careful what you say in public. You're bound to get frustrated at times – at the transport system, or the bureaucracy, or the beggars – but when this happens try to vent your feelings in private, not within earshot of local people who may find your remarks deeply offensive. Even if you whisper, your body language may betray your feelings.

You should also be wary about discussing politics in public places, particularly in countries with oppressive governments, such as Burma and Nigeria. It might be fascinating talking to ordinary people about their hopes and fears, but they may be putting themselves at risk by doing so. If you're interested in the politics of these countries – and every tourist should be, in my opinion – then read books and newspapers and try to talk to local journalists and political activists, who will be a lot better informed than people you meet in shops or bars.

Culture shock

● *How to go with the flow*

Understanding a new culture means getting to grips with social convention, manners and body language. It is as much about understanding ourselves as it is about understanding others. For instance, in the West we have a heightened sense of 'personal space' and tend to dislike anybody intruding on it (according to psychologists, our exclusion zone extends to about 18 inches). But in many parts of the world no such laws apply. Touching a stranger's arm or tugging on his shirt may be quite acceptable, and this can take a bit of getting used to.

There are no hard and fast rules, except to learn what's socially acceptable by watching local people. Be aware of the subtle differences in body language, how in India a tilt of the head may signal agreement, or how in Japan you should bow your head when introduced to a stranger. In many parts of the world it may be considered rude for a man to refuse a handshake, but ill advised for a woman to accept one. Kissing in public may be frowned on and nudity on beaches may be illegal.

Be prepared for poor timekeeping, particularly in countries with hot

Six hours before I was due to catch an internal flight in India I realised I had no cash. I left the hotel and found a rickshaw driver who said he'd take me to a bank. He couldn't find one. It took an hour to find a bank 300 yards from the hotel. The bank didn't have enough money to give me more than $30 worth of rupees.

I found another bank but that had no credit card facilities, so I had to go to the main branch where they said it would be no problem. After an hour of waiting I asked what was the problem. They said there was no problem. After another hour I asked again and they admitted that the telex machine was broken. (Remember telex?) They said they couldn't confirm my card transaction without the telex. When it was finally fixed they gave my cash to another customer.

Eventually, I got my money and arrived at the airport ten minutes before the flight left. The whole episode had taken six hours.

climates. Don't get upset if you arrange to meet somebody at a certain time and they're half an hour late. Not everybody in the world wears a watch. Equally, don't rely on transport connections to be bang on time. Most local people won't find this worrying and there's no point in you doing so – try to enjoy the fact that for once your life isn't ruled by the clock.

If you've been brought up in the West you may be shocked at how, in many parts of the world, women seem to be treated as second-class citizens. Women may be excluded from social situations or required to cover their hair in public. Some Hindu temples have signs outside them saying menstruating women are not allowed to enter. These rules and traditions are often the result of thousands of years of complex cultural development and religious belief. Even if they appear to us to be archaic and unfair they should be respected. Certainly, they won't be changed simply because they inconvenience you.

If you're a woman travelling alone you may find that, in order to fend off lecherous men, you have to go out of your way to appear modest and demure. It can also help if you tell a few white lies. Try wearing a ring on your wedding finger and carrying a photo of an imaginary husband. If you're travelling with a man – even just a friend – your life will be made a lot easier if you tell local people you're a married couple. You might consider adopting local dress, but first take sound advice about what is appropriate. You may be sending out the wrong messages by wearing something colourful that actually makes you look like a prostitute in the eyes of local people, or something with religious connotations that you don't fully understand. Some locals may find your attempts to 'go native' condescending or even insulting.

> **In some countries men assume foreign women are loose and available. Since learning this the hard way, I never wear make-up and I dress in a long skirt, long-sleeved shirt and head scarf.**

One of the great lessons to be learned in Asia is the art of avoiding confrontation. In the West we tend to admire people who speak their minds and say what they think. In many parts of the world, particularly in Asia, this is

meeting the locals.

considered unsophisticated and embarrassing behaviour. To get into a heated argument is undignified and can amount to a loss of face. Losing your temper is seen as a sign of weakness rather than strength. This method of dealing with problems by avoid confrontation is sometimes called 'the Asian way'. It can be frustrating if all you want is a straight answer to a question, but it can be a revelation, a new way of thinking and behaving that many travellers take home with them and benefit from for the rest of their lives.

Another unexpected delight of foreign travel is experiencing the hospitality and generosity of local people. If you're friendly to others you'll frequently find yourself being asked inside their homes and offered meals, drinks and presents. It may be considered rude to refuse such offers – but be wary. You may need to think on your feet: for instance, is the glass of water you have been given safe to drink? If not, just sip at it politely without swallowing it.

> Even the poorest people in the Third World are very proud and the fact they let you into their homes is a sign of friendship, not of their acceptance of poverty. Smile, say hello in the local language and leave your camera behind.

When accepting hospitality, you may feel you want to give something in return. To offer money might be considered offensive so it's worth having a few suitable gifts up your sleeve. There is no need to hand over your Walkman or your Oakley sunglasses, perhaps just a postcard or a souvenir from your home town, or a photograph of your family. Rather than selling your used paperbacks to other travellers, give them to local people who are learning English, or to a school.

Culture shock

If you travel with a camera you'll almost certainly want to take photos of people, whether they're friends you've made or simply ordinary men and women you see in the street. Some travellers might tell you this is intrusive and patronising but I find that most people – particularly children – enjoy having their picture taken and are flattered by your interest. Of course, that's no excuse for behaving like a member of the paparazzi and sneaking up on people with flashguns blazing. *Always* ask permission first and don't try to stage-manage the shot, but allow people to pose in a way that pleases them (think how you would feel if a tourist snatched a photo of you in your home town).

> I found people in Asia love having their picture taken so long as they have time to compose themselves. They can be embarrassed or angry if taken by surprise.

Many people you photograph in developing countries will ask you to send them a copy of the picture. You'd be amazed how much it means to some people, so don't promise to do so unless you intend to.

● *Politics, culture and religion*

In January 1996, a young British backpacker went missing in the popular tourist town of Kanchanaburi in Thailand. Within a few days the 23-year-old law graduate was found dead, the victim of an apparently random and motiveless murder. The news left travellers stunned and many parents of young backpackers were thrown into a panic at the thought that their children might be on their way to a similar fate. What seemed even more strange was that the killer, who later confessed to the police, was a young Buddhist monk who had made friends with the victim just hours before killing her. If you could not trust a monk in a country famed for its gentle and friendly people, then who could you trust?

This story is not repeated here to create a scare, but to illustrate the danger of making assumptions based on our own cultural backgrounds. In this case the victim may have trusted her killer because he was a monk, the ultimate symbol in the West of peace and abstinence. In Thailand, too, most monks are harmless, but not all of them are. Some young Thai men join a religious order because they have criminal convictions or a history of drug addiction and can't get a regular job. What the victim didn't know was that her killer was an active heroin addict.

Reading newspapers and books both before you leave and while you're away will help you to understand the endlessly fascinating culture that surrounds you. It will also make you aware of your own 'cultural baggage', the collection of assumptions and prejudices that interpret the things you see and guide the way you think and make decisions.

> In Buddhist countries you should not point with your feet or touch somebody's head, not even a small child's, because the head is considered sacred and feet unclean.

We all carry cultural baggage, whether we like it or not. One of the best ways of illustrating this is to ask visitors from abroad their impressions of your own country. Many visitors to Britain, for instance, see people spilling out of pubs and conclude that we're a nation of drunkards. The inability of most British people to speak foreign languages makes us seem rude and arrogant, and our reluctance to touch each other in public can make us seem cold and unfriendly. But it's all relative: Italians find us stuffy, yet Japanese complain that we're too informal.

> In Thailand it is illegal to climb on a Buddha image. One traveller took photographs of himself on a big statue and was arrested when he went to collect the film from the chemist in Chiang Mai.

Once you recognise your own cultural baggage you can start trying to shed it, or at least work around it. For instance, in the West we tend not to take religion very seriously, thinking that those people who live by their religious beliefs are a little odd. In fact, we are the odd ones because in most countries around the world religion is taken very seriously indeed. So, if you visit a temple and are asked to remove your shoes you should do so. And if a devout Muslim politely declines your offer of a beer he will not appreciate you trying to twist his arm.

> Always accept an offer of tea or coffee in the Middle East, even at a bank or travel agency. People are very persistent and saying no will just seem rude.

Similarly, in many parts of the world people have a greater respect for royalty and politicians than we do. People in Thailand, for instance, will be deeply offended if you insult their royal family and extremely puzzled if you rubbish your own. In some countries, tearing up banknotes or stepping on the national flag are criminal offences. This may seem extreme, but many people around the world have fought and died for democracy and political independence and, unlike us, they don't take it for granted.

● Being streetwise

We all like to think we're streetwise – knowing our way about, recognising the danger signs and being able to look cool and confident. As we go through life we develop a sixth sense that works a

bit like radar, a funny feeling we get when we know things aren't right. If we're smart we learn to trust this sixth sense. It can steer us out of trouble.

But when we travel abroad we enter a new world where all the little signals and nuances in people's behaviour are slightly different. We may be watchful and cautious but we no longer have our instincts because we don't understand what we should be looking for. We might think we're pretty clever, and we might even think we're pretty tough, but we're no longer streetwise.

> If you agree to meet people do it in a public place. Be wary of going to someone's house. If you must, let someone else know exactly where you are going or take a friend.

Once you realise that you're vulnerable simply because you're in an alien environment you're halfway to being safe. Arrogance and aggression will get you into trouble, not fend it off. In Britain, a survey showed that men are twice as likely as women to be the victims of random street violence.

Culture shock

Some tourists – out of arrogance or stupidity – take risks abroad that they would never consider taking at home, such as wandering around city streets at night or going back to a stranger's house. Obviously, this is pretty daft. Once you've spent a bit of time in a country you'll start to develop a new sixth sense as you subconsciously recognise the danger signals. Until then, it's worth reading newspapers and talking to other travellers, expats and local people and asking advice about where it's safe to go at night, and so on.

● *Haggling and tipping*

In some cultures haggling for goods and services is a way of life. Arguing over prices and playing games of bluff and counter-bluff can be fun at first, particularly if you're buying an interesting souvenir and you enter into the spirit of the deal, taking your time and perhaps sitting down for a cup of tea with a friendly shopkeeper. After a while, however, it can be downright boring. It's one thing haggling over a carpet, but quite another thing arguing over the price of a bottle of water when you're tired and thirsty. Most people find themselves at one time

during their travels reduced to a gibbering wreck and screaming: 'Just tell me the right price!'

Local people tend not to understand this reaction. To them, haggling is an enjoyable social experience and fixed prices represent a rip-off. In some countries there are no such things as fixed prices, so it's pointless wandering around a shop demanding to know the price of everything as if you were in your local supermarket. The price is simply the lowest figure the seller will accept or the highest the buyer is prepared to pay.

Don't haggle for something you don't really want because if the seller accepts your offer you may find it very awkward explaining

Culture shock

that you've been wasting his or her time. Be firm but calm and keep smiling throughout. Don't feel guilty about paying too little for something – no trader will sell it to you unless he's making a profit, despite what he tells you about his five hungry children.

Don't get obsessive about trying to shave a few pennies off the price of everything. But do take advantage of the laws of supply and demand. If, for instance, you arrive at a hotel that is clearly empty ask for a discount on the price of a room. Even in the West hoteliers will always drop their prices when business is slack.

Tipping can be another area of difficulty. Budget travellers are rarely obliged to tip and some never do because they're obsessed with saving money the whole time. I think this is pretty miserable and I would recommend you get in the habit of leaving small tips at hotels and restaurants. There is usually no need to tip taxi drivers or people running their own businesses, but employees such as waiters and room cleaners are often very poorly paid and will really appreciate your small change.

The purpose of tipping varies around the world. In America, in bars, hotels and restaurants, a tip is considered part of the bill and is almost obligatory. If you leave nothing you can often expect loud sarcastic comments and very poor service if you dare to come back. In Britain and other European countries a tip is thought of as a reward for good service, an opportunity for the customer to feel a bit generous.

But in developing countries a tip – sometimes called baksheesh – is a guarantee that something will be done. It should be given before the event, rather than after. So, when you arrive at a hotel give the room boy a small tip (it may be just a few coins) and you'll find that the service improves by several hundred per cent. A lightbulb is broken in your room? It will be fixed right away. You want a beer after the bar has closed? No problem. Think of tips as small investments that will make your life a lot easier.

● *Dealing with beggars*

There are no hard and fast rules on whether you should give money to beggars. It comes down to a matter of personal choice. But when you come across a beggar it's best to decide immediately whether or not you want to give something because dithering is uncomfortable for both of you and may mean you get hassled even more.

There is usually a clear distinction to be made between the genuinely impoverished – such as widows or disabled people – who rely on the charity of local people, and the opportunistic beggars who seem to target foreigners.

> Be firm in telling people to go away and ignore all sob stories, but don't be rude as often it is just over friendliness that makes people so irritating.

The sight of children begging may have you reaching into your pocket but bear in mind that some of them are controlled by adults and may supplement their income with a bit of pickpocketing on the side. Children in developing countries may be only opportunistic beggars and your 'generous' gift of sweets, pens or coins may be keeping them away from school and undermining their relationship with their parents. If you want to give real help to street children, a donation to an orphanage or homeless charity will be more constructive. Still, there are plenty of travellers who construct all sorts of clever arguments to explain why they should not give to beggars, when very often it's simply because they're too mean or jaded. At the end of the day, we all have to eat.

Not everybody who pesters you will be asking for money. Some will be touts or guides trying to earn a living and others will just be curious to talk to you. Try to get in the habit of being patient and polite. By losing your temper you'll look ridiculous and make your own life more stressful. Remember the essential difference between you and them is that you're there by choice, they by necessity. If you get fed up you can always go home.

● *Where to sleep*

Many first-time travellers dream of sleeping on tropical beaches. It sounds idyllic – turn up at a beautiful stretch of deserted sand, sling a hammock between two trees and doze under the stars. Unfortunately, the reality is rather less appealing. People who have camped out on beaches will tell you horror stories of being robbed, sexually assaulted or arrested in the middle of the night.

If you sleep on a beach you have no protection against thieves, insects or dangerous animals. You'll get drenched if it rains, there will be nowhere to shower and nowhere to leave your backpack during the day. I did it once and woke up at 5am covered in mosquito bites. Never again.

> My boyfriend and I arrived at St Raphael in the South of France at 10pm. We slept on a secluded part of the beach and I woke at 4am to find a man sexually assaulting me. Our sleeping bags had been burnt at the bottom where he had tried to get at our money. It was a bad idea.

Sleeping in a railway station or under a bridge – the traditional last resort of the penniless Inter-Railer – is an even worse idea. You might as well hang a sign around your neck inviting all the local criminals, drunks and weirdos to help themselves to your possessions. Think about it: would you sleep rough in your home town? Almost certainly not. If you arrive later in the day than anticipated and cannot find a room for the night, then find somewhere safe, like an all-night café, and stay awake for the night. You can look for somewhere to stay the next morning and catch up on your sleep later.

> If sleeping in an open place don't put your valuables at the bottom of your sleeping bag. At Salzburg station I saw thieves slashing open sleeping bags with swords.

You shouldn't ever need to sleep outdoors if you take a few sensible precautions. Firstly, think about what time of day you'll be arriving to look for a place to stay. The best time is mid-morning

when most hoteliers and hostel and guesthouse managers know which of their guests are going to check out that day. Even if the room isn't yet ready you can usually pay up front, leave your bags in a luggage room and wander off to have lunch, happy in the knowledge that you have somewhere to stay. If possible, don't arrive after dark when rooms in your price range may be full and you're left wandering the streets, an easy target for potential thieves.

Tourist Offices can help you find a place to stay, but will charge for booking accommodation. Most towns and cities have good, clean and cheap guesthouses, hotels and hostels to choose from. If there are two of you, take turns to search for rooms while the other waits with the bags at a café or in a busy square. Don't wait in bus and railway stations which always seem to attract dodgy characters. If there are three of you sharing, bear in mind that a hotel room may be no more expensive than a hostel.

It's usually much harder finding rooms at weekends and public holidays and at some popular places – such as Seville during Holy Week, Goa at Christmas, Ko Pha Ngan before a full-moon party – it may be well nigh impossible. Having said that, you'll almost always find somewhere to stay, particularly if you ask around.

If you arrive on an island by ferry – in Greece, Thailand or Indonesia, for instance – you'll often find a crowd of locals offering rooms. Don't barge them aside and stride disdainfully into town – they might be your only hope of finding somewhere to stay. Pick a respectable-looking individual, ask the price, the type of room they have, the distance from the beach and town (if they say 5 minutes, assume it's 10 or 15 minutes) and ask if they have any photos to show you. Once you agree to take the room you should not change your mind when you get there unless you feel you have been seriously misled.

> It is not worth camping in Africa because rooms are cheap and the ground is often too hard to sleep on. Carrying around a tent, a sleeping bag and all the other gear was a complete nightmare

Assuming you have a choice of places to stay, there are several factors to consider. Location is important, so is comfort, but top of your list should be security. Check that doors and windows can be locked from the inside and that there are no mysterious connecting doors. Take your own combination padlock which you'll be able to use when you're out to secure the door from the outside, or to lash your backpack to something solid like a water pipe or bedstead. If you have two padlocks you can do both. If there is a safe at reception, use it. If not, you could tape your valuables to the back of a drawer. At night, if you can't bolt the door from the inside, prop a chair under the handle or balance something behind the door that will wake you up if it's disturbed. Better still, use a rubber wedge under the door. And sleep with your money belt under your pillow.

If you are staying in a hostel you need to take extra precautions. Although sleeping in a dormitory can be fun, and a good way to meet new friends, there is a greater risk of being robbed, particularly by down-at-heel travellers who have run out of money and see you as a likely target. Keep your valuables hidden away, don't flaunt large amounts of cash or travellers cheques and use zip locks on your luggage. If you are given a locker, secure it with your own padlock – at least nobody else in the hostel will have a spare key.

You may decide you want to camp, either to save money or to enjoy the countryside. If so, find an official campsite with security guards, showers and maybe even secure lockers. You are particularly vulnerable in a tent, so think carefully and take advice before pitching up in a deserted spot. You will be safer if you are surrounded by other campers.

Don't assume if you're offered a room with air-conditioning that it will be better than one with a simple ceiling fan. Some air-conditioning units make an unbearable noise and many people wake up in the morning with a sore throat or a cold. This is because nasty infectious microbes tend to lurk in the extractor ducts if they're not serviced properly.

If mosquitoes are a problem, particularly in malarial areas, make sure the room has grilles on the windows or a mosquito net. Check the grilles and nets for tiny holes and ask for another room if you don't like what you see. Burn mosquito coils at night and don't leave lights on in the room once it starts to get dark because these will attract insects. (Mosquitoes are also attracted by the smell of perfume and soap, so one drastic way of keeping them at bay is to forget about washing for a few days. That, at least, is my excuse.)

● Public Transport

On August 12 1997, two young British tourists in Israel hitched a ride from the Red Sea resort of Eilat north to Jerusalem. Max Hunter and his girlfriend Charlotte Gibb, both students at Durham University, were taking a six-week backpacking holiday over their summer break. Charlotte had already spent several months in Israel, working in a kibbutz, and felt safe there. The man who stopped to give them a ride was middle-aged and looked perfectly respectable. Nobody could have predicted what would happen next.

Twenty miles into their journey the driver stopped the car for a cigarette break. Then, without a word, he drew a gun and started shooting at his two passengers. Max, 22, was killed instantly. Charlotte, 20, was shot in the face, arm and hand and left for dead. She was found an hour later and rushed to hospital where surgeons managed to save her life.

Such incidents happen only rarely, and Israel remains a relatively safe country, but there is a lesson here about hitchhiking. It's simple: don't do it. What was once a safe and fun way of travelling is now, sadly, a kind of Russian Roulette. There is simply no way of knowing whether you're getting into a car with a friendly local or a crazed psychopath. In America, drivers are so paranoid about being robbed by hitchers that most sensible people never give rides. Anybody who does stop for you is immediately suspect.

> I found hitch-hiking in America difficult. People regarded us as strange and some warned us of the kind of people who might pick us up

Trains are just about the safest and most comfortable way of getting about, although they're not always the fastest and you may have to book seats in advance. The view from a train is almost always better than the view from a bus – who would choose to breathe fumes while being thrown about on potholed roads when you could be gliding through open countryside in a comfortable carriage?

> At the end of my six months in Asia I had the option of flying from Calcutta to Bombay but I took a train instead. It took 36 hours but it was an amazing experience and gave me a very real sense of the sheer size of India.

Trains also tend to be good places to meet local people, particularly on long journeys which can take days rather than hours. Overnight sleepers provide a useful alternative to spending out on hotels, although on some routes you'll have to take precautions against robbery. Lock up your pack and chain it to your seat and keep all valuables in your money belt, worn under your clothes.

In Eastern Europe, take thick metal wire to secure the door of your compartment from the inside. In Russia, particularly on the line between Moscow and St Petersburg, thefts at night are commonplace and many passengers have been knocked out with chloroform before being robbed. If you feel uneasy, sleep in shifts making sure at least one person in the compartment is awake at any one time. Top bunks tend to be safer than bottom bunks.

> If you need to go to the toilet on a train take your valuables with you. Lock your rucksack to the luggage rack before settling down to sleep.

Rail networks don't cover every corner of the globe so sooner or later you'll find yourself using buses. These tend to be cheaper than trains and are often more convenient because in most towns the bus station is situated close to the cheapest accommodation. On the down side, buses are often uncomfortable and sometimes dangerous. Overcrowded buses driven at high speed on unmarked roads are a common sight in undeveloped countries.

Night buses are even more of a risk because they often travel extremely fast on unlit roads and the driver may be drunk or too tired to notice obstacles such as abandoned vehicles, bicycles or cattle. Try to avoid sitting near the back of a bus where the ride can be very bumpy – the most comfortable section is midway between the two axles – and stay well away from 'video buses' which ply long-distance routes all across the undeveloped world, keeping their passengers awake for hours on end with endless badly-dubbed B-movies played at top volume.

Another reason to avoid overnight buses is the fact that some crews take the opportunity to rifle through your luggage. The most notorious scam of this type is the 'luxury' tourist coach between Bangkok and Chiang Mai in Thailand, which has a spacious baggage compartment accessible from a trapdoor close to the driver. During the night the bus boy may go down below with a torch and work his way through every bag – picking locks if necessary – looking for valuables. He then neatly repacks the bags so that his victims only discover something is missing when they arrive at their hotel the following evening.

Occasionally, you may decide to take a domestic flight to save time or to avoid retracing your steps. In some countries flying is comparatively cheap but the safety record of domestic airlines may be dire, especially in countries such as China, Burma, India, Vietnam and parts of the former Soviet Union. Check the FCO website (see p. 96) for advice on using domestic airlines.

Ferries can also be dangerous, particularly in developing countries where they're often overcrowded and ill-equipped to deal with storms. The most notorious country for ferry disasters is the Philippines. On one day in August 1997 – bang in the middle of the typhoon season – 16 tourists died when a sightseeing boat capsized in Manila Bay, and dozens more drowned when a ferry sank in the Visayan Sea. That was just in one day. If you must go island hopping during the monsoon, take flights.

There is one form of transport that, in my view, is simply too dangerous to contemplate, and that is motorcycling. Renting a scooter or a bike is one of the most risky things you can do abroad, particularly if you're not an experienced rider. In many countries it's so easy to rent a bike that you won't even need to show a licence or wear a helmet. Sounds great, but chances are the bike will be in a terrible state of disrepair, the roads will be atrocious and truck drivers will use you for target practice. You may not even be covered on your insurance policy. Please – don't do it. Be careful about getting on the back of a motorcycle taxi with a heavy rucksack, because the weight can topple both you and driver over. If you're still not convinced, pay a visit to a nearby hospital and check out the conditions in the casualty ward.

● *Finding your way around*

In big cities the key is to look like you know where you're going. Try to memorise your route rather than standing around on a busy street corner grappling with a map. Be confident and walk with purpose. Use a pocket compass, which will at least let you know if you're heading in the right direction. If you do get lost, go into a shop or a café where you can study your map or ask somebody. A good trick in European cities is to carry a local newspaper under your arm so that people will assume you're a local.

> I found in Egypt that when I asked some people for directions they would start following me. I soon learned to ask people who were working in shops because they wouldn't be able to leave their posts

In some parts of the world you'll need to think about how to phrase questions. Local people may be so anxious to help you that they are reluctant to admit their ignorance (it's not because they're stupid – do you know where all the cheap hotels are in your home town?)

If you point down a street and ask somebody: 'Is this the way to the Hotel Fleapit?' they may answer yes even if they haven't got a clue. Instead, you should rephrase your question and simply ask: 'Where is the Hotel Fleapit?' If they know,

they'll tell you. If not, ask somebody else. In developing countries it's often useless showing maps and guidebooks to local people. They may not be able to read English – and may not even have seen a map before – but they will happily pass a little time idly thumbing through your guidebook trying to look knowledgeable.

When you eventually find the Hotel Fleapit and get a room, ask the receptionist to give you a business card or write down the address for you. This is particularly important if the local language is in a different script – Arabic, Thai or Chinese, for instance. Keep this piece of paper with you at all times. If you get in trouble you can always jump in a taxi and show it to the driver.

> In Mexico City I showed the taxi driver a map in my guide book. After saying 'Sí' he headed off in the wrong direction and we spent two hours going round in circles until we found a local woman who translated for him.

In cities you should stick to well-lit roads but in the countryside or beside beaches that isn't always possible. Paths and tracks may be pitch black. It's sensible to carry a torch with you, but try not to use it. Instead, concentrate on developing your night vision. Even when there seems to be no light at all, after a few minutes you'll find you can see enough to get by. It may feel eerie but you'll be a lot less vulnerable than if you advertise your presence with a torch.

● *Food and drink*

Most travellers worry about getting sick from eating infected food. That can happen but you're just as likely to fall ill because you're not eating enough or not drinking enough water. In hot weather you need to drink up to three litres of water a day just to replenish the fluid that your body loses naturally. When you sweat you also lose essential saline so you should add extra salt to your food.

Dehydration can be a nasty experience leading to headaches, muscle cramps, lethargy and nausea. The first signs that you're not drinking enough fluids are mild headaches and a darkening of your urine. If you pick up a stomach bug and suffer from diarrhoea it's particularly important to keep replacing lost fluid. Drink bottled water or flat Coke (for the sugar content). Live yoghurt – known as curd in India – is a proven defence against Delhi Belly. Some people chew cloves of raw garlic which they say prevents diarrhoea although the inevitable smell can make them unpopular roommates.

If you're in a hot and humid climate, you'll probably drink plenty of water because you'll notice that you're sweating profusely, but in somewhere hot and dry such as North Africa or the Australian Outback you won't realise how much fluid you're losing because your sweat will evaporate as soon as it reaches your skin. If a strong wind is blowing you may feel comfortably cool even as your bodily fluid dips to dangerously low levels. In these conditions you need to drink about six litres of water per day. You'll also find that alcohol has a more noticeable affect on you, so drink only in moderation and try to alternate beers with bottles of water.

Don't drink tap water unless you're sure it's safe (check the Directory for guidance) and don't assume that a flask of water left in your room has been boiled or sterilised. If you do attempt to boil water you'll need to do so for 20 minutes. You're much better off with bottled water, which can be bought just about anywhere – but check first that the factory seal hasn't been broken. It has been known for children to refill empty

bottles, leaving the seal apparently intact, so it's best to buy from shops or hotels rather than somebody who approaches you in the street. Check the Directory for information on how safe local food and drink is.

> I got used to cleaning my teeth without water. After a while it seems quite normal. With practice, I could even take my malaria tablets without swallowing water.

Get into the habit of drinking through a straw, especially from recycled bottles which may not have been properly cleaned in the factory or may have picked up some rust from the cap. If you don't think the tap water is clean enough to drink then you shouldn't brush your teeth with it or wash your hands in it before a meal or if you have a cut.

Avoid ice, which will have been made from tap water, and salad, which will have been washed in tap water, and be very wary of ice cream. Many cautious travellers have succumbed to the temptation of ice cream and spent the next couple of days kneeling over a toilet bowl.

You're less likely to get sick if you eat what the locals eat. The food will usually be well-prepared, fresh, cheap and won't have been lying around on a slab waiting for a customer. For this reason, try to go to restaurants and food stalls that are popular and have a high turnover. Be wary of cold buffets where food may have been sitting around for hours.

Eating at cheap street stalls, where the food is cooked in front of you, is usually safer – and cheaper – than splashing out on a meal at a five-star hotel. But when you eat on the street always make sure your hands are clean. You're just as likely to pick up a bug from something you've touched as from infected food. The only thing I always avoid at street stalls is seafood which can make you very ill indeed.

If you're setting off on a long journey stock up on provisions so that you don't arrive feeling tired and undernourished. The best things to pack are mineral water, bananas, biscuits, peanuts and bread. On buses and trains never accept food or drink from strangers, even those that seem incredibly friendly. I've lost count of the number of times I've heard of travellers waking up on a bus with a bad headache to find their new 'friend'

and their money belt have vanished into the night. This is not a threat to be taken lightly: in 1997, Edward Bravo, an American tourist, was given a drink of raki spiked with drugs in the Turkish resort of Egirdir. He not only lost his valuables, he never woke up.

● *Staying in touch*

If you're away from home for a long time your family is bound to worry about your safety, and friends will be curious to know what you're up to. Keep in touch. You might be having so much fun that it doesn't occur to you to call them. This is a bit selfish because, like it or not, your parents will worry about you, and your friends might resent the fact that you've 'forgotten' them.

Short frequent phone calls are best but don't make promises that you won't be able to keep. Don't commit yourself to phoning home every Sunday, for instance, and then one week find yourself on a remote beach or on a mountain trek where there's no phone. It might not seem worth you trying to get to a phone, but your parents will be climbing the walls with worry.

> I promised to phone home every week during my two months away. One time, I was talking to my mother when my money ran out and I walked away without a second thought. A week later I couldn't find a phone that worked. Then the lines went down for a week. By the time I did get through my mum was worried sick and I realised I'd been stupid.

Phoning from abroad isn't always expensive, particularly if you dial direct and avoid hotel switchboards. International dialling codes are listed by country in the Directory section; when ringing the UK from overseas don't forget to drop the 0 from the area code. If you plan to call your parents in the UK ask them to get you a BT contact card which can be used to dial their number from many places in the world. It's free and the charges appear on their home bill. If you want to be able to make calls to other numbers too, ask for a charge card. Details on 0800-345144.

You should phone somebody at home if you make significant changes to your travel plans or if you've been in an area where there's been a disaster, such as an air crash or an earthquake, just to reassure your folks that you're safe. It might not seem necessary to you but they may be besides themselves with worry.

If friends and relatives want to write to you, give them a list of poste restante addresses where mail will be held until you arrive. A good guidebook will tell you which post offices keep mail and how letters should be addressed. In some countries your first name is treated as your family name so it's best to write to 'SMITH, John' rather than 'John Smith'. When you go to pick up your mail ask the clerk to look under both your surname and your first name and, just to be sure, under 'M' for Mr or Miss.

Be cautious about where you tell people to send mail, bearing in mind that letters may take days or weeks to arrive. So if you plan to be in Sydney next week and Melbourne the week after, then Cairns the following week, tell them to write to Cairns. Poste restante mail is officially kept for just a month, but in practice it's often held for longer. When you collect mail you'll need proof of ID, ideally a passport.

American Express also runs a poste restante service for clients, which tends to be more efficient and reliable than local post offices. You don't need to be a cardholder to qualify, providing you have some Amex travellers cheques. Even just one $10 cheque is sufficient. The company won't keep parcels, for security reasons.

> When I met other travellers who were about to go home I would give them a letter to send on to my family. One guy even phoned my mum to say I was fine.

Sending mail home can be a hit-and-miss affair. Unless you have the money to use an international courier firm there's no guarantee that your letters and parcels will arrive. Occasionally this is because post office staff steal stamps then pocket the cash, so when you hand over your letter always stick on the stamps yourself, with glue if necessary, and insist on seeing them franked.

Modern technology has made keeping in touch a lot easier. One of the best innovations is the free e-mail service offered by an American company, Hotmail. Anybody can get their own email address – you don't need an Internet connection at home, or even a computer. Go to your college, to a library or a cyber café, and log on to www.hotmail.com. Once online, you will be given a free e-mail address which you can use to pick up messages anywhere in the world. The service is funded by online advertising, so you pay nothing. For a list of cyber cafés around the world where you can send and pick up messages, go to www.netcafeguide.com.

You can also rent your own voice-mail number while you are away. This works like an answering machine where friends and family can leave messages which you can pick up using a personal code. As you travel around you can also

Leave an itinerary with a friend back home or a member of your family. If you change your plans, move on earlier than anticipated or decide to stay longer, then let them know.

change your answer message so that people know where you are. The downside is that it can be expensive and you will be paying international phone rates each time you call your number. Details from Travellers Connections (0181 286 3065).

● *Getting work*

If you find yourself running out of money my advice is to go home. When you're broke and trying desperately to save cash you're at your most vulnerable and travel ceases to be enjoyable. If you insist on staying away, however, you'll probably have to get some sort of job.

It's worth doing some research about finding work before you head off on your travels. Don't believe the first person you meet who says you'll be able to walk into a job waiting tables in Sydney

or crewing a yacht in the Caribbean. Find out first if you'll need a work permit and whether you'll be able to work legally. If not, and you're relying on getting some sort of work, you may need to prepare a good story for immigration officials when you arrive. If you're caught and deported you may not be allowed back into the country.

If you are illegal you'll almost certainly be badly paid and you may be at the mercy of unscrupulous employers. Some will try to confiscate your passport and may even withhold your pay if you turn up late or they take a dislike to you. You are powerless to stop them – after all, you're illegal and your employer knows it.

> **I waitressed in France and did not have any formal agreement with my boss so when we had an argument he refused to pay me. I had been relying on that money to get me home.**

If you can't work legally don't agree to be paid more than a few days in arrears. Certainly don't believe any employer who says he will 'look after' your wages to help you save money. Remember, too, that if you are illegal a written agreement may not be worth the paper it's written on. If you feel there's nowhere secure to keep your earnings, open a bank account.

Be especially wary of employers who are looking exclusively for attractive young women. In Japan, foreign women can earn good money working in bars but some customers regard them as little more than prostitutes. The offers can be blatant and generous. Be warned: this is how many a respectable girl has been sucked into prostitution.

> I went to America for three months to nanny for friends and arrived with no return flight and no work permit. I was given a gruelling interrogation but fortunately I had a letter from my university in England confirming that I had a place to go back to.

There is an alternative to working abroad. It might not sound very glamorous but it's legal, well-paid and safe. It's working at home. Most young people find they save money more quickly if they get a job at home, partly because the pay is relatively good and partly because their costs are low, particularly if they can live with their parents. Working abroad, on the other hand, can be a treadmill where the money you spend on food, accommodation and the occasional night out means you can never save enough to move on. Eventually you are trapped, until you have to phone home and ask your parents or beg a friend to buy you a plane ticket home. Not very cool.

Don't be a victim

● *Theft*

Be warned: once you make the decision to go travelling all sorts of people will appear to tell you scare stories about gun-toting, drug-crazed thieves, muggers, bag slashers and white-slave traders. There are two things you can be sure of: (1) the more exotic your intended destination, the more dire the warnings will be; and (2) the people advising you not to go will not have been travelling themselves.

There is no need to panic about the threat of crime, provided you take sensible precautions. Remember that the most common forms of theft are simple pickpocketing and opportunistic bag snatching, both of which are largely confined to big cities. Surprisingly, they're far more common in countries like Spain, Italy and the Czech Republic than in far-away Thailand or Turkmenistan. My own experiences have borne this out. In the six months I spent travelling around 'dangerous' countries like El Salvador, Nicaragua and Guatemala my bags were only broken into once, and that was by baggage handlers at Miami airport.

Don't think that problems only occur in exotic parts of the world. Even on familiar territory and while travelling close to home, it is possible for things to go wrong.

The advice given in this book applies wherever you are in the world.

The Directory section of this book indicates which countries present the highest risk to travellers, or should be totally avoided, but petty crime can happen anywhere.

Most theft is easily preventable and need not ruin your trip. Keep all the items you can't afford to lose in your hotel safe or in your money belt which you should wear under your clothes. Don't take it off because you're hot, or bored with wearing it, and don't dip into it on the street. Keep enough cash in your front pocket to last you through the day but not enough so that losing it would be a tragedy. Put small padlocks on the side pockets of your bags.

Don't be a victim

Don't be a victim

Try not to let your luggage out of your sight. On a long bus journey it is a good idea to get out at stops to check that your bag is not unloaded.

In cities where there is extensive poverty, particularly in Africa and Latin America, don't wear any kind of jewellery on the street. Don't wear an expensive watch, or even a fake one that might look expensive to a passing thief. Be alert. Don't wear a personal stereo while walking on the street, standing on a crowded bus or in any public place (you wouldn't wear a blindfold so why deprive yourself of your sense of hearing?).

Trust your instincts and that sixth sense you've been developing. If anything weird happens – if you are shoved by a stranger on the street or find yourself suddenly surrounded by screaming children – you may have been targeted by thieves. Think clearly, don't panic and let people know you're aware that something is wrong. This is usually enough to scare them off. If you are with an organised group do not wander off by yourself. Remember it is your responsibility to stay in touch with the group leader.

If somebody offers to wipe some mysterious substance, such as ketchup or bird droppings, from your shoulder or back, congratulations! – you have just come across one of the oldest pickpocketing tricks in the book. As the stranger dabs at you with a handkerchief, either he or his accomplice will try to run off with your wallet or camera in the ensuing confusion. You have a couple of options – walk away briskly, or shout 'Thief!' and watch as your new friend takes to his heels. Don't get angry, because once you lose your cool your defences are down. (Incidentally, a survey of readers in the Sunday Times revealed that this mystery-substance-on-your-jacket scam is being used in Paris, Amsterdam, Mexico, Thailand, India, New York, Peru and Hungary. As far as thieves are concerned, it seems the old tricks are the good ones.)

People riding pillion on mopeds in Rome may snatch your bag and disappear down a narrow alleyway before you know what's going on. Carrying a rucksack makes you an easily recognisable target.

Don't be a victim

only had two encounters with bag snatchers. Both incidents happened on the same day in Barcelona, both outside cafés, both after dark. Neither was successful but I now keep my bag on my lap or hook the straps under the legs of my chair, or both.

> If you think it is safer to leave your passport and credit cards at your hotel than take them to the beach, wrap them in paper, bind them with masking tape then sign the tape. In this way you will know if someone has tampered with your belongings.

Bag snatchers are a problem particularly in Mediterranean countries, Eastern Europe and South America. They are usually unsophisticated and opportunistic, grabbing any bag they see and relying on the element of surprise. If you keep your valuables hidden away and your daypack strapped to your chest they should leave you alone. In all my travels I have

Despite some people's fears about thieves loitering on every street corner, you're just as likely to have things stolen by other travellers, particularly if you sleep in dorms or share rooms with strangers. Try to keep valuables locked away and get into the habit of taking your money belt to the bathroom with you and sleeping with it under your pillow or around your waist. Keep an eye on travellers who seem to have no money and loiter for hours in hostels and dorms.

HOW PICKPOCKETS POUNCE

1. Gangs operate at airports and bus stations looking for new arrivals knowing they're carrying money, credit cards and passports.

2. Young children are sometimes used to create a diversion. A child falls over and bursts into tears. As you bend to help, an adult accomplice picks your back pocket.

3. A crowded bus or train provides perfect cover for a pickpocket who may use a large scarf or overcoat draped over one arm to shield his roving hand.

4. A thief drops a handful of coins on the ground. As you bend to help pick them up your pocket is picked.

5. A gang member squirts ketchup or sun cream on to your shirt, jacket or shoe. A few minutes later his accomplice offers to wipe it away with a tissue, as your pocket is picked.

6. A man loiters at the side of a queue, reluctant to join it. He is waiting to identify a likely victim.

7. A mother hands her baby to you, so that you have to hold the child. While your hands are full, other children steal whatever they can.

8. Somebody rushes up to you saying you've been robbed. Your hand instinctively reaches for your wallet or money belt. You are about to be robbed.

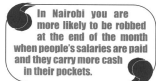

In Nairobi you are more likely to be robbed at the end of the month when people's salaries are paid and they carry more cash in their pockets.

If you're unlucky enough to be mugged don't resist and never run after the thief. He might pull a knife, or even a gun, and will probably be a lot more scared and desperate than you are. The experience will be over in a flash but the effects could be long-lasting. Try to stay calm, go back to your room, talk to friends and be aware that you might be in a mild state of shock.

● *Violence*

It's very unlikely that you'll encounter violence of any kind. The reason why the killings of backpackers make headlines across the world is that such incidents happen so rarely. There is a far higher chance of you being involved in a fatal road accident, or being washed out to sea than being the victim of a random killing. In fact, one magazine survey concluded that New Zealand was the most dangerous country for British travellers because of the number of deaths and injuries caused by bungee jumping, skiing and white water rafting.

By reading newspapers and listening to the radio you can keep up to date with political developments in unstable countries, and be aware of incidents that might put tourists at risk of violence or kidnapping. Don't listen to bogus advice from gung-ho travellers who tell you it's safe to walk around the streets of Port Moresby or surf in shark-infested waters. They're just trying to show off. Again, trust your instincts and don't take risks that you wouldn't take at home. In a city with a reputation for violence take taxis at night, rather than buses.

If you are black or Asian, you may come across racism of a type that you are not familiar with in Britain, even in developed countries. In Prague, for instance, British Asian tourists have been attacked by local skinhead gangs who mistook them for Romanian gypsies. There is no need to be paranoid, but be aware of the potential dangers and perhaps take extra care at night.

One of the best defences against violence is to look confident and walk tall. Be relaxed and alert. If you're trapped and think you're about to be attacked, breathe out to help you relax, adopt a passive stance and try to talk your way out of trouble. If that fails scream or yell at the top of your voice. Use physical self-defence only as a last resort. Remember, you could be accused of assault.

> I was groped whilst walking down a street in Malta. I ran after the man and hit him but in retrospect it would have been wiser to shout, not chase him.

● The black market

In countries where currency exchange rates are controlled by the central government a black market often emerges offering a better rate of exchange to tourists. A black market is, by nature, illegal and people caught using it can sometimes face large fines or even short stretches in prison.

Black markets usually exist in countries where the local currency is weak so the exchange rate is already pretty generous. Often the government sets exchange rates in a bid to maintain its foreign cur-

rency reserves. Tourists tend to take advantage of the black market because they're greedy, often unaware that they're helping to destabilise the local currency and further adding to the problems of the country they're visiting.

Is it worth it? The advantages of using the black market are usually inversely proportional to the risk. So if you're being offered a generous exchange rate that is, say, 20% better than at the bank, you run a high risk of being caught and fined, jailed or deported. If the rate is only 2% or 3% better than at the bank the risk is probably low, but you might ask yourself whether it's worth taking at all.

I think it's only worth using the black market if you're in a remote area many miles from the nearest bank and it's simply not convenient to use the official methods of exchange. Away from the big cities it's usually possible to make the deal safely and discreetly in a shop or your hotel. In a city you're far more likely to be caught or ripped off. As a rule, don't use the black market until you've spent enough time in the country to know the potential risks and rip-offs.

There are all sorts of elaborate and imaginative rip-offs pulled off by money changers. I've seen calculators wired up wrongly so that they produce false totals and conjuring tricks with wads of notes that any magician would be proud of. But most cons are variations on the old 'Here-comes-a-policeman' trick. In this scenario you follow a money changer into a shop doorway or down a darkened alley (really, how stupid can you get?) and just as you hand over your cash there is a commotion. Usually, the money changer claims he has spotted a policeman and before you have time to blink the money changer runs off with your cash or he is 'arrested' and your money is 'confiscated'. Either way, you lose.

● *Drugs*

The best advice is – don't do them. As well as being illegal (in most places), you put yourself at a disadvantage as soon as you take them. If you want to do drugs while you're away you'll find plenty of opportunities, so don't get overexcited and take undue risks the first time you think you see a chance to get off your face. The most important point to remember is that, compared to most countries, Western Europe is very tolerant of individual drug use. In Britain, for instance, most people

arrested with small quantities of cannabis escape with a mild ticking off, rather than face a conviction. But in some countries the penalties are incredibly harsh and, surprisingly, these are often the places where you might think the government would be most relaxed.

> We met a Scot whose bungalow was raided by police after a full moon party on Ko Pha Ngan. They found a tiny quantity of cannabis and jailed him for two weeks then charged him £500 to get out.

Don't be a victim

In Brazil, for instance, you can be jailed for 15 years for possessing small quantities of cocaine. India, where every other person you meet seems to be stoned, has very strict laws covering possession. In 1994, Stephanie Slater, a British backpacker was caught with a small quantity of cannabis in the southern Indian state of Kerala, and jailed for 10 years. She was later released, but only after serving two years in a filthy overcrowded prison.

> On a bus in Namibia the man in front of me was offering hash to other passengers. Another man on board turned out to be a plain-clothes policeman who told the driver to stop at a police station and drop them both off.

In 1997, nearly 2000 British citizens were being held in foreign jails, about 55% of whom were on drugs charges. Most of those were not international smugglers or big-time dealers but ordinary travellers. Many had probably assumed that drug-taking was legal or, at least, widely tolerated. Some would have been reported to the police by the very person who sold them the drugs – dealers often supplement their income by collecting rewards for turning in 'addicts'.

In some countries governments encourage courts to hand down the maximum possible sentences to Western travellers in order to deter others from taking the same risks, and to send out a message to the international community that they're making every effort to 'fight the war on drugs'. In this way they hope their supply of foreign aid won't run dry. If you are arrested for carrying drugs, the Foreign and Commonwealth Office will look after your welfare, but they never interfere with another country's judicial processes. Don't expect any sympathy from your own government, either. Politicians don't like to associate themselves with drug users.

● *Sexual harassment*

Wolf whistles, indecent proposals, lecherous glances, bottom pinching, wandering hands. They all happen and, sadly, in some countries they're a fact of life for Western women and, occasionally, for Western men. You may even decide that the promise of sexual harassment makes it worth avoiding some countries altogether.

There are various ways to defend yourself against sexual harassment but your best protection is an understanding of the local culture. Watch how locals behave. If local women cover their arms, legs and hair and refuse to talk to strange men then that's what you should do. You may have to abandon for a short while your convictions about sexual equality and think purely in terms of how your actions and appearance are seen by others.

> I got fed up with hassle from men in Egypt so I asked a local woman what to do. She told me to hold my hand to my face and flick it away dismissively. It worked and I never got hassled badly again.

A few general rules for women. Avoid direct eye contact with men and try not to behave in ways that might be construed as being flirtatious. Don't wear swimsuits, bikinis or high-cut shorts in towns. In the Middle East wearing a sleeveless blouse can be tantamount to going topless in the street. Ignore lewd comments. Talking to strange men – even waving or replying to a friendly 'hello' – might be interpreted as a sexual come-on. If you need to ask directions always approach a woman. If you're followed, don't speed up but find a policeman or go into a shop and explain what's happening. Somebody will help you.

> In Italy we were followed by a man for three hours who even sat behind us at a cafe blowing smoke in our faces. Eventually we found a policeman who took pity on us and held on to the man for ten minutes while we got a head start.

● Get-rich-quick schemes

Watch out for anybody who claims to know a way of making easy money. Of all the scams and tricks played on travellers get-rich-quick schemes are easily the most effective. It seems the one sure way of persuading people to part with their hard-earned cash is to convince them they can make a big profit out of nothing.

Don't be a victim

The most common scam involves gemstones. Travellers in countries such as India and Thailand will be invited to visit a 'factory' where they can see precious stones being polished. Once there, they will be told that if they buy a stone on their credit card they can make a huge profit by selling it once they get home. A variation on this is the friendly local who approaches you in the street, cheerily says he is off to buy some rubies at rock-bottom prices and generously invites you to come along too. This is particularly common in Bangkok.

> **I bought a string of pearls in Beijing which seemed cheap but I later found the dealer had added a zero to the total on my credit card slip which I had to pay.**

Once you get to the 'factory' you may catch a quick glimpse of somebody polishing a stone then you'll be hustled into a back room and offered a drink which may contain drugs of some kind. You will be told how easy it is to sell the stones for profit and that it's

If you want to meet up with local people and think they are genuine, then arrange to meet in a public place of your choosing, such as a café. If they are genuine in their intentions and want to know more about your country, they should be happy to meet on your terms.

perfectly legal, then you may be shown fake letters from other travellers who have supposedly made large sums of money themselves (though why they should write back to say so is beyond me). You may even be given the addresses of non-existent dealers in your home town who will pay you vast sums of money for the gems.

When I witnessed this scam in operation (at Agra in Northern India) a Swedish traveller was then produced who looked heavily sedated and who weakly tried to persuade me to sign credit card slips to the tune of several thousand dollars. If you find yourself in a similar situation, walk away immediately. Don't even admit to carrying a credit card. Some of these people are frighteningly persuasive.

Don't be a victim

● *Other tricks and scams*

I could fill a whole book with the hundreds of different methods used by crooks and con artists around the world but it would probably only make you needlessly paranoid. Anyway, most scams are easily recognisable once you learn to spot the signs.

The most simple approach – and one that is used the world over – is the stranger who claims to recognise you. 'Don't you remember me, I work at your hotel?' he will say. Or, 'I was your bus driver', or 'I saw you on the plane'. Inevitably, you won't recognise this person because you've not seen him before. But you can guarantee that he'll look offended, hoping you in turn will feel guilty. Be firm. If you pretend to recognise him he'll have won because he now has you in conversation.

In this situation your first thought may be to ask the stranger a question of verification such as 'Where am I staying?' or 'Which bus did I get?' or 'When did I arrive?' This isn't a good idea because any good conman can either make an intelligent guess or will have followed you from your hotel. If he answers correctly he has won you over and made you feel bad for doubting him. Be polite but insist that he's got the wrong person, then make an excuse, perhaps saying you're off to meet a friend. Not all these conmen are clever – one optimistic young man in Kenya tried the same line on me two days running. The second time we met I slapped him on the back and said with a smile: 'Yes, I think I do recognise you!'

Other con artists work by asking you a barrage of questions, most of which are perfectly harmless but a few of which may be more sinister, such as 'Where are you staying?' It might seem rude to refuse to answer this question but you can either say you don't remember the name of the hotel or give the name of another nearby (the cheaper the better, so you don't look too wealthy). If your new friend asks your room number or wants to see your room key you should be very suspicious. Also be wary of answering questions about your friends or fellow travellers. The conman might try to use this information to surprise them by 'knowing' their personal details.

Another type of scam is the good Samaritan who magically pops up just when you need help. He may be able to help you find a cheap

HOW TO SPOT A BOGUS COP

1. Bogus cops operate all over the world from Prague to Pretoria. They usually flash a bit of fake ID and claim to be plain-clothes. Nine times out of ten if you keep your cool and suggest you all go to the nearest police station to discuss the problem they will fade into the crowd.

2. The most common trick is to stop a tourist in the street to check for coun-terfeit or black market cash. As they inspect your money they may either palm a few notes, confis-cate them or just grab the whole wad and run off.

3. If you're driving a car you may be pulled over and robbed or have the car stolen. If you're in Mexico in a car with US plates, even the real police might do this!

4. In Nairobi and other African cities you may be approached by a student asking for money. If you give him anything the bogus cops will pounce, claiming you're funding a political dissident and demanding a large on-the-spot fine.

5. Conmen will occasionally pose as immigration officials claiming to be carrying out random passport checks. They may demand a 'fine' if you aren't carrying your passport. Show them a photocopy and say you're broke. They are unlikely to persist.

Don't be a victim

room or show you around the kasbah (then present you with a bill for his efforts). At a train station he might offer to help you beat the queues by buying a ticket for you. This is a common trick in Paris where con artists loiter at ticket machines offering change to tourists. Some will take your 43.50FF for a train ticket to the airport then hand you a Metro ticket that has cost them just 7FF.

In some countries tourists are occasionally drugged and robbed. This happens with alarming frequency in the Philippines where even experienced travellers can be taken in by the most plausible and charming people, sometimes even heavily pregnant women.

One common scam is for a friendly young man to tell you his sister is going to your country the following week to work as a nurse and is desperately anxious to talk to somebody about life there.

DEALING WITH DANGER

All the practical advice given in this book will help if you find
yourself in a situation where you feel threatened. Your valuables will be hidden and your hands should be free. If facing
a potential danger, this will make you less vulnerable. Follow
the cultural advice in this book – you may inadvertently upset
someone with a careless remark. We might poke fun at our
politicians, but criticising another country's politicians and
political history might cause great offence.

IF THINGS GO WRONG, OR IF YOU FEEL THREATENED:

Stay calm. Breathe out slowly, breath in slowly, then repeat.
This helps you relax.

Follow your instincts. Your intuition is telling you something
is not right – don't ignore this feeling, act on it. Think about
where you could go where you would feel safer.

Don't become aggressive. You may not be able to speak the
language, but you can still sound calm. Body language differs
from country to country, so try to remain in a passive stance.

Avoid looking down at your assailant. Maintain eye contact
from time to time, but not constantly.

Back away gradually, then walk away as fast as you can – don't
run, as this will make you less stable and easier to push over.

Walk away quickly, heading for somewhere safer, where you
can ask for help, such as a café or a shop.

If someone is determined to take your money or belongings, let them go. Don't risk attack.

Don't assume the only threat comes from men. Women and children participate in, and carry out, attacks and scams (see p. 74).

IF YOU ARE ATTACKED:

If you carry a personal alarm, hold this up to the ear of an attacker and let it off. The Suzy Lamplugh Trust recommend one particular gas shriek alarm (p. 96). Activating an alarm near the ear of an attacker will shock and disorientate, to give you valuable extra seconds to get away. The purpose of the alarm is not generally to attract help. If you have a personal alarm, you may be restricted from carrying it in your hand luggage on an airplane, so it should go with the rest of your baggage in the hold.

Shouting or screaming into an assailant's ear will also disorientate them and give you a few seconds to move away. Pretend to vomit, as your attacker will probably pull away.

If trapped, yell or scream. Shout out for the police.

If you are grabbed, try to break free and walk away as quickly as you can.

Report any incident to the police.

If you have been attacked or sexually assaulted, you may be uncertain about how the local police will respond to your report. Get in touch with the Embassy or the Consul to seek help. In a very few countries there is no British representation, so contact the consul of another EU country for advice.

Diana Lamplugh OBE, The Suzy Lamplugh Trust

Don't be a victim

Once you're in his house you may be offered a cup of coffee or a beer that tastes slightly strange. Next thing you know you wake up in a ditch dressed in only your underpants. I've met two people who've fallen for variations of this trick.

The most common tricks are simply those that involve charming the money from your pocket. Carpet sellers the world over seem to have a near magical ability to persuade tourists to buy rugs that they can't really afford, and don't really want. Some might even tell you their carpets sell for many times over in your country. This is almost always untrue. In fact, they may be cheaper at home.

It usually starts with a cup of tea for which you feel slightly indebted. A common trick is to lay out dozens of carpets in front of you, starting with a tiny one and slowly building up to a huge, very expensive one. As each of the carpets is then slowly and laboriously rolled back up, the salesmen look at you pleadingly and you shake your head and say you can't afford it. The salesmen look increasingly downcast, worrying how they will feed their wives and children, until finally the last tiny carpet is revealed. And that is the one you will buy because it seems so cheap compared with the rest. It works every time. My advice is this: if you don't want to buy a carpet, don't go to a carpet shop.

● *Getting sick*

From time to time, you're bound to get sick and spend a few days clutching your midriff and making darting runs to the nearest bathroom. The experience will not be very pleasant but chances are you won't have contracted dysentery or cholera, just a mild stomach bug brought on by a combination of unfamiliar food, heat and poor personal hygiene. Your body will fight it naturally and in the process will build up the various bacteria it needs to prevent you being struck down again.

Once you fall ill, stay out of the sun and drink plenty of water because there's a danger of becoming seriously dehydrated. Slow down and don't make any long journeys. If possible, check into a hotel room with a clean, comfortable bathroom (after all, you'll be spending a lot of time there). If you're travelling alone, try to find another traveller or a friendly hotel worker who will keep an eye on you and deliver food and drink.

If the diarrhoea persists for more than about five days call a doctor or go to a clinic. You might need to provide a stool sample (again, not a fun experience) to check you don't have something more persistent like amoebic dysentery or giardia. These need to be treated with specific drugs and will not simply go away of their own accord.

If things go wrong

> I got worms in Hanoi from eating pork and went to a chemist who gave me some tablets from an unmarked box. They turned out to be the wrong medicine and made my condition far worse. I should have gone to a doctor.

Don't take antibiotics unless advised by a doctor because these not only attack the infection but also strip away all the 'good' bacteria in your stomach. Eating plenty of yoghurt can help to build them back up again. If you suspect you have malaria (the usual symptoms are headaches, sweats, aches and a high temperature, like a very bad dose of flu that may get better after a couple of days then come on again with greater severity) you need to get to a doctor immediately. Dozens of Western travellers die of malaria every year.

In many countries it's possible to buy strong drugs over the counter. Be careful, unless you know what you're doing. It's better to see a doctor and have the correct drugs prescribed. In Europe, you can often get good advice from pharmacists in an emergency. If you're on medication, or have a recurring health problem, keep a note of the drug's generic name and a copy of your doctor's prescription.

● Reporting crime

Don't immediately assume because your passport or travellers cheques have mysteriously vanished that you've been robbed. You may have simply mislaid them. Try not to panic, but think where and when you last saw them. It's very easy to lose things when you travel so get into the habit of checking down the backs of seats, under beds and at the backs of drawers and lockers. I once cleverly hid a sizeable amount of cash inside a hotel wardrobe, then left it there.

It's not a good idea to accuse somebody of stealing from you. If you're wrong, you'll have needlessly insulted them and made yourself look stupid. If you're right, they may turn nasty. Either way, you won't get your things back. If you're convinced you know who's responsible (a hotel worker, for instance) give that person a chance to hand back your possessions without losing face or risking arrest. Go to them, tell them how distraught you are at the loss and that, naturally, you'll be calling the police to have the place searched. Then ask politely whether it's worth them having one last look to check that nobody has handed in your valuables. You may find they magically appear. If they do, smile, say thank you and put it down to experience.

> After my bag was snatched in Saigon the police asked me to go to the station to identify the thief. He was cowering in a corner covered in blood. One policeman showed me the stun gun they had used on him. I felt awful that this had happened because I hadn't taken enough care of my bag.

If that doesn't work you'll need to report the theft to the police, not because you expect them to get your things back, but to get a report for your insurers. Go as soon as is realistically possible, preferably within 24 hours. If you can't speak the language try to persuade a friendly local to go with you. Wear your smartest clothes and be patient.

Don't expect any sympathy from the police and prepare for a mountain of paperwork. Reporting a crime can be a long-winded and infuriating process and you may need to pay a bribe just to get it done. Wait until you're asked – never offer a bribe.

> My camera equipment was stolen from an overhead locker on a flight from London to New York. I reported it stolen on arrival at JFK but because I didn't get a police report as well my insurers wouldn't pay up.

In any dealings with officials you need to be careful not to cause offence or appear arrogant. Watch how other people behave in the queue in front of you – do they sit or stand, do they bow their heads slightly, or hold their hands behind their backs? You don't want to cause yourself more problems by using the wrong body language, such as folding your arms and puffing out your chest. In some countries it is a bad idea for a single woman to visit a police station alone. Take advice from a local person.

If things go wrong

> When my passport, tickets and bank cards were stolen I was treated as if it was my fault. You have to be thick-skinned and don't leave the police station until you have proof of what's been taken, where and when.

If an official insists on keeping a document ask him to make you a photocopy, sign it and give you a receipt. Don't agree to go off with the police in search of the culprit. This is a pointless public relations exercise occasionally put on to impress tourists. It's a waste of time, you won't get your valuables back and you might just be putting yourself in danger.

Once you have the police report, if it is made out in another language, you may need to get it translated, preferably on paper with an official-looking letterhead, say a local university. Stay in town for a day or two just in case your things turn up, but don't hold out too much hope.

Read your insurance documents carefully. If you need to contact your insurers write or phone (if a toll-free number has been provided) with all the necessary details. Note the name of the person you speak to and get a reference number. Keep all receipts, ticket stubs and a note of all the money you spend that you may be able to claim back later.

> Having things stolen needn't be the end of the world. Try to minimise the fuss, be patient, get documentation and don't worry.

Above all, don't let the experience get you down and persuade you into going home. Turn to other travellers for help and support and decide what items you really need to replace and what you can live without. Some victims of theft find the experience strangely liberating – they find they can get by with a lot less stuff than they thought they needed.

● Getting in trouble with the police

With the best will in the world it isn't always easy to stay on the right side of the law, particularly when you're moving from one country to another. You may be hauled up for what appears to be a trifling offence – jaywalking or getting on a train without a ticket – and find yourself in all sorts of trouble.

Countries that might at first sight seem the most liberal can have the most petty laws. In the Philippines, a place that seems to be permanently on the brink of outright lawlessness, I was pulled over by three armed policemen on the island of Cebu for 'disembarking from a minibus at an unofficial stop'. It would have been tempting to burst out laughing but the cops seemed to be taking it very seriously indeed. I was interrogated at length, then let off with a fine of 10 pesos (about 25p).

In situations like this the police may be perfectly aware that the charge is ridiculous but they may be waiting to see your response, goading you into an argument that only they can win. Needless to say, you should always be respectful, well-spoken and cooperative. Look suitably shame-faced if you're being told off, even if you know you're in the right. Don't just smile stupidly, because your idea of a charming grin might be their idea of a conceited smirk.

> In Bangkok you can now be fined up to 2000 baht (£25) just for dropping litter in the street. I was fined for dropping a cigarette butt.

Paying bribes isn't as common as some people would have you believe. If you offer a policeman or immigration official a back-hander you run the risk of insulting them and getting yourself into even deeper trouble. This time you might have to pay a very hefty fine (or an even bigger bribe!). If you do have to hand over money, be careful what you say. Call it a gift, a donation or baksheesh, never a bribe. If an official names a figure do not be afraid to plead poverty and haggle.

> Paying bribes to policemen in Mexico is so common that Mexicans even have a phrase for it. A bribe is known as *una mordita* – a little bite.

Be particularly cautious at airports and border crossings where security is often very tight. It may be illegal to take photographs of airports, bridges and military installations. If you're caught doing so, the best course is to apologise immediately and offer to hand over the film. Losing a few pictures is better than being carted off to a police station, strip-searched and fed on a diet of rice soup for three days.

● *Embassies and consulates*

If you do get in trouble or lose your passport or all your money, you should ask for help at your country's embassy or consulate. Don't expect the red-carpet treatment or a 'Get-out-of-jail-free' card. In some countries, diplomats deal with young, down-at-heel travellers who are simply angling for a free loan. They can see you coming. Again, put on your smartest clothes and be respectful.

In an emergency, a consular officer will contact your family and issue you with a temporary passport, though this is a lot quicker and easier if you have a photocopy of your stolen one. In exceptional circumstances, and when you can show that you're broke and have exhausted all ways of getting money, a consular officer

may give you a ticket to get home. However, your passport may be withdrawn until you have repaid the cost.

If you land in prison you must insist on a consul being informed. An official should then visit you to check on the conditions in which you are being held, and pass on a message to your family. However, the consul cannot offer legal advice, pay bail money, intervene in court proceedings or try to investigate the crime. Nor can a consular officer arrange for you to have special treatment – you'll just have to rot there with all the other suspects until your case comes up in court.

● *Back to reality*

If you're on your way home after a long time abroad you probably can't wait to see your friends and family and enjoy a few home comforts. Be prepared for disappointment. Many travellers find that coming home can be a depressing and weird experience. Even the trip from the airport can be deeply unsettling.

Remember all that stuff about culture shock? Well, after several weeks or months abroad you've probably become so adjusted to travel that coming home is a kind of culture shock in itself. Britain can seem very drab and unwelcoming after Asia, Africa or Australia. People at home may seem anxious and stressed all the time, not like the friendly locals you've got used to. And the freedom that you've enjoyed, making decisions about your own life and not having to answer to parents or bosses, is stripped away in an instant. It's little wonder that so many travellers vow to go away again as soon as they save enough money.

> I found it deflating getting home and realising time had stood still while I'd been having this massive experience. I need to keep reminding myself I've been away.

If you're prepared for this reaction you can at least put on a brave face when you do get home. Those people close to you who have waited so long to see you again will be upset and confused if you appear unhappy to see them, so try to be positive.

You might want to think about maintaining some of the good things that happened to you while you've been away. Reread your diaries (you did keep diaries, didn't you?) and try to put into practice some of the lessons that travel has taught you. If you've been learning a language while you were away, keep studying it. Perhaps get in touch with people from the countries you've visited

Going home

who live near you – after all, you now have a lot in common. And don't forget to send prints to those people you photographed and promised a copy. It's your turn now to repay some of the hospitality you've enjoyed.

There are practical considerations too. If you've recently been in a malarial zone, keep taking the tablets for four weeks after your return. If you develop a fever and flu-like symptoms go immediately to your doctor and tell him or her where you've been. Malaria can develop in travellers up to three months after their return home. Also see your doctor if you have persistent diarrhoea.

● *Have your say*

Finally, let us know how your trip went. Much of the advice in this book comes directly from the experiences of ordinary travellers like you. So if you think I've missed anything out, or got something wrong, or you've got an interesting story to tell, please write to Mark Hodson and The Suzy Lamplugh Trust, care of the Project Editor, Thomas Cook Publishing, PO Box 227, Thorpe Wood, Peterborough, PE3 6PU, or by e-mail at books@thomas cook.com, and let me know about it so that I can use your comments and stories in the next edition of this book. Have a great trip!

● *Travellers' tips*

Lonely Planet publishes a free quarterly newsletter, *Planet Talk* (from **Lonely Planet**, 10 Barley Mow Passage, Chiswick, London W4 4PH, UK. 0181-742 3161) and has an interesting website at http://www.lonelyplanet.com.

The full text of selected **Rough Guide** books is at: http://hotwired.com/rough/

More information and readers' updates are at: http://roughguides.com

Time Out city guides at: http://www.timeout.co.uk

Moon Travel Guides at: http://www.moon.com

● *Usenet newsgroups*

rec.travel.africa
rec.travel.asia
rec.travel.australia+nz
rec.travel.latin-america
rec.travel.usa-canada
rec.travel.misc

● *Maps and guidebooks*

Stanfords: branches in London's Covent Garden (0171-836 1915) and Bristol (0117-929 9966).

Stanfords sell a very wide range of books and maps. Larger independent bookshops and bigger branches of the high street chains usually have a section devoted to maps and guides.

● *Staying in touch*

Email

Hotmail: www.hotmail.com

Voicemail

Travellers Connections: Tel: 0181-286 3065.

Phonecards

British Telecom: 0800 345144

More information

● Travel safety and health advice

Healthy Travel: Bugs, Bites and Bowels by Dr Jane Wilson Howarth (Cadogan, £9.99).

Foreign and Commonwealth Office travel advice: Ceefax page 470;
http://www.fco.gov.uk

US State Department travel information. Tel: 202-647 5225;
http://travel.state.gov

Centers for Disease Control and Prevention (USA):
http://www.cdc.gov/travel

Travellers Guide to Health, available free from doctors' surgeries or the Central Office of Information (0800-555777).

● Personal alarms

The Suzy Lamplugh Trust sell their recommended personal gas shriek alarm (£6.99 plus £1 p&p). Tel: 0181 392 1839; fax 0181 392 1830.

● Voluntary work

Archaeology Abroad, 31-34 Gordon Square, London SW1H 0PY.

British Trust for Conservation Volunteers, 36 St Mary Street, Wallingford, Oxfordshire OX10 0EU. (01491-839766).

Kibbutz Representatives, 1a Accommodation Road, Golders Green, London NW11 8ED. (0181-458 9235).

● Overland truck companies

Acacia (0181-960 5747). Africa.

African Trails (0181-742 7724). Africa, Middle East.

Dragoman (01728-861133). Africa, Asia, Americas.

Encounter Overland (0171-370 6951). Africa, Asia, South and Central America.

Exodus (0181-675 5550). Africa, Asia, South America.

Explore Worldwide (01252-319448). Africa, America, Australia, Central Asia.

Guerba (01373-826611) Africa.

Intrepid (contact The Imaginative Traveller, 0181-742 3113). South East Asia.

Kumuka (0171-937 8855). Africa, Asia, South America.

Tracks (01303-814949). Africa, Europe

Truck Africa (0171-731 6142). Africa

● *Expedition companies*

Raleigh International (0171-371 8585). 10-week expeditions to Malaysia, Zimbabwe, Chile, Uganda, Belize and Namibia. Ages 17-25.

Trekforce Expeditions (0171-824 8890). Supporting science and conservation projects in Belize and Indonesia.

Frontier Environmental Expeditions (0171-613 1911). Conservation projects in Tanzania, Mozambique, Uganda and Vietnam.

● *Working abroad*

Work Your Way Around the World by Susan Griffith (Vacation Work, £12.95).

Payaway (quarterly directory, £8 per year) available from Ransom Publications, 57 Dafforne Road, London SW17 8TY.

● *Women and travel*

More Women Travel, ed. Natania Jansz and Miranda Davies (Rough Guides, £9.99).

● *World Wise Directory*

The need for this Directory was conceived by The Suzy Lamplugh Trust, who commissioned it from Oxford Brookes University with funding from the Prince's Trust.

This section contains information on over 200 countries around the world, including basic safety, health, visa and currency facts, and, where appropriate, the level of risk for travellers to that country. It also provides important cultural information so that you are aware of local codes of dress and behaviour, details that help you to stay safer.

Each page of the Directory is devoted to one country. The country's capital is given first, followed by information plotted against a symbol. What each of these symbols indicate is explained in the key, opposite.

The Directory is also accessible on the World Wise website at http://www.brookes.ac.uk/worldwise. The listings in the Directory section were up to date at the time of publication, but this information is subject to change. Funded by the Foreign and Commonwealth Office, the website is regularly updated, so check this before you embark on your travels.

Directory

Key to symbols

 TIME ZONE
indicates local time zone in relation to Greenwich Mean Time (GMT).

 TELEPHONE SERVICES
shows the dialling code FROM UK; then if you can use International Direct Dialling (IDD) from that country; followed by the OUTGOING CODE if you want make an international call from that country.

 EMERGENCY TELEPHONE NUMBERS
We list numbers for the emergency services – Ambulance, Fire and Police. In some countries there is a different telephone number for each service.

 REPRESENTATION IN THE UNITED KINGDOM
This details the address of the country's Embassy, Consulate or High Commission in the UK.

 UK REPRESENTATION
gives the address of the British Embassy or Consulate in the country.

TOURIST INFORMATION IN THE UK
The contact point, such as tourist office or Consulate, for more information about the country.

 LOCAL TOURIST INFORMATION
indicating contact details within the country itself for tourist information.

 PASSPORT INFORMATION
lists passport details for UK passport holders and other entry requirements.

 VISA INFORMATION
indicates whether or not a visa is required by a UK passport holder for travel to this country.

NB: Because details vary so widely, the Passport and Visa sections provide information appropriate only to holders of UK passports. Please also note that, because regulations are liable to change, you should double-check the passport and visa requirements with the country's Embassy or Consulate before you go. Don't forget that the World Wise website (http://www.brookes.ac.uk/worldwise) is updated regularly.

 PROHIBITED ITEMS
indicates which articles cannot be brought into (or taken out of) the country, or are not permitted without the appropriate licence or documentation.

Key to symbols

Key to symbols

 AIRPORT TAX
indicates if this is payable and in which currency it should be paid.

 RESTRICTED ENTRY
gives any specific details or requirements that need to be met to allow entry into the country.

HEALTH MATTERS
This shows, firstly, if immunisation against the following is recommended (indicated by 'R' against the disease):
HEPATITIS A, POLIO, TYPHOID.
Then, information about the presence of MALARIA is given, followed by recommended precautions against YELLOW FEVER.
Finally, there is a listing of any other health risks that exist in this country.

 FOOD AND DRINK
Where there is no indication, the water is regarded as drinkable, and normal precautions should be observed with food. Otherwise, the following applies:
W1 indicates that the water is untreated and not safe to drink. Avoid dairy products as they are not pasteurised. Fruit and vegetables should be peeled before consumption.
W2 indicates that water is untreated and not safe to drink.

 CURRENCY
This section starts by indicating the local currency and its units. This is followed by information about foreign exchange, the acceptance of credit cards and travellers cheques, and the preferred currency denomination for travellers cheques. This is concluded with a note on ATM (automatic teller machine/cashpoint) availability within the country.

 MONEY WIRING SERVICES
gives local contact details for MoneyGram and Western Union.

 CREDIT CARD EMERGENCY NUMBERS
lists the telephone number to call if your American Express, Diners Club, MasterCard or Visa credit card is lost or stolen.

 TRAVELLERS CHEQUES EMERGENCY NUMBERS
gives the telephone number to call (often toll-free/reverse charges) if your American Express, Thomas Cook or Visa traveller's cheques are lost or stolen. These are often local numbers, but a global emergency number may be given.

 BANKING HOURS
notes the normal bank opening hours

COST OF LIVING
notes factors that may affect local prices. For instance, in some countries tourists have to pay higher prices for goods and services than local people.

LANGUAGES
details the main languages spoken in the country.

WEATHER
provides brief information on the climate.

RELIGIONS
lists the main religions observed in each country. (See pp. 106–108.)

NATIONAL HOLIDAYS
lists the national holidays for 1998 and 1999. An asterisk (*) next to a entry indicates that this is an approximate date.

ELECTRICITY
indicates the local voltage and the type of plug used.

POST
shows approximately how long it will take a letter to reach Europe or the UK.

RADIO FREQUENCIES
lists the local frequencies for finding the BBC World Service (BBC) and the Voice of America (VOA).

WOMEN IN SOCIETY
gives information on how women are expected to dress and appropriate cultural information of particular interest to women travellers. This section may also give safety information for lone female travellers, or notes on society in general.

SAFE TRANSPORTATION
looks at road, rail and air travel within the country, highlighting the safer and most appropriate forms of travel. It may also give information about car hire and the documentation needed to either hire a car or take your own car into the country.

SPECIFIC INFORMATION
gives varied cultural information such as modes of behaviour and dress and the importance of religion. Also included is information appropriate to the safety of travellers, such as which crimes are prevalent and which areas should be avoided. It may also indicate what should not be photographed.

Most importantly, this section notes any warnings from the Foreign and Commonwealth Office (FCO) that apply to travellers intending to visit the country. If the FCO has a warning about the level of risk to visitors, then this is indicated.

Key to symbols

● *Abbreviations*

A few abbreviations appear throughout the Directory to save space.

BBC	British Broadcasting Corporation
FCO	Foreign and Commonwealth Office (Note: usually refers to the Travel Advice Unit of the FCO).
IDD	International Direct Dialling
IDP	International Driving Permit
Jan, Feb	January, February
Mon, Tues	Monday, Tuesday etc
R	Recommended (as in recommended vaccinations)
TO	Tourist Organisation/Tourist Office
VOA	Voice of America
Y	Yes

● *Health advice*

This section details the diseases listed throughout the Directory (where the presence of diseases and other health problems in each country is noted). It also gives advice on immunisation and prevention. Don't forget that health advice is also given on pages 29–31 and 87–88 of this book.

AIDS/HIV

All travellers should be aware of the risk of AIDS, which is present throughout the world. There is no cure for the disease, caused by the HIV virus. This is spread through unprotected sex with an infected person; use of infected needles, medical instruments or tattooing equipment; and transfusions of infected blood. Avoid having sex with anyone other than your usual partner; use a condom if you have sex with a new partner. If you need a blood transfusion while you are away, insist that you are given screened blood.

Bilharzia

Bilharzia (schistosomiasis) is caused by a worm that penetrates the skin. Prevention is by avoiding contact with stagnant water or swimming in waterways in countries where the disease is present.

Cholera

Cholera causes severe diarrhoea, which may lead to dehydration and possibly even death. It is transmitted by contaminated food and water. Immunisation is regarded as ineffective: prevention is by good hygiene and exercising caution with food and drink.

Dengue Fever

This is a disease transmitted by the bite of an infected mosquito. There is no immunisation against the disease, which causes flu-like symptoms.

Diptheria

Most adults in the UK will already have been immunised against this disease, caught by contact with a person infected with the disease. Vaccines are available for those who do not already have this protection.

Hepatitis

There are two forms of this viral infection of the liver – hapatitis A and hepatitis B. Hepatitis A is sometimes known as infectious hepatitis, transmitted by contaminated food and water, faeces and

Health matters

from a carrier of the disease. The most appropriate vaccination for this strain depends on the length of time you will spend travelling, so consult your doctor once you have decided on your travel plans.

Hepatitis B is spread in the same way as the HIV virus (see above). You can be vaccinated against this strain of the disease, but it takes six months to become effective.

Japanese B Encephalitis

Is a viral disease spread by mosquito. Because this disease can be fatal, those intending to spend some time in risk areas of southeast Asia (especially during the monsoon) are advised to seek immunisation.

Malaria

Malaria is spread by bite from infected mosquitoes and causes a fever and other complications. It can be fatal. Precautions are outlined on page 30. Anti-malaria tablets should be taken for a month after returning home. If you develop a fever or flu-like symptoms while you are travelling, or up to three months after your return home, seek medical attention. There are several strains of malaria: falciparum being the most serious. In some parts of the world, falciparum and vivax strains are becoming resistant to

anti-malaria treatments. See also p.30

Meningitis

This bacterial disease can be fatal and is transmitted by contact with a carrier. There is an effective vaccination against strains A and C, but no immunisation against the strain most prevalent in the UK.

Polio

Polio (poliomyelitis) is a viral infection that causes meningitis and paralysis. It is transmitted through faeces and contaminated water. If you have been immunised over ten years ago, a booster can be taken. Those who have not received the vaccine before should have the full course of three doses. (This is the vaccine usually given on sugar lumps.)

Rabies

This is an infection of the nervous system, and once symptoms have developed – muscle spasms and delirium – it is usually fatal. The disease is spread by bite or scratch from an infected animal. If bitten, seek treatment immediately. Wash the wound, apply alcohol and go to the nearest doctor or hospital. Treatment is by a course of injections. Vaccinations are available, but you still need to seek the same treatment if bitten.

Health matters

Tetanus

Tetanus is transmitted through cuts and wounds, and causes painful muscle spasms. The spores that carry it live in the soil, and can be transmitted by an injury as minor as a scratch from a thorn. Immunisation is by a series of three injections and, if this was within the last ten years, a booster can be given.

Tick-borne Encephalitis/ Lyme Disease

A vaccination is available for Tick-borne Encephalitis, but none for Lyme Disease. Prevention is by covering up in areas affected by the disease, especially if hiking or camping. Both diseases are transmitted by a bite from an infected tick – encephalitis is inflammation of the brain, whilst Lyme Disease produces arthritic pain, swollen joints and a rash. Early treatment of Lyme Disease is effective, if left too late, treatment will not work.

Tuberculosis

Most adults in the UK will already have been vaccinated against this respiratory disease. If not, immunisation is advisable if you are going to work or stay for more than a month in a country where TB is common.

Typhoid

Typhoid fever is transmitted via contaminated food and water. Those travelling to areas where sanitation is poor should be immunised and care should be taken when handling food.

Yellow Fever

This is transmitted by mosquito bite. Some countries (see the Directory) require a vaccination certificate in order to gain entry. The vaccination is highly effective, lasting for ten years, but can only be given at a designated centre. Ask your own doctor for advice on obtaining the vaccination.

● *Religions*

This is not the place for a full introduction to the religious cultures you may encounter on your travels. You should learn as much as you can from guidebooks and reference sources for the areas you intend to visit. The purpose of this section is to acquaint you with some considerations about behaviour and sensitivity to the more widespread religions. These will apply to many of the countries in the following directory – to save repeating them everywhere, they are outlined here.

Always, in any event, be guided by the local customs you observe. In particular, if you wish to visit a place of worship, always ensure that you adhere to appropriate dress codes. For example, women visiting a mosque should always cover their heads. Look for any notices giving guidance about what should be worn, or observe how other worshippers are dressed.

Christianity

The main differences in customs between Christian cultures are less to do with sects and more to do with strictness of observance, which is often connected to how traditionally society is organised. For example, in southern European countries both Roman Catholic and Greek Orthodox communities impose a much stricter dress code on visitors to churches than would be the case in northern Europe. Unless the contrary is obvious from the conduct of other visitors, assume that in churches and other Christian sites bare arms and legs are frowned upon and may result in entry being denied. Women may have to cover their heads, if only with a shawl. In nearly all Christian countries it is still the custom for men to uncover their heads whilst in a church, on the other hand. Entry may also be denied or restricted during religious services, and even when not, visitors are expected to maintain silence.

Be prepared also for a greater deference or respect towards priests in many communities than you would expect in your own country, and take care not to flout it, which will cause offence or worse.

World religions

Buddhism

Originating in India as an offshoot of Hinduism, this religion has spread throughout southern and eastern Asia over the last two millennia. Its most obvious manifestations are statues or images of the Buddha, as well as temples, festivals and communities of priests or monks.

Buddhist monks, who are invariably treated by the locals with the greatest of respect, which you should emulate. Buddhist monks do not live separately from the community, like Christian monks, and they may in some respects seem quite worldly to an outsider; but they should not be criticised. Nor should you touch a monk, even accidentally. Monks may not accept money directly (put it in their bowl), or anything at all from a woman.

Dress and conduct in Buddhist temples and shrines should resemble that in Muslim and conservative Christian places of worship, i.e. no bare arms and legs, and remove shoes before entering. Respect for the image of the Buddha is important, and this means not climbing on one, or even posing for a photograph with one.

Islam

Islamic belief has its principles in the existence of the one God, Allah. The words of Allah were given to the prophet Mohammed and became known as the Koran. Adherence to Islam permeates all areas of daily life in Muslim countries.

Muslims must perform the five Pillars of Islam: to publicly pronounce 'There is no God but God and Mohammed is the messenger of God'; to pray five times a day; the giving of alms; to fast during the month of Ramadan; to make the haj – the annual pilgrimage to Mecca.

Prayers may take place anywhere, but the worshipper always faces the direction of Mecca. A visitor should not display embarrassment if prayers are offered in front of him/her, by a shopkeeper on his premises, for instance.

During Ramadan, Muslims abstain from food and drink between the hours of sunrise and sunset. Shops may close afternoons, and some may open again at night. It is usually possible for non-Muslim travellers to obtain food and refreshment, in the main cities and western-style hotels, at any rate, but to eat, drink or smoke in public during Ramadan would be considered insulting.

Muslims abstain from alcohol and from the consumption of pork. Non-Muslim visitors may drink alcohol, with more or less discretion according to the strictness of local observance, but drunkenness is always considered beyond contempt.

Women, even in the more liberal Muslim countries, dress conservatively, generally showing their face and hands only; in stricter cultures faces may be veiled and indeed women may not be visible in public much at all.

Shoes should not be worn inside a house or mosque, and to show the soles of the feet towards another person is considered an insult. In mosques very often there is a barrier beyond which non-believers should not enter. If giving or receiving gifts, always use the right hand. Hospitality towards others is an integral part of Islam; to refuse an offer of hospitality may be considered an insult.

Other religions

A number of significant religions, with worldwide or extensive regional followings, are also noted throughout the Directory, for example Hinduism, Judaism, Sikhism and Taoism. Where these have a major impact on the culture of the country you will be visiting, find out what you can about them beforehand.

Afghanistan

CAPITAL: Kabul

 GMT + 4.5

No. Telephone, fax, telex, telegram or postal services available.
IDD: None

 Not present.

Embassy of the Islamic State of Afghanistan, 31 Princes Gate, London SW7 1QQ
Tel: (0171) 589 8891. Fax: (0171) 581 3452.

British Embassy, Karte Parwan, Kabul, Afghanistan. Tel (93) 88888. NOTE: At the time of writing the British Embassy is closed. Some consular assistance may be provided by the High Commission in Pakistan.

Refer to Embassy in London.

Afghan Tourist Organisation (ATO), Ansari Wat, Shar-i-Nau, Kabul, Afghanistan. Tel: (93) 30323.

 Return Ticket required. Requirements may be subject to short-term change. Contact the relevant authority before departure.
VALID PASSPORT REQUIRED.

 Required by all except travellers holding re-entry permits issued by Afghanistan. and travellers holding confirmed onward tickets and continuing their journey to another country by the same aircraft within 2 hours.

 Alcohol. The export of antique carpets and furs is prohibited without licence. All valuable goods must be declared on arrival.

 Af 200

 Nationals of Israel require special authorisation from the Embassy for entry.

 POLIO, TYPHOID: R
MALARIA: Exists in the falciparum and vivax varieties.
YELLOW FEVER: A vaccination certificate is required if arriving from endemic or infected areas. Travellers arriving from non endemic areas should note that vaccination is strongly recommended for travel outside the urban areas.
OTHER: Cutaneous leishmaniasis, cholera, tick-borne relapsing fever, typhus, and rabies are present.

 W1

 Afghani (Af) = 100 puls. Credit cards and travellers cheques are not accepted.
ATM: Unavailable.

 MONEYGRAM and WESTERN UNION: Unavailable.

 No local contact numbers

No local contact numbers

 Generally 0800–1200 and 1300–1630 Sat to Wed, 0830–1330 Thur. At the time of writing many banks are closed.

 Limited accommodation and commodities in Kabul. All are inexpensive.

 Pashtu and Dari Persian. English, French, German and Russian are also spoken.

 Regions above 2500m are extremely cold. There are considerable differences between temperatures in the summer and winter, and between day and night in lowland regions and the valleys.

 Islamic majority (mostly Sunni); Hindu, Jewish and Christian minorities.

 1998: Jan 29–31*; Mar 21; Apr 7–10* 17, 28; May 1, 7; July 6*; Aug 19.
1999: Jan 29–31*; Mar 21; Apr 7–10* 17, 28; May 1, 7; July 6*; Aug 19.

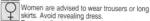 220 volts AC, 50 Hz.

Postal services unavailable.

 BBC 15.58 12.10 9.410 1.413
VOA 15.379 9.762 9.645 6.110

Women are advised to wear trousers or long skirts. Avoid revealing dress.

 Buses, trolley buses and taxis operate in Kabul. It is essential to check these services with the relevant airline offices.

 The FCO advises against travel to Afghanistan. Continuing tension between different Afghan groups has led to outbreaks of fighting throughout the country. Those who propose to travel, despite the warning, are strongly advised to check the situation before setting out.
Religion has a strong influence over daily life. Exercise care when taking photographs and do not photograph military installations.

CAPITAL: Tirana

 GMT + 1 (GMT + 2 from last Sunday in March to Saturday before last Sunday in October).

FROM UK: 355.   IDD: Y, to major towns.
OUTGOING CODE: 00

Police 24445, Fire 23333,
Ambulance 22235

Embassy of the Republic of Albania, 4th Floor, 38 Grosvenor Gardens, London SW1W 0EB.
Tel: (0171) 730 5709. Fax: (0171) 730 5747.

British Embassy, Office of the British Charge d'Affairs c/o French Embassy, Rruga Skënderbeu, 14 Tirana, Albania.
Tel: (42) 34250.

Alfturist (Travel Agency) c/o Regent Holidays (UK) Limited, 15 John St, Bristol BS1 2HR.
Tel: (01179) 211 711. Fax: (01179) 254 866.

Albanian Ministry of Construction and Tourism, Marketing and Promotion Department, Bulevardi Dëshmorët e Kombit, Tirana, Albania.
Tel: (42) 28123. Fax: (42) 27931.

Return Ticket required. Requirements may be subject to short term change. Contact the relevant authority before departure.
VALID PASSPORT REQUIRED.

Export permits are required for precious metals, antique rolls and scrolls, books, works of art. NOTE: Passing through customs can take a long time and is a difficult procedure.

US$10 levied on all foreign departures.

 Proof of sufficient funds to finance stay may be required.
POLIO, TYPHOID: R.
YELLOW FEVER: A vaccination certificate is required from travellers over 1 year of age coming from infected areas.
OTHER: Hepatitis A and B, Rabies.

 W1

 CURRENCY: Lek (Lk) = 100 qindarka. Exch: Banks offer the best rate of exchange. CC; MasterCard and EuroCard are accepted by banks and major hotels. AMEX is not accepted. TC: Accepted by some banks. MasterCard and Eurocheques are accepted in banks and some hotels. Travellers cheques will be cashed by some banks. US dollars are preferred.
ATM AVAILABILITY: None.

 MONEYGRAM: 00 800 0010 then 800 592 3688.
WESTERN UNION: (42) 34979

 AMEX: +44 1273 696933
DINERS CLUB: no local number
MASTERCARD: 1 314 542 7111.
VISA: no local number
AMEX: +44 1273 571 600
THOMAS COOK: +44 1733 318650
VISA: 0181 667 1393

 0700–1500 Mon to Fri.

 Albania is one of the poorest countries in Europe, although its economy is improving. Visitors will be charged a far higher rate for services and goods than locals.

 Albanian. In the south, Greek is spoken. Italian may also be spoken.

 Temperate climate. Warm and dry periods occur between June–Sept. Cool and wet between Oct–May. Best time to visit is May–June and mid Sept.

 Mostly Muslim with Greek Orthodox. Protestant and Roman Catholic minorities.

 1998: Jan 1, 2; Apr 12; May 1, 15*; Nov 28; Dec 25.
1999: Jan 1, 2; Apr 4; May 1, 15*; Nov 28; Dec 25.

 220 volts AC 50 Hz.

 May take up to 2 months. Send recorded delivery to avoid loss.

BBC: 17.64 15.07 9.410 6.180
VOA: 15.20 9.760 6.040 1.260

 Women are expected to dress modestly, although attitudes are becoming slightly more relaxed.

RAIL: mainly single track, dilapidated and overcrowded. ROAD: Most are in poor condition and driving standards are low. BUS: The major form of transportation in Albania. TAXIS: Can be found in the capital in front of the main hotels.

The FCO advises against all but essential travel to Albania. The crime rate is steadily rising, and criminal gangs are active throughout the country. Foreign visitors and their vehicles are an attractive target for criminals. Visitors should not overtly display valuables. Avoid remote areas especially at night. It is greatly appreciated if you attempt to speak Albanian.

Algeria

CAPITAL: Algiers

 GMT + 1

 FROM UK: 213, IDD: Y 00

 Not present.

 Embassy of the Democratic and Popular Republic of Algeria, 54 Holland Park, London, W11 3RS. Tel: (0171) 221 7800. Fax: (0171) 221 0448

British Embassy, BP 43, Résidence Cassiopée, Bâtiment B, 7 Chemin des Glycines, 16000 Alger-Gare, Algiers. Tel: 62 24 11. Fax: 69 24 10

Algerian Consulate, 6 Hyde Park , London, SW7 5EW. Tel: (0171) 589 6885. Fax: (0171) 589 7725

 VALID PASSPORT REQUIRED
Return Ticket Required – may be subject to change at short notice. Contact the Consulate before travelling.

 Visa required.

 Personal Jewellery weighing more than 100g will be subject to a temporary importation permit which ensures its re-exportation.

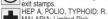 AD 1000, payable in local currency.

 Evidence of sufficient funds required. Visa not granted for those with Israeli visas and exit stamps.

 HEP A, POLIO, TYPHOID: R.
MALARIA: Limited Risk.
YELLOW FEVER: Recommended. Certificate is required if arriving from infected areas.
Bilharzia present

W2

 Algerian Dinar (AD) = 100 centimes. NOTE: when exchanging money a receipt is required that should be presented on departure. Foreign money must be declared via a declaration form and stamped at arrival. Very limited acceptance of credit cards. Travellers cheques can only be changed in 4-star hotels. French francs are the preferred currency.
ATM AVAILABILITY: Over 100 locations.

MONEYGRAM: Unavailable
WESTERN UNION: Unavailable

 AMEX: +44 1273 696933
MASTERCARD: 1 314 542 7111
VISA: (1) 410 581 9091

 AMEX: +44 1273 571 600
THOMAS COOK: +44 1733 318950
VISA: +44 1733 318949

 0900–1630 Sun–Thur

 Visitors should expect to pay much more than local people.

 Arabic, French and English are spoken in tourist centres.

 During the Summer the temperatures can be very high with humid weather in the North. Travel delays can be caused by sandstorms and coastal towns are also prone to storms.

 Islam (mostly Sunni). Few Roman Catholics and Protestants.

 1998: Jan 1, 30*–31; Apr 7 – 8, 28; May 1, 7; June 19; July 5, 6*; Nov 1.
1999: Jan 1, 29–30*; Apr 6–7, 28; May 1, 6*; June 19; July 5, 6*; Nov 1.

 127/220 Volts. Plugs = European 2-pin

 Airmail from the main cities takes 3–4 days, from elsewhere it takes much longer.

 BBC: 17.70 15.07 12.09 9.410
VOA: 15.21 9.760 6.040 5.995

 Strict dress codes for women prevail; only one eye can be shown. Women should cover themselves in accordance with Islamic religion.

RAIL: Daily services between the main centres. COACH: Not recommended for long journeys. ROAD: Most are in good condition. NOTE: For desert travel, vehicles must be in good working order as breakdown facilities are virtually non-existent. Water and petrol supplies must be carried. DOCUMENTATION: IDP is required.

NOTE: EXTREME RISK. There have been a number of recent attacks on tourists. The FCO advises against all travel to Algeria. Note that Algiers airport is considered a potential terroritst target. British nationals should have armed protection.
The land borders between Morocco and Algeria remain closed.

CAPITAL: Pago Pago

GMT–11

FROM UK: 684. IDD: Y. OUTGOING CODE: 00

All services – 911.

United States of America, 24–32 Grosvenor Square, London W1A 1AE. Tel: (0171) 499 9000. Fax: (0171) 629 9124

No British Representation.

Not present.

Office of Tourism, Convention Centre, Pago Pago, AS 96799. Tel: 6331091. Fax: 6331094.

Return Ticket Required. Regulations may be subject to change at short notice. Contact the embassy before departure.
Passports required by all except nationals of the USA with other proof of identity with a valid onward return ticket for stays of up to 30 days. Passports must be valid for at least 60 days beyond the period of stay.

Not required for tourist purposes providing a confirmed reservation and documentation for onward travel is held. Passengers wishing to stay for more than 30 days will be required to obtain special permission.

Narcotics.

US$10 on all international departures.

POLIO, TYPHOID: R
YELLOW FEVER: A vaccination certificate is required by those arriving from infected areas.

W2

US Dollar (US$) = 100 cents. Amex is widely accepted. Other credit cards have more limited use. Travellers cheques, preferably in US dollars, are widely accepted. ATM AVAILABILITY: 4 locations.

MONEYGRAM: Unavailable.
WESTERN UNION: 800 543 4080.

AMEX:+44 1273 696933
DINERS CLUB: No local number
MASTERCARD: 1 800 307 7309
VISA: (1) 410 581 9091

AMEX: (61) 2 886 0689
THOMAS COOK: 1 800 223 7373
VISA: 1 800 732 1322

0900–1500 Mon to Fri.

Relatively expensive, although local guest-houses are cheaper.

Samoan. English is widely spoken.

Hot tropical climate with heavy rainfall from Dec–Apr. Most comfortable time is May–Sept.

Christian Congregation, Roman Catholicism, Latter day Saints and Protestant.

1998: Jan 1; Feb 16; Apr 17; May 19; July 4; Sept 3; Nov. 20; Dec 25, 26.
1999: Jan 1; Feb 16; Apr 1; May 19; July 4; Sept 3; Nov. 20; Dec 25, 26.

110/220 Volts AC 60 Hz.

1–2 weeks. Poste Restante: General Delivery, Pago Pago, American Samoa, 96799.

BBC: 17.83 15.34 9.740 11.95
VOA: 5.985 11.72 9.525 5.180

Traditional Samoan society is bound by very strict customs. The government issues a list of behaviour and dress codes for both Western and American Samoa. Traditional clothing is preferred. Samoans' social behaviour conforms to strict and rather complicated rituals.

CAR HIRE: Drivers must be 25 or older (except for a few local companies). DOCUMENTATION: National driving licence is acceptable or IDP. BUS: A local service operates between the airport and capital. TAXI: Plentiful, fixed fare.

Beach wear should be kept for the beach. Local culture should be respected. Do not interrupt evening prayer rituals. Some villages will not allow swimming or fishing on Sundays.

Andorra

CAPITAL: Andorra-la-Vella

GMT + 1 (GMT + 2 from last Sunday in March to the Saturday before the last Sunday in September)

FROM UK: 376. IDD: Y.
OUTGOING CODE: 0

Emergency medical service: 825 225, Ambulance and Fire: 118, Police: 110

Embassy of Spain, 39 Chesham Place, London, SW1X 8SB. Tel: (0171) 235 5555. Fax: (0171) 259 5392.

British Consulate, (in Barcelona), 13th Floor, Edificio Torre de Barcelona, Avenida Diagonal 477, 08036 Barcelona, Spain. Tel: (3) 419 9044. Fax: (3) 405 2411.

Andorra Tourist Board, 63 Westover Road, London SW18 2RF. Tel: (0181) 874 4806

Sindicat d'Initiative de las Valls d'Andorra, Carrer Dr Vilanova, Andorra la Vella, Andorra. Tel: 820214. Fax: 8825823.

Return Ticket required. Requirements may be subject to short-term change. Contact embassy before departure. Paasports required except for nationals of France or Spain providing they are holding a valid ID card.

Not required for stays of up to 3 months.

Pornography, radio transmitters, certain food-stuffs, plants, flowers, animals and birds. Items made from endangered species are prohibited.

Nearest airport is Barcelona, Spain.

Rabies

Most currencies are accepted but the main currency in circulation is the Spanish Peseta and to a lesser extent the French Franc. Travellers cheques and all major credit cards are accepted. Spanish pesetas, French francs and US dollars are the preferred currency.
ATM: 150 locations.

MONEYGRAM: 0 800 99 0011 then 800 592 3688.
WESTERN UNION: Unavailable.

AMEX: +44 1273 696933
DINERS CLUB: no local number
MASTERCARD: 900 97 1231
VISA: (1) 410 581 9091

AMEX: +44 1273 571 600
THOMAS COOK: 900 99 4403
VISA: 900 97 4447

0900–1300 and 1500–1700 Mon to Fri, 0900–2000 Sat.

Similar prices to the rest of Western Europe.

Catalan, Spanish and French are also spoken.

Summers are generally warm and winters are cold, but the climate is generally temperate. There is rain throughout the year.

Roman Catholic.

1998: Jan 1, 6; Mar 14; Apr 10, 13; May 1, 8, 19, 29; Aug 15; Sept 8; Nov 1; Dec 8, 25, 26.
1999: Jan 1, 6; Mar 14; Apr 2, 5; May 1, 8, 19, 29; Sept 8; Nov 1; Dec 8, 25, 26.

Sockets 240 volts AC 50 Hz. Lighting 125 volts AC.

Approx. 1 week to Europe. Internal mail services are free.

BBC: 12.09 9.410 6.195 3.995
VOA: 5.995 6.040 11.96 15.20

Similar to other European countries.

ROAD: A good road runs from the Spanish to the French border. DOCUMENTATION: A national driving licence is sufficient.

Usual social courtesies, as in Western Europe, should be applied.

Angola

CAPITAL: Luanda

 GMT +1

 FROM UK: 244. IDD: N
OUTGOING CODE: Calls through the operator are booked in advance

 Not present.

 Embassy of the People's Republic of Angola, 98 Park Lane, London W1Y 3TA. Tel: (0171) 495 1752. Fax: (0171) 495 1635.

 British Embassy, CP 1244, Rua Diogo Cão 4, Luanda, Angola. Tel (2) 392 991. Fax: (2) 333 331.

 No visas are issued for tourists therefore there is no representation.

 National Tourist Agency, CP 1240 Palácio de Vidro, Luanda, Angola,. Tel: 2) 372 750.

 Return Ticket required. May be subject to short-term change. Contact Embassy before departure. PASSPORT REQUIRED BY ALL

 Required by all. Tourist travel is not permitted. Business Visas granted.

 Firearms and Ammunition.

 Persons arriving without a visa are subject to possible arrest or deportation.

 HEP A, POLIO, TYPHOID: R.
MALARIA: R. Falciparum variety present.
YELLOW FEVER: R. with vaccination certificate if arriving from an infected area.
OTHER: Bilharzia, Cholera and Rabies.

 W 1.

 New Kwanza (NKW) = 100 lwie (LW). Note: All imported currency should be declared on arrival. Export of local currency is prohibited. Credit cards and travellers cheques are not accepted.
ATM AVAILABILITY: Unavailable

 MONEYGRAM: Unavailable.
WESTERN UNION: Unavailable.

 AMEX: +44 1273 696933
DINERS CLUB: No local number
MASTERCARD: No local number
VISA: No local number

AMEX: No local number
THOMAS COOK: No local number
VISA: No local number

 0845–1600 Mon–Fri

 High inflation present due to the country's unstability.

 Portuguese. African languages are spoken by the majority of the population.

 North: Hot and wet in the summer months (Nov to Apr), winter is slightly cooler and mainly dry. South: Hot throughout the year with a slight decrease in the winter months.

 Roman Catholic, Protestant and Animist.

 1998: Jan 1, 4; Feb 4, 24; Mar 8; May 1; June 1; Sept 17; Nov 11; Dec 25.
1999: Jan 1, 4; Feb 4, 24; Mar 8; May 1; June 1; Sept 17; Nov 11; Dec 25.

 220 Volts Ac, 60 Hz. Plugs = Continental 2 pin.

 5–10 days for airmail.

 BBC: 21.66 17.88 15.40 9.600
VOA: 21.49 15.60 9.525 6.035

 Women are generally self-sufficient due to the decimation of most of the male population in civil war.

 FLIGHTS: Between main centres. RAIL: Erratic with no sleeping cars or air conditioning. ROAD: Many roads are unsuitable for travel. Local advice is needed. DOCUMENTATION: ID papers to be carried at all times. All travel is strictly controlled and some business travel is prohibited.

 NOTE: HIGH RISK. The FCO advises against travel to Angola, unless on essential business. Much of the country is still mined and banditry and car-jacking are common.

CAPITAL: The Valley

 GMT-4

 FROM UK: 1809   IDD: Y
OUTGOING CODE: 011

 911

No Embassy in the UK.

Anguilla Tourist Office, 3 Epirius Road, London SW6 7UJ. Tel: (0171) 937 7725. Fax: (0171) 938 4793.

Department of Tourism, The Secretariat, The Valley, Anguilla. Tel: 497 2759 or 497 2451. Fax: 497 3389.

 Return Ticket required. Requirements may be subject to short term change. Contact embassy before departure.
VALID PASSPORT REQUIRED BY ALL:

 May be required by some nationals, check with the Passport office, Clive House, Petty France, London SW7.

 Narcotics.

 EC$ 13, payable in local currency, for international departures.

 POLIO, TYPHOID: R.
YELLOW FEVER: A vaccination certificate is required from passengers over 1 year of age arriving from infected areas

 W2

 Eastern Caribbean Dollar (EC$) = 100 cents. Exch; Currency may be exchanged in the capital. Amex is the most widely used credit card. Visa has a limited acceptance. Traveller's cheques in US dollars are the easiest to exchange.
ATM AVAILABILITY: Unavailable.

 MONEYGRAM: Unavailable
WESTERN UNION: 497 2653.

 AMEX: +44 1273 696933
DINERS CLUB: No local number
MASTERCARD: No local number
VISA: (1) 410 581 9091

 AMEX: (1) 801 964 6665
THOMAS COOK: 1 800 223 7373
VISA: 1 800 732 1322

 0800–1500 Mon to Thur. 0800–1700 Fri.

 Hotels range from deluxe class to self-catering, but all are expensive.

 English.

 Generally hot. Oct–Dec is the rainy season, July–Oct hurricanes may occur.

 Roman Catholic, Anglican, Baptist, Methodist and Moravian with Hindu, Jewish, and Muslim minorities.

 1998: Jan 1; Apr 10, 13; May 1, 26, 30; June 16; Aug 4, 7, 8; Dec 19, 25, 26.
1999: Jan 1; Apr 2, 5; May 1, 26, 30; June 16; Aug 4, 7, 8; Dec 19, 25, 26.

 110/220 volts AC, 60 Hz.

 4 days to 2 weeks.

 BBC: 9.300 5.975 6.195 7.325
VOA: 15.12 11.58 9.775 5.995.

Although equality prevails, women are still expected to fulfil traditional housekeeping roles.

 ROAD: There is a good but basic network of roads. TAXIS: Are available at the airport and seaports with various fixed prices to hotels and resorts. CAR HIRE: Agencies are present. DOCUMENTATION: A temporary licence can be issued by the police station in the capital on presentation of a valid national driving licence.

Relaxed lifestyle with predominant English culture. Beachwear should be confined to the beach and resort areas.

Antigua and Barbuda

CAPITAL: St Johns

GMT-4

FROM UK: 1809   IDD: Y
OUTGOING CODE: 011

999/911

Antigua and Barbuda High Commission, 15 Thayer Street, London W1M 5LD. Tel: (0171) 486 7073/4/5. Fax: (0171) 486 9970.

British High Commission, PO Box 483, 11 Old Parham Road, St John's, Antigua. Tel: 462 0008/9. Fax: 462 2806 or 482 271.

Refer to High Commission.

Antigua Department of Tourism, PO Box 363. Long and Thames Streets, St John's, Antigua. Tel: 462 0408. Fax: 462 2483.

Return Ticket required. Requirements may be subject to short-term change. Contact embassy before departure.
VALID PASSPORT REQUIRED BY ALL: Nationals of the USA do not require a passport providing they have other documents with proof of their identity. A valid passport is required by all other nationalities. Passports have to be valid for at least 6 months beyond the intended period of stay.

Required if stay is longer than 6 months.

Contact the High Commission for a full list.

US$35 foreign national departure tax except children under 16 years of age.

POLIO, TYPHOID: R.
YELLOW FEVER: A vaccination certificate is required from passengers over 1 year of age arriving from infected areas.

W2

Eastern Caribbean Dollar (EC$) = 100 cents. Exch: US$ and Sterling can be exchanged at hotels and larger shops.
All credit cards are accepted. Travellers cheques can be exchanged at banks, large hotels and shops. US dollars are the preferred currency.
ATM AVAILABILITY: Over 70 locations.

MONEYGRAM: 1 800 543 4080.
WESTERN UNION: 497 2653.

AMEX: +44 1273 696933
DINERS CLUB: No local number.
MASTERCARD: 1 800 307 7309
VISA: (1) 410 581 9091

AMEX: (1) 801 964 6665
THOMAS COOK: 1 800 223 7373
VISA: 1 800 732 1322

0800–1400 Mon to Thur. 0800–1700 Fri.

Can be very expensive, especially in the tourist centres. Accommodation is cheaper in the summer than in the winter.

English, English Patois is also spoken.

Tropical, warm climate. Rainfall is minimal.

Anglican, Methodist, Moravian, Roman Catholic, Pentecostal, Baptist and Seventh Day Adventists.

1998: Jan 1; Apr 10, 13; May 1, 19; Jul 7; Aug 4, 5; Nov 1; Dec 25, 26.
1999: Jan 1; Apr 2; 5. May 1, 19; Jul 7; Aug 4, 5; Nov 1; Dec 25, 26.

220/110 volts AC 60 Hz. American style 2-pin plugs are generally used. Some hotels have outlets for 240 volts to be used in which case European type 2-pin plugs are used.

5–7 days.

BBC: 17.84 15.22 6.195 5.975
VOA: 15.20 11.70 6.130 9.455.

Usual precautions should be taken. Do not walk alone at night or in quiet areas.

ROAD: Mostly all weather. Buses are irregular. TAXI: Available everywhere charging standard rates, US$ commonly accepted. CAR HIRE: Can be arranged before arrival although is easy to arrange on arrival. DOCUMENTATION: A national driving licence is acceptable but a local licence must be obtained.

Embracing is the common method of greeting friends and family. Dress should be appropriate for the occasion and location i.e. keep beachwear for the beach/pool. Special events, such as International Sailing Week (in Apr/May) and Tennis Weeks (July–Aug), require accommodation to be booked well in advance.

CAPITAL: Buenos Aires

GMT–3

FROM UK: 54
OUTGOING CODE: 00

IDD: Y

Police – 101/107.

Embassy of the Argentine Republic, 53 Hans Place, London, SW1X 0LA. Tel: (0171) 584 6494

British Embassy, Casilla 2050, Dr Luis Agote 2412/52, 1425 Buenos Aires, Argentina. Tel: (1) 803 7070/1. Fax: (1) 803 1731

Argentine Consulate, Fifth Floor, Trevor House, 100 Brompton Road, London, SW3 1ER. Tel: (0171) 589 3104. Fax: (0171) 584 7863.

Secretaría de Turismo de la Nación, Calle Suipacha 1111, 21º, 1368 Buenos Aires, Argentina. Tel: (1) 312 5621. Fax: (1) 313 6834.

Return Ticket Required by Australia, Japan and others. May be subject to change at short notice. Contact the Consular authority before departure. Valid passport required

Visas required by all for business purposes. Refer to the relevant authority for visa requirements for tourists.

Animals and birds from Africa and Asia (except Japan), parrots and fresh food stuffs. All gold must be declared.

US\$ 13. Transit passengers and those under two years of age are exempt. This can not be paid in other currencies.

POLIO, TYPHOID: R. MALARIA: Exists in the Vivax variety in rural and areas below 1200m. OTHER: N. Rabies, noteworthy risk of Hepatitis A, Trypanosomiasis, Gastroentiritis, Intestinal Parasitosis and Anthrax. W2

Nuevo Peso (P) = 100 centavos. Diners Club, American Express and MasterCard are accepted. Travellers cheques can be exchanged in larger towns: US Dollars preferred. ATM: Over 800 locations.
MONEYGRAM: 001 800 54288 then 800 592 3688
WESTERN UNION: 1 311 4900.
AMEX: +44 1273 696933
DINERS CLUB: (54) (1) 721 6356
MASTERCARD: 08002-2002
VISA: No local number
AMEX: (1) 313 1823
THOMAS COOK: +44 1733 318950
VISA: +44 1733 318949

1000–1500 Mon to Fri.

Budget travel is not impossible. Reasonably priced lodging, food and transport is available. Allow for fluctuating prices between cities and rural areas.

Spanish is the official language. English, German, French and Italian are sometimes spoken.

The central area is hot and humid Dec–Feb, cooler in winter. The north has a sub-tropical climate, the south has a sub-arctic climate.

Roman Catholic, Protestant minority.

1998: Jan 1; Apr 9, 10; May 1, 25; June 8, 15, 20; July 9; Aug 17; Oct 12; Dec 8, 25, 31.
1999: Jan 1; Apr 1, 2; May 1, 25; June 8, 15, 20; July 9; Aug 17; Oct 12; Dec 8, 25, 31.

220 Volts AC, 50 Hz. Plugs = older buildings require 2-pin , but 3-pin can be used in more modern buildings.

Airmail to Europe takes between 5 to 10 days. Surface mail can take as long as 50 days, so airmail is advisable.
BBC: 17.79 15.19 11.75 9.915
VOA: 15.12 11.91 9.590 6.130

Women's roles differ greatly from those in cities and large towns to simple traditional customs in the lower Andes. Catholocism maintains a high profile on society in general. Lone women travellers will find Argentina generally safer than most Latin American countries, although caution is still advised. Single women in Buenos Aires may encounter some unwanted attention.

FLIGHTS: Air travel is the most convenient way to get around the main cities but is often in heavy demand and subject to delay.
ROADS: Cross-country high ways are well built, although road conditions off the main routes can be unreliable. DOCUMENTATION: IDP is required and this must be stamped at the offices of the Automovil club Argentina. Minor violations are subject to large fines. RAIL: One of the largest domestic rail networks in the world. It has good facilities and lower class travel can be good value.

Avoid casual discussion of the Falklands/ Malvinas islands. Due to an increase in crime, occasionally involving violence, avoid poorly-lit areas at night. Avoid carrying large amounts of cash at all times. Beachwear is not suitable for town. Avoid military installations, which usually allow no stopping. Theft is rife in Buenos Aires; do not offer resistance if robbery is attempted.

Armenia

CAPITAL: Yerevan

 GMT + 4.

 FROM UK: 374   IDD: Available to Yerevan. Outgoing calls to countries outside the CIS must be made through the operator. Long waits are inevitable.

 Not present.

 Embassy of the Republic of Armenia, 25A Cheniston Gardens, London W8 6TG. Tel: (0171) 938 5435. Fax: (0171) 938 2595. British Embassy, 28 Charents Street, Yerevan, Armenia. Tel: (2) 151 842. Fax: (2) 151 807.

 Intourist, 219 Marsh Wall, Isle of Dogs, London E14 9PD. Tel: (0171) 538 8600. Fax: (0171) 538 5967.
Not present.

 Requirements may be subject to change at short notice. Contact the relevant authority before travelling. Required by all and must be valid for 3 months from the point of departure.

 Visa required

 Pornography, loose pearls and anything owned by a third party to be carried for that third party. Works of art and antiques, lottery and state loan tickets can not be exported. A full list is available from Intourist.

 POLIO, TYPHOID: R.
OTHER: Rabies

 W1

 The official currency is the Armenian Dram introduced to replace the Rouble in 1993. The exchange rate is stabilising but rapid inflation is possible. US Dollars and Russian Roubles are sometimes used in official transactions. NOTE: The import and export of local currency is prohibited for non-residents. Import and export of foreign currency is unlimited by non-residents if declared on arrival. Neither credit cards or travellers cheques are accepted.
ATM AVAILABILITY: 2 locations.

 MONEYGRAM: Unavailable.
WESTERN UNION: 2 58 9367.

 No local contact numbers

 No local contact numbers

 0930–1730 Mon to Fri.

 High inflation: all luxury goods are very expensive and in short supply.

 Armenian and Russian.

 Continental climate: Summers are hot and dry but temperatures fall at night. Winters are very cold with heavy snowfalls.

 Christian (mostly Armenian Aspotolic Church). Russian Orthodox and Muslim minority.

1998: Jan 1, 6; Apr 24; May 9, 28; Sept 21; Dec 7, 31.
1999: Jan 1, 6; Apr 24; May 9, 28; Sept 21; Dec 7, 31.

 220 volts Ac, 50 Hz. Power cuts are frequent.

 International services are severely disrupted and extremely erratic with infrequent deliveries made. Letters may be more efficiently handled if posted via Paris but may still be subjected to considerable delay.

BBC: 15.57 11.76 9.410 6.195
VOA: 9.760 6.040 1.197

 Women tend to be less retiring than in nearby Muslim areas. There have recently been attacks on single women walking alone in Yerevan at night. Vigilance is recommended.

 ROAD: Surfaces can be very poor even in the case of major highways. Supplies of fuel and parts are limited. COACHES: Run between major centres of population.

 NOTE: A cease-fire has been in place since May 1994 but the dispute over Nagrony Karabakh remains unresolved and border areas with Azerbaijan should still be avoided. Travel at night outside the capital Yerevan should be avoided if possible. It is not clear whether maintenance procedures for local aircraft are observed. Visitors are advised to travel by an International airline departing from outside Armenia. Visitors should avoid discussing politics with the local population.

CAPITAL: Oranjstad

GMT–4

FROM UK: 2978   IDD: Y
OUTGOING CODE: 00

Police: 11000, Ambulance: 74300, Fire: 115

No Embassy on the UK.
EUROPE: Office of the Minister Plenipotentiary of Aruba, Schimmelpennincklaan 1, 2517 JN The Hague, The Netherlands. Tel: (70) 356 6200 or 365 9824. Fax: (70) 345 1446.
Not present.

Caribbean Tourism, Vigilant House, 120 Wilton Road, London SW1V 1JZ. Tel: (0171) 233 8382. Fax: (0171) 873 8551.
Aruba Tourism Authority, PO Box 1019, L G Smith Boulevard 172, Oranjstad, Aruba. Tel: (8) 21019 or 23777. Fax: (8) 34702.

Return Ticket required. Requirements may be subject to short-term change. Contact embassy before departure.
Valid passport required.

All nationals may enter for a period of 14 days for tourist purposes providing they have onward or return tickets and proof of sufficient funds for the length of stay.

Duty free is only available to persons over 18 years.

Approx. US$20 per person for all travellers over 2 years of age.

YELLOW FEVER: R.
A Yellow Fever vaccination certificate is required from travellers over 6 months of age arriving from infected areas.

W2

Aruba Florin (AFL) = 100 cents. Exch: The US$ is widely accepted. Local currency can not be exchanged outside Aruba. Travellers cheques in US dollars are widely accepted. MasterCard is widely accepted.
ATM AVAILABILITY: 10 locations.

MONEYGRAM: 800 1554.
WESTERN UNION: 2978 22473.

AMEX: +44 1273 696933
MASTERCARD: 800 1561
VISA: No local number

AMEX: 1 801 964 6665
Thomas Cook: 1 800 223 7373
VISA: 1 800 732 1322

0800–1200 and 1300–1600 Mon to Fri.

Hotels on the Palm Beach and Eagle Beach resorts are very expensive. Rates for other accommodations are much lower in the summer season.

Dutch, English, Spanish and Papiamento are also spoken.

Warm and dry climate. Average temperature 28°C. The months of October, November and December experience short showers.

Roman Catholic, Protestant and Jewish minorities.

1998: Jan 1, 25; Feb 23; Mar 18; Apr 10, 12, 13, 30; May 1, 8; Dec 25, 26.
1999: Jan 1, 25; Feb 22; Mar 18; Apr 2, 4, 5, 30; May 1; 8; Dec 25, 26.

110 volts Ac 60 Hz.

Up to 1 week.

BBC: 17.84 15.22 9.915 5.975
VOA: 15.12 11.58 9.590 6.130

Usual precautions should be taken. Do not walk alone at night or in quiet areas.

FLIGHTS: Air Aruba offers domestic services between other Caribbean islands. ROAD very good system of roads throughout the island. BUS: Bus services operate between the towns and hotels. TAXI: Fares are fixed and should be checked before journey. CAR HIRE: The most pleasant way of getting around the island. Many cars are available. DOCUMENTATION: A valid national or IDP is required. Minimum age is 23 for driving.

Beachwear should only be worn around the beach/pool.

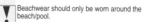

CAPITAL: Canberra

East GMT + 10, Central + 9.5, West + 8.

FROM UK: 61   IDD: Y
OUTGOING CODE: 0011

Emergency services: 000.

High Commission for the Commonwealth of Australia, Australia House, The Strand, London. WC2B 4LA. Tel: (0171) 379 4334. Fax: (0171) 465 8218.

British High Commission, Commonwealth Avenue, Yarralumba, Canberra ACT 2600, Australia. Tel: (6) 270 6666. Fax: (6) 273 3236.

Australian Tourist Commission, Gemini House, 10–18 Putney Hill, London, SW1S 6AA. Tel: (0181) 780 2227. Fax: (0181) 780 1496.

Australian Tourist Commission, PO Box 2721 Level 3, 80 William Street, Woolloomooloo. Sydney, NSW 2011, Australia. Tel: (2) 360 1111. Fax: (2) 331 3385.

Return Ticket Required. Regulations may be subject to change at short notice. Contact the embassy before departure.
VALID PASSPORT REQUIRED.

Visa required.

Strict regulations on non–prescribed drugs, weapons, foodstuffs and potential sources of disease and pestilence.

YELLOW FEVER: A vaccination certificate will be required if travelling from an infected area.

Australian Dollar (A$) = 100 cents. NOTE: Import or export of A$5000 must be reported to customs at entry or departure. All major credit cards and traveller's cheques, in any international currency, are widely accepted. ATM AVAILABILITY: Over 6000 locations.

MONEYGRAM: 0011 800 66639472.
WESTERN UNION: 1 800 649 565.

AMEX: +44 1273 696933
DINERS CLUB: (61) (3) 8054444
MASTERCARD: 1 800 120 113
VISA: 1 800 125 161

AMEX: (02) 886 0689 (Sydney only), 1 800 251 902 (outside Sydney).
THOMAS COOK: 1 800 127 495

VISA: 1 800 127 477

0930–1600 Mon to Thur, 0930–1700 Fri. These hours vary throughout the country.

Comparatively cheap compared to the UK and USA. Caters for all.

English and many minority languages.

Extreme varieties of climate from tropical to temperate. Nov–Mar warm or hot everywhere. Apr–Sept occasional rain in the South which can be intense.

Mainly Protestant, Roman Catholic and many minorities.

1998: Jan 1, 8, 2;. Feb 10; Mar 2, 9, 16; Apr 10, 11, 13, 14, 24; Apr 25; May 4 (NT, QL), 18 (SA); June 1 (WA), 8 (AC, NS, NT, QS, SA, TS, VI); July 3, 10, 17, 24, 25 (NT); Aug 3, 12. (NT); Sept 28 (WA); Oct 5, 8. (AC, NS, SA); Dec 25, 26.
1999: Jan 1, 8, 26; Feb 10; Mar 2, 9, 16; Apr 2, 4, 5, 6, 24; Apr 25; May 4 (NT, QL), 18 (SA); June 1 (WA), 8 (AC, NS, NT, QS, SA, TS, VI); July 3, 10, 17, 24, 25 (NT); Aug 2, 12. (NT); Sept 28 (WA); Oct 5, 8. (AC, NS, SA); Dec 25, 26.

240/250 Volts AC 50 Hz. Unique 3 pin plugs used–adaptor required.

7–10 days.

BBC: 15.36 11.95 9.740 7.145
VOA: 21.50 11.72 9.525 5.985.

Relatively safe for women travellers although a patriarchal culture still prevails, especially in the outback.

FLIGHTS: Vast size of Australia makes this the most convenient form of intercity travel. ROAD: In the outback a full set of spares should be carried, with water, food and petrol. DOCUMENTATION: National licence, valid for 3 months, must be carried whilst driving.

If travelling into the interior, specific precautions should be taken, for instance, take adequate supplies, and leave information of your whereabouts. Special care and respect of natural habitats is recommended.
Always ask permission before photographing aborigines. Tourists should exercise care in Sydney, as a number of backpackers have been attacked. Be cautious when using ATMs.

Austria

CAPITAL: Vienna

GMT + 1 (GMT + 2 from last Sunday in March to the Saturday before the last Sunday in Sept)

FROM UK: 43   IDD: Y
OUTGOING CODE: 00

Police: 133, Ambulance: 144, Fire: 122.

Embassy of the Republic of Austria, 18 Belgrave Mews West, London, SW1X 8HU. Tel: (0171) 235 3731/4. Fax: (0171) 235 8025.

British Embassy, Jauresgasse 12, A–1030 Vienna, Austria. Tel: (1) 713 1575. Fax: (1) 714 7824.

Austrian National Tourist Office, 30 St George Street, London, W1R 0AL. Tel: (0171) 629 0461. Fax: (0171) 499 6038.

Österreich Werbung (ANTO), Margaretenstrasse 1, A-1040 Vienna, Austria. Tel: (1) 58866. Fax: (1) 588 6620.

Valid passport required. Requirements may be subject to short term change. Contact embassy before departure.

Visa required by all except: Nationals of EU countries with a valid ID card.

Rabies. Ticks also pose a problem, and may transmit Lyme disease.

Austrian Schilling (Ssch) = 100 Groschen. Exch: All banks, exchange counters at airports, railway stations. Credit cards are not as widely used in Austria as they are in the USA and the United Kingdom, however most major cards will be accepted in large towns. Travellers cheques are accepted in towns and tourist areas.
ATM AVAILABILITY: Over 3000 locations.

MONEYGRAM: 022 903 011..
WESTERN UNION: (0222) 798 4400

AMEX: +44 1273 696933
DINERS CLUB: (43) (1) 5046667
MASTERCARD: 0660 8235
VISA: (1) 410 581 9091

AMEX: 0660 6840
THOMAS COOK: 0660 6266
VISA: 0660 7320

0800–1230 and 1330–1500 Mon, Tues, Wed and Fri. Thur 0800–1230 and 1330–1730 . Various provinces will have different opening times.

Relatively expensive, similarly to other Western European countries.

German.

Moderate continental climate. Winter – high snow levels but sunny. Summer – warm days cool nights.

Mostly Roman Catholic, some Protestant.

1998: Jan 1, 6; Apr 13; May 1, 8, 19, 29; Aug 15; Oct 26; Nov 1; Dec 25, 26.
1999: Jan 1, 6; Apr 5; May 1, 8, 19, 29; Aug 15; Oct 26; Nov 1; Dec 25, 26.

220 volts AC 50 Hz. Round 2 pin European plugs are used.

2–4 days within Europe.

BBC: 11.78   9.410   6.195   3.955
VOA: 15.20   9.760   6.060   5.995.

RAIL: An efficient rail service operates throughout Austria. Special offers / discounts can often be found. ROAD: Excellent network of roads. There is free assistance from the Austrian motoring association. (OAMTC). DOCUMENTATION: Green card is strongly recommended for driving. The British driving licence is usually recognised.

It is customary to greet people with the salute Grüss Gott. Austrians tend to be quite formal. The church holds a high position in Austrian society which should be kept in mind by the visitor. It is customary to dress up for the opera or theatre.

Azerbaijan

CAPITAL: Baku

 GMT + 4. (GMT + 5 during the summer).

 FROM UK: 994   IDD Available to Baku. All international calls must be made through the operator.

 Not present.

 Embassy of the Azerbaijan Republic, 4 Kensington Court, London W8 5DL. Tel: (0171) 938 5482. Fax: (0171) 937 1783.

British Embassy, 2 Izmir Street, 370065 Baku, Azerbaijan. Tel: (12) 985 558. Fax: (12) 922 739.

 Refer to the Embassy.

 Ministry of Foreign Affairs, Ghanjlar meydani 3, 370004 Baku, Azerbaijan. Tel: (12) 933 012. Fax: (12) 937 969 or 930 743.

 Return Ticket required. Requirements may be subject to short-term change. Contact the relevant authority before departure. VALID PASSPORT REQUIRED BY ALL: Must be valid for at least the length of the visa.

 Visa required.

 Antiques, works of art, precious metals, state loan certificates, lottery tickets, siaga horns, punctuate and red deer antlers and punctuate deer skins.

 MALARIA: Exists exclusively in the vivax variety throughout the year in Southern areas of Azerbaijan. OTHER: Rabies, Cutaneous and visceral leishmaniasis occur. Trachoma is common.

 W1

 CURRENCY: 1 Manat (AM) = 100 gyapik. Travellers cheques and credit cards are not accepted. It is generally a cash-only economy. ATM AVAILABILITY: Unavailable.

 MONEYGRAM: Unavailable. WESTERN UNION: Unavailable.

 No local numbers.

 No local numbers.

 0930–1730 Mon to Fri

 Since the dispute with Armenia, shortage of commodities has forced prices to rise.

 Azerbaijani.

 Continental climate.

 Mostly Shia Muslim.

 1998: Jan 1, 30*; Mar 8; May 7*, 28; Oct 9, 18; Nov 17; Dec 14*, 30*, 31. 1999: Jan 1, 18*; Mar 8; May 7*, 28; Oct 9, 18; Nov 17; Dec 9, 14*, 30*, 31.

 220 volts AC 50 Hz.

 International postal services are severely disrupted. Long delays are inevitable and may take months. Parcels may not arrive in tact.

 BBC: 15.57 11.76 9.410 7.160 VOA: 9.760 6.040 1.197 0.792

 Local women, especially in rural areas tend to be retiring. Initially foreign women are treated with courtesy, which may lead to unwelcome attention. Women are advised to dress conservatively and act in a cool manner.

 ROAD: Most of the road network is paved. Military operations and mass migration of refugees may delay journeys considerable. NOTE: Special permission from the Ministry of Interior will be required to visit regions in restricted areas.

NOTE: Travel to this region should be avoided. Recent incidents against foreigners have included robberies and have in some cases been violent. Visitors must be vigilant at all times. Use officially marked taxis, which you should not share with strangers. It is not known whether aircraft used on internal flights are subject to thorough maintenance procedures and therefore internal flights should not be used.

CAPITAL: Nassau

GMT–5

FROM UK: 1809   IDD: Y
OUTGOING CODE: 011

All services: 911

High Commission of the Commonwealth of the Bahamas, 10 Chesterfield Street, London, W1X 8AH. Tel: (0171) 408 4488. Fax: (0171) 499 9937.

British High Commission, PO Box N-7516, Third Floor, Bitco Building, East Street Nassau, The Bahamas. Tel: 325 7471/2/3. Fax: 323 3871.

Bahamas Tourist Office, 3 The Billings, Walnut Tree Close, Guildford, Surrey GUI 4UL. Tel: (01483) 448 900. Fax: (01483) 448 990.

Bahamas Ministry of Tourism, PO Box N-3701, Bay Street, Nassau, The Bahamas. Tel: 322 7500 or 322 8634. Fax: 328 8634. Fax: 328 0945.

Return Ticket required. Requirements may be subject to short term change. Contact embassy before departure.
PASSPORT REQUIRED BY ALL.

Visa Not Required by Nationals of EU countries for visits of less than 8 months.

Radio transmitters.

Ba$15, payable in local currency. Children under 3 years of age and transit passengers are exempt.

YELLOW FEVER: A vaccination certificate is required from travellers over 1 year of age arriving within 6 moths of visiting an infected area.

W2

Bahamian Dollar (Ba$) = 100 cents. All major credit cards are accepted. Travellers cheques, preferably in US dollars or Pound sterling, are accepted.
ATM AVAILABILITY: Over 25 locations.

MONEYGRAM: 1 800 543 4080.
WESTERN UNION 327 5170.

AMEX: +44 1273 696933
DINERS CLUB: No local number
MASTERCARD: 1 800 307 7309
VISA: (1) 410 581 9091

AMEX: (1) 801 964 6665
THOMAS COOK: 1 800 223 7373
VISA: 1 800 732 1322

0930–1500 Mon to Thur, 0930–1700 Fri.

Avoid the tourist centres when looking for cheaper accommodation and food. Staying in the Bahamas may prove difficult for the budget traveller.

English.

The Bahamas are slightly cooler than other islands in the Caribbean.

Baptist, Anglican and Roman Catholic.

1998: Jan 1; Apr 10, 13; May 26; June 1, 5; July 10; Aug 4; Oct 12; Dec 25, 26.
1999: Jan 1; Apr 2, 5; May 26, 31; June 5; July 10; Aug 3; Oct 12; Dec 25, 26.

120 volts AC 60 Hz

5 days.

BBC: 17.84 15.22 9.915 5.975
VOA: 15.21 11.70 6.130 0.930

Usual precautions should be taken. Do not walk alone at night or in quiet areas.

SEA: A mail boat serves the outer island which may also be used by passengers. ROAD: Inexpensive and frequent buses are available. TAXIS: Metered. CAR HIRE: Major companies have agencies at the airport and in Nassau. DOCUMENTATION: A valid British driving licence is valid for 3 months.

Bahamas has 700 islands in total. The tourist may consider visiting those that are less commercial. Beach wear is not acceptable in towns where informal dress should be worn. It is illegal to work without a work permit. Employment is scarce so do not expect to find work to finance your visit. Violent crime is increasing and a number of incidents have taken place in tourist areas. Lock balcony doors in hotel rooms. Penalties are severe for involvement in drugs.

CAPITAL: Manama

 GMT + 3.

 FROM UK: 973. IDD Y.
OUTGOING CODE: 0

 All services: 999.

 Embassy of the State of Bahrain, 98 Gloucester Road, London SW7 4AU. Tel: (0171) 370 5132/3. Fax: (0171) 835 1814. British Embassy, PO Box 114, 21 Government Avenue, Manama, 306, Bahrain. Tel: 534 404 or 534 865/6. Fax: 531 273.

 Refer to Embassy.

 Bahrain Tourism Company (BTC) PO Box 5831, Manama, Bahrain. Tel: 530 530. Fax: 530 867.

 Return Ticket required. Requirements may be subject to short-term change. Contact the relevant authority before departure.
VALID PASSPORT REQUIRED BY ALL
Visa required by citizens of the UK for a maximum of 4 weeks (providing their full passport is valid for 6 months).

 Jewellery and all items originating in Israel may only be imported under licence. Pearls are under strict import regulations.

 BD3 for international departures, payable in local currency.

 Holders of Israeli passports. Holders of passports with visas or endorsements for Israel (valid or expired) are permitted to transit Bahrain providing they do so by the same aircraft.

 POLIO, TYPHOID: R.

OTHER: Cutaneous leishmaniasis, typhoid fevers and hepatitis A and B occur.

 Dinar (BD) = 100 fils. All credit cards and travellers cheques are accepted. US dollars are the preferred currency.
ATM AVAILABILITY: Over 60 locations.

 MONEYGRAM: 800 010.
WESTERN UNION: 214021.

 AMEX: +44 1273 696933
DINERS CLUB: (973) 530188
MASTERCARD: 800 087
VISA: (1) 410 581 9091

 AMEX: (973) 256 834
THOMAS COOK: +44 1733 318950
VISA: +44 1733 318949

 0800–1200 and usually 1600–1800 Sat to Wed. 0800–1100 Thur.

 Can be relatively cheap if you travel around by foot and make purchases from the souk. Accommodation ranges from the deluxe to cheaper family-run guest houses

 Arabic. English may also be spoken.

 Summers are very hot. Winters are much cooler. Rainfall is only likely in the winter. Spring and autumn are pleasant.

 Muslim (Shia and Sunni). Christian, Bahai, Hindu and Parsee minorities.

 1998: Jan 1, 30*; Apr 7*, 28; May 7*; July 6*; Dec 16.
1999: Jan 1, 31*; Apr 7*, 28; May 8*; July 7*; Dec 16.

 230 volts AC, single phase and 400 volts, 50 Hz. (Awali–100 volts AC, 60 Hz.) Plugs are normally the 13-amp pin type.

 3–4 days to Europe.

 BBC: 15.58 12.10 11.76 9.410
VOA: 15.20 11.83 9.700 7.205.

 Attitudes towards women are more liberal than in many other Gulf states. It is acceptable to wear short dresses. However, it is advisable to avoid wearing revealing clothes. Bahrain is described as one of the friendliest countries in the Gulf to travel in.

 SEA: Transport between the smaller islands is by motor boat or dhow. ROAD: Manama is served by an excellent road system. BUS: Routes now serve most towns and villages. TAXI: Identifiable by their orange and red colouring. Those waiting outside hotels may charge more and between midnight and 0500 – fares increase by 50 %.

 Bahrain is relatively liberal in comparison to other Gulf countries. Non Muslims may not enter mosques except during prayer times. Violent crime is quite rare, but visitors should avoid village areas, especially after dark. It is polite to drink 2 small cups of tea when offered.

Bangladesh

CAPITAL: Dhaka

 GMT + 6.

 FROM UK: 880   IDD: Y. Limited.
OUTGOING CODE: 00

 High Commission for the People's Republic of Bangladesh, 29 Queen's Gate, London SW7 5JA. Tel: (0171) 584 0081. Fax: (0171) 225 2130.

 British High Commission, PO Box 6079, United Nations Road, Baridhara, Dhaka 1212, Bangladesh. Tel: (2) 882 705 or 883 666 (consular/immigration). Fax: (2) 883 437.

 Refer to High Commission.

 Bangladesh Parjatan Corporation (National Tourism Organisation) 33 Old Airport Road, Tejgaon, Dhaka 1215, Bangladesh. Tel: (2) 325 155. Fax: (2) 817 235.

Return Ticket required. Requirements may be subject to short-term change. Contact the relevant authority before departure.
VALID PASSPORT REQUIRED BY ALL

 Visa required.

Animals.

Tk300, payable in local currency. Passengers in transit are exempt.

POLIO, TYPHOID: R. MALARIA: Exists throughout the year in the whole country, except Dhaka City. The falciparum variety is reported to be highly resistant to chloroquine. YELLOW FEVER: A vaccination certificate is required if arriving from an infected area. OTHER: Cholera, Rabies, Filariasis, Visceral leishmaniasis, Dengue Fever, Dysentery and Hepatitis A, B and E are present.
W1

 Bangladeshi Taka (Tk) = 100 poisha. Exchange: Many shops in cities offer better rates than banks. NOTE: All currency exchange must be entered on a currency declaration form. Diners Club and Amex accepted. Travellers cheques can be exchanged at Dhaka Airport. ATM: Unavailable.
MONEYGRAM: Single location at capital city. WESTERN UNION: (2) 9554733.

AMEX: +44 1273 696933
DINERS CLUB: 880 2 258128
MASTERCARD: No local number
VISA: No local number

AMEX: (1) 801 964 6665
THOMAS COOK: +44 1733 318950
VISA: +44 1733 318949

0900–1500 Sat to Wed, 0900–1300 Thur.

 Can be cheap if willing to sacrifice luxuries.

 Bengali (Banga). English is spoken in Government and commercial circles.

 Generally a hot tropical climate with a monsoon season Apr–Oct when temperatures are highest. The cool season is Nov–Mar.

 Mainly Muslim with Hindu, Buddhist and Christian minorities. Since 1988 Islam has been the official state religion.

 1998: Jan 27*, 30; Feb 21; Mar 26; Apr 7, 14; May 1, 7, 10; July 1, 6; Aug 15; Sept 4; Oct 22; Dec 6, 16, 25, 31.
1999: Jan 27*, 30; Feb 21; Mar 26; Apr 7, 14; May 1, 7, 10; July 1, 6; Aug 15; Sept 4; Oct 22; Dec 6, 16, 25, 31.

 220/240 volts AC, 60 Hz. Plugs are of the British 5 an 15 amp, 2 or 3 pin 9 (round) type.

 Airmail takes 3–4 days to Europe. Surface mail can take several months.
BBC: 17.79 15.31 11.75 9.740
VOA: 17.74 15.42 9.760 6.110

 Women should wear trousers or long skirts especially when attending religious places. Women should not be photographed unless it is clear there will be no objection.

 RAIL: A slow but efficient system sometimes limited by the geography of the country. ROAD: It is possible to reach almost everywhere by road, but given the country's geography with frequent ferry crossings. Poor driving and vehicle maintenance as well as unlit buses and lorries cause frequent accidents. BUS: Serve all major towns, fares are generally low. TAXI: Available at airports and major hotels. Agree fares in advance. CAR HIRE: Available at airports and major hotels. DOCUMENTATION: IDP or national licence.

 NOTE: New arrivals should register with the High Commission in Dhaka. Money must not be given as gifts as it causes offence. Religious customs should be respected by all visitors. PHOTOGRAPHY: In rural areas people are unused to tourists and therefore respect should be shown. Do not take photographs of military installations. SPECIAL PRECAUTIONS: Visitors should avoid demonstrations and crowded places where outbreaks of violence have occurred. Major roads between towns are subject to night time armed banditry.

Barbados

CAPITAL: Bridgetown

 GMT-4

FROM UK: 1809   IDD: Y
OUTGOING CODE: 011
Police: 112; Ambulance: 115; Fire: 113.
All services: 119.

Barbados High Commission, 1 Great Russell Street, London, WC1B 3JY. Tel: (0171) 631 4975. Fax: (0171) 323 6872.

British High Commission, PO Box 676, Lower Collymore Rock, St Michael, Barbados. Tel: 436 6694. Fax: 436 5398.

Barbados Tourism Authority, 263 Tottenham Court Road, London, W1P AA. Tel: (0171) 636 9448. Fax: (0171) 637 1496.

Barbados Tourism Authority, PO Box 242 Harbour Road, Bridgetown, Barbados. Tel: 427 2623/4. Fax: 426 4080.

Return Ticket required.
VALID PASSPORT REQUIRED: must be valid for 6 months after date of entry.

Visa not required by nationals of EU countries for stays up to 6 months.

Import of foreign rum and ammunition and firearms. Permits are required for plants and animals.

Bds$25 in local currency, for all departures.

POLIO, TYPHOID: R
YELLOW FEVER: A vaccination certificate if required from passengers over 1 year of age coming from infected areas.

 Barbados Dollar (Bds$) = 100 cents. All major credit cards are accepted. Travellers cheques, preferably in US dollars and Pound sterling, are accepted.
ATM AVAILABILITY: 45 locations.

MONEYGRAM: 1 800 543 4080.
WESTERN UNION: 436 6055.

 AMEX: +44 1273 696933
DINERS CLUB: No local number.
MASTERCARD: 1 800 307 7309
VISA: (1) 410 581 9091

 AMEX: (1) 801 964 6665
THOMAS COOK: 1 800 223 7373
VISA: 1 800 732 1322

0800–1500 Mon to Thur, 0800–1300 and 1500–1700 Fri.

Generally expensive. Avoid the tourist centres if travelling on a budget, although prices throughout the island are quite expensive.

English. Local Bajan dialect is also spoken.

Subtropical climate cooled by sea breezes. Wet season – July till Nov when brief showers occur. Dry season – Dec till June.

Christian (Protestant majority, Roman Catholic minority). Small numbers of Jews, Hindus and Muslims are also present.

1998: Jan 1, 21; Apr 10, 13; May 1; June 1; Aug 1, 3; Oct 5; Nov 30; Dec 25, 26.
1999: Jan 1, 21; Apr 2, 5; May 1, 31; Aug 1, 3; Oct 5; Nov 30; Dec 25, 26.

110 volts AC 50 Hz American style 2-pin plug are used.

Up to 1 week.

BBC: 17.84 15.22 6.195 5.975
VOA: 15.12 11.91 9.590 5.995

Usual precautions should be taken. Do not walk alone at night or in quiet areas.

 FLIGHTS: Several operators run flights between neighbouring islands. ROAD: A good network of roads run throughout the island. BUS: Frequent comprehensive coverage of the island. Although cheap buses are crowded during the rush hour. CAR HIRE: Various vehicles can be hired at the airport or large hotels. DOCUMENTATION: A Barbados driving licence is required, a valid national or IDP should be held.

Attacks and thefts are rare although persistent salesmen are likely to continually approach you. Visitors should exercise common sense precautions such as not exhibiting conspicuous signs of wealth and not to visit deserted beaches at night.

Belarus

CAPITAL: Minsk

GMT + 2

FROM UK: 7. IDD: Y in all major cities.
OUTGOING CODE: International calls go
through the operator.

Police: 02; Ambulance: 03; Fire: 01.

Embassy of the Republic of Belarus, 6
Kensington Court, London W8 5DL. Tel:
(0171) 937 3288.

British Embassy, Zakharova 26, 220034
Minsk, Belarus. Tel: (172) 368 687. Fax:
(172) 144 7226.

Intourist, 219 Marsh Wall, Isle of Dogs,
London E14 9FJ. Tel: (0171) 538 8600. Fax:
(0171) 538 5967.

Belintourist, Maserava 19, 220078, Minsk,
Belarus. Tel: (172) 269 840. Fax: (172) 231
143.

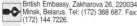
Return Ticket required. Requirements may be
subject to short term change. Contact
embassy before departure.
VALID PASSPORT REQUIRED: must be
valid for 6 months after departure.

Required by all except nationals of the CIS
republics. Transit visas are required if crossing Belarus to reach Ukraine or the Baltic
States. Visas not available on arrival.

Pornography, loose pearls, anything owned
by a third party that is to be carried in for that
third party.

Not present.

OTHER: Poliomyelitis, Rabies.

Belarusian Rouble. Exchange: Should only
take place at authorised bureaus and the
transaction must be entered on the currency
declaration form which will be issued on
arrival. Amex and Visa are accepted in larger
towns. Travellers cheques are not widely
accepted, but are preferable to cash. It is
advisable to take hard currency as well.
ATM AVAILABILITY: 5 locations.

MONEYGRAM: Unavailable.
WESTERN UNION: 095 119 8250.

AMEX: +44 1273 696933
DINERS CLUB: No local number
MASTERCARD: No local number
VISA: (1) 410 581 9091

AMEX: +44 1273 571 600
THOMAS COOK: +44 1733 318950
VISA: +44 1733 318949

0900–1730 Mon to Fri.

An improving economy exists with cheap to
moderately priced goods available.

Belarusian, but Russian is also spoken by
13% of the population.

Temperate continental climate.

Christian, mainly Eastern Orthodox and
Roman Catholic with small Jewish and
Muslim minorities.

1998:Jan 1, 7; Mar 8, 15; Apr 12, 13, 28;
May 9; July 3; Dec 27, 31.
1999: Jan 1, 7; Mar 8, 15; Apr 4, 5, 28; May
9; July 3; Dec 27, 31.

220 volts AC 50 Hz, adapters are
recommended.

At least 10 days. Larger hotels offer Poste
Restante facilities.

BBC: 17.64 15.07 9.410 6.195
VOA: 15.20 11.96 7.170 6.040.

Traditionally, a patriarchal society, but
younger women are becoming more
liberated.

RAIL: 5590 km of rail track is in use. ROAD:
Tourists can only drive on approved routes.
Valid visa and passport, insurance certificate
and customs form guaranteeing the visitor
will not take the car out of the country,
Intourist documentation with the approved
route and accommodation to be used must
be carried at all times. DOCUMENTATION:
IDP is required.

The people of Belarus offer a welcoming and
friendly hospitality to visitors. It is advisable
to take warm clothing in winter and water-
proofs throughout the year. Avoid dairy produce and mushrooms, which can carry high
levels of radiation. Theft is a problem so
exercise caution in major cities.

Belgium

CAPITAL: Brussels

 GMT + 1

 FROM UK: 32   IDD: Y
OUTGOING CODE: 00

Police: 101; Fire, Ambulance: 100

Embassy of the Kingdom of Belgium,
103–105 Eaton Square, London, SW1W
9AB. Tel: (0171) 470 3700 (general
enquiries) or (0891) 600 255 (recorded message) Fax:(0171) 259 6213.

British Embassy, 85 rue d'Arlon, B-1040
Brussels, Belgium. Tel: (2) 287 6211. Fax: (2)
287 6355.

Belgian Tourist Office, 5th Floor, 29 Princes
Street, London W1R 7RG. Tel: (0171) 629
3977 or (0891) 887 799 (recorded message)
Fax: (0171) 629 0454.

Office de promotion du Tourisme Wallonie-
Bruxelles, 61 rue Marché-aux-Herbes, B-
1000 Brussels, Belgium. Tel: (2) 504 0200.
Fax(2) 513 6950.

Return Ticket required. Requirements may be
subject to short term change. Contact
embassy before departure.
Valid Passport Required by all except nationals of EU countries providing they carry a
national ID card.

 Unpreserved meat products. Other preserved
food stuffs must be declared.

 BFr250/530.

 Rabies

 Belgian Franc (Bfr) = 100 centimes. Credit
cards and Travellers cheques are widely
accepted. US dollars are the preferred
currency.
ATM AVAILABILITY: Over 2000 locations.

 MONEYGRAM: 0800 7 1173.
WESTERN UNION: 0800 99088.

 AMEX: +44 1273 696933
DINERS CLUB: No local number
MASTERCARD: 0800 1 5096
VISA: 0800 7 1460

AMEX:0800 12112
THOMAS COOK: 0800 1 2121
VISA: 0800 7 1645

0900–1200 and 1400–1600 Mon to Fri.
Some banks are open 0900–1200 Sat.

Relatively expensive, similarly to other
Western European countries.

Flemish and French.

Warm May–Sept, and snow likely during the
winter months.

Mostly Roman Catholic with small minorities
of Protestants and Jews.

1998: Jan 1; Apr 13; May 1, 21, 22; July 21;
Aug 15, 17; Nov 1, 11; Dec 25.
1999: Jan 1; Apr 5; May 1, 20, 22; July 21;
Aug 15, 16; Nov 1, 11; Dec 25.

220 Volts AC 50 Hz. Plugs are the 2 pin
round type.

2–3 days to other European destinations.
Poste Restante is available in the main cities.

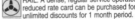 BBC:11.78 6.195 3.955 0.648
VOA: 15.20 11.97 9.670 6.040

Similar values as in the rest of Western
Europe.

RAIL: A dense, regular service operates. A
reduced rate card can be purchased for
unlimited discounts for 1 month period.

 Flemings often prefer to speak English,
rather than French, to all foreign visitors.

CAPITAL: Belmopan

 GMT–6

 FROM UK: 501   IDD: Y
OUTGOING CODE: 00

 All services: 911

 Belize High Commission, 22 Harcourt House, 19 Cavendish Square, London, W1M 9AD. Tel: (0171) 499 9728. Fax: (0171) 491 4139.

Belize High Commission, 22 Harcourt House, 19 Cavendish Square, London, W1M 9AD. Tel: (0171) 499 9728. Fax: (0171) 491 4139.

British High Commission, PO Box 91, Embassy Square, Belmopan, Belize, CA. Tel: (8) 22146/7. Fax: (8) 22761.

Caribbean Tourism, Vigilant House, 120 Wilton Road, London SW1V IJZ. Tel: (0171) 233 8382. Fax: (0171) 873 8551.

Belize Tourist Board, PO Box 325, 83 North Front Street, Belize City, Belize, CA. Tel: (2) 77213. Fax: (2) 77490

 Return Ticket Required. Requirements may change at short notice. Contact the High Commission before departure. Passports valid for 6 months beyond the intended length of stay are required by all.

 Visa Required by all, but it is advisable to contact the High Commission before departure as regulations are subject to change.

 Narcotics and firearms.

 BZ$22.50 departure tax with BZ$ 2.50 security tax is levied on all passengers except transit passengers and those under 12 years of age. Payable in the local currency.

 POLIO, TYPHOID: R.
MALARIA: Exists throughout the year, excluding the urban areas, predominately in the benign Vivax form.
YELLOW FEVER: A vaccination certificate is required for travellers arriving from infected areas.
OTHER: Rabies

 W1

 Belizean Dollar (BZ$) = 100. Amex and Visa are widely accepted. MasterCard can also be used but to a more limited extent. US Dollars is the preferred currency for travellers cheques.
ATM AVAILABLITY: Unavailable.

 MONEYGRAM: 555 then 800 592 3688.
WESTERN UNION: (2) 72678.

 AMEX: +44 1273 696933
DINERS CLUB: No local number
MASTERCARD: 1 314 542 7111
VISA: (1) 410 581 9091
AMEX: (1) 801 964 6665
THOMAS COOK: +44 1733 318950
VISA: +44 1733 318949

 0800–1300 Mon to Thur, 0800–1200 and 1500–1800 Fri.

 Caters for all travellers and budgets.

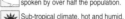 English is the official language but Spanish is spoken by over half the population.

 Sub-tropical climate, hot and humid. Monsoon season June–September.

 Roman Catholic, Anglican, Methodist, Mennonite, Seventh Day Adventist, Pentecostal minorities.

 1998: Jan 1; Mar 9; Apr 10–13; May 1, 24; Sept 10, 21; Oct 12; Nov 19; Dec 25–26.
1999: Jan 1; Mar 9; Apr 2–5; May 1, 24; Sept 10, 21; Oct 12; Nov 19; Dec 25–26.

 110/220 Volts Ac 60 Hz.

 Up to 5 days to Europe

 BBC: 17.82 15.22 9.590 7.325
VOA: 11.91 9.775 6.130 5.995

 Culture is influenced by Caribbean, Latin and colonial heritage. Women tend to restrict their activities to simple craft-making and household chores. Visitors may experience pestering from the local men, which should not be a problem if ignored.

 FLIGHTS: Charter and scheduled flights operate between the main towns. ROAD: All weather roads link the main towns in the country although torrential rain during the monsoon season often makes these impassable. CAR HIRE: International companies exist in the main cities. DOCUMENTATION: A national driving licence is acceptable.

 Petty crime is common and mugging is a problem in major cities. Travel in groups if possible. Common sense rules should be applied. It is inadvisable to discuss politics with the locals.

Benin

CAPITAL: Porto Novo

 GMT +1

 FROM UK: 229   IDD: Y
OUTGOING CODE: 00

30 14 31 (UK Embassy)

Republic of Benin Consulate, Dolphin House, 16 The Broadway, Stanmore, Middlesex HA7 4DW. Tel: (0181) 954 8800. Fax: (0181) 954 8844.

The British High Commission in Lagos deals with enquiries relating to Benin.

Refer to Embassy.

Office National du Tourisme et de l'Hôtellerie (ONATHO), BP 89, Contonou, Benin. Tel: 315 402.

 Return Ticket Required. May be subject to short term change. Contact the Embassy before departure.
VALID PASSPORT REQUIRED

 Visa Required.

 Foreign currency.

 Departure tax levied CFA 2500 or US$ 9.

 POLIO, TYPHOID: R.
MALARIA: Required, Falciparum variety present.
YELLOW FEVER: Required with a vaccination certificate if arriving from an infected area.
OTHER: Bilharzia, Meningitis, Rabies, Trypanosomiasis, Cholera, Hepatitis A.

 W 1

 CFA Franc = 100 centimes. Benin is part of the French Monetary Area. Only currency issued by the Banque des Etats de l'Afrique Centrale is valid. Credit cards are accepted on a very limited basis. French francs are the preferred currency in traveller's cheques.
ATM AVAILABILITY: Unavailable.

 MONEYGRAM: Unavailable
WESTERN UNION: 31 40 23

 AMEX: +44 1273 696933
DINERS CLUB: No local number
MASTERCARD: 1 314 542 7111
VISA: (1) 410 581 9091
AMEX: No local number
THOMAS COOK: +44 1733 318950
VISA: +44 1733 318949

0800–1100 and 1500–1600 Mon to Fri

 Moderate growth resulting in continuous rising prices.

French. A variety of languages are also spoken by ethnic groups. Some English is spoken.

 South: hot and dry from Jan to Aug. Rainy season is May–July and Sept–Dec. North: hot and dry from Nov to Jun and cooler and very wet July–Oct.

 Mostly Animist / Traditional with Muslim and Christian (mainly Roman Catholic).

 1998: Jan 1, 10, 30*; Apr 7*, 13; May 1, 21; June 1; July 6*; Aug 1, 15; Nov 1; Dec 25.
1999: Jan 1, 10, 30*; Apr 6*; May 1, 21, 31; July 5*; Aug 1, 15; Nov 1; Dec 25.

 220 Volts AC 50 Hz.

 3–5 days for airmail.

 BBC: 17.85 15.40 15.07 7.16
VOA: 21.49 15.65 9.575. 6.035

 A predominantly patriarchal society, but with the changing economy, roles are modifying.

 RAIL: 600 km of track runs from Contonou to Pobé, Ouidah, Seg boroué and Patakou.
ROAD: these are reasonably good but most are impassable during the rainy season. It is advisable to clear your itinerary with the authorities. Foreigners travelling outside Contonou are subject to restrictions and visitors are advised to check their position before travelling. TAXI: Settle fares in advance. CAR HIRE: A number of local car hire firms now exist. DOCUMENTATION: International Driving License is required.

 NOTE: Recent attacks and armed robberies require the visitor to be vigilant. Importance is placed on religious beliefs which should be respected.

CAPITAL: Hamilton

GMT–4

FROM UK: 441   IDD: Y
OUTGOING CODE: 011

All services: 911.

British Dependant territories Visa Section, The Passport Office, 70–78 Clive House, Petty France, London, SW1H 9HD. Tel: (0171) 271 8552. Fax: (0171) 271 8645

Not present.

Bermuda Tourism, 1 Battersea Church Road, London SW11 3LY. Tel: (0171) 734 8813. Fax: (0171) 352 6501

Bermuda Department of Tourism, Global House, 43 Church Street, Hamilton HM 12, Bermuda. Tel: 292 0023. Fax: 292 7537

Return Ticket Required. Requirements may change at short notice. Contact the Embassy before departure.
VALID PASSPORT REQUIRED.

Visas are not required for stays of up to 3 weeks.

Spear guns for fishing, firearms and non-prescribed drugs.

Bda$20. Levied on passengers over 12 years old. Passengers in immediate transit are exempt. This is payable in local currency.

Bermuda Dollar (Bda $) = 100 cents. Export of local currency is usually limited to Bda$ 250. US Dollar cheques are widely accepted. Mastercard, American Express Visa, and Diners Club are all accepted, in hotels, shops and restaurants.
ATM AVAILABILITY: 54 locations.

MONEYGRAM: 1 800 543 4080.
WESTERN UNION: Available.

AMEX: +44 1273 696933
DINERS CLUB: 800 468 4033
MASTERCARD: 1 800 307 7309
VISA: (1) 410 581 9091

AMEX: (1) 801 964 6665
THOMAS COOK: 1 800 223 7373
VISA: 1 800 732 1322

0930–1500 Mon to Thur, 0930–1500 and 1630–1730 Fri.

Very Expensive. Bermuda is a holiday destination for affluent tourists.

English is the official language. There is a small community of Portuguese speakers.

Semi-tropical climate, with cool sea breezes. Showers can occur at any time of the year.

Anglican, Episcopal, Roman Catholic, Christian.

1998: Jan 1; Apr 10; May 25; June 15; July 30, 31; Sept 7; Nov 11; Dec 25–26.
1999: Jan 1; Apr 1; May 24; June 14; July 30, 31; Sept 7; Nov 11; Dec 25–26.

110 Volts AC 60 Hz. American flat, 2-pin plugs are used.

Airmail: 5–7 days to Europe.

BBC: 17.84 15.22 9.515 5.975
VOA: 15.21 11.70 6.130 5.995

Bermuda has a very English air about it. The pace is relaxed and polite. Usual precautions should be taken. There is no need for additional concern.

ROAD: Visitors are not allowed to drive in Bermuda. TAXI: Official taxis display a small blue flag.

Most hotels and restaurants require jacket and tie in the evening. Social conventions are mostly British influenced.

CAPITAL: Thimphu

 GMT + 6.

 FROM UK: 975.
IDD: Restricted to main areas.
OUTGOING CODE: 00

 No representation.

 No representation. Nearest Consulate in Calcutta.

 Not present.

 Bhutan Yod Sel Tours and Treks. PO Box 574, Thimpu, Bhutan. Tel: (2) 23912. Fax: (2) 23589

 Return Ticket required. Requirements may be subject to short-term change. Contact the relevant authority before departure.
VALID PASSPORT REQUIRED BY ALL

 Visa Required by all except for nationals of India. NOTE: There are two ways of entering Bhutan; by air to Paro Airport or by road to the Bhutanese town of Phuntosholing. All travellers entering by road must ensure they have the necessary documentation for transiting through India.

 Gold and silver bullion and obsolete currency. The export of antiques, religious objects, manuscripts, images and anthropological materials is strictly prohibited.

 Nu 300, payable in local currency.

 POLIO, TYPHOID: R.
MALARIA: Exists throughout the year in the Southern belt. Resistance to chloroquine has been reported in the falciparum variety of the disease.
YELLOW FEVER: A vaccination certificate is required if coming from an infected area.
OTHER: Cholera, Rabies, Meningitis.

 W1

1 Ngultrum (NU) = 100 chetrum (Ch). Exch: Leading foreign currencies can be exchanged at the Bank of Bhutan. Major hotels may also exchange currency. Amex and Diners Club have a very limited acceptance. Traveller's cheques can be exchanged at the Bank of Bhutan branches.
ATM AVAILABILITY: Unavailable.

 MONEYGRAM: Unavailable/
WESTERN UNION: Unavailable.

 AMEX: +44 1273 696933
DINERS CLUB: Not present.
MASTERCARD: No local number
VISA: No local number

AMEX: (1) 801 964 6665
THOMAS COOK: +44 1733 318950
VISA: +44 1733 318949

 0900–1700, with an hour's closure at lunchtime, Mon–Fri

 Caters for all budgets, but predominantly very inexpensive. Accommodation varies from hotels in the capital to guesthouses and cottages elsewhere.

 Dzongkha is the official language. A large number of local dialects are spoken due to the isolation of many villages. Nepali is common in the South of the country.

 June–Aug: The temperatures drop dramatically as this is the monsoon period. Nights are cold. Generally Oct, Nov and Apr–mid Jan are the best times to visit when rainfall is slight and temperatures are pleasant.

 Mahayana Buddhism is the state religion; the majority of Bhutanese people follow the Drukpa school of the Kagyupa sect.

 1998: Jan 1*, 30; Apr 6. 7, 28; June 25, 26; July 6, 26, 27; Sept 24; Nov 3, 11, 12, 20.
1999: Jan 1*, 30; Apr 6, 7, 28; June 25, 26; July 6, 26, 27; Sept 24; Nov 3, 11, 12, 20.

 220 volts Ac, 50 Hz.

 Airmail to Europe can take up to 2 weeks.

 BBC: 17.79 15.31 11.75 9.740
VOA: 17.74 15.40 11.71 7.125

 Equal rights exist between men and women.

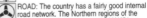 ROAD: The country has a fairly good internal road network. The Northern regions of the High Himalayas have no roads. YAKS/ PONIES/MULES: The main form of transportation. DOCUMENTATION: IDP required.

 Religion has a strong influence on traditional ways of life. Travel to the country has been restricted to visitors for many years and some areas are closed to foreigners. The country must be entered via India or Bangladesh.

Bolivia

CAPITAL: La Paz

 GMT-4

 FROM UK: 591. IDD: Y.
OUTGOING CODE: 011

 Embassy and Consulate of the Republic of
Bolivia, 106 Eaton Square, London, SW1W
9AD. Tel: (0171) 235 4248 or 235 2257. Fax:
(0171) 235 1286.
British Embassy, Avienda Arce 2732, Castilla
694, La Paz, Bolivia. Tel: (2) 357 424. Fax:
(2) 391 063.

 Contact the Embassy or Consulate.

 Direccón Nacionale de Turismo, Calle
Mercado 1328, Casilla 1868, La Paz, Bolivia.
Tel: (2) 367 463. Fax: (2) 374 630.

 Valid Passport Required by all.

 Visa Required for all tourist purposes.

 Cameras must be declared.

 US$20 for all international departures. This
can not be paid in other currencies.

 POLIO, TYPHOID: R.
MALARIA: Exists in rural and low lying areas
below 2500m in the Vivax variety. Resistance
to chloroquine has been reported.
YELLOW FEVER: Vaccination is recommended to all. Those arriving from infected
areas must have a vaccination certificate.

 W2

 Boliviano (B) = 100 centavos. Sterling can not
be exchanged. Most money is changed at
Gambios and Hotels. All major credit cards
have very limited acceptance. US Dollars
travellers cheques are the most acceptable
form of currency to take with you. Sterling
cheques can be changed with difficulty.
ATM AVAILABILITY: 70 locations.

 MONEYGRAM: 0 800 1112.
WESTERN UNION: (2) 379 422
AMEX: +44 1273 696933
DINERS CLUB: No local number.
MASTERCARD: 1 314 542 7111
VISA: (1) 410 581 9091
AMEX: (1) 801 964 6665
THOMAS COOK: 1 800 223 7373
VISA: 1 800 732 1322

 0830–1200 and 1430–1730 Mon to Fri.

 Caters for all budgets. Reasonable prices for
comfortable accommodation and eating out.

 Spanish, English, Inca and other local
dialects spoken.

 There can be extreme temperature changes
between day and night especially in the
mountain areas. The wet season is between
November and February. Le Paz has very
thin air due to its high altitude.

 Roman Catholic, Protestant.

 1998: Jan 1; Feb 10, 23, 24; Apr 10, 15; May
1, 25; June 11; July 16; Aug 6; Sept 14, 24;
Nov 1, 2, 10, 18; Dec 25.
1999: Jan 1; Feb 10, 22, 23; Apr 2, 15; May
1, 25; June 10; July 16; Aug 6; Sept 14, 24;
Nov 1, 2, 10, 18; Dec 25.

 110/220 Volts AC in La Paz. 220 Volts AC in
the rest of the country, 50 Hz. Plugs: most
houses have 2-pin sockets for both electrical
currents. Variations may occur.

 3–4 days. A Poste Restante service is
available.

 BBC: 11.86 11.75 7.325 5.970
VOA: 15.12 11.58 9.590 5.995

 Women's roles are dependent on their geographical location within Bolivia. Women
travelling alone will arouse suspicion.
Unwelcome attention from men may occur.
Dress should be conservative.

 During the rainy season all modes of public
transport including airlines may suspend services for weeks at a time without explanation. ROAD: Work is in progress to improve
the condition of the road network. Standards
of driving are often low which may make rail
a preferred option. When driving, a full set of
spares, tools, extra petrol, food and water
should be carried. DOCUMENTATION: IDP
is required. When entering Bolivia a circulation card 'Hoja de Ruta' must be obtained
from the 'Servicio National de Transito' at the
border of Bolivia. These will be presented
and stamped at all police posts.

 Respect for traditions should be observed.
Rural Bolivians should be referred to as
campesinos, rather than Indians, which is
considered an insult. Petty theft is an
occasional problem.

Bonaire

CAPITAL: Kralendijk

 GMT-4.

FROM UK: 599   IDD:Y.
OUTGOING CODE: 00

Police: 11; Ambulance: 14.
All services: 5997 8004.

No embassy in the UK.
EUROPE: Office of the Minister Plenipotentiary of the Netherlands Antilles, Badhuisweg 173–175, 2597 JP The Hague, The Netherlands. Tel: (70) 306 6111. Fax: (70) 351 2722.
The British Consulate in Curacao deals with enquiries relating to Bonaire.

Caribbean Tourism, Vigilant House, 120 Wilton Road, London SW1V 1JZ. Tel: (0171) 233 8382. Fax: (0171) 873 8551
Tourism Corporation Bonaire, Kaya Simon Bolivar 12, Kralendijk, Bonaire, Netherlands Antilles. Tel: 78322. Fax: 78408.

Return Ticket required. Requirements may be subject to short-term change. Contact Embassy before departure.
VALID PASSPORT REQUIRED

Nationals of the UK are allowed to stay for 90 days without a visa providing they have a return or onward ticket. NOTE: Enquire at the Ministers office at the Hague for a complete, up to date list of regulations regarding individual countries.

 Narcotics and firearms.

 NAG 22.50 for passengers over two years of age on international flights. US$5.75 for inter-Caribbean flights.

 POLIO, TYPHOID: R.
YELLOW FEVER: A vaccination certificate is required from travellers over one year of age coming from an infected area.

 Netherlands Antilles Guilder or Florin (NAG) = 100 cents. NOTE: Import and export of local currency is limited to NAG 200. Credit cards are accepted in large establishments. Travellers cheques in US currency is the most welcomed.
ATM AVAILABILITY: 10 locations approximately.

 MONEYGRAM: Unavailable.
WESTERN UNION: Unavailable.

 AMEX: +44 1273 696933
DINERS CLUB: Not present.
MASTERCARD: 001 800 307 7309
VISA: (1) 410 581 9091

AMEX: (1) 801 964 6665
THOMAS COOK: 1 800 223 7373
VISA: 1 800 732 1322

0830–1200 and 1330–1600 Mon to Fri.

Generally inexpensive goods, especially perfume, jewellery and alcohol.

Dutch. Papiamento, English and Spanish are also spoken.

Hot throughout the year with cooling sea winds. Wet season Oct to Dec.

Roman Catholic. Protestant and a variety of Evangelical church minorities.

1998: Jan 1; Apr 10, 13, 30; May 1, 21; Sept 6; Dec 25, 26.
1999: Jan 1; Apr 2, 5, 30; May 1, 20; Sept 6; Dec 25, 26.

 127 volts AC 50 Hz.

 4–6 days.

BBC: 17.82 11.78 9.640 5.975
VOA: 15.20 11.91 9.590 5.995

Society is heavily influenced by South American culture.

ROAD: Reasonably good but a 4-wheel drive may be required for extensive tourism of the island. CAR HIRE: Firms are located at the airport and large hotels. DOCUMENTATION: A valid national licence will be sufficient but drivers must be 23 years or older. TAXI: A good taxi service exists on he island

 Beachwear is only suitable for the beach or poolside. Most bars and restaurants outside the two main hotel resorts are closed by midnight.

Bosnia-Herzegovina

CAPITAL: Sarajevo

 GMT + 1 (GMT + 2 during the summer).

 FROM UK: 387.
IDD AVAILABLE: Formally internationally
IDD-connected as part of the former
Yugoslav federation.
OUTGOING CODE: 99

 It is advisable to consult the foreign office in
your country of residence before departure,
regarding emergency assistance.

 Embassy of the Republic of Bosnia-
Herzegovina, 320 Regent Street, London
W1R 5AB. Tel: (0171) 255 3758. Fax: (0171)
255 3760.

 British Embassy, 8 Tina Ujavica, 7100
Sarajevo, Bosnia-Herzegovina. Tel: (71) 444
429. Fax: (71) 666 131.

 Not present.

 Ministry of Foreign Affairs, Vojvode Putnika 3,
71000 Sarajevo, Bosnia-Herzegovina. Tel:
(71) 213 777. Fax: (71) 653 592.

 The partition of the republic make legal border crossing and airport (Sarajevo) entry for
all foreign nationals dificult. Check before
travelling to the country.

 Narcotics.

 DEM20.

 Rabies

 W1

 Yugoslav Dinar (YuD) = 100 paras. Croatian
Kuna (K) = 100 lipa. In the Serb controlled
areas, only the Yugoslav Dinar is legal
tender, while in Croat controlled areas only
the Kuna is accepted. NOTE: German marks
are the only generally accepted currency.
Pound sterling is of little value and rarely
used. Credit cards not travellers cheques are
accepted anywhere in Bosnia-Herzegovina.
ATM AVAILABILITY: Unavailable.

 MONEYGRAM: Unavailable.
WESTERN UNION: 7221418.

 AMEX: +44 1273 696933
DINERS CLUB: No local number
MASTERCARD: No local number
VISA: No local number

 AMEX: No local number
THOMAS COOK: No local number
VISA: No local number

 0730–1530 Mon to Fri.

 Limited commodities and high inflation as a
result of the war.

 Serbo-Croat (Serbs) and Croato-Serb
(Croats).

 The climate is variable with moderate continental conditions. It is usually cold in the winter and hot in the summer.

 Slavic Muslims, Serbian Orthodox and a
minority of Roman Catholic Croats.

 1998: May 01–02; July 27; Nov 25.
1999: May 01–02; July 27; Nov 25.

 220 volts AC, 50 Hz.

 Uncertain service due to the civil war.

 BBC: 15.58 12.10 9.410 6.195
VOA: 1.197 9.760 6.040 0.792.

 Revealing clothes should not be worn.

Civil war prevents any transport being safe.

The Foreign and Commonwealth Office
advises care in planning travel to Bosnia-
Herzegovina. Although fighting has stopped,
there are violent incidents. Check the situation before travelling.

Botswana

CAPITAL: Gaborone

 GMT +2

 FROM UK: 267. IDD: To over 80 Countries.
OUTGOING CODE: 00

 Police: 351161

 Botswana High Commission, 6 Stratford Place, London W1N 9AE. Tel: (0171) 499 0031. Fax:(0171) 495 8595.

 British High Commission, Private Bag 0023, Gaborone, Botswana. Tel: 352 841 / 2/ 3. Fax: 356 105

 Refer to Embassy.

 Dept of Tourism, Ministry of Commerce and Industry. Private Bag, 0047, Gaborone, Botswana. Tel: 353 024 0r 313 314. Fax: 308 675

  Return ticket required. May be subject to change at short notice. Contact the relevant authority before departure.
VALID PASSPORT REQUIRED BY ALL and must be valid for 6 months.

 Military clothing and some agricultural products, without obtaining prior permission.

 Pula 80, payable in local currency.

 POLIO, TYPHOID: R.
MALARIA: Falciparum variety present.
OTHER: Bilharzia, Cholera, Rabies, Ticks, Hepatitis A, Sleeping sickness present.

W 1

Pula (P) = 100 thebes Note: Export of local currency is limited to P500. Credit cards are accepted on a limited basis. Travellers cheques are accepted, but the surcharge may be high.
ATM AVAILABILITY: 27 locations.

MONEYGRAM: Unavailable
WESTERN UNION: Available.

 AMEX: +44 1273 696933
DINERS CLUB: No local number.
MASTERCARD: 1 314 542 7111
VISA: (1) 410 581 9091

 AMEX: +44 1273 571 600
THOMAS COOK: +44 1733 318950
VISA: +44 1733 318949

 0900–1430 Mon, Tues, Thur and Fri.
Wed: 0815–1200 and Sat 0815–1045.

 Comparable with Western Europe.

 English and Setswana.

 Oct–Apr = Hot and Wet season.
May–Sept = Cooler and Drier.

 Mostly traditional with Christian minority. Islam and Bahá'í faith represented.

 1998: Jan 1, 2; Apr 10, 11, 13; May 1, 25; July 1, 20, 21; Sept 30; Dec 25, 26.
1999: Jan 1, 2; Apr 2, 3, 5; May 1, 20; July 1, 20, 21; Sept 30; Dec 25, 26.

 220/240 Volts AC, 50 Hz Plug s= 13 amp socket.

 1–3 weeks by airmail

 BBC: 17.88 11.94 6.190 3.255
VOA: 21.49 15.60 9.525 6.035

 Men and women are socially and culturally equal.

 AIR, RAIL AND BUS: Major cities are linked by these networks. ROAD: tarmacked roads are limited mostly being sand tracks. Reserves of water and fuel should always be taken. DOCUMENTATION: IDP is recommended for stays up to 6 months, after which a Botswana driving license must be obtained.

 Casual clothing is acceptable. Respect for the traditional way of life must be displayed. Do not take photographs of airports, official residences and military and defence establishments.

CAPITAL: Brasilia

 Spans several time zones: Eastern Standard Time = GMT–3, North East States and East Pará = GMT–3, Western Standard Time = GMT–4, Amapa and West Pará time = GMT–4, Acre State = GMT–5, Fernando de Noronha Archipelago = GMT–2.

 FROM UK: 55. IDD: Y.
OUTGOING CODE: 00

 All services: 0.

 Brazilian Consulate General, 6 St Albans Street, London, SW1Y 839 8958.
British Embassy, Caixa Postal 07-0586, Seto de Embaixadas Sul, Quadra 801, Conjunto K, 70.408 Brasilia DF, Brazil. Tel: (61) 225 2710. Fax: (61) 225 1777.
Brazilian Tourist Office and Embassy of the Federal Republic of Brazil, 32 Green Street, London, W1Y 4AT. Tel: (0171) 499 0877. Fax: (0171) 493 5105.

 Centro Brasileiro de Informacao Turistica (CEBITUR), Rua Mariz e Barros 13, 6º andar, Praca de Bandeira, 20.270 Rio de Janeiro, Brazil. Tel: (21) 293 1313. Fax: (21) 273 9290.

 Return Ticket required. Requirements may change at short notice. Contact the embassy before departure.

 VALID PASSPORT REQUIRED BY ALL. Visas required unless travelling as tourists for stays of under 3 months.

 US$ 17–18 is levied on international departures, payable in local currency only.
Meat and cheese products from various countries. Contact the consular authority.

 POLIO, TYPHOID: R. MALARIA: Exists throughout the year below 900 m in some rural areas. Falciparum variety has been reported as being highly resistant to chloroquine. YELLOW FEVER: A vaccination certificate is required by all travellers arriving from infected areas. OTHER: Bilharzia, Rabies.

 W1

 'Real' (RI) = 100 centavos. All banks and Gambios exchange foreign currency. All major credit cards are accepted. Travellers cheques can be easily exchanged. US Dollar cheques are the preferred currency.
ATM AVAILABILITY: Over 10, 000 locations.

 MONEYGRAM: Limited to larger towns
WESTERN UNION: Unavailable.

 AMEX: +44 1273 696933
DINERS CLUB: (55) (11) 2356628
MASTERCARD: 000 811 887 0553
VISA: 000 811 481 0554
AMEX: (11) 545 5018
THOMAS COOK: 000 811 870 0553
VISA: 000 811 784 0553

 1000–1630 Mon to Fri.

 Deluxe hotels are generally restricted to the cities in the south whilst all other accommodation may be found in habitated areas.
Portuguese. French, German, Italian and English are also spoken.

 Climate varies considerably, from arid scrubland in the interior to the impassable tropical rain forest of the northerly amazon jungle and the tropical eastern coastal beaches.
Rainy season: south = Jan–Apr; north = Apr–July; Rio and Sao Paulo = Nov–Mar.

 Roman Catholic.

 1998: Jan 1, 20, 25, 26; Feb 2, 23–25; Mar 19; Apr 9, 10, 11, 21; May 1; June 11; July 2, 16; Aug 15; Sept 7, 8; Oct 12; Nov 1, 2, 15; Dec 8, 24, 25, 31.
1999: Jan 1, 20, 25, 26; Feb 2, 22–24; Mar 19; Apr 1, 2, 3, 21; May 1; June 10; July 2, 16; Aug 15; Sept 7, 8; Oct 12; Nov 1, 2, 15; Dec 8, 24, 25, 31.

 Brasilia–220 Volts AC, 60 Hz. Rio de Janeiro and Sao Paulo–100 Volts AC, 60 Hz. 2 pin plugs are used.

 4–6 days. Reasonably reliable. Sending mail registered or franked will eliminate the risk of having stamps steamed off.

 BBC: 17.83 15.19 11.75 9.640
VOA: 15.12 11.58 9.590 5.995

 Women play diverse roles, depending upon geography, religion and education. Women travellers will arouse curiosity and possible unwelcome attention from males. Maintaining a low profile is advisable.

 TAXI: Recognised by red number plates and fitted with meters. DRIVING: Car hire is possible but parking is difficult as is driving through the congested city streets. DOCUMENTATION: IDP is required. RAIL: Limited services exist between the major cities but there has been a substantial decline in the number of long distance services operated.

 SPECIAL PRECAUTIONS: Crime is a growing problem, particularly in Rio de Janeiro and Sao Paulo. Taking extreme caution and avoidance of showing expensive possessions is recommended. By law, a passport should be carried at all times.

CAPITAL: Road Town

 GMT–4

 FROM UK: 180949   IDD: Y.
OUTGOING CODE: 001

 Police: 114; Ambulance: 112.

 British Dependant Territories Visa Section, The Passport Office, Clive House, 70–78 Petty France, London, SW1H 9HD. Tel: (0171) 271 8552. Fax: (0171) 271 8645.

 Refer to Home Office.

 British Virgin Islands Tourist Board, 11 St Martins Lane, London, WC2N 4DY. Tel: (0171) 240 4259. Fax: (0171) 240 4270.

 British Virgin Islands Tourist Board, PO Box 134, Waterfront Drive, Roadtown, Tortola, British Virgin Islands. Tel: 43134. Fax: 43866.

Return Ticket required. Requirements may be subject to short-term change. Contact embassy before departure.
VALID PASSPORT REQUIRED

Nationals of Great Britain, Australia, Canada, the USA, and Japan may stay up to 6 months without a visa.

Import licences are needed for some goods mainly foodstuffs.

US$8 for all international departures.

POLIO, TYPHOID: R

W2

US Dollar (US$) = 100 cents. All major credit cards are accepted. Travellers cheques, preferably in US dollars, are accepted.
ATM AVAILABILITY: 6 locations.

MONEYGRAM: Limited availability
WESTERN UNION: 494 5381.

 AMEX: +44 1273 696933
DINERS CLUB: No local number.
MASTERCARD: 1 800 307 7309
VISA: (1) 410 581 9091

 AMEX: 1 800 221 7282
THOMAS COOK: 1 800 223 7373
VISA: 1 800 732 1322

 0900–1500 Mon to Thur, 0900–1700 Fri.

 Generally expensive and may prove difficult for the budget traveller.

English.

 Tropical climate with cooling winds. Low rainfall and comfortable night temperatures.

Methodist. Also church of God, Anglican, Adventist, Baptist and Roman Catholic.

 1998: Jan 1; Mar 9; Apr 10, 13; May 19; June 1; July 1; Aug 3, 5, 6; Oct 21; Nov 14; Dec 25, 26.
1999: Jan 1; Mar 9; Apr 2, 5; May 19, 31; July 1; Aug 2, 5, 6; Oct 21; Nov 14; Dec 25, 26.

 110/60 volts AC 60 Hz. American 2 pin plugs are used.

 Up to 1 week.

 BBC: 17.82 15.2 9.590 5.975
VOA: 15.21 11.91 9.455 5.995.

Usual precautions should be taken.

 ROAD: There is a good road network. TAXI: Usually operate according to fixed rates.
CAR HIRE: There are 9 car hire companies.
DOCUMENTATION: A temporary British Virgin Islands licence is required which will be issued for a small fee on production of a valid foreign licence.

Backpacking is actively discouraged. Beachwear should be kept for the beach or pool. Sixty islands to explore.

Brunei

CAPITAL: Bandar Seri Begawan

 GMT + 8

 FROM UK: 673   IDD: Y.
OUTGOING CODE: 00

Not present.

High Commission of Brunei Darussalam, 19/20 Belgrave Square, London SW1X 8PG. Tel: (0171) 581 0521. Fax: (0171) 235 9717. Consular Section: 19A Belgrave Mews West, London SW1X 8HT. Tel (0171) 581 0521. Fax: (0171) 235 9717

British High Commission, PO Box 2197, 3rd Floor, Hong Kong Bank Chambers, Jalan Pemancha, Bandar Seri Begawan, Brunei. Tel: (2) 222 231 or 222 6001 (consular section). Fax: 226 002.

Refer to High Commission / Consular section.

Information Bureau Section, Information Department, Prime Ministers Office, Bandar Seri Begawan 2041, Brunei. Tel: (2) 240 400. Fax: (2) 244 104.

 Return Ticket Required. Requirements may change at short notice. Contact the embassy before departure.
VALID PASSPORT REQUIRED BY ALL, with assured re-entry facilities to country of origin or domicile required by all. Passports must be valid for at least 6 months after entry.

Visa Not Required by nationals of the UK for stays of up to 30 days. NOTE: All visitors must be able to display proof of sufficient funds on entry.

 Pornography, non-prescribed drugs – the penalty for carrying non-prescribed drugs is harsh.

Br$15.

Nationals of Cuba, Israel and North Korea will be refused admission.

 POLIO, TYPHOID: R
YELLOW FEVER: A vaccination certificate is required by those who have visited an infected area within the previous six days.

 W1

 Brunei Dollar (Br$) = 100 sen. Foreign currency and travellers cheques can be exchanged at any bank. Hotels and department stores may also exchange travellers cheques.

Credit cards are generally accepted by major establishments. NOTE: The export of local currency is limited to Br$1000. Preferable currency for travellers cheques is US dollars. All credit cards are generally accepted by major establishments.
ATM AVAILABILITY: Over 25 locations.

 MONEYGRAM: Unavailable.
WESTERN UNION: Unavailable.

 AMEX: +44 1273 696933
DINERS CLUB: No local number.
MASTERCARD: 1 314 542 7111
VISA: (1) 410 581 9091
AMEX: (852) 885 9331
THOMAS COOK: +44 1733 318950
VISA: +44 1733 318949

 0900–1200 and 1400–1500 Mon to Fri, 0900–1100 Sat.

 Accommodation can be very expensive. Transport and food are comparable with prices in the rest of East Malaysia.

Malay. English Chinese dialects are also spoken.

 Tropical climate most of the year. Monsoon = Oct–Mar when there is very heavy rainfall.

 Mostly Sunni Muslims. Also Buddhist, Confucian, Daoist and Christian minorities.

 1998: Jan 1, 31*; Apr 7*, 10, 13, 26; May 1*; July 6, 7*; Sept 8; Dec 25, 26.
1999: Jan 1, 31*; Apr 2, 5, 7*, 26; May 1*; July 6, 7*; Sept 8; Dec 25, 26.

 230 Volts AC 50 Hz. Plugs are either square or round 3 pin.

 2–5 days.

 BBC: 17.83 15.31 11.95 6.195
VOA: 15.42 11.76 9.770 7.120

 Women should ensure that head, knees and arms are well covered. Women are not expected to shake hands. Generally safe for women travellers.

ROAD: BUS: operate to main centres. CAR HIRE: Available at the airport and large hotels. DOCUMENTATION: IDP is required. A temporary licence can be obtained on presentation of a national licence.

 Avoid passing or receiving with the left hand or pointing the soles of the feet towards companions. Shoes should be removed when entering Muslim homes. If offered refreshments by a host it is considered rude to refuse. Accommodation is impossible to find outside the main towns.

CAPITAL: Sofia

GMT + 2

FROM UK: 359.   IDD: Y to main cities.
OUTGOING CODE: 00, some calls go through the international operator.

Ambulance: 150; Fire: 160; Police: 166.

Embassy of the Republic of Bulgaria, 186–188 Queens Gate , London SW7 5HL. Tel: (0171) 584 9400 or 584 9433. Fax: (0171) 584 4948.
British Embassy, Boulevard Vasil Levski 65 67, Sofia 1000, Bulgaria. Tel: (2) 885 361/2 or 885 325. Fax: (2) 656 022.

Balkan Holidays (Travel Agency), Sofia House, 19 Conduit Street, London W1R 9TD. Tel: (0171) 491 4499. Fax: (0171) 491 7068.
Balkantourist, Boulevard Vitosha 1, Sofia, Bulgaria. Tel: (2) 43331.

Requirements may change at short notice. Contact the relevant authority before finalising travel arrangements.
VALID PASSPORT REQUIRED BY ALL: A valid passport with at least 6 months remaining validity at time of departure is required.

Visa required by all.

Pornography. NOTE: Many items must be declared e.g. antique rolls and scrolls, books and works of art. Check with embassy for a full list.

US$3 levied on all foreign departures.

An aids test may be required if stay is longer than 1 month.

W2

Lev (Lv) = 100 stotinki. Exch: A bordereau receipt will be given and must be kept until departure. NOTE: Import and export of local currency is prohibited. Amounts of currency over US$1000 have to be declared. Diners Club, American Express and Visa have limited acceptance. Travellers cheques can be exchanged in major banks. US dollars and Pound sterling are the preferred currency. ATM AVAILABILITY: Over 100 locations (MasterCard/Cirrus only).

MONEYGRAM: 00800 0010 then 800 592 3688.
WESTERN UNION: Unavailable.

AMEX: +44 1273 696933
DINERS CLUB: 359 2 84131
MASTERCARD: No local numbe
VISA: (1) 410 581 9091

AMEX: +44 1273 571 600
THOMAS COOK: +44 1733 318950
VISA: +44 1733 318949

0800–1130 and 1400–1800 Mon to Fri, 0830–1130 Sat.

Inexpensive when compared with Western Europe.

Bulgarian. English is spoken in resorts. Turkish, Russian, French and German may also be spoken.

Summers are the warmest with some rainfall. Winters are cold with snow. Rain falls frequently in the Spring and Autumn.

Eastern Orthodox Church, Muslim and Roman Catholic minorities.

1998: Jan 1; Mar 3; Apr 17, 20; May 1, 24; Dec 25.
1999: Jan 1; Mar 3; Apr 2, 5; May 1, 24; Dec 25.

220 volts AC, 50 Hz. Plugs are 2 pin.

4 days to 2 weeks to Western Europe.

BBC: 17.64 15.07 9.410 6.180
VOA: 9.760 6.040 5.995 1.521

FLIGHTS: Air travel is only slightly more expensive than rail and much more convenient. RAIL: Reservations are essential, 1st Class is advisable. ROAD: Speed limits are strictly enforced as a drinking and driving penalties. CAR HIRE: Can be arranged through hotels. DOCUMENTATION: AN IDP should be obtained although foreign driving licences are acceptable for short journeys. A 'Green' card is compulsory.

A nod of the head means 'No' and shaking the head means 'Yes'. Dress should be conservative but casual. It is advisable to register with the police, a hotel or guesthouse within 48 hours of arrival. Do not accept food or drink from strangers. Exercise caution in Sofia, particularly at night.

CAPITAL: Ouagadougou

GMT

FROM UK: 226   IDD: Y.
OUTGOING CODE: 00

Information unavailable.

Honorary Consulate of Burkina Faso, 5
Cinnamon Row, Plantation Wharf, London
SW11 3TW. Tel: (01710) 738 1800. Fax:
(0171) 738 2820
British Embassy, 01 BP 2581 Third Floor,
Abidjan 01, Cote d'Ivoire. Tel: 2268 50/1/2
and 328209. Fax: 22 32 21.

Refer to Consulate

Direction de l'Administration Touristique et
Hôtelière, BP 624, Ouagadougou 01, Burkina
Faso. Tel: 306 396

Return Ticket Required.
VALID PASSPORT REQUIRED

VISA REQUIRED BY ALL.

Sporting guns can only be imported under
licence.

US$ 13, is payable on international
departures.

HEP A, POLIO, TYPHOID: R.
MALARIA: R. Falciparum variety present.
YELLOW FEVER: R. with vaccination certifi-
cate if arriving from an infected area.
OTHER: Bilharzia, Rabies, Cholera, River
Blindness and Sleeping Sickness.

W 1

CFA Franc (CFA Fr). Visa and MasterCard
have limited acceptance. Travellers cheques
are accepted on a limited basis. French
francs are the preferred currency.
ATM AVAILABILITY: Unavailable.

MONEYGRAM: Unavailable.
WESTERN UNION: Unavailable.

AMEX: +44 1273 696933
DINERS CLUB: No local number
MASTERCARD: 1 314 542 7111
VISA: (1) 410 581 9091

AMEX: No local number
THOMAS COOK: +44 1733 318950
VISA: +44 1733 318949

0730–1130 + 1500–1600 Mon to Thur,
0730–1130 + 1530–1700 Fri.

Burkina Faso is the sixth poorest country in
the world.

French with several indigenous languages.

Tropical climate. Dec–Mar are the best
months. Rainy season is June–Oct. Winds
blow Nov–Feb which brings cool and dry
weather.

Animist. With Muslim and Christian (Roman
Catholic) minorities.

1998: Jan 1, 3; Mar 8; Apr 7, 13; May 1, 21;
July 6; Aug 4, 5, 15; Oct 15; Nov 1; Dec 11,
25.
1999: Jan 1, 3; Mar 8; Apr 5, 7; May 1, 20;
July 6; Aug 4, 5, 15; Oct 15; Nov 1; Dec 11,
25.

220/380 volts AC 50 Hz. Plugs = 2 pin.

Up to 2 weeks by airmail. There are few post
offices. Poste Restante is available with a
mail- charge for collection of letters.

BBC: 17.83 15.40 15.07 12.09
VOA: 21.49 15.60 9.525 6.035

Society and culture is predominantly
patriarchal.

ROAD: Most are impassable during the rainy
season. Police check points often cause
delay. FLIGHTS: there are few domestic
flights. DOCUMENTATION: Temporary driving licences are available from local authorities if you present a valid national driving
license.

Customs should be respected especially in
traditional rural areas. Clothing can be casual
and should be appropriate for the hot
weather.

Burundi

CAPITAL: Bujumbura

 GMT +2

 FROM UK: 257   IDD: Y.
OUTGOING CODE: 90

 All travellers are advised to consult the foreign office in their country of residence regarding emergency assistance.

No Embassy in the UK. Europe: 46 Square Marie-Louise, B-1040 Brussels, Belgium. Tel: (2) 230 4535 or 230 4548. Fax: (2) 230 7883.

British Consulate, BP 1344, 43 avenue Bubanza, Bujumbura, Burundi. Tel: (2) 23711.

Refer to the Embassy in Belgium.

Office National du Tourisme, BP902, 2 ave des Euphorbes, Bujumbura, Burundi. Tel: (2) 24208. Fax: (2) 29390.

 Return Ticket Required. Regulations may be subject to change at short notice. Contact the Embassy before departure.
VALID PASSPORT REQUIRED BY ALL

 Visa required by all. Tourist and Business. Passengers arriving at Bujumbura airport will be issued entry stamps, providing they have previously informed their travel agency of their passport number and identity.

 All baggage must be declared and duty may be required for cameras, radios and type-writers.

 A departure tax equivalent to 5 US$ is levied for alien residents. Transit passengers are exempt.

 HEP A, POLIO, TYPHOID: R.
MALARIA: R. Falciparum variety exists of which resistance to chloroquine has been reported. The recommended prophylaxis is mefloquine.
YELLOW FEVER: Strongly recommended. If arriving from an endemic area a vaccination certificate will be required.
OTHER: Cholera, Bilharzia, Rabies, Meningitis present.
NOTE: Visitors may be asked to show proof of vaccination against meningococcal meningitis.

 W 1

 Burundi Franc (BIF) = 100 centimes. Unlimited import of foreign currency, subject to declaration, export limited to amount declared on import. Import and Export of local currency is limited to BIF 2000. Limited acceptance of MasterCard and Diners Club. Travellers cheques are not currently accepted.
ATM AVAILABILITY: Unavailable

 MONEYGRAM: Unavailable
WESTERN UNION: Unavailable.

 AMEX: +44 1273 696933.
DINERS CLUB: No local number.
MASTERCARD: 1 314 542 7111
VISA: No local number.
AMEX: No local number.
THOMAS COOK: No local number.
VISA: No local number.

 0800–1130 Mon to Fri. There are banks in Bujumbura and Gitega.
Due to the coup of 1996 the country's economy has been all but wiped out.

 French and Kirundi, Kiswahili is also spoken.

 The climate is mostly mild and pleasant, although a hot equatorial climate is found near Lake Tanganyika and in the Ruzizi river plain.

 Mostly Roman Catholic with local Animist beliefs. Also Anglican and Pentecostalism.

 1998: Jan 1; Feb 5; May 1, 21; July 1; Aug 15; Oct 13, 21; Nov 1; Dec 25.
1999: Jan 1; Feb 5; May 1, 20; July 1; Aug 15; Oct 13, 21; Nov 1; Dec 25.

 220 Volts 50 Hz

 There is a main post office in Bujumbura. Delivery times are uncertain.

 BBC: 21.47 17.88 15.42 6.005
VOA: 21.49 15.60 9.525 6.035

 A volatile tribal culture predominates.

 FLIGHTS: There are no regular internal flights. ROADS: Most are sealed but often impassable during the rainy season.
DOCUMENTATION: IDP is required.

 NOTE: EXTREME RISK. The FCO advises against all travel to Burundi. People outside the cities may not be used to visitors. Therefore respect should be shown for local traditions. Dress should be conservative.

CAPITAL: Phnom Penh

GMT + 7

FROM UK: 855   IDD: Y.
OUTGOING CODE: Calls must go through the operator.

Not present.

No Embassy in the UK.

British Embassy, 29 Street 75, Phnom Penh, Cambodia. Tel: (23) 427124. Fax: (23) 427125.

No Tourist Office in the UK.

Ministry of Tourism, 3 Monivong Boulevard, Phnom Penh, Cambodia. Tel: (23) 26107. Fax: (23) 24607.

Requirements may change at short notice. Contact the embassy before departure. VALID PASSPORT REQUIRED.

Required by all. Tourist and Business types granted. Tourist visas available at airport.

Narcotics.

US$15 levied on international departures.

POLIO, TYPHOID: R.
MALARIA: Exists all year throughout the country in the Falciparum variety, which has been reported as being highly resistant to chloroquine.
YELLOW FEVER: A vaccination certificate is required if arriving from an infected area.
OTHER: Bilharzia, Plague, Poliomyelitis, Rabies.

W1

CURRENCY: Riel (CRI) = 100 sen. Exch: US$ are widely accepted and exchanged. Other currencies are not readily recognised. NOTE: Import and export of local currency is prohibited. Travellers cheques and credit cards are not accepted currently.
ATM AVAILABILITY: Unavailable.

MONEYGRAM: Unavailable.
WESTERN UNION: Unavailable.

AMEX: +44 1273 696933.
DINERS CLUB: No local number.
MASTERCARD: No local number.

VISA: No local number.

AMEX: No local number.
THOMAS COOK: No local number.
VISA: No local number.

0800–1500 Mon to Fri.

Due to civil war, prices fluctuate, although restaurants are in abundance in Phnom Penh.

Khmer. Chinese and Vietnamese are also spoken. French is spoken by older generations and English taught to younger generations.

Tropical Monsoon Climate. May–Oct is the Monsoon. Winters in the North can be cold. Temperatures throughout the country are fairly constant.

Mostly Buddhist with a Christian and Muslim minority.

1998: Jan 1, 7; Feb 11; Mar 8; Apr 14–16; May 1, 10, 14;. June 1, 18; July 1; Sept 21, 24; Oct 23, 30; Nov 3, 4, 5 ,9; Dec 10.
1999: Jan 1; Mar 8; Apr 13–15; May 1, 24, 25–27; June 1, 18; Sept 24; Oct 11–13, 23, 30; Nov 1, 9, 24–26; Dec 10.

220 Volts AC 50 Hz. Power cuts are frequent an power is only available in the evenings outside Phnom Penh.

4–5 days.

BBC: 15.36 11.95 9.740 6.195
VOA: 17.73 15.42 11.76 6.110

Mostly servile in nature and custom.

Independent travel is restricted. ROAD: Travel permits are required to cross provincial borders. Most roads are in poor condition. DOCUMENTATION: IDP is required.

HIGH RISK. Foreigners have been kidnapped and others may be targeted. NOTE: The FCO advises against travel outside the capital. If you have to travel outside Phnom Penh you should contact the embassy for advice. Venturing outside areas under government control will carry a higher degree of risk and bandity is rife. Slow down when approaching check points. PHOTOGRAPHY: Ask permission before taking photos and extra courtesy should be shown towards monks.

Cameroon

CAPITAL: Yaoundé

 GMT +1

 FROM UK: 237   IDD: Y.
OUTGOING CODE: 00

 Not present.

 Embassy of the Republic of Cameroon, 84 Holland Park, London W11 3SB. Tel: (0171) 727 0771. Fax (0171) 792 9353.
British Embassy, BP 547, avenue Winston Churchill, Yaoundé, Cameroon. Tel: 220 545 or 220 796. Fax: 220 148.

 Refer to the Embassy

Société Camerounaise de Tourisme (SOCA-TOUR) BP 7138, Yaoundé, Cameroon. Tel: 233 219.

 Return Ticket Required. Requirements may be subject to change at short notice. Contact the Embassy before departure.
VALID PASSPORT REQUIRED BY ALL
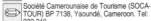 Visas Required. Tourist and Business visas issued.

 Radios, cameras and alcoholic beverages must be declared on arrival and are usually admitted free of duty if there is only one of each of them.

Departure Tax: CFA Fr10,000 for International flights, Fr500 for domestic flights, payable in local currency.
HEP A, POLIO, TYPHOID: R. MALARIA: R. Falciparum variety present, resistance to chloroquine has been reported. YELLOW FEVER: R. A vaccination certificate is required by all visitors over one year of age. OTHER: Bilharzia, Cholera, Meningitis and Rabies present.

 W1

 CFA Franc (CFA Fr) = 100 centimes. NOTE: Only notes issued by the 'Banque des Etats de l'Afrique Centrale' are valid and not those issued by 'Banque des Etats de l'Afrique de l'Ouest'. It is advisable to exchange French Francs or US Dollars with Sterling. Both have very limited acceptance. French francs are the preferred currency in traveller's cheques, although pound sterling is also accepted. ATM AVAILABILITY: Unavailable.

 MONEYGRAM: Unavailable.
WESTERN UNION: Unavailable.

 AMEX: +44 1273 696933
DINERS CLUB: No local number.
MASTERCARD: 1 314 542 7111
VISA: (1) 410 581 9091

AMEX: +44 1273 571 600
THOMAS COOK: +44 1733 318950
VISA: +44 1733 318949

0730–1130 and 1430–1630 Mon to Fri

The economy has deteriorated due to civil unrest.

French and English are given equal importance in the constitution although French is more commonly spoken. Many local African languages are spoken.

South is hot and dry from Nov to Feb. Rainy season mainly July to Oct although there is some rain Mar to June. Temperatures in the North vary.

Mainly Animist and Christian. A minority with Muslim faith.

1998: Jan 1; Feb 11; Apr 7, 10; May 1, 20, 21; Aug 15; Dec 25.
1999: Jan 1; Feb 11; Apr 2, 7; May 1, 20; Aug 15; Dec 25.

110/220 Volts Ac 50 Hz.
Plugs = round 2 pin.

Approximately 1 week.

BBC: 17.83 15.40 9.600 7.160
VOA: 21.48 15.58 9.575 6.035

A patriarchal culture prevails.

FLIGHTS: The most efficient means of internal travel. RAIL: Slow and cheap, a limited few have restaurant facilities and air conditioning. Couchettes are available on some trains.

There has been an increase in violent crime and highway robbery is prevalent in the North. Avoid the North-west of the country. The North is mainly Muslim and traditions and customs should be respected, for example, visitors should never step inside a Muslim prayer circle of rocks. In rural areas traditional beliefs predominate, so it is essential to use tact. Cameras should be used with discretion and permission obtained before taking photographs. Do not take photographs of anything connected with the military.

CAPITAL: Ottawa

 6 time zones from GMT–3.5 in New Foundland to GMT–8 on the Pacific Coast.

 FROM UK: 1   IDD: Y.
OUTGOING CODE: 011

 911 or 0 (depending on province).

Canadian High Commission, Macdonald House, 1 Grosvenor Square, London, W1X 0AB. Tel: (0171) 258 6600. Fax: (0171) 258 63333.

British High Commission, 80 Elgin Street, Ottawa, Ontario, K1P 5K7. Tel: (613) 237 1530. Fax: (613) 237 7980. Consulates in Edmonton, Halifax, St Johns, Montreal, Toronto, Vancouver, and Winnipeg.

 Visit Canada Centre, 62–65 Trafalgar Square, London WC2N 5DT. Tel: (0171) 930 8540 (trade) or (0891) 715 000 (general information).

Tourism Canada, Industry Canada, 4th Floor East, 235 Queens Street, Ottawa, Ontario, K1A 0H5. Tel (613) 954 3851. Fax: (613) 952 7906.

 Return Ticket Required. Requirements may change at short notice. Contact the embassy before departure.
VALID PASSPORT REQUIRED BY ALL: Valid for at least one day beyond the intended departure date from Canada.

 Visa Not Required by British passport holders. NOTE: Visa regulations are subject to change at short notice; it is advisable to check with the nearest Canadian Consulate, Embassy or high commission prior to travel.

 Firearms and explosives, endangered species of animal and plants, animal products, meat, food and plant material is subject to restrictions. Dogs and cats may be imported from certain rabies free countries subject to restriction and formalities.

 Can $10 levied on international departures, payable in local currency.

Canadian Dollar (Can $) = 100 cents. Credit cards are widely accepted. Travellers cheques in Canadian dollars are preferred. ATM AVAILABILITY: Over 13,000 locations.

 MONEYGRAM: 1 800 933 3278.
WESTERN UNION: 800 235 0000.

 AMEX: +44 1273 696933
DINERS CLUB: 1 800 554 7608
MASTERCARD: 1 800 307 7309
VISA: 1 800 847 2399

AMEX: 1 800 221 7282
THOMAS COOK: 1 800 223 7373
VISA: 1 800 732 1322

 1000–1500 Mon to Fri. Some banks in major centres have extended hours–check locally.

 Prices are similar to Western Europe. They are also dependent on season and province.

 English. Quebec–French.

 Summers are warm and sunny whilst winters can be very cold, especially in the North.

 Roman Catholic. United church of Canada, Anglican and others.

 1998: Jan 1, 2; Feb 16, 28 (AL); Mar 9, 17; Apr 10, 13, 20; May 18; June 6, 24 (QU); July 1, 5, 6, 10; Aug 3 (BC/NB), 17 (YT); Sept 7; Oct 12; Nov 11; Dec 25, 26, 28. 1999: Jan 1, 2; Feb 16, 28 (AL); Mar 9, 17; Apr 2, 5, 20; May 18; June 6, 24 (QU); July 1, 5, 6, 10; Aug 3 (BC/NB), 17 (YT); Sept 7; Oct 12; Nov 11; Dec 25, 26, 28.

 110 Volts AC 60 Hz. American style flat, 2 pin plugs are standard.

 5–7 a day.

 BBC: 11.86   9.640   7.325   5.975
VOA: 17.84   11.86   9.515   5.975

 Equality between men and women is the norm. Culture, generally is influenced by France in Quebec and England/America elsewhere.

 FLIGHTS: About 75 airlines operate national services. RAIL: Services are extensive across Canada. ROADS: Extensive covering vast distances. COACH: One of the cheapest and most convenient ways of travelling the country. Each region is well served by networks of coach-lines. CAR HIRE: Available in all cities and airports to drivers with full licences over 21 years of age. DOCUMENTATION: Visitors may drive with their national driving licences for up to 3 months in all provinces.

 Smoking has been barred from most public places.

Cape Verde

CAPITAL: Cidade de Praia

 GMT -1

 FROM UK: 238
IDD: Possible to main cities. Some calls to and from the country must go through the international operator.
OUTGOING CODE: Outgoing calls must go through the local operator.

 All services: 87

 No Embassy in the UK. EUROPE: Koninginnegracht 44, 2514 AD The Hague, The Netherlands. Tel: (70) 346 9623. Fax: (70) 346 7702.
British Consulate, c/o Shell Cabo Verde, Sal Avenue, Amilcar, Cabral, CP4, Sal, Cape Verde. Tel: 314 470 or 314 605 or 314 232. Fax: 314 755

 Refer to Embassy

 Instituto Nacional do Tourismo–INATUR, CP294, Chã da Areia, Praia, São Tiago, Cape Verde. Tel: 631 173. Fax: 614 475

 Return Ticket Required. Requirements may change at short notice. Contact the Embassy before departure.
VALID PASSPORT REQUIRED BY ALL: With a minimum validity of at least 6 months

 Visa Required.

 HEP A, POLIO, TYPHOID: R. MALARIA: R. YELLOW FEVER: Vaccination certificate required from visitors over one years of age arriving from an area where incidents of yellow fever have been reported within the last six years. OTHER: Cholera.

 W1

 Cape Verde Escudo (CVEsc) = 100 centavos. Note: Import and export of local currency is prohibited. Import of foreign currency unlimited but declaration on arrival required. Maximum export of foreign currency is CVEsc 25000 or the amount declared on arrival, whichever is the larger. Credit cards and travellers and cheques are not usually accepted.
ATM AVAILABILITY: Unavailable

 MONEYGRAM: Unavailable.
WESTERN UNION: Unavailable.

 AMEX: +44 1273 696933.
DINERS CLUB: No local number.
MASTERCARD: No local number.
VISA: No local number.

 AMEX: No local number.
THOMAS COOK: No local number.
VISA: No local number.

 0800–1400 Mon to Fri.

 Tourism is very undeveloped, but this may change with the government's recent decision to promote tourism.

 Portuguese, Creole and some English and French

 Temperate with a low rainfall.

 Almost entirely Roman Catholic with a Protestant minority.

 1998: Jan 1, 20; May 1, 19; Aug 15; Nov 1; Dec 25.
1999: Jan 1, 20; May 1, 19; Aug 15; Nov 1; Dec 25.

 220 Volts 50 Hz

 To and from Europe – over 1 week.

 BBC: 17.83 15.40 9.600 6.005
VOA: 21.49 15.60 9.525 6.035

 Culture is predominantly patriarchal.

 ROAD: There are 2250 km of road on the islands, of which one third are paved. There is currently a road improvement programme taking place. BUS: Services are satisfactory. TAXI: Fares should be agreed in advance. DOCUMENTATION: IDP is recommended.

Usual European social courtesies should be observed.

Cayman Islands

 GMT–5.

 FROM UK: 1809
IDD: Possible to North America and Europe.
OUTGOING CODE: 0

 Police: 911; Ambulance: 555.
All services: 911.

 Cayman Islands Government Office and
Department of Tourism, 6 Arlington Street,
London, SW1A 1RE. Tel: (0171) 491 7772
(Government Office) or 491 7771
(Department of Tourism). Fax (0171) 491
7944 (Government Office) or 409 7773
(Department of Tourism).

 UK Passport Agency, Clive House, Petty
France, London, SW1H 9HD. Tel: (0171) 279
3434.

 At Government House.

 Cayman Islands Department of Tourism, The
Cricket Square, Elgin Avenue, PO Box 67,
Grand Cayman. Tel: (94) 90623. Fax: (94)
94053.

 Return Ticket required. Requirements may be
subject to short-term change. Contact
embassy before departure.
Valid passport required by all except nationals of Canada, the UK and the USA, if proof
of nationality is provided and return or
onward tickets shows that the visitor will
leave the Cayman islands within 6 months.

 Visa Not Required by UK Nationals.

 Pet owners require a permit from the Cayman
Islands' Department of Agriculture.

 CI$ 8 or US$ 10 payable by all travellers over
12 years of age.

 POLIO, TYPHOID: R

Cayman Islands Dollar (CI$) = 100 cents.
Exchaange: US currency circulates freely.
Major credit cards are widely accepted.
Travellers cheques in US dollars are widely
welcomed.
ATM AVAILABILITY: 4 locations.

MONEYGRAM: 1 800 543 4080.
WESTERN UNION: 949 7822.

 AMEX: +44 1273 696933
DINERS CLUB: Not present.
MASTERCARD: 1 800 307 7309
VISA: (1) 410 581 9091

 AMEX: (1) 801 964 6665
THOMAS COOK: 1 800 223 7373
VISA: 1 800 732 1322

 0900–1600 Mon to Thur, 0900–1630 Fri.

 Extremely expensive.

 English. Local dialects are also spoken.

 Warm tropical climate throughout the year.
Wet season – May to Oct with generally brief
showers.

 Presbyterian with large numbers of
minorities.

 1998: Jan 1; Feb 25; Apr 10, 13; May 18;
June 16; July 1; Nov 9; Dec 25, 26.
1999: Jan 1; Feb 25; Apr 2, 5; May 18; June
16; July 1; Nov 9; Dec 25, 26.

 110 volts 60 Hz. American style (flat) 2 pin
plugs are used.

 5–7 days.

 BBC: 17.84 15.22 9.740 3.915
VOA: 15.21 11.70 6.130 0.930.

 Normal precautions should be followed.

 ROAD: A good road network connects the
coastal towns of all three main islands. BUS:
A cheap but infrequent bus service operates
between George Town and the West Bay.
CAR HIRE: By far the best way to get
around. DOCUMENTATION: An IDP is
required in addition to insurance. Drivers
must be over 21 years of age.

! Beachwear should be kept to the beach /
pool.

CAPITAL: Bangui

GMT +1

FROM UK: 236
IDD: Y but some calls still go through the operator.
OUTGOING CODE: Calls should go through the operator.

Not present.

No embassy in the UK. EUROPE: Embassy of the Central African Republic, 30 rue des Perchamps, 75016 Paris, France. Tel: (1) 42 24 42 56. Fax: (1) 42 88 98 95.
British Consulate, c/o SOCACIG, BP 728, Bangui, Central African Republic. Tel: 610 300 or 611 045. Fax: 615 130

Refer to the Embassy.

Office National Centrafican du Tourisme (OCATOUR) BP 655, Bangui, Central African Republic. Tel: 614 566

Return Ticket Required. Requirements may be subject to change at short notice. Contact the embassy before departure.
VALID PASSPORT REQUIRED.

Visa Required.

Firearms. Animal skins and diamonds must be declared on departure.

Departure tax of US$5 is levied on all international flights.

HEP A, POLIO, TYPHOID: R.
MALARIA: R. falciparum form is prevalent. Resistance to chloroquine has been reported.
YELLOW FEVER: A vaccination certificate is required on arrival, by all travellers over one year of age. OTHER:Cholera. A vaccination certificate is required by all travellers.
Bilharzia, Meningitis and Rabies also present.

W1

CFA franc (CFA Fr) = 100 centimes. Very limited acceptance of credit cards and travellers cheques and commission is very expensive.
ATM AVAILABILITY: Unavailable.

MONEYGRAM: Unavailable.
WESTERN UNION: Unavailable.

AMEX: +44 1273 696933
DINERS CLUB: Not present.
MASTERCARD: 1 314 542 7111
VISA: (1) 410 581 9091
AMEX: +44 1273 571 600
THOMAS COOK: +44 1733 318949
VISA: +44 1733 318949

0730–1130 Mon–Fri

Tourists can expect to pay high prices.

French is the official language and essential for business. The native language is Sango.

Hot all year round especially in the Northeast. The Monsoon in the south is May–Oct.

Animist, Christian and a minority follow Islam.

1998: Jan 1; Mar 29; Apr 13; May 1, 21; June 1; Aug 13, 15; Nov 1; Dec 1, 25.
1999: Jan 1; Mar 29; Apr 5; May 1, 20, 31; Aug 13, 15; Nov 1; Dec 1, 25.

220/380 Volts Ac 50 Hz

Airmail takes 1 week, although it is often much longer. Poste Restante is available in Bangui. Postal and telecommunication systems are currently being developed.
BBC: 21.66 17.83 15.40 9.600
VOA: 21.49 15.60 9.525 6.035

Women should respect the Muslim dress and are segregated in the towns.

FLIGHTS: Domestic flights are limited to chartered planes. RIVER: River-boats operate along the Ubangi but can be very slow. ROAD: Good roads connect the main towns but are impassable during the rainy season. Travellers must carry as much petrol as possible as deliveries to stations outside the towns are infrequent. DOCUMENTATION: IDP is required.

The FCO advise against travel unless essential. The border with Cameroon is closed, and armed guards are targetting visitors. Visitors should dress modestly in Muslim areas and respect customs. Ensure you do not smoke or drink in public places during Ramadam. PHOTOGRAPHY: Be cautious and ask permission before taking photographs.

Chad

CAPITAL: N'Djamena

 GMT + 1

 FROM UK: 235 It may be necessary to go through the operator.   IDD: N
OUTGOING CODE: Calls must go through the operator.

 Not present.

 No embassy in the UK. Europe: 65 rue des Belles Feuilles, 75116 Paris, France. Tel (1) 45 53 36 75. Fax (19) 45 53 16 09.

British Consulate BP 877, Avenue Charles de Gaulle, N'djamena, Chad. Tel: 513 064. Telex 5234 (a/b ACT KD).

 Refer to the Embassy.

 Direction du Tourisme, des Parcs Nationaux et Réserves de Faune BP 86, N'djamena, Chad. Tel: 512 303. Fax: 572 261.

 Return Ticket Required. Requirements may be subject to change at short notice. Contact embassy.
Valid Passport Required.

 Visas Required.

 Narcotics.

 There is a departure tax for tourists of CFA Fr 7500, payable in local currency.

 Evidence of sufficient funds may be necessary. Travel outside the capital requires special authorisation from the minister of the Interior which must be obtained on arrival. There may be difficulty obtaining it.

 HEP A, POLIO, TYPHOID: R.
MALARIA: R: falciparum variety present.
YELLOW FEVER: R, with certificate of vaccination.
OTHER: Bilharziasis, River blindness, Sleeping sickness and Meningitis.

 W1

CFA Franc (CFAfr) = 100 centimes. Advisable to bring US Dollars rather than sterling into the country. Credit cards and travellers cheques are not accepted. ATM AVAILABILITY:Unavailable.

MONEYGRAM: Unavailable.
WESTERN UNION: Unavailable.

 AMEX: +44 1273 696933.
DINERS CLUB: No local number.
MASTERCARD: No local number.
VISA: No local number.
AMEX: No local number.
THOMAS COOK: No local number.
VISA: No local number.

0900–1400 Mon to Fri

The economy is very unstable due to civil unrest.

French. Arabic and Sara are also widely spoken. There are over 50 local languages.
The climate is hot and tropical. South has a rainy season from May–Oct. Central has a rainy season from Jun–Sept. The North has little rain. It is often cool in the evenings.

Muslim and Animist with a Christian minority.

1998: Jan 1, 30*; Apr 7*, 13; May 1, 25; July 6; Aug 11; Nov 1, 28; Dec 1, 25.
1999: Jan 1, 29*; Apr 13, 16*; May 1, 25; July 6; Aug 11; Nov 1, 28; Dec 25.

20 Volts AC 5o Hz. Plugs = 3 Pin.

Airmail takes about one week.

BBC: 17.83 15.22 11.75 5.970
VOA: 15.21 11.58 9.775 5.995

There is strict segregation of women especially in towns. Dress should be conservative in respect of Muslim laws.

 FLIGHTS: Very limited. ROAD: N'Djamena needs 4-wheel drive and permits are usually required. Due to security conditions and lack of petrol and repair facilities the government have prohibited travel especially in central and northern areas. Most roads are impassable during the rainy season. DOCUMENTATION: Carnet de passage is required and is issued by the Tourist Association in the country of origin. An IDP is also required and either a Green card or ALL RISKS insurance obtained in Chad. Documentation must be obtained at all times as travellers may encounter road-blocks.

NOTE: MODERATE RISK. Visitors to Chad should be vigilant at all times. Respect for traditional beliefs and customs is expected. SPECIAL PRECAUTIONS: Chad's Northern provinces bordering Libya constitute a military zone and remain heavily mined. Travel to and from this area is very dangerous and should be avoided.

Chile

CAPITAL: Santiago

 GMT-4 (GMT-3 from second Sunday in October to second Sunday in March). Easter Island: GMT-6 (GMT-5 from second Sunday in Oct to second Saturday in March).

 FROM UK: 56   IDD: Y.
OUTGOING CODE: 00

 Police: 133; Fire: 132.

 Embassy and Consulate of the Republic of Chile, 12 Devonshire Street, London, W1N 2DS. Tel: (0171) 580 6392.
British Embassy, Casilla 72 D or Casilla 16552, Avenida El Bosque Norte 0125, Santiago 9, Chile. Tel: (2) 231 3737. Fax: (2) 231 9771.

 Refer to Embassy or Consulate.

 Servicio Nacionale de Turismo (SERNATUR), Casilla 14082, Avenida Providencia 1550, Santiago, Chile. Tel: (2) 696 0474. Fax: (2) 236 1417.

 Return Ticket Required. Requirements may change at short notice. Contact the embassy before departure.
VALID PASSPORT REQUIRED. Passports have to remain valid for 6 months after departure. NOTE: Passports of children must contain a photo and state the nationality.

 As the regulations are always subject to change at short notice, check with the Chilean Consulate for the latest information.

 Meat products, flowers, fruit and vegetables.

 US$18 or the Peso equivalent.

 POLIO, TYPHOID: R

 W1

 Peso (Ch$) = 100 centavos. Exch: Many outlets will exchange currency. NOTE: Visitors should avoid black market exchange rates. All major credit cards are accepted. Travellers cheques in US dollars are preferred, but must be exchanged before midday.
ATM AVAILABILITY: Over 1000 locations.

 MONEYGRAM: 123 0 020 3725.
WESTERN UNION: 800 200 102.

 AMEX: +44 1273 696933
DINERS CLUB: 56 2 3383473 80
MASTERCARD: 1230 020 2012
VISA: 1230 020 0127
AMEX: (1) 801 964 6665
THOMAS COOK: 1 800 223 7373
VISA: 1 800 732 1322

 0900–1400 Mon to Fri.

 Chile is no longer a bargain. Modest lodgings, food and transport however are still cheaper than Europe, North America or Argentina.

 Spanish. English is also widely spoken.

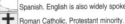 Roman Catholic, Protestant minority.

 1998: Jan 1; Apr 10, 11; May 1, 21; June 11, 29; Aug 15; Sept 11, 18, 19; Oct 12; Nov 1; Dec 8, 25, 31.
1999: Jan 1; Apr 2, 3; May 1, 21; June 11, 29; Aug 15; Sept 11, 18, 19; Oct 12; Nov 1; Dec 8, 25, 31.

 220 Volts AC 50 Hz. 3 pin plugs and screw type bulbs are used.

 Daily airmail services to Europe take approximately 3–4 days.

 BBC: 17.83 15.2 11.75 5.970

 Chile's diverse geographical variants, ranging from arid grasslands to the Atacama desert (the driest in the world) governs women's role and occupation in society. Women should not wear shorts outside rural areas.

 FLIGHTS: There are frequent services to main towns. The southern part of the city relies heavily on air links. Reservations are essential. ROADS: Generally in good condition . It is advisable in remoter areas to carry spare parts, and petrol. Tyres must be hard wearing in the remoter areas. DOCUMENTATION: IDP is required. BUSES: Inter-city buses are cheap and reliable. TAXI: Agree the fare in advance.

 Violent crimes are rare but purse snatching in Santiago is not unusual. Crime is common in the beach resorts during the summer. In the event of an emergency always carry your identification and contact your embassy for advice. PHOTOGRAPHY: Avoid taking photographs of anything connected to the military.

CAPITAL: Beijing

GMT + 8.

FROM UK: 86   IDD: Y.
OUTGOING CODE: 00

Police: 110; Fire: 119.

Embassy of the People's Republic of China (Consular Section), 31 Portland Place, London, W1 3AG. Tel: (0171) 636 5637. Fax (0171) 636 9756.

British Embassy, 11 Guang Hua Lu, Jian Guo Men Wai, Beijing, Peoples Republic of China. Tel: (1) 532 1961/5 or 532 1930/1938/9. Fax: (1) 532 1937.

China National Tourist Office, 4 Glentworth Street, London NW1 5PG. Tel: (0171) 935 9427. Fax: (0171) 487 5842.

China International Travel Service (CITS), Head Office, 103 Fuximgmenni Avenue, Beijing, People's Republic of China. Tel: (1) 601 1122. Fax: (1) 601 2013.

Return Ticket Required. Requirements may change at short notice. Contact the embassy before departure.

VALID PASSPORT REQUIRED BY ALL
Visa Required by all

Radio transmitters/receivers, exposed but undeveloped film. Baggage declaration forms must be completed on arrival. A copy must be given to customs when leaving the country.

Yuan 90.

POLIO, TYPHOID: R   MALARIA: Exists throughout the country below 1500 m in the Falciparum variety, which has been reported s being highly resistant to Chloroquine.
YELLOW FEVER: A vaccination certificate is required by anyone arriving from infected areas. OTHER: Bilharzia, Cholera, Rabies.

W1

Yuan (Renminbi RMB) = 10 chiao/jiao or 100 fen. Exchange: there is only one national bank which has 30,000 branches. In hotels and certain stores, luxury items such as spirits may be bought in Western currency. All credit cards are valid in major provincial cities in designated establishments. US dollars are the preferred currency in travellers cheques. ATM AVAILABILITY: Over 60 locations.

MONEYGRAM: 10811 then 800 592 3688.
WESTERN UNION: (10) 6318 4313.

AMEX: +44 1273 696933
DINERS CLUB: No local number.
MASTERCARD: 10 800 110 7309
VISA: (1) 410 581 9091
AMEX: (852) 885 9331
THOMAS COOK: +44 1733 318950
VISA: +44 1733 318949

0930–1200 and 1400–1700 Mon to Fri, 0900–1700 Sat.

China is predominantly an agrarian community in spite of the recent Westernisation of its major cities. Consequently, prices vary substantially from region to region and city to city.

Mandarin Chinese. Cantonese, Fukienese, Xiamenhua and Hakka. English may sometimes be spoken.

Great variations in climate. Northeast = Hot and Dry summers with very cold winters. North and central has a continental rainfall, hot summers and cold winters. Southeast = Substantial rainfall, with semi tropical summer and a cool winter.

Buddhism, Daoism and Confucianism. Also Muslim, Protestant and Roman Catholic.

1998: Jan 1, 2, 28–30; May 1, 2; Oct 1, 2.

220/240 Volts AC, 50Hz.

Approx. 1 week. Address all postal communications 'People's Republic of China'.

BBC: 15.36 15.28 11.82 7.18
VOA: 17.74 11.76 7.275 1.575

Women in major cities are becoming more culturally free, however this is still limited due to tight censorship legislation. Women in rural areas continue to live a feudal, peasantry existence, in accordance with tradition.

Independent travel is increasingly possible. Further information can be obtained from the Chinese National Tourist Office (address above). ROAD: Most places can be reached by road but many are of poor quality. BUS: Reasonable services operate in main cities.

Visitors are sometimes greeted by applause as a sign of welcome. The usual response is to applaud back. PHOTOGRAPHY: Do not take photos of airports and always seek permission. Personal theft is common. People often stare and spit. Since 1988 free travel to Tibet has ceased. China issues approx. 1000 visas a year for guided excursions only.

Colombia

CAPITAL: Santa Fe de Bogota

GMT–5

FROM UK: 57
IDD: Y, to most areas. Calls to remoter areas may have to be made through the operator.
OUTGOING CODE: 90

All services: 112 (01 in smaller towns and rural areas)

Embassy of the Republic of Colombia, Flat 3A, 3 Hans Crescent, London, SW1X 0LR. Tel: (0171) 589 9177. Fax: (0171) 581 1829.
British Embassy, Apdo Aereo 4598, Torre Propaganda Sancho, Calle 98, No 9-03, Piso 4, Santa Fe de Bogota DC, Colombia. Tel: (1) 218 5111. Fax: (1) 218 2460. Consulates in Baranquilla, Cali and Medellin.

Refer to the Embassy.

Corporacion Nacional de Turismo, Apdo Aereo 8400, Calle 28, No 13A-15, 16º-18º, Santa Fe de Bogota DC, Colombia. Tel: (1) 283 9466. Fax: (1) 284 3818.

Return Ticket Required. Requirements may change at short notice. Contact the embassy before departure. Passports with 6 months validity required by all.
Not required by tourists staying less than 90 days. NOTE: Visitors must show proof of sufficient funds to cover their stay. All visitors must obtain an exit stamp from the security police before leaving. (Best obtained at the airport or in the main cities).

Emeralds, gold and platinum require receipts of purchase, which must be presented to customs on departure.

US$17 or the equivalent in Pesos. This tax is double for stays of more than 60 days.

POLIO, TYPHOID: R.
MALARIA: Exists in throughout the year in low-lying and rural areas in the Falciparum variety. Resistance to chloroquine has been reported.   YELLOW FEVER: R.
OTHER: Cholera, Hepatitis and Rabies.

W1

Peso (Col$). Exch: US$ is the easiest to exchange at hotels, banks, shops, travel agencies. All major credit cards accepted. Travellers cheques in US dollars are preferred and are easier to exchange in larger towns.
ATM AVAILABILTY: Over 2500 locations.

MONEYGRAM: 980 12 0834.
WESTERN UNION: 9800 15690.

AMEX: +44 1273 696933
DINERS CARD: (57) (1) 3455177
MASTERCARD: 980 12 1303
VISA: (1) 410 581 9091
AMEX: (1) 801 964 6665
THOMAS COOK: 1 800 223 7373
VISA: 1 800 732 1322

0900–1500 Mon to Fri.

Accommodation and commodities are moderately priced in the cities.

Spanish. Local Indian dialects and English is also spoken.

Hot and humid with a rainy season between May–Nov. Cooler climate in the upland areas.

Roman Catholic. Protestant and Jewish minorities.

1998: Jan 1, 12; Feb 25; Mar 23; Apr 9, 10, 11; May 1, 25; June 15, 22, 29; July 20; Aug 7, 17; Oct 12; Nov 2, 16; Dec 8, 25.
1999: Jan 1, 12; Feb 24; Mar 23; Apr 1, 2, 3; May 1, 24; June 14, 21, 29; July 20; Aug 7, 17; Oct 12; Nov 2, 16; Dec 8, 25.

110/120 Volts AC, US 2 pin plugs are used.

Airmail usually takes 5–7 days. International post boxes are yellow.

BBC: 17.82 15.2 7.325 5.970
VOA: 15.21 11.58 9.575 5.995

Travelling alone is not advised as violent attacks have recently increased in Colombia. Inequality between men and women can be a problem. Roman catholicism is practised by 95% of the population and subsequently has a major influence on society.

FLIGHTS: There is an excellent network of domestic flights and the large distances between cities makes this method of transport more convenient. ROAD: Highways connecting the main cities have recently been completed. Roads are usually passable except during the rainy season.
DOCUMENTATION: An IDP is required.

Corruption is commonplace in Colombia. Personal safety and possessions are at risk at all times. Kidnapping and criminal violence remain problems. Extreme caution is therefore required.

Comoro Islands

CAPITAL: Moroni

 GMT +3

 FROM UK: 269   IDD: N.
OUTGOING CODE: Calls must go through the operator.

 Not present.

 No embassy in the UK. Europe: Embassy of he Federal Republic of the Comoros, 20 rue Marbeau, 75106 Paris, France. Tel: (1) 40 67 90 54. Fax: (1) 40 67 72 96.

 British Embassy in Madagascar deals with enquiries relating to the Comoro Islands: British Embassy, BP 167, First Floor, Immeuble 'Ny Havana', Cité de 67 Ha, Antananarivo, Madagascar. Tel: (2) 27749 or 27370. Fax (2) 26690.

 Refer to the Embassy.

 Société Comorienne de Tourisme et d'Hôtellerie (COMOTEL) Itsandra Hotel, Njazidja, Comoros. Tel: 732 365.

 Return Ticket Required. Requirements may be subject to short term change. Consult embassy before departure.
VALID PASSPORT REQUIRED BY ALL

 Required by all. Transit and Tourist. Visas are issued by the Immigration officer on arrival. Exit permits are required by all.

 Weapons, Ammunition and Radio Transmission Equipment. Plants or Soil.

 Departure Tax CFA Fr 500 or Ffr 100.

 HEP A, POLIO, TYPHOID: R.
MALARIA: R. Falciparum variety present.
YELLOW FEVER: If travelling from an infected area a vaccination certificate may be required.

 W1

CFA Franc (CFA Fr) = 100 centimes. There is a very limited acceptance of credit cards, restricted to mainly hotels. French Franc travellers cheques are recommended. The Banque Internationale des Comoros is the only bank that will exchange traveller's cheques.
ATM AVAILABILITY: Unavailable.

 MONEYGRAM: Unavailable.
WESTERN UNION: Unavailable.

 AMEX: +44 1273 696933
DINERS CLUB: No local number.
MASTERCARD: 1 314 542 7111
VISA: (1) 410 581 9091

 AMEX: +44 1273 571 600
THOMAS COOK: +44 1733 318950
VISA: +44 1733 318949

 0730–1300 Mon to Thur, 0730–1100 Fri.

 Tourists can expect to pay higher prices than on the mainland.

 French and Arabic. The majority speak Comoran and there is a blend of Arabic and Swahili.

 Climate is tropical and very warm. Coastal areas are very hot and humid (Dec–March) with some rain and cyclones. Upland areas = cooler and have more rain.

 Muslim with a Roman Catholic minority.

 1998: Jan 29*; Apr 9*; May 9, 25; July 6, 18*; Nov 27*.
1999: Jan 29*; Apr 16*; May 9, 25; July 6, 18*; Nov 26*.

 220 Volts AC, 50 Hz

 At least 1 week.

 BBC: 17.88 15.42 11.94 6.190
VOA: 21.49 15.60 9.525 6.035

 Culture is predominantly patriarchal.

Private vehicles are the only form of transport on the Islands. 4 wheel drives are needed for the interior and outlying islands, especially in the rainy season.
DOCUMENTATION: IDP is required.

! Religious customs should be respected especially during Ramadam. French residents and tourists tend to be quite relaxed about what they wear, although dress should be conservative.

Congo

CAPITAL: Brazzaville

 GMT + 1

 FROM UK: 242   IDD: Y.
OUTGOING CODE: 00

 Not present.

 Honorary Consulate of the Republic of Congo, Alliance House 12 Caxton Street , London SW1H 0QS. Tel: (0171) 222 7575. Fax: (0171) 233 2087.

 Refer to British Embassy in Kinshasa, Zaïre. BP 8049, avenue de Trois Z, Kinshasa-GGombe, Zaïre. Tel: (243) (12) 34775/8.

 Europe: Embassy of the Republic of Congo and the Tourist Office, 37 bis rue Paul Valery, 75016 Paris, France. Tel: (1) 45 00 60 57. Fax: (1) 40 67 70 86.

 Direction Générale du Tourisme et des loisirs, BP 456, Brazzaville, Congo. Tel: 830 953.

 Return Ticket Required. Requirements may be subject to change at short notice. Consult embassy before departure.
VALID PASSPORT REQUIRED BY ALL

 Required by all, except nationals of Gabon. Tourist, and Business, 15 or 30 days.

 A licence is required for sporting guns.

 Departure tax of CFAFr 500, payable in local currency.

 HEP A, POLIO, TYPHOID: R.
MALARIA: R. Falciparum variety exists, resistance to chloroquine has been reported. YELLOW FEVER: Vaccination is required by all visitors over one year of age.
OTHER: Biharzia, Cholera, River blindness and Sleeping sickness are also prevalent.

 W1

CFA Franc (CFA Fr) = 100 centimes. Credit cards and travellers cheques are not widely accepted.
ATM AVAILABILITY: Unavailable.

MONEYGRAM: Unavailable.
WESTERN UNION: Unavailable.

 AMEX: +44 1273 696933.
DINERS CLUB: No local number.
MASTERCARD: No local number.
VISA: No local number.

 AMEX: No local number.
THOMAS COOK: No local number.
VISA: No local number.

 0630–1300 Mon to Fri. Counters close at 1130.

 Tourists can expect to pay high prices for services.

 French. Other languages are Likala and Kikongo. English is spoken very little.

 Rainy Season = Oct–Apr. Dry Season = May–Sept. The Climate is Equatorial

 Majority of the population believe in Animism. Also Roman Catholics and a minority of Protestants and Muslims.

 1998: Jan 1, 4; May 1; June 30; Nov 2; Dec 25.
1999: Jan 1, 4; May 1; June 30; Nov 2; Dec 25.

 220/230 Volts AC 50Hz

 Unreliable Internal Service

 BBC: 21.66 17.83 15.40 9.600
VOA: 17.80 15.41 9.575 6.035

 Culture is predominantly patriarchal.

 RAIL: Advance booking is recommended. Services can be erratic. ROAD: The roads are mostly tracks and are suitable for 4-wheel drive. Several car-hire firms in Brazzaville. DOCUMENTATION: IDP is required.

 The FCO advises against all travel, except to Pointe Noire. Travellers should contact the Consul on arrival, and should exercise caution after dark. PHOTOGRAPHY: Do not photograph public buildings.

Cook Islands

CAPITAL: Avarua

 GMT–10

 FROM UK: 682.
IDD: Y, although operator assistance may be required.
OUTGOING CODE: 00

 Police: 999. Ambulance and hospital: 998.
Fire: 996.

 Queries to New Zealand High Commission.

 The British High Commission, PO BOX 1812, 44 Hill Street, Wellington 1, New Zealand.
Tel: (4) 472 6049. Fax: (4) 471 1974.

 Tourism Council of the South Pacific, 375 Upper Richmond Road West, London, SW14 7WX. Tel: (0181) 392 1838. Fax: (0181) 392 1318.
Cook Islands Tourist Authority, PO Box 14, Raratonga, Cook Islands. Tel: 29435. Fax: 21435.

 Return Ticket Required. Regulations may be subject to change at short notice. Contact the embassy before departure.
Valid Passport Required by all except nationals of New Zealand. Passports should be valid for 12 months after the intended date of departure.

 Visa Required for business purposes. Not required for tourist purposes if staying for less than 31 days. NOTE: Proof of arranged accommodation and sufficient funds for length of stay will be required.

 Fruit, meat, fireworks, ammunition and gun powder.

 NZ$25, payable in local currency, for passengers over 12 years. NZ$ 10 for passengers between 2 and 12 years.

 POLIO, TYPHOID: R

 New Zealand Dollar (NZ$) = 100 cents. Both credit cards and travellers cheques are accepted. Australian dollars are the preferred currency in travellers cheques.
ATM AVAILABILITY: Unavailable.

MONEYGRAM: Unavailable.
WESTERN UNION: Available.

 AMEX: +44 1273 696933
DINERS CLUB: No local number.
MASTERCARD: 0800 44 9140
VISA: (1) 410 581 9091
AMEX: (61) 2 886 0689
THOMAS COOK: 0800 44 0112
VISA: 0800 44 0110

 0900–1500 Mon to Fri.

 Can be expensive in the tourist centres. However, accommodation is increasing yearly, which may bring a price decrease in the resorts.

 Maori. English widely spoken

 Hot climate throughout the year. Most rain Nov–Apr.

 Cook Islands Christian Church. Roman Catholic. Latter Day Saint. Seventh day Adventists and Assembly of God.

 1998: Jan 1; Apr 10, 13; June 1; July 25, 27; Aug 4; Oct 26; Dec 25, 26, 28.
1999: Jan 1; Apr 2, 5; June 1; July 25, 27; Aug 4; Oct 25; Dec 25, 26, 28.

 240 Volts Ac, 50 Hz

 Up to 2 weeks.

 BBC: 15.36 9.740 11.96 7.145
VOA: 18.82 15.18 9.525 1.735

 A conservative Christian society prevails. Cover arms and shoulders in church. Be careful in secluded areas, especially at night.

 The cheapest way to travel around the island is on an Inter-Island cargo ship. On Rarotinga there is a bus service and plenty of taxis. ROAD: Vehicles can be hired from a number of outlets. DOCUMENTATION: A current Cook Islands driving licence is required and available from the police station in Avarua on presentation of a national licence or IDP.

 Religious celebrations, for instance Gospel Day in October, are taken very seriously and should be respected. Beach-wear should not be worn in the towns. Usual social courtesies should be followed.

Costa Rica

CAPITAL: San Jose

 GMT–7

FROM UK: 506   IDD: Y
OUTGOING CODE: 00

Police: 104; Fire: 103; Ambulance: 225/1436 and 228/2187.

Embassy and Consulate of the Republic of Costa Rica, Flat 1, 14 Lancaster Gate, London, W2 3LH. Tel: (0171) 706 8844. Fax: (0171) 706 8655.

British Embassy, Apartado 815, 11th Floor, Edificio Centro Colón, 1007 San José, Costa Rica. Tel: 221 5566 or 221 5716 or 221 5816. Fax: 233 9938.

Refer to the Embassy.

Instituto Costarricense de Turismo, Apartado 777, Edificio Genaro Valverde, Calles 5 y 7, Avenida 4a 1000 San José, Costa Rica. Tel 223 1733. Fax: 255 4997.

Return Ticket Required. Requirements may change at short notice. Contact the embassy before departure.
Valid Passport Required by all, with a minimum validity of 6 months from date of arrival.

Visas not normally required. Check with the embassy and consulate for latest information.

Narcotics and firearms.

US$ 37 or local equivalent, payable if staying in Costa Rica for longer than 48 hours by everyone .

Gypsies and persons of unkempt appearance will be deported.

POLIO, TYPHOID: R.
MALARIA: Exists throughout the year in the Vivax variety in the rural areas below 700 m.
OTHER: Bilharzia.

W2

 Costa Rican Colón = 100 centimos. Exch: Gambios will give the best exchange rates. All major credit cards accepted. Travellers cheques in US dollars only will be accepted. ATM AVAILABILITY: Over 150 locations.

 MONEYGRAM: 001 800 824 2220.
WESTERN UNION: 283 6336.

 AMEX: +44 1273 696933
DINERS CLUB: 506 2571766
MASTERCARD: 980 12 1303
VISA: (1) 410 581 9091

 AMEX: (1) 801 964 6665
THOMAS COOK: 1 800 223 7373
VISA: 1 800 732 1322

 0900–1500 Mon to Fri.

More expensive than other central American countries but still cheaper than North America. All accommodation is graded.

Spanish. English is also spoken.

Roman Catholic.

 Coastal areas are much hotter than inland valleys. The rainy season is May–Nov.

 1998: Jan 1; Apr 9, 10, 11; May 1; July 25; Aug 2, 15; Sept 15; Oct 12; Dec 25, 29–31.
1999: Jan 1; Apr 1, 2, 11; May 1; July 25; Aug 2, 14; Sept 15; Oct 12; Dec 25, 29–31.

 110/220 Volts 60 Hz. 2 pin lugs are standard.

 6–10 days.

 BBC: 17.84 15.26 95.90 5.975
VOA: 15.12 11.91 9.590 6.130

 Roman catholicism influences all aspects of daily living. Women may receive unwelcome male attention.

 FLIGHTS: A number of operators offer domestic flights, but reservations can not be made out side of San José. ROADS: Generally very good standard but heavy traffic can make driving arduous. DOCUMENTATION: A national driving licence is required. BUS: Services operate between most towns but book in advance because overcrowding is common.

Christian names are preceded by Don for a man and Donna for a woman. Casual dress is acceptable for most occasions but beachwear should be confined to the pool/beach. Muggings and theft from cars are common.

Côte d'Ivoire

CAPITAL: Yamoussoukro

 GMT

 FROM UK: 225   IDD: Y.
OUTGOING CODE: 00.

Not present.

Embassy of the Republic of Côte d'Ivoire, 2
Upper Belgrave Street, London SW1X 8BJ.
Tel: (0171) 235 6991. Fax: (0171) 259 5439.

British Embassy, 01 BP 2581, Third Floor
Immeuble 'Les Harmonies', angle boulevard,
Carde et Avenue Dr Jamot, Plateau Abidjan
01, Côte d'Ivoire. Tel: 226 850/1/2 or 328209.
Fax: 223 221.

Refer to the Embassy.

Office Ivoirien du Tourisme et de l'Hôtellerie,
BP V184, Abidjan, Côte d'Ivoire. Tel: 206
528. Fax 225 924.

 Return Ticket Required. Requirements may
be subject to change at short notice. Consult
embassy before departure.
VALID PASSPORT REQUIRED BY ALL

Visa Required. Tourist and Business visas
available. Transit visas not usually required
by travellers not leaving the airport.

 Sporting guns may only be imported under
licence. Limits are placed on the importation
of certain personal affects. Contact the consulate prior to departure.

 Departure tax domestic: CFA Fr 800
International: £5.90 . Transit passengers are
exempt.

 HEP A, POLIO, TYPHOID: R.
MALARIA: The falciparum variety is present.
Resistance to chloroquine has been reported.
YELLOW FEVER: A vaccination certificate is
required from all visitors over 1 year of age.
OTHER: Bilharzia, Meningitis, Rabies

 W1

 CFA Franc (CFAFr) = 100 centimes.
Exchange available in airport, banks and
hotels. Amex and MasterCard are widely
accepted. Visa and Diners Club are only
accepted on a limited basis. Traveller's
cheques are accepted in major hotels and
some shops. French francs are the preferred
currency.
ATM AVAILABILITY: Unavailable.

 MONEYGRAM: 00 111 11.
WESTERN UNION: 22 12 12.

 AMEX: +44 1273 696933
DINERS CLUB: No local number.
MASTERCARD: 1 314 542 7111
VISA: (1) 410 581 9091
AMEX: +44 1273 571 600
THOMAS COOK: +44 1733 318950
VISA: +44 1733 318949

 0800–1130 and 1430–1630 Mon to Fri.

 Services and prices are generally expensive.

 French. Local dialects of Dioula and Baoule
are also spoken.

 Dry season : Dec–Apr and Aug– Sept. Rainy
Season: May–July and Oct–Nov.

 Mostly traditional beliefs. Also Muslim and
Christian.

 1998: Jan 1, 29*; Apr 10, 13; May 1, 8, 19;
Aug 15; Nov 1; Dec 7, 25.
1999: Jan 1, 29*; Apr 2, 5; May 1, 7, 18; Aug
15; Nov 1; Dec 7, 25.

 220 Volts Ac 50 Hz. Plugs = round two pin.

 Airmail can take up to 2 weeks.

 BBC: 17.83 15.07 11.83 6.005
VOA: 21.485 15.58 9.527 6.035

 Women can expect to enjoy a more multi-
cultural society than in the rest of West
Africa.

 ROAD: Good road system of tarmac roads
with frequent petrol stations in the North. Hire
cars are available in the main towns. TAXIS
are available in the main cities. FLIGHTS :
regular domestic flights operate between the
main cities. RAIL: Fast, regular trains operate
throughout the day between the main cities.

! There is extreme ethnic and linguistic variety
which distinguishes it from many other
African countries. Swimming off the coast is
dangerous.

Croatia

CAPITAL: Zagreb

 GMT + 1 (+ 2 from the last Sunday in March to the Saturday before the last Sunday in September).

 FROM UK: 385   IDD: Y
OUTGOING CODE: 99

 Police: 92; Fire: 93; Ambulance: 94.

 Embassy of the Republic of Croatia, 21 Conway Street, London W1P 5HL. Tel: (0171) 387 1144. Fax: (0171) 387 3276.

 British Embassy, PO Box 454, 2nd Floor, Astra Tower, Tratinska, 41000 Zagreb, Croatia. Tel: (1) 334 245. Fax (1) 338 893.

 Croatian National Tourist Office, 2 The Lanchesters, 162-164 Fulham Palace Road, London W6 9ER. Tel: (0181) 563 7979. Fax: (0181) 563 2616.

 Ministry of Tourism, Avenija Vukovar 78, 41000 Zargreb, Croatia. Tel: (1) 613 9444. Fax(1) 611 3216.

 Return Ticket Required, may be subject to change at short notice. Contact the Embassy before travelling.
VALID PASSPORT REQUIRED.

 Visa not required by British passport holders.

 US$8 on international flights from Zagreb.

 Rabies

 W1

 The Kuna (Kn) = 100 Lipa (Lp). Exch: The only true repositories of value and real medium of exchange locally are the German DM and the US$ (Sterling is rarely used). NOTE: The import and export of local currency is limited to Kn 2000. All major credit cards are accepted. German DM is the preferred Traveller's cheque currency.
ATM AVAILABILITY: Over 80 locations.

 MONEYGRAM: 99 385 0111 then 800 592 3688
WESTERN UNION: Unavailable.

 AMEX: +44 1273 696933
DINERS CLUB: No local number.
MASTERCARD: 1 314 542 7111
VISA: (1) 410 581 9091

  AMEX: +44 1273 571 600
THOMAS COOK: +44 1733 318950
VISA: +44 1733 318949

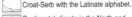 0700-1500 Mon to Fri, 0800-1400 Sat.

 The Croatian economy is still recovering after civil war. Visitors may be charged higher prices than locals.

 Croat-Serb with the Latinate alphabet.

 Continental climate in the North and Mediterranean on the Adriatic cost.

 Roman Catholic Croats. Eastern Orthodox Serbs.

 1998: Jan 1; Apr 13; May 1, 30; June 22; Aug 5, 15; Nov 1; Dec 25, 26.
1999: Jan 1; Apr 5; May 1, 30; June 22; Aug 5, 14; Nov 1; Dec 25, 26.

 220 volts AC, 50Hz

 May take several days.

BBC: 15.07 12.09 9.410 6.195
VOA: 9.670 6.040 5.995 1.260

ROAD/RAIL: The main road/rail route to and from Western Europe now effectively stops at Zagreb (coming from Ljubljiana) with extensive detours via Hungary for international traffic going South to and from Serbia, Republic of Macedonia and Greece. DOCUMENTATION: National or IDP required. A 'Green' card should be carried by visitors taking their own car into Croatia.

The situation has now calmed in most parts of Croatia. Avoid travel in the Eastern Slavonia/Baranja area where tensions remain high. There is, however, a continued risk of a deterioration in the security situation in some areas so visitors should remain cautious. For up to date information, contact the FCO travel advice unit before travelling. Certain restrictions exist on taking photographs in some areas.

CAPITAL: Havana

 GMT–4

 FROM UK: 53   IDD: Y to Havana only.
OUTGOING CODE: 00. (From Havana only.
All other calls must go through the operator.)
All services: 26811.

Embassy of the Republic of Cuba, 167 High
Holborn, London, WC1V 6PA. Tel: (0171)
240 2488. Fax: (0171) 836 2602. Cuban
Consulate, 15 Grape Street, London WC2
8DR. Tel: (0171) 240 2488 or (0891) 880 820
(recorded message). Fax: (0171) 836 2602.
British Embassy, Calle 34, 708 Miramar,
Havana, Cuba. Tel: (7) 331 771 or 331 049
(Commercial section). Fax (7) 338 104.
Cuba Tourist Office, 167 High Holborn,
London, WC1V 6PA. Tel: (0171) 379 1706.
Fax: (0171) 379 5455.
Empresa de Turismo Internacional (Cubatur),
Calle 23, No 156, entre N y O, Apartado
6560, Vedado, Havana, Cuba. Tel: (7) 324
521. Fax: (7) 333 104.

 Return Ticket required. Requirements may be
subject to short-term change. Contact
Embassy before departure.
Valid Passport Required by all: must be valid
for at least 6 months beyond length of stay.
 Visa Required by all, except holders of a
tourist card.

 Natural fruits or vegetables, meat and dairy
products, weapons and ammunitions, all
pornographic material and drugs.

US$15.

POLIO, TYPHOID: Low risk present.
OTHER: Rabies

W2

Cuban Peso (Cub$) = 100 centavos. At offi-
cial tourist shops purchases can only be
made in US Dollars. Exch: Should only be
made at authorised money exchanges as
there are severe penalties for black market
money exchanging. NOTE: Keep all
exchange receipts which will be required
when making purchases. Do not enter the
place or date details on any cheque until
ready to make the transaction or the cheque
will be refused. The import of local currency
is prohibited. Generally a maximum of
Cub$10 can be reconverted to foreign curren-
cy when leaving on presentation of an official

exchange form. Visa and MasterCard are
widely accepted. US Dollars (not drawn from
a US bank) and Sterling are excepted in traveller's cheques.
ATM AVAILABILITY: Unavailable.

 MONEYGRAM: Unavailable.
WESTERN UNION: Unavailable.

 AMEX: No local number.
DINERS CLUB: No local number.
MASTERCARD: 1 314 542 7111
VISA: (1) 410 581 9091
AMEX: (1) 801 964 6665
THOMAS COOK: 1 800 223 7373
VISA: 1 800 732 1322

 0830–1200 and 1330–1500 Mon to Fri,
0830–1030 Sat.

 Not as expensive as some of the other
Caribbean Islands.

 Spanish. English and French may also be
spoken.
 Hot all year round. Rainy season May–Oct.
Hurricane possible Aug–Nov. Cooler
between Nov–Apr.

 Roman Catholic majority.

 1998: Jan 1, 28; Feb 24; Mar 13, 28; Apr 16,
19; May 1, 17; July 25–27, 30; Aug 12; Oct
8, 10, 28; Nov 27; Dec 2, 7.
1999: Jan 1, 28; Feb 24; Mar 13, 28; Apr 16,
19; May 1, 17; July 25–27, 30; Aug 12; Oct
8, 10, 28; Nov 27; Dec 2, 7.

 110/220 volts Ac 60 Hz. American style
plugs are used except for large hotels, which
may use European type plugs.

 Can take up to several weeks.

 BBC: 17.84 15.22 6.195 5.975
VOA: 17.84 15.22 9.640 5.975

 Normal precautions should be followed.
Avoid venturing out alone at night and keep
to busy areas.

 FLIGHTS: Cubana operates scheduled services between the main towns. It is essential
to book in advance.

 The tourist industry is rapidly developing,
with growing tolerance of Western influences. Shorts should only be worn at the
beach or pool. The penalties for drug traffick-
ing are severe.

Curaçao

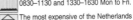

CAPITAL: Willemstad

 GMT-4

 FROM UK: 599   IDD:Y to Europe.
OUTGOING CODE: 00

 Police: 114; Ambulance: 112.
All services: 444444.

 Office of the Plenipotentiary of the Netherlands Antilles, Antillenhuis, Badhuisweg 173–175, 2597JP The Hague, The Netherlands. Tel: (70) 306 6111. Fax: (70) 351 2722.

 British Consulate, Heintje Kool, Z/N, Willemstad, Curaçao, NA. Tel: (9) 695 968. Fax (9) 695 964.

 Caribbean Tourism, Vigilant House, 120 Wilton Road, London, SW1V 1JZ. Tel: (0171) 233 8382. Fax: (0171) 873 8551.

 Curaçao Tourism Development Bureau, Pietermaai 19, Willemstad, Curaçao, NA. Tel: (9) 616 000. Fax: (9) 612 305.

 Return Ticket required. Requirements may be subject to short-term change. Contact embassy before departure.
VALID PASSPORT REQUIRED.

 Nationals of the UK are allowed to stay for 90 days without a visa provided they have onward or return tickets. NOTE: Contact the embassy for an up to date complete list of visa regulations, which are complex and may change at short notice.

 Narcotics and firearms.

 NAG22.50 , or US$ 12.50 per person. Children under 2 years of age and transit passengers are exempt.

 POLIO, TYPHOID: R.
YELLOW FEVER: A vaccination certificate is required from travellers over 6 months of age arriving from infected areas.

Netherlands Antilles Guilder or Florin (NAG) = 100 cents. Credit cards are accepted in large establishments. US dollar travellers cheques are the most welcomed.
ATM AVAILABILITY: 10 locations.

 MONEYGRAM: 001 800 872 2881.
WESTERN UNION: 5999 9 617472.

 AMEX: +44 1273 696933
DINERS CLUB: No local number.
MASTERCARD: 001 800 307 7309
VISA: (1) 410 581 9091

 AMEX: (1) 801 964 6665
THOMAS COOK: 1 800 223 7373
VISA: 1 800 732 1322

 0830–1130 and 1330–1630 Mon to Fri.

 The most expensive of the Netherlands Antilles.

 Dutch. English, Spanish Papiamento are also used.

 Hot all year round with cooling winds. Rainy season Oct–Dec.

 Roman Catholic.

 1998: Jan 1; Feb 23; Apr 10, 13, 30; May 1, 21; June 2; Dec 25, 26.
1999: Jan 1; Feb 22; Apr 2, 5, 30; May 1, 21; June 2; Dec 25, 26.

 110/220 volts AC 50 Hz.

 4–6 days.

 BBC: 17.82 11.86 9.640 5.975
VOA: 15.20 11.91 9.590 5.995.

 Usual precautions should be taken. Women tend to be conservative in accordance with the island's dominant religion.

ROAD: An IDP is required. BUS: A good bus service operates throughout the island and many hotels operate their own mini-buses to the capital. TAXI and CAR HIRE: Plentiful.

Swim wear for beach/pool-side only.

Cyprus

CAPITAL: Nicosia

GMT +2 (GMT + 3 from the last Sunday in March to the Saturday before the last Sunday in September).

FROM UK: 357   IDD: Y.
OUTGOING CODE: 00

All services: 199.

High Commission of the Republic of Cyprus, 93 Park Street, London W1Y 4ET. Tel: (0171) 499 8272. Fax: (0171) 491 0691. Consular Section Tel: (0171) 629 5350. Fax: (0171) 491 0691.

British High Commission, PO Box 1978, Alexander Pallis Street, Nicosia, Cyprus. Tel: (2) 771 131. Fax: (2) 781 758.

Cyprus Tourism Organisation, 213 Regent Street, London W1R 8DA. Tel: (0171) 734 9822 or 734 2593. Fax: (0171) 287 6534.

Cyprus Tourism Organisation, PO Box 4535, 19 Limassol Avenue, Melkonian Building, Nicosia, Cyprus. Tel: (2) 337 715. Fax: (2) 331 644.

Return Ticket Required, may be subject to change at short notice. Contact consulate before travelling.
VALID PASSPORT REQUIRED BY ALL: must be valid for 3 months after date of departure for visitors not requiring visas. Those requiring visas must have passports valid for at least 6 months from the point of departure.

Visa Not Required by Nationals of Great Britain.

Narcotics.

C(£)7, payable in local currency.

Passports stamped with 'Turkish Republic of Northern Cyprus'.

Cyprus Pound (C£) = 100 cents. Travellers cheques can be cashed in all banks, US dollars, Pound sterling and the Deutschemark are all accepted currencies. All major credit cards are accepted.
ATM AVAILABILITY: Approx. 200 locations.

MONEYGRAM: Available at all Avis Rent-a-Car locations.
WESTERN UNION: Available.

AMEX: +44 1273 696933
DINERS CLUB: 357 2 446974
MASTERCARD: 080 90569
VISA: (1) 410 581 9091

AMEX: +44 1273 571 600
THOMAS COOK: 080 91029
VISA: 080 91028

Generally 0815–1230, in tourist areas 1530–1730 (winter) and 1630 -1830 (summer).

Slightly cheaper than Western Europe.

Mostly Greek with some Turkish. English, German and French are also spoken.

Mediterranean climate. Hot Dry Summers with mild winters. Rainfall is most likely during the winter.

Greek Orthodox and Muslim minorities.

1998: Jan 1, 6; Mar 2, 25; Apr 1, 17, 20, 21; May 1; June 8; Aug 15; Oct 1, 28; Dec 25, 26.
1999: Jan 1, 6; Mar 1, 25; Apr 1, 2, 5, 6; May 1; June 7; Aug 15; Oct 1, 28; Dec 25, 26.

240 volts AC 50 Hz.

Approx. 3 days to Europe. Poste Restante facilities are available in the main cities and resorts.

BBC: 15.07 12.09 9.410 6.180
VOA: 11.90 9.700 9.530 6.060.

Traditional roles persist among the older generation. Around the capital city views are influenced by western culture. Usual precautions should be observed.

ROAD: BUS: Services are cheap and efficient. CAR HIRE: Widely available and considered to be the best way of seeing the island, but check car is roadworthy. DOCUMENTATION: IDP or National driving licence is accepted.

It is considered impolite to refuse an offer of Greek coffee or a cold drink. Casual wear is usually accepted, but beachwear should be confined to the beach or poolside. Respect should be shown for religious beliefs. Visitors can expect a warm and hospitable reception from Cypriots.

CAPITAL: Prague

GMT + 1 (GMT + 2 from last Sun in Mar to the Sat before the last Sun in Sept).

FROM UK: 42   IDD: Y.
OUTGOING CODE: 00

Ambulance: 155; Fire: 150; Police: 158.

Embassy of the Czech Republic, 26–30 Kensington Palace Gardens, London, W8 4QY. Tel: (0171) 243 1115. Fax: (0171) 727 9654.
British Embassy, Thunovská 14, 11 800 Prague 1, Czech Republic. Tel: (2) 24 51 02 39. Fax: (2) 539 927.
Czech Tourist Centre 78 Finchley Road, London NW3 6BP. Tel: (0171) 794 3263. Fax: (0171) 794 3265.
Czech Tourist Authority (Information Centre), Národní trída 28, 110 01 Prague !, Czech Republic. Tel: (2) 24 21 14 58.

Requirements may be subject to short term change. Contact embassy before departure. VALID PASSPORT REQUIRED. Passports must be valid for at least 8 months at the time of application, and in a reasonable state. Nationals of EU countries do not require a visa (except those with the endorsement British Overseas Citizen who do require a visa).

Pornography. All items of value, e.g. cameras and tents must be declared on arrival to allow clearance on departure.

W2

Koruna (Kc) or Crown = 100 hellers. Exch: All banks, exchange offices, main hotels and cross border crossings. NOTE: The import and export of local currency is prohibited by non–residents. All major credit cards are accepted in main hotels, restaurants and shops. Travellers cheques are widely accepted. The preferred currencies are US dollars, Sterling and German DM.
ATM AVAILABILITY: Over 1000 locations.

MONEYGRAM: 00 42 000 101.
WESTERN UNION: (02) 2422 9524.

AMEX: +44 1273 696933
DINERS CLUB: No local number.
MASTERCARD: 1 314 542 7111
VISA: (1) 410 581 9091

AMEX: +44 1273 571 600
THOMAS COOK: +44 1733 318950
VISA: +44 1733 318949

Generally 0800–1800 Mon to Fri.

Currently cheaper than Western Europe. However as visitors are increasing so are the prices, and it can be expected to become increasingly difficult for the budget traveller.

Czech (spoken with Bohemia and Moravia). Slovak, Russian, German and English are also spoken.

Mild summers and cold winters.

Roman Catholic. Protestant including Methodist, Moravian, Unity of Czech Brethren and Baptist, Judaism.

1998: Jan 1; Apr 13; May 1, 8; July 5, 6; Oct 28; Dec 24, 25, 26.
1999: Jan 1; Apr 5; May 1, 8; July 5, 6; Oct 28; Dec 24, 25, 26.

Generally 220 volts AC 50 Hz.

There is a 24 hour service available at the main post office in Prague. Poste Restante is available throughout the country.

BBC: 15.07 12.09 6.195 3.955
VOA: 15.20 9.670 6.040 5.995.

Traditional roles are still maintained by the older generation, whereas western values are developing among the younger members of society.

FLIGHTS: Very cheap, quick and convenient. RAIL: Fares are low but supplements are payable for travel by express trains. Reservations should be made in advance for long journeys. BUS: Efficient and comfortable. They are more reliable than the train but it is advisable to book in advance. CAR HIRE: Available from several companies. DOCUMENTATION: A national driving licence will be sufficient.

When using public transport ensure you pay the correct amount which will avoid paying any extra money to persistent train/bus conductors. Pickpocketing is rife. PHOTOGRAPHY: Do not take photographs of anything connected with the military.

CAPITAL: Copenhagen

GMT + 1 (+2 from the last Sunday in March to the Saturday before the last Sunday in September.)

FROM UK: 45   IDD: Y.
OUTGOING CODE: 00

Police and Ambulance: 112 (in Copenhagen).

Royal Danish Embassy, 55 Sloane Street, London SW1X 9SY. Tel: (0171) 333 0200 or 333 0265. Fax: (0171) 333 0270 or 333 0266.
British Embassy, Kastelsvej 36–40, DK -2100 Copenhagen Ø, Denmark. Tel: 35 26 46 00. Fax: 33 32 15 01.

Danish Tourist Board, 55 Sloane Street, London SW1X 9SY. Tel: (0171) 259 5958/9. Fax (0171) 259 5955.
Danmarks Turistråd (Tourist Board), Vesterbrogade 6D, DK-1620 Copenhagen V, Denmark. Tel 33 11 14 15. Fax: 33 93 14 16.

Requirements may be subject to short term change. Contact embassy before departure.
VALID PASSPORT REQUIRED.
Visa Not Required by Nationals of the UK with full British Passports.

Meat or meat products can not be imported into Denmark.

Danish Krone (Dkr) = 100 øre. Exchange: Eurocheques are cashed by hotels and banks and may also be used at most restaurants and shops. Personal cheques cannot be used by foreigners in Denmark. Some banks may refuse to exchange large foreign bank notes. All major credit cards accepted. Travellers cheques can be cashed by banks and hotels, and can be used at most hotels and shops. US dollars and Deutschmarks are the preferred forms of currency.
ATM AVAILABILITY: Over 2500 locations.

MONEYGRAM: 8001 0010 then 800 592 3688.
WESTERN UNION: 800 10711.

AMEX: +44 1273 696933
DINERS CLUB: (45) 36723672
MASTERCARD: 8001 6098
VISA: (1) 410 581 9091

AMEX: 800 10100
THOMAS COOK: 800 1 01 10
VISA: 800 1 77 46

0930–1700 Mon, Tues, Wed and Fri, 0930–1800 Thur. Several exchange bureaus are open until midnight.

Slightly cheaper than other Scandinavian countries but still relatively expensive.

Danish. English, German and French may also be spoken.

Summer June–Aug. Winter Oct–Mar which is wet with period of frost. Feb is the coldest month. Spring and Autumn are generally mild.

Mainly Evangelical Lutheran with a small Roman Catholic minority.

1998: Jan 1; Apr 9, 10, 13; May 8, 21; June 1, 5; Dec 24, 25, 26.
1999: Jan 1; Apr 1, 2, 5; May 8, 20, 31; June 5; Dec 24, 25, 26.

220 volts AC 50 Hz. Continental 2 pin lugs are used.

2–3 days to rest of Europe.

BBC: 12.09 9.410 6.195 3.995
VOA: 11.96 9.760 6.140 5.995.

Relatively safe in comparison to other countries for women. There is little inequality between men and women.

PUBLIC TRANSPORT: Extensive service provided. SEA: There are frequent ferry services between the islands. RAIL: The main cities on all islands are connected by the rail network. Express trains operate and 'Inter-Rail' and 'Nord-Tourist' pass (which can be used throughout Scandinavia) can provide good value. CAR HIRE: Available to drivers over the age of 20. DOCUMENTATION: National driving licence is acceptable. Visitors taking their own car are advised to obtain a 'Green Card' as without will limit their insurance coverage.

Usual social courtesies should be observed. Casual dress is suitable for most places. Railway porters and washroom attendants will expect a tip.

CAPITAL: Djibouti

GMT + 3

FROM UK: 253   IDD: Y.
OUTGOING CODE: 00

Not present.

No embassy in the UK. Europe: Embassy of the Republic of Djibouti, 26 rue Emile Ménier, 75116, Paris, France. Tel: (1) 47 27 49 22. Fax: (1) 45 53 50 53.

British Consulate, BP 81 Gellatly, Hankey et Cie, Djibouti, Djibouti. Tel: 351 940. Fax: 353 294.

Refer to the Embassy.

Office Nationale du Tourisme et de l'Artisanat (ONTA), BP 1938, place du 27 juin, Djibouti, Djibouti. Tel: 353 790. Fax: 356 322.

Return Ticket Required. Requirements may be subject to change at short notice. Contact the appropriate diplomatic or consular authority before finalising travel arrangements. VALID PASSPORT REQUIRED.

Visa Required for a maximum stay of 3 months. An extension may be granted in Djibouti on request to the headquarters of the Police Nationale. Entry and Transit Visas are granted

Gold objects apart from personal jewellery.

Departure tax DFr5000, payable in local currency.

POLIO, TYPHOID: R.
MALARIA: R. Falciparum variety exists throughout the year. Resistance to chloroquine has been reported.
YELLOW FEVER: Required. A vaccination certificate is required for visitors over one year of age arriving from infected areas.
OTHER: Cholera.

W1

Djibouti Franc (DFr) = 100 Centimes. Credit cards are accepted by airlines and large hotels only. French franc is the preferred currency in traveller's cheques, but they are only accepted if marked as an External Account or Pour Compte Etranger. Sterling and US Dollars also accepted.
ATM AVAILABILITY: Unavailable.

MONEYGRAM: Unavailable.
WESTERN UNION: Unavailable.

AMEX: +44 1273 696933
DINERS CLUB: No local number.
MASTERCARD: 1 314 542 7111
VISA: (1) 410 581 9091

AMEX: +44 1273 571 600
THOMAS COOK: +44 1733 318950
VISA: +44 1733 318949

0715–1145 Sat to Thur.

Expensive and should be avoided by those with tight budgets.

Arabic and French. English is spoken by hoteliers, taxi drivers and traders.

Very hot and dry between June and Aug. Slightly cooler between Oct and Apr with occasional rain.

Muslim with Roman Catholic, Protestant and Greek Orthodox Minorities.

1998: Jan 1, 30–31; Apr 7–8, 12, 28; May 1; June 27; July 6*; Nov 17*; Dec 25.
1999: Jan 1, 29–30; Apr 4, 7–8, 28; May 1; June 27; July 6*; Nov 17*; Dec 25.

220 Volts Ac 50 Hz

Approximately 1 week to Europe by Airmail

BBC: 17.88 11.86 6.630 6.005
VOA: 21.49 15.60 9.525 6.035

Due to a predominantly Muslim faith, culture remains patriarchal.

TAXIS: Fares increase 50% after dark. CAR HIRE: 4-wheel drive is recommended. Water and petrol supplies must be carried. RAIL: There is only 1 service to Ethiopia which tourists and business people are prohibited from using.

NOTE: Areas of the country are closed, and risk of banditry and fighting is prevalent in certain areas. Check with the Foreign and Commonwealth Travel Advice unit before departure. Visitors should register with their Embassy or Consulate shortly after arrival. Despite Djibouti being a Muslim country, casual wear is acceptable. However, beachwear should not be worn in the towns.

CAPITAL: Roseau

 GMT–4.

 FROM UK: 1809 IDD: Y.
OUTGOING CODE: 1 (for the USA, Canada and most Caribbean Islands), 011 for other countries.

 999

 Dominica High Commission, 1 Collingham Gardens, South Kensington, London, SW5 0HW. Tel: (0171) 370 5195. Fax: (0171) 373 8743.
The British High Commission in Barbados deals with enquiries relating to Dominica.

 Caribbean Tourism, Vigilant House, 120 Wilton Road, London SW1V 1JZ. Tel: (0171) 233 8382. Fax: (0171) 873 8551.
National Development Corporation (NDC)–Division of Tourism, PO Box 73, Valley Road, Roseau, Dominica. Tel: 448 6032. Fax: 448 5840.

 Return Ticket required. Requirements may be subject to short-term change. Contact embassy before departure.
VALID PASSPORT REQUIRED.

 Visas not required by: Nationals of commonwealth countries for stays of up to 6 months. Enquire at the nearest Embassy or High Commission for the latest, complete list of regulations regarding visas.

 Narcotics and firearms.

 EC$ 25 or US$ 10.

 POLIO, TYPHOID: R.
YELLOW FEVER: A vaccination certificate is required from travellers over 1 year of age coming from infected areas.

 W2

 East Caribbean Dollar (EC$) = 100 cents. Travellers cheques are accepted in most hotels – US Dollars preferred. All major credit cards have limited acceptance.
ATM AVAILABILITY: 1 location.

 MONEYGRAM: 800 543 4080.
WESTERN UNION: 448 2181.

 AMEX: +44 1273 696933
DINERS CLUB: No local number.
MASTERCARD: 1 800 307 7309
VISA: (1) 410 581 9091

 AMEX: (1) 801 964 6665
THOMAS COOK: 1 800 223 7373
VISA: 1 800 732 1322

  0800–1500 Mon to Thur, 0800–1700 Fri.

 Not as expensive as some of the other Caribbean islands.

 English. Creole French is spoken by most of the population.

 Hot, subtropical climate all year round. Rainy season June–Oct, which is also the hottest time.

 Roman Catholic.

 1998: Jan 1; Feb 23–24; Apr 10, 13; May 1, 19; June 1; Aug 3; Nov 3, 4; Dec 25, 26.
1999: Jan 1; Feb 23–24; Apr 2, 5; May 1, 19, 31; Aug 2; Nov 3, 4; Dec 25, 26.

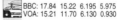 220/240 volts AC 50 Hz.

 Post to Europe takes approximately 14 days. There is no Poste Restante service.

BBC: 17.84 15.22 6.195 5.975
VOA: 15.21 11.70 6.130 0.930

 Women tend to be conservative in accordance with the dominant religion of the island.

ROAD: There are more than 700 km of well maintained roads on the island, although even these can be difficult when driving. BUS: Service exists but is unpredictable. TAXIS: Are the most efficient means of transport. CAR HIRE: Available but driving can be difficult. DOCUMENTATION: IDP is recommended. A valid foreign licence can be used to get a temporary visitors licence.

Beach wear should be kept to the beach or pool side. PHOTOGRAPHY: Permission should be asked before taking photos of local people.

Dominican Republic

CAPITAL: Santa Domingo

GMT-4

FROM UK: 1809   IDD: Y
OUTGOING CODE: 011

711/809 472 7111

Honorary Consulate of the Dominican Republic, 6 Queens Mansions, Brook Green, London W6 7EB. Tel: (0171) 602 1885.

British Consulate, Saint George School, Abraham Lincoln 552, Santo Domingo DR, Dominican Republic. Tel: 540 3132. Fax: 562 5015. (Consulate also in Puerto Plata.)

Caribbean Tourism, Vigilant House, 120 Wilton Road, London SW1V 1JZ. Tel: (0171) 233 8382. Fax: (0171) 873 8551.

Dominican Tourism Promotion Council, Desiderio Arias 24, Bella Vista, Santo Domingo, Dominican Republic. Tel: 221 4660. Fax: 682 3806.

Return Ticket required. Requirements may be subject to short-term change. Contact Embassy before departure.
VALID PASSPORT REQUIRED BY ALL: . Must remain valid for 6 months following date of departure.

Visa Not Required by Nationals of the UK, as tourists only for a maximum of 90 days, and foreign nationals who are legal residents of the UK. NOTE: Refer to the nearest consulate for a complete, up-to-date list of regulations for all countries.

Agricultural or horticultural products.

US$10. Passengers under 2 years of age and those in direct transit are exempt.

POLIO, TYPHOID: R – Polio is endemic.
MALARIA: Exists throughout the year in particular areas in the Falciparum variety, which has been reported as being highly resistant to chloroquine.
OTHER: Rabies, Bilharzia and Hepatitis

W1

Dominican Republic Peso (RD$) = 100 centavos. NOTE: Import and export of local currency is prohibited. All major credit cards are accepted. Traveller's cheques, in any international currency, are accepted by some banks. ATM AVAILABILITY: Over 100 locations.

MONEYGRAM: 1 800 543 4080.
WESTERN UNION: 200 1163.

AMEX: +44 1273 696933
DINERS CLUB: No local number.
MASTERCARD: 1 800 307 7309
VISA: (1) 410 581 9091
AMEX: (1) 801 964 6665
THOMAS COOK: 1 800 223 7373
VISA: 1 800 732 1322

0800–1600 Mon to Fri.

The best buys are the island's own handicrafts, such as amber jewellery and decorative pieces encasing insects, leaves or dewdrops. Other bargains are wood-carvings, limestone carvings and Dominican turquoise.

Spanish. English is also spoken.

Hot tropical climate. Rainy season June –Oct when possible hurricanes may also occur.

Roman Catholic. Protestant and Jewish minorities.

1998: Jan 1, 6, 21, 26; Feb 27; Apr 10; May 1; Aug 16; Sept 24; Dec 25.
1999: Jan 1, 6, 21, 26; Feb 27; Apr 2; May 1; Aug 16; Sept 24; Dec 25.

110 volts AC 60 Hz.

7 days. Advisable to post all mail from the central post office in Santo Domingo.

BBC: 17.84 15.22 6.195 5.975
VOA: 15.21 11.91 9.590 6.130.

Although a strong Roman Catholic heritage prevails, women are influenced by American culture, highlighted by the high divorce rate.

ROAD: There is a reasonable network of roads although not all are all weather and 4 wheel drives are recommended for wet weather. BUS: Cheap and efficient service runs from the capital to the main towns. CAR HIRE: Several car hire companies are present. DOCUMENTATION: IDP or national licence can be used. NOTE: Min. age for driving is 25. Credit cards are recommended when paying for car hire.

The Dominican Republic is now a major tourist destination. A variety of activities are available for all types of traveller, from casinos to classical concerts. Store valuables in hotel safety deposit boxes.

Ecuador

CAPITAL: Quito

GMT − 5, Galapagos Island GMT − 6

FROM UK: 593　　　　　IDD: Y
OUTGOING CODE: 00

Police: 101; Ambulance: 131.

Embassy of the Republic of Ecuador, Flat 3B, 3 Hans Crescent, Knightsbridge, London, SW1X 0LS. Tel: (0171) 584 1367. Fax: (0171) 823 9701.

British Embassy, Casilla 314, Calle Gonzalez Suarez 111, Quito Ecuador. Tel: (2) 560 669 or 560 670/1. Fax: (2) 560 730.

Refer to the Embassy.

Asociación Ecuatoriana de Agencias de Viajes y Turismo (ASECUT), Casilla 9421, Edificio Banco del Pacífico, 5º Piso Avenida, Amazonas 720 y Veintimilla, Quito, Ecuador. Tel: (2) 503 669. Fax: (2) 285 872.

Return Ticket Required. Requirements may change at short notice. Contact the embassy before departure.
VALID PASSPORT REQUIRED BY ALL: Passports must be carried at all times.

Visa Not Required by Nationals of the UK for stays of up to 90 days. All nationals wishing to stay in Ecuador for stays of between 3 and 6 months for business reasons. The visa will cost US$50.

Fresh and dry meats, plants, vegetables, require special permission prior to the journey.

US$25 payable in dollars.

POLIO, TYPHOID: R.
MALARIA: Exists throughout the year below 1500 m in the Falciparum variety. Resistance to chloroquine has been reported.
YELLOW FEVER: Vaccination is strongly recommended for travellers wishing to leave urban areas, a vaccination certificate is required if arriving from infected areas.
OTHER: Cholera, Hepatitis, Rabies.

W1

Sucre (Su) = 100 centavos. All major credit cards are accepted. Traveller's cheques in US dollars are widely accepted.
ATM AVAILABILITY: Over 160 locations.

MONEYGRAM: 999 119 then 800 592 5755.
WESTERN UNION: (2) 565 059.

AMEX: +44 1273 696933
DINERS CLUB: (593) (2) 981 441
MASTERCARD: 1 314 542 7111
VISA: (1) 410 581 9091

AMEX: (1) 801 964 6665
THOMAS COOK: 1 800 223 7373
VISA: 1 800 732 1322

0900–1330 and 1430–1830 Mon to Fri, some open 0930–1400 Sat.

Standard prices outside the main towns. Relatively low costs for travelling and food.

Spanish. Indian dialects and English are also spoken.

Warm subtropical climate. Andean areas are cooler. High rainfall in coastal and jungle areas.

Roman Catholic.

1998: Jan 1; Apr 10; May 1; Aug 10; Oct 9; Nov 2, 3; Dec 25.
1999: Jan 1; Apr 2; May 1; Aug 10; Oct 9; Nov 2, 3; Dec 25.

110/120 Volts AC, 60 Hz.

Up to 1 week

BBC: 17.82　15.22　9.915　7.325
VOA: 18.82　15.18　9.525　1.735

Roman catholic plays a major part in daily living. The rural areas are precipitated by local tribal customs. Usual precautions are advised for lone female travellers.

FLIGHTS: are the usual form of inter-city transport. ROAD: Conditions vary due to previous earthquakes and flooding. Improvements are being made to the extensive road network. CAR HIRE: Several international companies operate. DOCUMENTATION An IDP is not required. BUS: Can be a convenient way of getting around, but avoid at night.

The Panecillo Hill area of Quito should be avoided due to local dispute and the Mount Cotopaxi National Park should be visited after seeking local expert advice. Tourist muggings do occur. Visitors should register with the Embassy on arrival.

CAPITAL: Cairo

GMT + 2

FROM UK: 20   IDD: Y.
OUTGOING CODE: 00

Not present.

Embassy of the Arab Republic of Egypt, 26 South Street, London W1Y 8EL. Tel: (10171) 499 2401. Fax: (0171) 355 3568

British Embassy, Sharia Ahmad Raghab, Garden City, Cairo, Egypt. Tel: (2) 354 0850 or 354 0852. Fax: (2) 354 0859. Consulates in Alexandria, Suez, Port Said, and Luxor.

Egyptian State Tourist Office, 170 Piccadilly, London, W1V 9DD. Tel: (0171) 493 5282. Fax: (0171) 408 0295. Opening hours Mon to Fri 0930–1630.

Egyptian General Authority for the Promotion of Tourism Misr Travel Tower, Abassia Square, Cairo, Egypt. Tel: (2) 823 570 02 282 8430.

Return Ticket Required. requirements may be subject to change at short notice. Contact the appropriate consular authority before finalising travel arrangements.
VALID PASSPORT REQUIRED BY ALL, and must be valid for at least 6 months beyond the intended stay in Egypt.

Visa Required by nationals of UK. Tourist and Business, single or multiple entry types granted.

Check with the embassy or tourist office for a comprehensive list. NOTE: All cash, travellers cheques, credit cards and gold over £E 500 must be declared on arrival.

Departure tax is £E21, payable in local currency.

POLIO, TYPHOID: R.
MALARIA: No risk in Cairo or Alexandria but falciparum and vivax varieties exists from June to October in the El Faiyoum area.
YELLOW FEVER: A vaccination certificate is required if arriving from infected areas. Check with embassy as to which areas Egypt considers infected.
OTHER: Bilharzia, Malaria, Rabies.

W1

Egyptian Pound (£E) = 100 piastres. There are 5 national banks and 78 branches of foreign banks. All major credit cards are accepted. Traveller's cheques in US dollars are the preferred currency.
ATM AVAILABILITY: 88 locations.

MONEYGRAM: Available at Thomas Cook and American Express locations
WESTERN UNION: 357 83 65.

AMEX: +44 1273 696933
DINERS CLUB: 202 575 4537
MASTERCARD: 1 314 542 7111
VISA: (1) 410 581 9091
AMEX: +44 1273 571 600
THOMAS COOK: +44 1733 318950
VISA: +44 1733 318949

0830–1400 Sun to Thur.

Tourists can expect to pay higher prices than locals.

Arabic, English and French are widely spoken.

Hot and dry during the summer with dry winters with chilly days. Dusty winds from the Sahara prevail during April.

Islam. All types of Christianity are represented especially the Coptic Church.

1998: Jan 7, 30*; Apr 6*, 7, 19, 20, 25, 28; May 1; July 1*, 6, 23; Oct 6.
1999: Jan 7, 18*; Apr 6*, 7, 11, 20, 25, 28; May 1; July 1*, 6, 23; Oct 6.

220 Volts 50 Hz are most common. 110/380 volts AC may also be used.

Approximately 5 days by airmail. There are Poste Restante facilities at the main post office in Cairo; a small fee is charged when the mail is collected.

BBC: 17.64 15.07 12.09 1.323.
VOA: 21.45 11.82 9.700 6.060.

Revealing clothes should not be worn by women especially in he religious areas.

RAIL: A good rail network exists. TAXIS are available in the cities. Agree the fare in advance.

Following action by extremist groups against tourists, visitors are advised to be vigilant and heed advice given by the authorities. Ask permission before photographing people.

El Salvador

CAPITAL: San Salvador

 GMT – 6

 FROM UK: 503.
IDD: Y to Europe, USA and others.
OUTGOING CODE: 00

 All services: 123/121.

 Embassy of the Republic of El Salvador, Tennyson House, 159 Great Portland Street, London, W1N 5FD. Tel: (0171) 436 8282 or (0891) 444 580. Fax: (0171) 436 8181.
British Embassy, PO Box 1591, Paeso General Escalón 4828, San Salvador, El Salvador. Tel: 298 1763. Fax: 298 3328.

 Refer to the Embassy.

 Instituto Salvadoreño de Turismo (ISTU), Calle Rubén Dario 619, San Salvador, El Salvador. Tel: 222 0960. Fax: 222 1208.

 Return Ticket Required. Requirements may change at short notice. Contact the embassy before departure.
VALID PASSPORT REQUIRED BY ALL
Visa not required by nationals of the UK for stays of up to 90 days.

 Narcotics and firearms.

 US$24 when leaving the country.

 Contact the Embassy for the latest information.

 POLIO, TYPHOID: R
MALARIA: Exists all year throughout the country in the Vivax variety. Risk is greater in low-lying areas.
YELLOW FEVER: Vaccination certificates are required by travellers over 6 months of age coming from infected areas.
OTHER: Rabies, Visceral leishmaniatis, Mucocutaneous leishmanisis.

 W1

 Colón Esc (colloquially Peso) = 100 cen-tavos. MasterCard, Visa and Amex are widely accepted. Traveller's cheques are accepted in banks and hotels on production of a pass-port. US dollar cheques are preferred.
ATM AVAILABILITY: Over 20 locations.

MONEYGRAM: 1 800 824 2220.
WESTERN UNION: 279 1902.

 AMEX: +44 1273 696933
DINERS CLUB: 503 23 2888
MASTERCARD: 1 314 542 7111
VISA: (1) 410 581 9091
AMEX: (1) 801 964 6665
THOMAS COOK: 1 800 223 7373
VISA: 1 800 732 1322

 0900–1300 and 1345–1600 Mon to Fri.

 The main hotels are in the capital. Prices fluctuate, depending on festivals and national events.

 Spanish. English is also widely spoken.

 Hot subtropical climate. Rainy season is May–Oct. The upland areas are cooler.

 Roman Catholic.

 1998: Jan 1; Apr 8–10; May 1; June 30; Aug 5–6; Sept 15; Nov 2; Dec 25, 30, 31.
1999: Jan 1; Mar 31; Apr 1, 2; May 1; June 30; Aug 5–6; Sept 15; Nov 2; Dec 25, 30, 31.

 110 Volts AC, 60 Hz

 7 days.

 BBC: 17.84 15.26 9.590 5.975
VOA: 15.21 11.70 6.130 5.995

 Since the civil war ended officially, women have become independent and forthright due to the mass disappearances of many of the male population, at the height of the war. Roman catholicism continues to influence society.

 ROADS: Approx. 1/3 of roads are suitable for all weather conditions. DOCUMENTATION: AN IDP or national driving licence is required. RAIL: Links main cities. BUS: A good service exists between major towns. TAXI: Are plentiful but are not metered so agree fare in advance.

El Salvador portrays a more stable political climate than for many years, however the infrastructure remains fragile with rival fac-tions contesting territorial supremecy. Travellers should still contact their embassies for current developments. Tourists should exercise great caution. Youths with guns are a growing problem on the streets of towns and cities. Seek advice as to which areas are safe. Extreme political unrest and crime rate. Avoid using cameras around military areas.

Equatorial Guinea

CAPITAL: Malabo

 GMT + 1

 FROM UK: 240   IDD: Y.
OUTGOING CODE: Operator assistance may be required.

Not present.

No Embassy in the UK. EUROPE: Embassy of the Republic of Equatorial Guinea, 6 rue Alfred de Vigny, 75008 Paris, France. Tel: (1) 47 66 44 33 or 47 66 95 70. Fax: (1) 47 64 94 52.

Consulate in Cameroon now deals with enquiries: British Consulate, Winston Churchill Avenue, BP 547, Yaoundé, Cameroon. Tel: (237) 220 545. Fax: (237) 20 148

Not present.

The Centro Cultural Hispano-Guineano gives out good maps of the Island and mainland.

Return Ticket Required. Requirements may be subject to change at short notice. Contact the relevant consular authority before finalising travel arrangements.
VALID PASSPORT REQUIRED BY ALL

Visa Required by all.

Spanish Newspapers.

 POLIO, TYPHOID: R.
MALARIA: Required. Falciparum exists throughout the country and resistance to chloroquine has been reported.
YELLOW FEVER: Vaccination certificate required by arrivals from infected areas. However, vaccination is advised for all travellers.
OTHER: Bilharzia, river blindness in unchlorinated water, oriental lung fluke (recently reported) and Cholera are present.

W1

CFA Franc (CFA Fr) = 100 centimes. NOTE: Export of local currency is limited to CFA Fr3000. CFA Franc can not be easily exchanged outside of the CFA Fr area. Diners Club is accepted on a limited basis in large towns only. Traveller's cheques are not accepted.
ATM AVAILABILITY: Unavailable.

 MONEYGRAM: Unavailable.
WESTERN UNION: Unavailable.

 AMEX: +44 1273 696933
DINERS CLUB: No local number.
MASTERCARD: No local number.
VISA: No local number.
AMEX: No local number.
THOMAS COOK: No local number.
VISA: No local number.

0800–1200 Mon to Sat.

Tourists can expect to pay high prices for services.

Spanish, African dialects including Fang and Bubi are spoken.

Tropical climate throughout the year. Rainfall throughout the year although less falls between Dec and Feb.

There are no official religions but the majority of the population are Roman Catholic with Animist minority.

1998: Jan 1; Apr 10; May 1; June 5, 11; July 25; Aug 3, 15; Oct 12; Nov 17; Dec 10, 25.
1999: Jan 1; Apr 2; May 1; June 5; 10. July 25; Aug 3, 15; Oct 12; Nov 17; Dec 10, 25.

220/240 Volts. AC

Approximately 2 weeks

BBC: 21.66 17.83 15.40 7.160
VOA: 21.49 15.60 9.525 6.035

Women should take extra precautions if travelling in Equatorial Guinea.

FLIGHTS: Advisable to book in advance.
ROADS: There are few tarred roads and car hire companies are unavailable but taxis can be hired. SEA: there is a ferry between Malabo, Bata and Doula, allow 12 hours for the trip.

Although the current situation is calm, caution should be exercised. Travelling after dark should be avoided. Europeans are likely to be met with curiosity and even suspicion. Foreign cigarettes are often accepted as gifts. PHOTOGRAPHY: A photo permit, available from the embassy, is essential.

Eritrea

CAPITAL: Asmara

 GMT + 3

 FROM UK: 291.
IDD: Y to Asmara, Massawa and Assab.
OUTGOING CODE: Operator assistance
required for outgoing international calls.

 Not present.

 Eritrean Consulate, 96 White Lion Street,
London N1 9PF. Tel: (0171) 713 0096.
Fax:(0171) 713 0161.
British Consulate, PO Box 5584, c/o Mitchell
Cotts Building, Emperor Yohnanes Avenue 5,
Asmara, Eritrea. Tel: (1) 120 145. Fax (1) 120
104.

 Refer to the Consulate.
Eritrean Tour Service (ETS) PO Box 889, 61
Harnet Avenue, Asmara, Eritrea. Tel: (1) 124
999. Fax: (1) 126 366

 Return Ticket Required. Requirements may
be subject to change at short notice. Contact
the relevant consular authority before finalising travel arrangements.
VALID PASSPORT REQUIRED BY ALL
Visa required by all. Business and Tourist
granted. Transit passengers who do not
leave the airport do not need a visa.

 US$20 for international departures + Br 3
service charge.

 POLIO, TYPHOID: R.
MALARIA: Exists throughout the year and
high resistance to chloroquine has been
reported. YELLOW FEVER: A vaccination
certificate is required by all arrivals over one
year of age arriving from infected areas.
However, everyone is advised to have the
vaccination for travel outside the urban areas.
OTHER: Bilharzia, Cholera, Hepatitis,
Rabies, Meningitis are present. Tetanus
injection is also recommended.

 W1

 Ethiopian Birr (Br) used in Asmara and the
South. The Sudanese Dinar is in circulation in
the North and West. US Dollars in cash is the
best form of currency. MasterCard and
Diners Club have limited acceptance.
ATM AVAILABILITY: Unavailable.

 MONEYGRAM: Unavailable.
WESTERN UNION: 1 11 33 57.

 AMEX: +44 1273 696933
DINERS CLUB: No local number.
MASTERCARD: 1 314 542 7111
VISA: No local number.
AMEX: +44 1273 571 600
THOMAS COOK: +44 1733 318950
VISA: +44 1733 318949

 0800–1200 and 1400–1700 Mon to Fri,
0800–1200 Sat.

 Prices are generally lower in Eritrea than in
surrounding countries.

 Arabic and Tigrinya. English and Italian also
spoken.

 Hottest period is Apr to Jun but it can be very
cold at night. June–Feb rainy season
depending on the area of the country.

 50% Ethiopian Orthodox and 50% Muslim.

 1998: Jan 1, 7, 19, 29*; Mar 8; Apr 9*; May
1, 24; June 20; July 16*; Sept 1, 12, 28; Dec
25.
1999: Jan 1, 7, 19; Mar 8; Apr 2*; May 1, 24;
June 20; July 16*; Sept 1, 12, 28; Dec 25.

 110 Volts AC in Asmara different voltage
exists outside the capital. There are occasional power surges.

 Delays should be expected.

 BBC: 21.47 17.89 15.42 11.73
VOA: 21.49 15.58 9.530 6.035

 Women must avoid wearing revealing
clothes.

 No internal flights or railways. ROADS:
Reasonable between tourist and business
centres. Improvements are being made.
BUSES: Connect all larger towns and cities.
TAXIS: Can be found in the capital and at
the airport, fares should be agreed in
advance.

 Travel to the Sudanese border should be
avoided. The Hanish islands and their coast-
lines are also unsafe for travellers. Only take
accommodation in the larger towns as there
many landmines in rural Eritrea. Avoid travel
after dark. Casual wear is suitable for most
places.

Estonia

CAPITAL: Tallinn

GMT + 2 (+2 from the last Sunday in March to the Saturday before the last Sunday in September.)
FROM UK: 372   IDD: Y
OUTGOING CODE: 810

Ambulance: 03 (Tallinn: 003); Police: 02 (Tallinn: 002); Fire: 01 (Tallinn: 001).

Embassy of the Republic of Estonia, 16 Hyde Park Gate, London SW7 5DG. Tel: (0171) 589 3428. Fax: (0171) 589 3430.
British Embassy, Kentmanni 20, EE-0100 Tallinn, Estonia. Tel (3726) 313 353 or 313 461/2. Fax: (3726) 313 354.

Not present.

Estonian Tourist Board, Pikk Street 71, EE-0001 Tallinn, Estonia. Tel (2) 601 700. Fax: (2) 602 743.

Requirements may be subject to short term change. Contact embassy before departure.
VALID PASSPORT REQUIRED BY ALL

Visa not required by nationals of Great Britain. For the latest information contact the relevant authorities at least 3 weeks before finalising travel arrangements.

Pornography.

Rabies.

1 Kroon = 100 sents. Exchange: US$ and Deutsch Marks are widely accepted. Credit cards are accepted on a limited basis. Traveller's cheques can be exchanged at most banks. Preferred currency is US dollars. ATM AVAILABILITY: Over 200 locations.

MONEYGRAM: 8 00 8001001.
WESTERN UNION: 2 640 5023.

AMEX: +44 1273 696933
DINERS CLUB: No local number.
MASTERCARD: 1 314 542 7111
VISA: (1) 410 581 9091

AMEX: +44 1273 571 600
THOMAS COOK: +44 1733 318950
VISA: +44 1733 318949

0930–1630 Mon to Fri.

Estonian. Some Russian may also be spoken.

There is rainfall throughout the year with the heaviest falling in Aug. Heavy snow falls are likely in the winter months. The climate has large temperature variations. Summer can be quite warm but winter, lasting from Oct–Mar, can be very cold.

Protestant (Lutheran).

1998: Jan 1; Feb 24; Apr 10, 12; May 1, 31; June 23, 24; Dec 25, 26.
1999: Jan 1; Feb 24; Apr 2, 4; May 1, 30; June 23, 24; Dec 25, 26.

220 volts AC, 50 Hz. European 2 pin plugs are used.

Approx. 6 days.

BBC: 15.07 12.09 9.410 6.195
vOA: 11.97 9.760 6.040 5.995

Traditionally a patriarchal society, but gender roles becoming more equal.

RAIL: The rail system is underdeveloped but the most major cities are connected to the network. SEA/RIVER: Ferries connect the mainland with the main Islands. ROAD: There is a high density of roads although there are few major highways. Careful driving is advised and driving at night is not recom-mended. It is best to remember that spare parts are not always available. CAR HIRE: Hertz agencies are present in Tallinn. DOC-UMENTATION: European nationals should be in possession of the new 'European Driving Licence'. BUS: A wide network of routes are operated including express ser-vices. Prices are very low and buses are still the most important means of transport. TAXIS: Agree fare in advance.

It is advisable to take a supply of medicines as they are unlikely to be available (Aspirin etc.). Visitors should take care to respect Estonians' sense of national identity. Crime is an increasing problem for tourists in Tallinn.

Ethiopia

CAPITAL: Addis Ababa

GMT + 3

FROM UK: 251   IDD: Y
OUTGOING CODE: Calls must be made through the International operator.

Not present.

Embassy of Ethiopia, 17 Princes Gate, London, SW7 1PZ. Tel: (01710) 589 7212. Fax: (0171) 584 7054.

British Embassy, PO Box 858, Fikre Mariam, Abatechan Street, Addis Ababa, Ethiopia. Tel: (1) 612 354. Fax (1) 610 588.

Refer to Embassy.

Ethiopian Commission for Hotels and Tourism, PO Box 2183, Addis Ababa, Ethiopia. Tel: (1) 517 470. Fax: 513 899.

Return Ticket Required. Requirements may be subject to change at short notice. Consult the relevant consular authority before finalising travel arrangements.
VALID PASSPORT REQUIRED BY ALL
Visa required. Tourist, business and transit visas granted. The latter is not required if remaining in the airport before an onward journey.

Narcotics.

US$ 10 is payable on departure, in US dollars only.
Entry into Ethiopia can normally only be made by air transport via Addis Ababa international airport. Special permission will be required for alternative entry.

POLIO, TYPHOID: R.   MALARIA: R.
Resistance to chloroquine has been reported.
YELLOW FEVER: Vaccination strongly recommended. A vaccination certificate will be required by all travellers over one year of age arriving from infected areas. OTHER: Bilharzia, Cholera, Meningitis and Rabies.

W1

Ethiopian Birr (Br) = 100 cents. US$ currency is the most convenient. NOTE: Import and export of local currency is limited to Br100. Foreign currency is unlimited but must be declared on arrival. MasterCard and Diners Club are accepted in the capital only. Traveller's cheques have limited acceptance, US dollars the preferred currency.
ATM AVAILABILITY: Unavailable.

MONEYGRAM: Unavailable.
WESTERN UNION: 1 51 24 37.

AMEX: +44 1273 696933
DINERS CLUB: No local number.
MASTERCARD: 1 314 542 7111
VISA: +44 1273 696933
AMEX: +44 1273 571 600
THOMAS COOK: +44 1733 318950
VISA: +44 1733 318949

0800–1200 and 1300–1700 Mon to Thur, 0830–1130 and 1300–1700 Fri.
Prices are generally lower than surrounding countries

Amharic. English is the second official language. Italian and French are also spoken.
Lowlands – hot and humid, Warm in the hill country and cool in the uplands. Rain – mostly from June to Sept.

North – mainly Christian. East and South – mainly Islam.

1998: Jan 7, 19, 30*; Mar 2; Apr 7, 17, 19; May 1, 28; July 6*; Sept 11, 27.
1999: Jan 7, 18, 18*; Mar 2; Apr 7, 9, 11; May 1, 28; July 6*; Sept 11, 27.

220 Volts AC 50 Hz.

Approximately 2 weeks.

BBC: 17.88   11.86   9.630   6.005
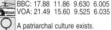
VOA: 21.49   15.60   9.525   6.035

A patriarchal culture exists.

FLIGHTS: Erratic internal flights operate to over 40 towns. ROADS: A good network of all-weather roads exists. NOTE: Frequent fuel shortages can make travel outside Addis Ababa very difficult. TAXI: Fares should be agreed in advance. DOCUMENTATION: A British driving licence is valid for 1 month after which a temporary Ethiopian licence will be required.

NOTE: Mugging and hijacking is increasingly posing a threat. Tourists should confine themselves to recognised tourist areas and avoid travel after dark. Border areas should be avoided. Travelling alone is discouraged. Casual wear is suitable for most places.
NOTE: Ethiopia uses the pre-Julian Solar Calendar with 12 months of 30 days and the 13th month of 5 or 6 days. It is important to check dates before travelling.

Falkland Islands

CAPITAL: Port Stanley

GMT – 4

FROM UK: 500   IDD: Y.
OUTGOING CODE: 0

All services: 999.

Falkland Islands Government and Tourist Office, Falkland House, 14 Broadway, London, SW1H 0BH. Tel (0171) 222 2542. Fax: 22619.

No British Embassy present.

See government office.

Falkland Islands Tourist Board, Old Transmitting Station, Stanley, East Falkland. Tel: 22215. Fax: 22619.

Return Ticket Required. Requirements may change at short notice. Contact the embassy before departure.
VALID PASSPORT REQUIRED BY ALL

All nationals must complete visitor forms from the government office before, or on, arrival.

Uncooked or cured meat and plants are only allowed under licence. No livestock allowed on any incoming aircraft.

Falkland Islands Pound (Fl£) = 100 pence. FE facilities: available in Stanley and the Standard Chartered Bank. Cheques issued by the main UK bank (up to £50) can be cashed with a valid cheque card. Credit cards have only a limited acceptance.
ATM AVAILABILITY: Unavailable.

MONEYGRAM: Unavailable.
WESTERN UNION: Unavailable.

AMEX: +44 1273 696933
DINERS CLUB: No local number.
MASTERCARD: 1 314 542 7111
VISA: 0800 96 3833

AMEX: 0800 521 313
THOMAS COOK: +44 1733 318950
VISA: +44 1733 318949

0830–1200 and 1330–1500 Mon to Fri.

Comparable with United Kingdom but tends to be more expensive, due to the importation of most requirements.

English.

Temperate climate conditioned by the surrounding sea.

Christianity.

1998: Jan 1; Apr 10, 13, 21; June 16; Oct 5; Dec 8, 25–29.
1999: Jan 1; Apr 2, 5, 21; June 16; Oct 4; Dec 8, 25–29.

240 Volts AC, 50 HZ.

4–7 days.

BBC: 17.79 11.75 9.915 5.970
VOA: 15.21 11.58 9.775 5.995

Usual precautions should be taken that apply in Western Europe. The close knit community means crime is of no particular problem.

FLIGHTS: Light aircraft services can be used to travel between most of the Islands. ROAD: A 4 -wheel drive is recommended if travelling outside the capital where vehicles may become bogged down.

To visit the Falkland Islands an application has to be made to the Falkland Islands Government Office as they provide the transportation. The islands are made up of a small population, living in and around the capital.

Fiji

CAPITAL: Suva

GMT + 12

FROM UK: 679   IDD: Y
OUTGOING CODE: International calls are made through the operator.

All services: 000.

Embassy of the Republic of Fiji, 34 Hyde Park Gate, London, SW7 5DN. Tel: (0171) 839 2200. Fax: (0171) 839 9050.

British Embassy, PO Box 1355, Victoria House, Gladstone Road, Suva, Fiji. Tel: 311033. Fax: 301406.

Refer to Embassy.

Fiji Visitors Bureau, PO Box 92, Suva Fiji. Tel: 302 433. Fax: 300 907.

Return Ticket Required. Regulations may be subject to change at short notice. Contact the embassy before departure.
VALID PASSPORT REQUIRED BY ALL and must be valid for 6 months from the date of entry.

Nationals of the UK do not require a visa.

Fruit and Plants may be confiscated on entry.

F$20, payable in local currency. Children under 16 years of age are exempt.

POLIO, TYPHOID: R.
YELLOW FEVER: A vaccination certificate will be required of arriving from an infected area (excluding those under 1 year of age).

W2

Fijian dollar (F$) = 100 cents. NOTE: Export of local currency is limited to F$100, export of foreign currency as cash is limited to F$500. All major credit cards are accepted. Travellers cheques, preferably in Australian dollars, can be easily exchanged. ATM AVAILABILITY: 10 locations.

MONEYGRAM: Unavailable.
WESTERN UNION: 314 812.

AMEX: +44 1273 696933
DINERS CLUB: No local number.
MASTERCARD: 1 314 542 7111
VISA: (1) 410 581 9091

AMEX: (61) 2 886 0689
THOMAS COOK: +44 1733 318950
VISA: +44 1733 318949

0930–1500 Mon to Thur, 0930–1600 Fri.

Can be expensive in the tourist centres, but cheaper dormitory-style accommodation is gradually being introduced. Different islands cater for different needs and are budgeted accordingly.

Fijian and Hindi. English is widely spoken.

Tropical climate, rainy season = Dec – Apr.

Methodist and Hindu. Roman Catholic and Muslim minorities.

1998: Jan 1; Mar 13; Apr 10, 11, 13; May 29; June 15; July 6*, 27; Oct 12, 19; Dec 25, 26.
1999: Jan 1; Mar 13; Apr 2, 4, 5; May 29; June 15; July 5*, 19; Oct 12, 19; Dec 25, 26.

240 Volts AC, 50 Hz.

Up to 10 days.

BBC: 15.36 11.95 9.740 7.145
VOA: 18.82 11.72 9.525 5.985

Fijian society is friendly and open. There is no discrimination between men and women. Saris are worn by women.

FLIGHTS: Shuttle services are available between islands, although more expensive than other methods. SEA: Ferries operate inexpensive crossings between islands. Arrangements should be confirmed before the vessel leaves port. ROAD: Car Hire is available. DOCUMENTATION: Foreign driving licence is acceptable. TAXI: Metered in towns. BUS: Services operate between large towns and on suburban routes. ROAD: Car Hire is available DOCUMENTATION: Foreign driving licence is acceptable. TAXI: Metered in towns. BUS: Services operate between large towns and on suburban routes.

A multi-racial culture prevails. Beach-wear is not acceptable in towns.

CAPITAL: Helsinki

GMT + 2 (GMT + 3 from the last Sunday in March to the Saturday before the last Sunday in September.)

FROM UK: 358   IDD: Y
OUTGOING CODE: 990 (for international enquiries from Finland dial 92020).

Helsinki Police: 002; Doctor: 008; Ambulance and Fire: 000.

Embassy of the Republic of Finland, 38 Chesham Place, London SW1X 8HW. Tel: (0171) 235 9531. Fax (0171) 235 3680.
British Embassy, Itainen Puistotie 17, 00140 Helsinki, Finland. Tel: (0) 661 293. Fax (0) 661 342.

Finnish Tourist Board, 30–35 Pall Mall, London SW1Y 5LP. Tel: (0171) 839 4048 or 930 5871 (trade only). Fax: (0171) 321 0696.
Embassy Matkailun edistämiskeskus (Tourist Board) PO Box 625, Töölönkatu 11, 00101 Helsinki, Finland. Tel: (0) 403 011. Fax: (0) 40 30 13 33.

Requirements may be subject to short term change. Contact embassy before departure.
VALID PASSPORT REQUIRED
Visa not required by nationals of Great Britain (holders of British Hong Kong passports do require a visa). NOTE: Many other nationals do not require visas – check with the nearest authority for a complete up-to-date list of visa requirements for Finland.

Food, plants, medicine, works of art are subject to restrictions. Import of drinks with more than 60% volume of article are prohibited.

Markka (FMK) = 100 penniä. Exch: banks and exchange bureaux at ports, airports, stations. All major credit cards are widely accepted. Travellers cheques are accepted throughout the country. US dollars are the preferred currency.
ATM AVAILABILITY: Over 2000 locations.

MONEYGRAM: 0 800 1 115198.
WESTERN UNION: 9 800 20440.

AMEX: 9 125 1600
DINERS CLUB: (358) 8009 5555
MASTERCARD: 08001 156234
VISA: (1) 410 581 9091

AMEX: 9800 12000
THOMAS COOK: +44 1733 318950
VISA: +44 1733 318949

0915–1615 Mon to Fri.

Relatively expensive, similar to other Scandinavian countries.

Finnish. Swedish and English may also be spoken.

The climate is temperate, but with considerable variation in temperatures. Summers are warm whilst winters Oct–Mar are very cold. The North has snow cover from mid Oct to mid May.

Mostly Lutheran with others including; Finnish Orthodox, Baptists, Methodists, Free Church, Roman Catholic, Jews and Muslim.

1998: Jan 1, 6; Apr 9, 10, 13; May 1, 21; June 19; Dec 6, 24, 25, 26, 31.
1999: Jan 1, 6; Apr 1, 2, 5; May 1, 20; June 19; Dec 6, 24, 25, 26, 31.

220 volts AC, 50 Hz. Plugs are continental 2 pin type.

3 days within Europe.

BBC: 15.07 12.09 9.410 6.195
VOA: 11.97 9.760 6.040 5.995

Women in general should encounter few problems. Whilst usual precautions should be taken, the crime rate is quite low and there is little inequality between men and women.

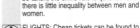

FLIGHTS: Cheap tickets can be found to the various airports throughout the country.
RAIL: Cheap and efficient, various discount schemes operate depending on status e.g. group travel 'Interail' and 'Scanrail'. ROAD: A well developed road system, use of horns is frowned upon and signs will indicate warnings of reindeer and other wildlife when collision are possible. BUS: An excellent network of routes are available offering cheap offers to specific groups. CAR HIRE: Normally drivers should have at least 1 years driving experience. DOCUMENTATION: Usually National or IDP is required with insurance. A 'Green' card is recommended.

Finnish people often appear reserved.
PHOTOGRAPHY: Check with the Russian Embassy if you wish to take photos near the Western border. During the summer mosquitoes and gnats can be nuisance, especially in the North where a good supply of repellent is recommended.

CAPITAL: Paris

 GMT + 1 (GMT + 2 from the last Sunday in March to the Saturday before the last Sunday in September).

 FROM UK: 33   IDD: Y
OUTGOING CODE: 19

 Police: 17; Fire: 18; Ambulance: 15.

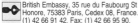 French Consulate General, (Visa Section) PO Box 57, 6A Cromwell Place, London SW7 2EW. Tel: (0171) 838 2000. Information Service – (0891) 887 733. Fax: (0171) 838 2046.
British Embassy, 35 rue du Faubourg St Honore, 75383 Paris, Cedex 08, France. Tel: (1) 42 66 91 42. Fax: (1) 42 66 95 90.
French Government Tourism Office, 178 Piccadilly, London W1V 0AL. Tel:(0891 244 123 (France Information Line). Fax: (0171) 493 6594.
Maison de la France (Tourist Information Agency), 8 avenue de l'Opéra, 75001 Paris, France. Tel (1) 42 96 10 23. Fax: (1) 42 86 80 52.

 Advisable to have a return ticket as proof of sufficient funds to finance stay, although this is not an absolute requirement. Requirements may be subject to short term change. Contact embassy before departure.
VALID PASSPORT REQUIRED.

 NOTE: British citizens who have retained Commonwealth passports may require a visa. Check with the visa section of the consulate.

 Gold jewellery, other than personal jewellery below 500 g in weight must be declared.

 Ffr 3, or equivalent in any currency. French Franc (Ffr) = 100 centimes. American Express, Diners Club and Visa credit cards are all widely accepted. Travellers cheques are accepted almost everywhere. French francs preferred.
ATM AVAILABILITY: Over 25,000 locations.

 MONEYGRAM: 00 800 66639472.
WESTERN UNION: 01 43 35 60 60

 AMEX: +44 1273 696933
DINERS CLUB: (33) (1) 47627575
MASTERCARD: No local number.
VISA: 0800 9 01235

 AMEX: 05908600
THOMAS COOK: 0800 90 8330
VISA: 0800 91 5617

 0900–1200 and 1400–1600 Mon to Fri. Some banks close on Mon and close at 1200 the day before a bank holiday.

 Similar to other Western European countries. Cities and tourism centres are more expensive than less commercial areas.

 French. Basque is spoken in the Southwest by some and Breton in Brittany. Some English is spoken by much of the population.

 Temperate climate in the North. Rainfall throughout the year. Some snow may fall in the winter. Mediterranean climate in the South. Relatively mild temperatures in the West. Summers can be very hot and sunny, inland areas can be mild.

 Mostly Roman Catholic with a Protestant minority.

 1998: Jan 1. Apr 11, 13; May 1, 8, 21; June 1; July 13, 14; Aug 15; Nov 1, 11; Dec 24, 25.
1999: Jan 1; Apr 3, 5; May 1, 8, 20, 31; July 12, 14; Aug 15; Nov 1, 11; Dec 24, 25.

 220 volts AC 50Hz. Plugs are the 2-pin type.

 2–3 days within the rest of Europe.

 BBC: 9.410 6.195 3.995 0.648
VOA: 15.21 9.760 6.040 5.995

 Roles vary depending on the region women live. Generally, there is little inequality in urban areas.

 RAIL: Excellent service. ROAD: BUS: Very few long distance bus services exist. CAR HIRE: A list of agencies can be obtained from the tourist information office. DOCUMENTATION: A national driving licence is sufficient. Nationals from the EU are strongly advised to take a 'Green' card. The car registration documents must also be carried.

 Casual wear is common but the French are renown for their stylish dress sense. Topless sunbathing is tolerated on most beaches but naturism is restricted to certain beaches. Be aware of pick pockets and bag snatchers at railway stations and tourist areas. Do not expect to find work to finance your stay as France currently has a relatively high rate of unemployment.

CAPITAL: Cayenne

 GMT – 3

 FROM UK: 594   IDD: Y
OUTGOING CODE: 19 (16 for France)

 Same as France.

French Consulate General, PO Box 57, 6a
Cromwell Place, London, SW1 2JN. Tel:
(0171) 838 2051. Fax: (0171) 838 2046.

British Honorary Consulate., 16 avenue
President, Monnerville, Cayenne, French
Guiana. Tel: 311 034. Fax: 304 094.

 Not present.

Comité du Tourisme de la Guiana, BP 801,
rue de la Lalouette, 97338 Cayenne, French
Guiana. Tel 300 900. Fax: 309 315.

 Return Ticket Required. Requirements may
change at short notice. Contact the embassy
before departure.
VALID PASSPORT REQUIRED BY ALL.

Same as for France. A valid visa for France
is also valid for French Guiana, although the
visitor should make it clear that they intend to
visit French Guiana when applying for a visa
for France.

 Same as for France.

 US$20, payable in French francs.

 POLIO, TYPHOID: Y.
MALARIA: Exists in the Falciparum variety.
Resistance to chloroquine has been reported.
YELLOW FEVER: A vaccination certificate is
required for visitors over 1 year of age arriv-
ing from all countries.
OTHER: Rabies.

 W2

 French Franc (FFr) = 100 centimes. Exch:
The Banque de la Guyane will exchange
money, there are no exchange facilities at the
airport. There are two currency exchange
offices in Cayenne. All major credit cards are
accepted except for Diners Club. Traveller's
cheques have limited acceptance. French
francs preferred.
ATM AVAILABILITY: Unavailable.

 MONEYGRAM: Unavailable.
WESTERN UNION: Unavailable.

 AMEX: +44 1273 696933
DINERS CLUB: No local number.
MASTERCARD: 1 314 542 7111
VISA: (1) 410 581 9091

  AMEX: (1) 801 964 6665
THOMAS COOK: 0800 90 8330
VISA: 0800 9105617

 0745–1130 and 1500–1700 Mon to Fri.

 Expensive in relation to surrounding
countries.

 French. English and Creole are also spoken.

Tropical climate. Rainy season Jan–June.
Hot all year with cool nights.

 Roman Catholic.

 1998: Jan 1; Feb 24, 25; Mar 17; Apr 10, 13;
May 1, 8, 21; June 1, 10; July 14; Aug 15;
Oct 15; Nov 1, 2, 11; Dec 25.
1999: Jan 1; Feb 24, 25; Mar 17; Apr 2, 5;
May 1, 8, 20, 31; June 10; July 14; Aug 15;
Oct 15; Nov 1, 2, 11; Dec 25.

 220/127 Volts AC, 50 Hz

5–7 days.

BBC: 17.82 15.19 11.75 9.640
VOA: 15.21 11.74 9.815 6.030

 French and indigenous culture co-exist.

FLIGHTS: Air Guyane serves the interior of
the country from Cayenne. ROAD: There is a
road along the coast. DOCUMENTATION:
IDP is recommended. TAXI: Available in
Cayenne. CAR HIRE: Available at the airport
or in Cayenne.

 Modest beachwear is preferred. Lying off the
coast is the infamous Devil's Island, upon
which the book and subsequent film,
'Papillon' was based.

Gabon

CAPITAL: Libreville

 GMT + 1

 FROM UK: 241   IDD: Y
OUTGOING CODE: 00

 Not present.

Embassy of the Gabonese Republic, 27 Elvaston Place, London SW7 5NL. Tel: (0171) 823 9986. Fax: (0171) 584 0047.

British Embassy closed in 1991. The West African department of the Foreign and Commonwealth Office handles enquiries for Gabon. Tel (0171) 270 2516. Fax: (0171) 270 296.

 Refer to the Gabonese Embassy.

Office National Gabonaise du Tourisme, PO Box 161, Liberville, Gabon. Tel: 722 182.

Return Ticket Required. Requirements may be subject to short term change. Contact the relevant consular authority before finalising travel arrangements.
VALID PASSPORT REQUIRED BY ALL

Visa required by all. Tourist and business visas are granted.

Guns and ammunition can not be imported without a police permit.

Nationals of Angola, Cape Verde, Cuba, Ghana, Guinea-Bissau Haiti and Israel will be refused admission unless transiting by the same aircraft.

POLIO, TYPHOID: R.
MALARIA: Required. Falciparum variety prevalent, resistance to cholorquine has been reported.
YELLOW FEVER: A vaccination certificate is required by travellers over one year of age.
OTHER: Bilharzia, Choler, rabies, River blindness also present.

 W1

CFA Franc (CFA Fr) = 100 centimes. NOTE: Import of local currency is limited to CFA Fr 250,000. There is very limited acceptance of any credit cards or travellers cheques.
ATM AVAILABILITY: Unavailable.

 MONEYGRAM: Unavailable.
WESTERN UNION: 77 33 33

 AMEX: +44 1273 696933
DINERS CLUB: No local number.
MASTERCARD: 1 14 542 7111
VISA: (1) 410 581 9091

AMEX: +44 1273 571 600
THOMAS COOK: +44 1733 318950
VISA: +44 1733 318949

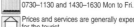 0730–1130 and 1430–1630 Mon to Fri.

Prices and services are generally expensive for the tourist.

 French and the African language – Fang.

May–Sept is the dry Season. Feb–Apr is rainy Season. Trade winds prevail during the dry season.

Mostly Christian with the remainder Muslim and Animist.

1998: Jan 1, 30*; Apr 7*, 13; May 1; June 1; Aug 15, 16; Nov 1; Dec 25.
1999: Jan 1, 18*; Apr 7*, 5; May 1, 19; July 16*; Aug 14, 15; Nov 1; Dec 25.

 220 Volts Ac 50 Hz

 Airmail at least 1 week to Western Europe.

 BBC: 21.66 17.83 15.40 9.600
VOA: 21.49 15.60 9.525 6.035

 A patriarchal society exists.

FLIGHTS: Regular domestic flights operate.
SEA: River barges and Ferries operate along the waterways. RAIL: Currently being expanded connects main cities. ROAD Mostly not tarred of poor standard, inadvisable during the rainy season. CAR HIRE: Possible from main hotels and airports.
DOCUMENTATION: IDP required.

CAPITAL: Banjul

GMT

FROM UK: 220   IDD: Y
OUTGOING CODE: 00

495 133 (Embassy)

High Commission of the Republic of the Gambia, 57 Kensington Court, London, W8 5DG. Tel: (0171) 937 6316/7/8. Fax: (0171) 937 9095.
British High Commission, PO Box 507, 48 Atlantic Road, Fajara, Banjul, The Gambia. Tel: 495 133/4 or 495 578. Fax: 496 134.

Refer to the High Commission.

Ministry of Information and Tourism, New Admin Building, Banjul, The Gambia. Tel: 226 706. Telex: 2204.

Return Ticket Required. Requirements may be subject to change at short notice. Consult the appropriate consular authority before finalising travel arrangements.
VALID PASSPORT REQUIRED BY ALL Nationals of Ireland do not require a visa. Nationals of the UK do not require a visa for the purpose of tourism only, for visits no longer than 3 months.

Narcotics.

Domestic and International departure tax is Di150 or US$20, payable in any currency.

POLIO, TYPHOID: R   MALARIA: Present throughout the year in the falciparum variety. Resistance to chloroquine has been reported. YELLOW FEVER: A vaccination certificate is required by all visitors over 1 year of age travelling from infected areas. Vaccination is recommended to all visitors planning to travel outside the urban areas. OTHER: Bilharzia, Cholera and Rabies are present.

W1

Gambian Dalasi (Di) = 100 bututs. Currency must be declared on arrival and export of foreign currency is limited to the amount imported. Black market currency exchange is strongly discouraged. Mastercard and Visa are accepted in large towns only. Travellers cheques are accepted, US dollars and pound sterling are the preferred currency.
ATM AVAILABILITY: Unavailable.

MONEYGRAM: Unavailable.
WESTERN UNION: 225 289.

AMEX: +44 1273 696933
DINERS CLUB: No local number.
MASTERCARD: 1 314 542 7111
VISA: (1) 410 581 9091
AMEX: +44 1273 571 600
THOMAS COOK: +44 1733 318950
VISA: +44 1733 318949

0800–1330 Mon to Thur, 0800–1100 Fri.

Services and prices for tourists will generally be expensive.

English

Generally recognised to have the most agreeable climate in West Africa. Mid Nov–mid May is dry in coastal areas. June–Oct is rainy season. Inland the cool season is shorter and day time temperatures are very hot between March and June.

Mostly Muslim. Remainder are Christian and Animist.

1998: Jan 1, 30*; Feb 18; Apr 7*, 10; May 1, 7*; July 6*, 22; Aug 15; Dec 25.
1999: Jan 1, 18*; Feb 18; Apr 2, 8*; May 1, 8; July 7*, 22; Aug 15; Dec 25.

220 Volts AC 50Hz. Plugs = either round or square 3 pin

BBC: 17.83 15.40 15.07 9.600
VOA: 21.49 15.60 9.525 6.035

Due to a predominant Muslim culture a patriarchal society exists.

ROADS: Few paved roads of which most are impassable during the rainy season. Road improvements programmes are in place.
TAXIS: Fares should be settled in advance.
CAR HIRE: Possible: check with company before travelling. DOCUMENTATION: IDP is required. RIVER: Ferries operate on a frequent basis along the river which connects Barra Point to Banjul. A weekly ferry operates between Banjul an Basse.

Beware of pickpockets and bag snatchers. Beach wear is not suitable for towns. Visitors should respect local laws and customs and dress conservatively. Do not expect to find work in the country. Sea swimming can be dangerous.

Georgia

CAPITAL: Tbilisi

 GMT + 4 (GMT + 5 during the summer).

 FROM UK: 995   IDD: Unreliable.
OUTGOING CODE: Calls to places outside of the CIS must be made through the operator. Long waits should be expected.

 Fire: 01; Police: 02; Ambulance: 03.

Georgian Embassy, 45 Avemore Road, London W14 8RT. Tel/Fax: (0171) 603 5325.
British Embassy, The Metekhi Palace Hotel, 380003 Tbilisi, Georgia. Tel (32) 955 497.

 Not present.

 Not present.

 Return Ticket required. Requirements may be subject to short-term change. Contact the relevant authority before departure.
VALID PASSPORT REQUIRED BY ALL: British passports must be valid for at least 6 months after leaving Georgia.

 Visas required.

 Pornography, loose pears and anything owned by a third party that is to be carried in for that third party. State loan certificates, lottery tickets and works of art antiques can not be exported.

 US$ 10, is levied on international travel.

 The Consulate/Embassies of the Russian Federation no longer issue tourist visas valid for Georgia.

 POLIO, TYPHOID: R   OTHER: Rabies.

 W2

At present Georgia remains in the Rouble zone, but a national currency the 'Lari' has now been introduced. Credit cards are accepted in some hotels. Travellers cheques are not accepted.
ATM AVAILABILITY: Unavailable.

 MONEYGRAM: Unavailable.
WESTERN UNION: 32 938921.

 AMEX: +44 1273 696933
DINERS CLUB: No local number.
MASTERCARD: 1 314 542 7111
VISA: (1) 410 581 9091

 AMEX: No local number.
THOMAS COOK: No local number.
VISA: No local number.

 0930–1730 Mon to Fri.

 Accommodation caters for all budgets, but the larger hotels do tend to inflate their prices.

 Mostly Georgian. Russian, Ossetian, Abkhazian and Adzharian.

 Hot summers with mild winters particularly in the Southwest. Low temperatures are common in Alpine areas and rainfall may be heavy in the subtropical Southwest.

 Christian mainly Georgian Orthodox and other Christian denominations. Eastern Orthodox. Muslim, Judaism.

 1998: Jan 1; Mar 3; Apr 9, 15; May 9, 26; Aug 15, 28; Oct 14; Nov 23.
1999: Jan 1; Mar 3; Apr 9, 15; May 9, 26; Aug 15, 28; Oct 14; Nov 23.

 220 volts AC, 50 Hz.

 International postal services are severely disrupted.

 BBC: 17.64 15.07 6.180 1.323
VOA: 9.760 6.040 1.197 0.792.

 At social occasions foreign women are likely to be the object of flattery. Those who do not like this should be careful not to show signs of encouragement.

 ROAD: An adequate supply of fuel must be purchased in Tbilisi if driving around Georgia as fuel may be hard to obtain in other areas. Reliable road maps and signs do not exist.
BUS: Provide a reliable if uncomfortable service between towns in the republic. TAXIS: Only use official taxis, which should not be shared with strangers in view of the incidents of crime.

 NOTE: Travel at night outside Tbilisi should be avoided if possible. The breakaway regions of Abkhazia and South Ossetia should be strictly avoided as they remain insecure. The Georgia–Russia land border is usually closed to Westerners. The Georgians are very friendly and hospitable. It is normal for most men in Georgia to carry firearms. Be vigilant against banditry and street crime.

CAPITAL: Berlin

GMT + 1 (GMT + 2 from the last Sunday in March to the Saturday before the last Sunday in September).
FROM UK: 49   IDD: Y
OUTGOING CODE: 00

Police: 110; Fire: 112.

Embassy of the Federal Republic of Germany, 23 Belgrave Square, 1 Chesham Place, London SW1X 8PZ. Tel: (0171) 824 1300. Fax: (0171) 824 1435. Consulate: Tel: (0891) 331 166 (recorded visa information) or (0171) 824 1465/6. Fax: (0171) 824 1449. Other Consulates in Manchester and Edinburgh.

British Embassy, Fredrich-Ebert-Allée 77, 53113 Bonn, Federal Republic of Germany. Tel: (228) 9167-0. Fax(228) 9167-331 or 9167-200. Consulates in Berlin, Bremen, Düsseldorf, Frankfurt/M, Hamburg, Hannover, Kiel, Munich, Nuremberg and Stuttgart.

German National Tourist Office, Nightingale House, 65 Curzon Street, London W1Y 8NE. Tel: (0891) 600 100 (recorded information) or (0171) 493 0080 (general enquiries). Fax: (0171) 495 6129.

Deutsche Zentrale für Tourismus e. V. (DZT), Beethovenstrasse 69, Frankfurt/M, Federal Republic of Germany. Tel (69) 75720. Fax: (69) 751 903.

Requirements may be subject to short term change. Contact Embassy before departure.
Valid Passport Required by UK Nationals.
Republic of Ireland: holders of national ID cards do not require valid passports.

Visas are required by nationals of the UK.

Rabies

Deutsche Mark (DM) = 100 pfennigs. TC: Banks, Post Offices, Travel Bureaux and Hotels. All major credit cards are accepted in 60% of shops, restaurants, hotels and petrol stations. Travellers cheques are accepted in all major currencies. ATM AVAILABILITY: Over 40,000 locations.

MONEYGRAM: 00 800 66639472
WESTERN UNION: (0681) 933 3328.

AMEX: +44 1273 696933
DINERS CLUB: (49) 5921 86 1818
MASTERCARD: 0130 81 9104
VISA: 0130 810991

AMEX: 0130 853100
THOMAS COOK: 0130 85 9930
VISA: 0130 82 4719

Generally 0830–1300 and 1400/30–1600 Mon to Fri, Thur until 1730 in main cities. Main branches do not close for lunch.
East Germany is still slightly cheaper than West Germany in small towns, although prices are reaching Western levels in cities.

German. English and French may also be spoken.

Temperate climate throughout the country. Summers are warm and winters are cold. There is rain throughout the year.

Mostly Protestant. Roman Catholic and other Christian denominations are also practised.

1998: Jan 1, 6; Feb 23–24; Apr 10, 13; May 1, 21; June 1, 11; Aug 15; Oct 03, 31; Nov 1, 18; Dec 24, 25, 26, 31.
1999: Jan 1, 6; Feb 22–23; Apr 2, 5; May 1, 20, 31; June 10; Aug 15; Oct 3, 31; Nov 1, 18; Dec 24, 25, 26, 31.

220 volts AC, 50 Hz.

An efficient service operates.

BBC: 15.07 12.09 6.195 6.180
VOA: 15.20 9.760 6.040 5.995.

There is little inequality between men and women.

RAIL: A modern, sophisticated rail system operates in the West. It will take some time for Eastern Germany to be brought up to Western standards. ROAD: Western area is covered by a modern network of motorways. Motorways in the East are of a reasonable standard but this may not be the case for secondary roads. CAR HIRE: Available at most towns and railway stations. NOTE: It may be difficult to use credit cards at petrol stations. DOCUMENTATION: Foreign drivers may use their national driving licence for up to 1 year or IDP. Carry car registration details. EU citizens taking their own cars are strongly advised to take a 'Green Card' for full insurance coverage. BUS: Tend to run in towns. There are few intercity services.
Red roses are only given to lovers and odd numbers should be given. Casual wear is widely accepted although formal wear may be required in upmarket restaurants. Shops, businesses, schools begin at 0800 or earlier.

Ghana

CAPITAL: Accra

 GMT

 FROM UK: 233
IDD: Available to major cities.
OUTGOING CODE: 00

 221 665 (Embassy)

 Ghana High Commission, (Visas), 04 Highgate Hill, London, N6 5HE. Tel: (0181) 342 8686. Fax: (0181) 342 8566/70.
British High Commission, PO Box 296, Osu Lik, off Gamel Abdul Nasser Avenue, Accra, Ghana. Tel: (21) 221 665 or 669 585. Fax: (21) 664 652.

Ghana High Commission (tourist information), 102 Park Street, London, W1Y 3RJ. Tel: (0171) 493 4901. Fax: (0171) 629 1730.
Ghana Tourist Board, PO Box 3106, Tesano, Nsawam Road, Accra, Ghana. Tel: (21) 231 779. Fax: (21) 231 779.

 Return Ticket Required. Requirements may be subject to change at short notice. Consult embassy before departure.
VALID PASSPORT REQUIRED BY ALL.

 Visa required.

 Animals, firearms, ammunition, explosives and milk with a high fat content.

 Departure tax is US$10.

 POLIO, TYPHOID: R.
MALARIA: Precaution advised. Falciparum form exists and resistance to chloroquine has been reported.
YELLOW FEVER: A vaccination certificate is required by all.
OTHER: Bilharzia, Rabies, a vaccination against cholera is strongly recommended, a vaccination certificate is required if arriving from an infected area.

 W1

Cedi (c) = 100 pesewas. Only authorised foreign exchange dealers must be used. NOTE: Import and export of local currency is limited to c3000 and should be recorded in passport.
Credit cards and travellers cheques have very limited use.
ATM AVAILABILITY: Unavailable.

 MONEYGRAM: 0191 then 800 592 3688
WESTERN UNION: 21 66 27 58.

 AMEX: +44 1273 696933
DINERS CLUB: No local number.
MASTERCARD: 1 314 542 7111
VISA: (1) 410 581 9091

 AMEX: +44 1273 571 600
THOMAS COOK: +44 1733 318950
VISA: +44 1733 318949

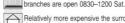 0830–1400 Mon–Thur, 0830–1500 Fri. A few branches are open 0830–1200 Sat.

 Relatively more expensive the surrounding areas.

 English and local African languages are spoken.

 The climate is hot and humid throughout the year. Apr–July is the rainy season.

 Christian, Muslim, and traditional beliefs. All forms of religion have a strong influence on daily life.

 1998: Jan 1, 30*; Mar 6; Apr 7, 10, 13; May 1; June 4; July 1; Dec 4, 25, 26.
1999: Jan 1, 18*; Mar 6; Apr 2, 5, 8; May 1; June 4; July 1; Dec 4, 25, 26.

 220 Volts Ac 50 Hz Plugs = 3 pin in larger buildings, older buildings have 2 use plugs.

 2 weeks or more to Europe.

 BBC: 17.83 15.40 11.83 7.160
VOA: 21.48 15.58 9.575 6.035

 Not as patriarchal as surrounding West Africa.

 RAIL: Limited. CAR HIRE: Available but very expensive. DOCUMENTATION: British driving licence valid for 90 days. IDP is recommended. BUSES: Extensive bus services operate in Accra.

Take local advice about security matters. Exercise care with possessions at the main airport. Ghanaians should always be addressed formally. PHOTOGRAPHY: Be discreet with cameras especially around the Castle in Accra or at the Akosombo Dam. Do not take photos of anything connected with the military.

CAPITAL: Gibraltar

 GMT + 1 (GMT + 2 from the last Sunday in March to the Saturday before the last Sunday in September).

 FROM UK: 350   IDD: Y
OUTGOING CODE: 00

 All services: 999.

 Gibraltar's Foreign Affairs are handled by the UK Foreign and Commonwealth Office, King Charles Street, London SW1A 2AH. Tel: (0171) 270 2862. All other enquiries g to the Gibraltar Information Bureau.

 Gibraltar Information Bureau, Arundel Great Court, 179 The Strand, London WC2R 1EH. Tel: (0171) 836 0777. Fax: (0171) 240 6612.

 Gibraltar Information Bureau, Engineer's battery, 32 B Rosia Road, Gibraltar. Tel: 74950. Fax: 74943.

 Requirements may be subject to change at short notice. Contact Consulate before travelling.
Valid passport required by all, except EU nationals in possession of a valid identity card..

 Visa not required. Contact the Foreign and Commonwealth office for the latest information.

 Gib£10, payable in local currency.

 Pound Sterling (Gib £) = 100 new pence. It is advisable to change unused currency from Gibraltar before leaving the area as UK banks charge for conversion. All major credit cards and travellers cheques are accepted. Pound sterling is the preferred currency. ATM AVAILABILITY: 3 locations.

MONEYGRAM: 8800 then 800 592 3688
WESTERN UNION: 51 999.

 AMEX: +44 1237 696933
DINERS CLUB: +44 (252) 375252
MASTERCARD: 1 314 542 711
VISA: 0800 96 3833

 AMEX: 0800 521313
THOMAS COOK: +44 1733 318950
VISA: +44 1733 318949

 0900–1530 and 1630–1800 Fri.

 Certain goods may be cheaper due to its duty free status. Otherwise similar to Spain.

 English and Spanish.

 The climate is warm throughout the year. Summers are hot and can be quite humid. Winters are mild.

 Mainly Roman Catholic. Church of England, Judaism, Hindu and other minorities are also represented.

 1998: Jan 1; Mar 9; Apr 10, 13; May 1, 25; June 15; Aug 31; Sept 10; Dec 25, 26.
1999: Jan 1; Mar 9; Apr 2, 5; May 1, 24; June 15; Aug 30; Sept 10; Dec 25, 26.

 220/240 volts AC 50 Hz.

 1–5 days within Europe. Poste Restante facility available in the Post Office in Main Street.

 BBC: 15.07 12.09 6.195 3.995
VOA: 15.20 9.760 6.040 5.995

 Usual precautions should be taken. No additional risks apply.

 BUS: There are good local bus services operating at frequent intervals. TAXI: There are plenty of taxis and the drivers are required by law to produce on demand a copy of fares.

 Traditional British and Mediterranean customs are upheld.

Greece

CAPITAL: Athens

 GMT + 2 (GMT + 3 from the last Sunday in March to the last Sunday in September).

 FROM UK: 30 + 1 for Athens, 31 Thessaloniki, 81 Heraklion, 661 Corfu. IDD: Y throughout the mainland and islands. OUTGOING CODE: 00

 Police: 100; Ambulance: 166; Fire: 199.

 Embassy of the Hellenic Republic, 1A Holland Park, London W11 3TP. Tel: (0171) 221 6467 or (0891) 171 202 (visa information line). Fax: (0171) 243 3202.
British Embassy, Odos Ploutarchou 1, 106 75 Athens, Greece. Tel: (1) 723 6211. Fax: (1) 724 1872. Consulates in Crete, Corfu, Kavala, Patrai, Rhodes, Salonika, Samos and Volos.
National Tourist Organisation of Greece (GNTO), 4 Conduit Street, London W1R 0DJ. Tel: (0171) 734 5997. Fax: (0171) 287 1369.
Ellinikos Oragnismos Tourismou (EOT) (National Tourist Organisation of Greece), PO Box 1017, Odos Amerikis 2, 105 64 Athens, Greece. Tel: (1) 322 3111/19. Fax: (1) 325 2895.

 Requirements may be subject to change at short notice. Check before travelling.
VALID PASSPORT REQUIRED BY ALL for at least 6 months.

 Visa Not Required for a period of 3 months. NOTE: Visitors using chartered tickets, leaving Greece on an overnight trip to another country, may risk having their return ticket invalidated by the authorities.

 Plants, one surf board per person (if entered in passport). The export of antiques is prohibited unless permission is obtained from the Archaeological Service in Athens. Those who fail to comply will be prosecuted.

 Dr6000 incl. of ticket price.

 YELLOW FEVER: A vaccination certificate is required from visitors over 6 months of age coming from infected areas. OTHER: Rabies.

 W2

 Drachmar (Dr) Currency can be changed at banks and money exchangers. NOTE: Import of local currency is limited to Dr100,000 and export to Dr20,000 for non-residents and Dr40,000 for residents. All major credit cards are accepted. Travellers cheques are accepted in all major currencies, and can be easily changed at banks.
ATM AVAILABILITY: Over 1500 locations.

 MONEYGRAM: 00 800 11 293 0309.
WESTERN UNION: 01 927 1010.
AMEX: +44 1273 696933
DINERS CLUB: (30) (1) 9241345
MASTERCARD: 00 800 11 887 0303
VISA: 00 800 11 481 0304
AMEX: +44 1273 571 600
THOMAS COOK: 00 800 4412 8366
VISA: 00 800 4412 8455

 0800–1400 Mon to Fri. Many of the banks of the larger islands stay open longer, especially during the tourist season.
Tourist centres can be very cheap when compared to other European countries.
Greek. Most people working in tourism speak some English, German, Italian or French.
Warm Mediterranean climate. Nov–Mar is when most rain falls. Winters are mild in the South but much cooler in the North.
Mainly Greek Orthodox, and Muslim and Roman Catholic minorities.

 1998: Jan 1, 6; Mar 2, 25; Apr 17, 20; May 1; June 8; Aug 15; Oct 28; Dec 25, 26.
1999: Jan 1, 6; Mar 9, 25; Apr 24, 27; May 1; June 7; Aug 15; Oct 28; Dec 25, 26.

 220 volts AC 50 Hz.

 All post for overseas will be sent by airmail. Poste Restante is available at the post office.
BBC: 15.07 13.23 9.410 6.180
VOA: 15.20 9.760 6.040 5.995.

 Take usual precautions. Women from Northern and Western Europe may receive unwanted attention from Greek men, but this doesn't usually lead to problems if ignored. Women should not walk alone at night.

 RAIL: Regular trains operate between Athens and main cities. There is a 20% discount on return fares and other offers available.
ROAD: Good road network. BUS: Link Athens and all the main towns in Attica, Northern Greece and Peloponnese. TAXI: Run on a shared basis. Rates are reasonable, on a Km basis. Extra charge on journeys from/to airports, ports, stations. CAR HIRE: Most firms operate throughout Greece. DOCUMENTATION: A national driving licence is acceptable for EU nationals.

 Traditions and customs prevail throughout Greece. The Greek Orthodox church has an important place in the community. Throwing back the head is a negative gesture. It is an offence to sell your belongings and can lead to arrest.

Grenada

CAPITAL: St George's

 GMT –4

 FROM UK: 1809   IDD: Y.
OUTGOING CODE: International operator must be used.

 Police: 112; Ambulance: 434.
All services: 911.

 Grenada High Commission, 1 Collingham Gardens, Earls Court, London, SW5 0HW. Tel: (0171) 373 7809. Fax: (0171) 370 7040.
British High Commission, 14 Church Street, St George's, Grenada. Tel: 440 3222. Fax: 440 4939.

 Refer to High Commission.

 Board of Tourism, PO Box 293, The Carenage, St George's, Grenada. Tel: 440 2001. Fax: 440 6637.

 Return Ticket required. Requirements may be subject to short term change. Contact embassy before departure.
VALID PASSPORT REQUIRED BY ALL

 Visa not required.

 Narcotics and firearms.

 EC$25 per adult payable in cash, EC$17.50 is charged for children between 5 and 12 years old.

 POLIO, TYPHOID: R
YELLOW FEVER: A vaccination certificate is required from those over one year of age coming from infected areas.
OTHER: Rabies.

 Eastern Caribbean Dollar (EC$) = 100 cents. All travellers cheques and major credit cards are widely accepted. US dollars are the preferred currency.
ATM AVAILABILITY: Unavailable.

MONEYGRAM: 1 800 543 4080.
WESTERN UNION: 440 2198.

 AMEX: +44 1273 696933
DINERS CLUB: No local number.
MASTERCARD: 1 800 307 7309
VISA: (1) 410 581 9091

 AMEX: (1) 801 964 6665
THOMAS COOK: 1 800 223 7373
VISA: 1 800 732 1322

 0800–1400 Mon to Thur, 0800–1300 and 1400–1700 Fri.

 Moderate to expensive. Hotels need to be booked well in advance. Prices may vary with seasonal changes and specific events. Duty-free shops exist with an international market.

 English

 Tropical climate. Rainy season June–Dec. Dry season Feb–May.

 Roman Catholic. Anglican, Methodist and Seventh Day Adventist minorities.

 1998: Jan 1; Feb 7; Apr 10, 13; May 1, 19 June 1, 11; Aug 3, 10–11; Oct 25, 26; Dec 25, 26.
1999: Jan 1; Feb 7; Apr 2, 5; May 1, 19, 31; June 10; Aug 3, 9–10; Oct 25, 26; Dec 25, 26.

 220/240 volts AC, 50 Hz.

 Post will take approximately 14 days to reach Europe.

 BBC: 17.84 15.22 9.915 6.195
VOA: 15.21 11.70 9.590 5.995.

 Society is influenced by African and colonial heritage, resulting in a conservative and reserved outlook.

 SEA: Round island trips are very popular, small to large boats can be hired. ROAD: They are narrow and winding. CAR HIRE: A large variety if vehicles can be hired. DOCUMENTATION: IDP is recommended. BUS: Cheap but slow service operates.

 Beach-wear is not acceptable in town.

Guadeloupe

CAPITAL: Basse-Terre

GMT–4.

FROM UK: 590   IDD: Y
OUTGOING CODE: 19

Police: 17; Fire and Ambulance: 18.

As French Consulate General (for visa enquiries) or French Embassy (cultural).

The British Embassy in Bridgetown (Barbados) deals with enquiries relating to Guadeloupe.

Caribbean Tourism, Vigilant House, 120 Wilton Road, London SW1V 1JZ.

Office du Tourisme, BP 1099, 5 Square de la Banque, 97181 Pointe-à-Pitre, Guadeloupe. Tel: 820 930. Fax: 838 922.

Return Ticket required. Requirements may be subject to short term change. Contact the Embassy before departure.
VALID PASSPORT REQUIRED BY ALL: Same as for France.

See France, but specify Guadeloupe when making application.

Ffr 80, payable in local currency, is levied on all foreign nationals.

POLIO, TYPHOID: R
YELLOW FEVER: A vaccination certificate is required from visitors over 1 year of age coming from infected areas
OTHER: Bilharzia

W2

French Franc (Ffr) = 100 centimes. All major credit cards are accepted. Travellers cheques in French francs are welcomed.
ATM AVAILABILITY: Unavailable.

MONEYGRAM: Unavailable.
WESTERN UNION: Unavailable.

AMEX: +44 1273 696933
DINERS CLUB: Not present.
MASTERCARD: 1 314 542 7111
VISA: (1) 410 581 9091

AMEX: (1) 801 964 6665
THOMAS COOK: 1 800 223 7373
VISA: 1 800 732 1322

0800–1600 Mon to Fri

Expensive due to a 15–30% tax levied on services depending on the time of year.

French. Patois and English are widely spoken.

Warm weather all year round. Main rainy season June–Oct. High humidity at times.

Roman Catholic. Evangelical Protestant minority.

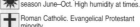
1998: Jan 1; Apr 10, 13; May 1, 8, 19; July 14, 21; Aug 15; Nov 1, 11; Dec 25.
1999: Jan 1; Apr 2, 5; May 1, 8, 19; July 14, 21; Aug 15; Nov 1, 11; Dec 25.

110/220 volts AC, 50 Hz.

Approx. 1 week to Western Europe.

BBC: 17.84 15.22 6.195 5.975
VOA: 15.21 11.70 6.130 0.930

Relaxed and equal society.

SEA: Regular ferry services move around the island. ROAD: BUS: There is a good bus service. CAR HIRE: Many companies are present. DOCUMENTATION: National driving licence is sufficient. One years driving experience is required. IDP is advised.

Guadeloupe is a French overseas department and the French culture is clearly evident.

Guam

CAPITAL: Agana

 GMT + 10

 FROM UK: 671   IDD: N
OUTGOING CODE: International calls must go through the operator.

 All services: 911.

 Refer to the USA entry.

 No British representation in Guam.

 Refer to USA entry.

 Guam Visitors Bureau, PO Box 3520, Suite 201–205, Boon's Building, 127 North Marine Drive, Upper Tumon, Agaña, Guam 96911. Tel: 646 5278/9. Fax: 646 8861.

 As for the USA.
VALID PASSPORT REQUIRED BY ALL except those entering directly from the USA.

 See USA Entry.

 See entry for the USA.

 See USA entry.

 POLIO, TYPHOID: R.

 W2

 US Dollar (US$) = 100 cents. Credit cards are widely accepted. Travellers cheques in US dollars can be exchanged.
ATM AVAILABILITY: Over 30 locations.

 MONEYGRAM: 0011 800 821 8192.
WESTERN UNION: Available.

AMEX: +44 1273 696933
DINERS CLUB: 800 525 9040
MASTERCARD: 1 800 307 7309
VISA: (1) 410 581 9091

 AMEX: (61) 2 886 0689
THOMAS COOK: 1 800 223 7373
VISA: 1 800 732 1322

 1000–1500 Mon to Thur, 1000–1800 Fri.

 Appropriate to all tastes and budget.

 English and Chamorro. Japanese and Tagalog also spoken.

 Tropical climate with rains July–Nov.

 Roman Catholic.

 1998: Jan 1, 19; Feb 16; Mar 4; Apr 10; May 25; July 4, 21; Sept 7; Oct 12; Nov 2, 11, 26; Dec 8, 25.
1999: Jan 1, 19; Feb 16; Mar 4; Apr 2; May 25; July 4, 21; Sept 7; Oct 12; Nov 2, 11, 26; Dec 8, 25.

 120 Volts AC 60 Hz.

 Up to 2 weeks.

 BBC: 15.36 11.95 9.740 6.195
VOA: 18.82 15.18 9.525 1.735

 Western culture is widely accepted due to a large naval presence. This is reflected in the status of women in Guam

 ROAD: BUS: A reasonable bus service is available on a limited number of routes. TAXI: Fare are metered. CAR HIRE: Available from most major companies. DOCUMENTATION: AN IDP is required.

 Guam's tourist industry is geared towards the Japanese market, which make up 80% of visitors. As a result other travellers will observe an abundance of Japanese customs in the tourist areas. Usual social courtesies should be applied.

CAPITAL: Guatemala City

GMT–6

FROM UK: 502   IDD: Y
OUTGOING CODE: 00
Police: 120 / 137 / 138; Fire: 122 / 123;
Ambulance: 125 / 128.

Embassy of the Republic of Guatemala, 13
Faucet Street, London, SW10 9HN. Tel:
(0171) 351 3042. Fax: (0171) 3765708.
British Embassy, 7th Floor, Edifice Centro
Financerio, Tower Two, 7a Avenida 5–10,
Zona 4 Guatemala City, Guatemala. Tel: (2)
321 601/2/4. Fax: (2) 341 904.

Refer to the Embassy.

Guatemala Tourist Commission, 7 Avenida
1–17, Centro Civico, Zona 4 Guatemala City,
Guatemala. Tel: (2) 311 333. Fax: (2) 318 893.

Return Ticket Required. Requirements may
change at short notice. Contact the embassy
before departure.
VALID PASSPORT REQUIRED BY ALL
Those on business from the UK or Republic
of Ireland require visas. Tourists from the UK
or Republic of Ireland may stay for a maximum of 90 days without a visa – a tourist
card will be issued by the authorities at the
airport.

Narcotics.

Q50 is levied on all international departures,
payable in local currency.

Contact the embassy for an up to date list of
countries, which have restricted entry.

POLIO, TYPHOID: R.
MALARIA: Exists throughout the year in
areas below 1500 m.
YELLOW FEVER: A vaccination certificate is
required by travellers arriving from infected
areas.
OTHER: Hepatitis, Rabies, Onchocerciasis,
American trypanosomiasis and Altitude sickness can occur in higher areas.

W1

Quetzal (Q) = 100 centavos Visa and Amex
are widely accepted. Other cards have only a
limited acceptance. Travellers cheques in US
dollars are recommended.
ATM AVAILABILITY: Over 120 locations.

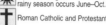
MONEYGRAM: 099 1350.
WESTERN UNION: (02) 312 860.
AMEX: +44 1273 696933
DINERS CLUB: 502 2 317955
MASTERCARD: No local number.
VISA: (1) 410 581 9091
AMEX: (1) 801 964 6665
THOMAS COOK: 1 800 223 7373
VISA: 1 800732 1322

0900–1500 (certain branches 0900–2000)
Mon to Fri.

Prices can be very reasonable. Accommodation is diverse and priced accordingly.
Food and local merchandise are relatively
inexpensive especially in markets.

Spanish. English and over 20 indigenous
languages are also spoken.

Climate varies according to altitude. Lower
altitudes being far hotter than highlands. The
rainy season occurs June–Oct.

Roman Catholic and Protestant.

1998: Jan 1; Apr 8–11; May 1, 10, 11; June
30; July 1; Aug 15; Sept 15; Oct 12, 20; Nov
1, 2; Dec 24–25, 31.
1999: Jan 1; Mar 31; Apr 1–3; May 1, 9, 10;
June 30; July 1; Aug 15; Sept 15; Oct 12, 20;
Nov 1, 2; Dec 24–25, 31.

110 Volts AC 60 Hz. There are some regional variations.

7–21 days.

BBC: 17.82 15.22 7.325 5.970
VOA: 15.12 11.58 9.775 5.995

Guatemala is the most populated South
American country, mainly Indian with Spanish influence. Culture is tribal, based on bar-
tering and selling home grown merchandise.
FLIGHTS: Air transport is by far the most
efficient means of internal travel since there
are over 380 airstrips. RAIL: A daily service
between the Pacific and Caribbean coasts.
ROAD: There is an extensive road network
but only a small amount are all weather.
BUS: The bus services are cheap but crowded. TAXI: A flat rate is often charged within
the city but prices are often expensive. CAR
HIRE: International companies operate in
Guatemala City and rates are low. DOCU-
MENTATION: A local licence will be issued
on presentation of a national driving licence.
Some regions may still be politically volatile.
Visitors should register with the Embassy
upon arrival. Violent crime is rife throughout
the country.

Guernsey

CAPITAL: St Peter Port

 GMT (GMT + 1 from March to October).

 FROM UK: 01481 (calls from overseas must be made using the UK country code: 44).
IDD: Y   OUTGOING CODE: 00

 All services: 999.

 Guernsey is an English Channel Island.

 Guernsey Tourist Office, PO Box 23, North Esplanade, St Peter Port, Guernsey, Channel Islands GY1 3AN. Tel: 726 611 (administration) or 723 552 (information). Fax: 721 246 or 714 951.

 Same as those for the rest of the UK – see the United Kingdom.

 See entry for the UK.

 £20, payable in local currency.

 Pound Sterling (£) = 100 pence. Exch: bureaux de change in banks, hotels. NOTE: Channels Islands notes and coins are not accepted in the UK although they can be reconverted at parity in UK banks. All major credit cards and travellers cheques are accepted.
ATM AVAILABILITY: Over 10 locations.

 MONEYGRAM: 800 666 39472.
WESTERN UNION: 800 833 833.

 AMEX: +44 1273 696933
DINERS CLUB: 01252 375252
MASTERCARD: 0800 96 4767
VISA: (1) 410 581 9091

 AMEX: 0800 521313
THOMAS COOK: 0800 622101
VISA: 0800 515884

 0930–1530 Mon to Fri. Some banks are open later on weekdays and on Saturday morning.

 The Channel Islands are largely a duty-free zone.

 English. Norman Patois is spoken in some parishes.

 The most popular holiday season is from Easter to October with temperatures averaging 20–21ºC. Rainfall is mainly during the cooler months.

 Church of England, Baptist, Congregational and Methodist.

 1998: Jan 1; Mar 17; Apr 10, 13; May 4, 25; Aug 3, 31; Dec 25, 26, 28.
1999: Jan 1; Mar 17; Apr 2, 5; May 3, 24; Aug 2, 30; Dec 25, 26, 27.

 240 volts AC, 50 Hz.

 Only Guernsey stamps will be accepted for outgoing mail.

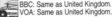 BBC: Same as United Kingdom.
VOA: Same as United Kingdom.

 Men and women are deemed equal.

 ROAD: BUS: A comprehensive bus service operates. CAR HIRE: Many companies have agencies in Guernsey. DOCUMENTATION: A full national driving licence is required.

 Casual wear is acceptable in most places. Usual social courtesies should be observed.

CAPITAL: Bissau

 GMT

FROM UK: 245
IDD: Y, but international calls must go through the operator.
OUTGOING CODE: All outgoing calls must go through the operator

Not present

Consulate General of the Republic of Guinea Bissau, 8 Palace Gate, London W8 4RP. Tel: (0171) 589 5253. Fax: (0171)589 9590.

British Consulate, Mavegro Int, Cp100, Bissau, Guinea Bissau. Tel: 201 224 or 201 216. Fax: 201 265.

Refer to the Embassy.

Centro de Inforação e Turismo, CP 294, Bissau, Guinea Bissau.

Return Ticket Required. Requirements may be subject to change at short notice. Consult embassy before departure.
VALID PASSPORT REQUIRED BY ALL

Visa Required (can be extended in central police station).

Alcohol.

US$12, levied on international departures.

POLIO, TYPHOID: R.
MALARIA: Falciparum variety exists throughout the year. resistance to chloroquine has been reported.
YELLOW FEVER: Strongly recommended to all visitors. A vaccination certificate must be provided by visitors arriving from infected areas.
OTHER: Bilharzia and Rabies.

W1

Guinea Bissau Peso (GBP) = 100 centavos. Travellers cheques can be cashed at major banks only. US dollars is the preferred currency. Credit cards are not accepted. ATM AVAILABILITY: Unavailable.

MONEYGRAM: Unavailable.
WESTERN UNION: Unavailable.

AMEX: No local number.
DINERS CLUB: No local number.
MASTERCARD: No local number.
VISA: No local number.

AMEX: No local number.
THOMAS COOK: No local number.
VISA: No local number.

0730–1430 Mon to Fri.

Guinea Bissau is one of the poorest countries in the world. Some hotels are very expensive.

Portuguese. The majority of the population speak Guinea Creole.

Tropical climate. May–Nov is wet season. Dec–Apr is dry season. Temperatures vary with altitude.

Mostly Animist with Muslim and Christian.

1998: Jan 1, 20, 30*; Mar 8; Apr 7*; May 1; Aug 3; Sept 24; Nov 14; Dec 25.
1999: Jan 1, 2, 18*; Mar 8; Apr 8*; May 1; Aug 3; Sept 24; Nov 14; Dec 9, 25.

Limited electricity supply on 200 volts AC 50 Hz.

Post to Europe will take over a week..

BBC: 17.83 15.40 11.84 6.005
VOA: 21.49 15.60 9.525 6.035

A patriarchal society exists.

FLIGHTS: The national airline provides regular internal flights. SEA/RIVER: most towns are accessible by ship. Coast hopping ferries operate from the North coast to Bissau. ROADS: Only 1/5 are tarred and suitable for all weather conditions. DOCUMENTATION: IDP is recommended though not legally required. A temporary driving licence can be obtained on presentation of a valid British Driving licence.

Tourism is developing in Guinea Bissau. Casual wear is acceptable. Social customs should be respected especially in the Muslim areas. PHOTOGRAPHY: It is forbidden to take photos of any public buildings or anything connected with the military.

CAPITAL: Conakry

 GMT

 FROM UK: 224   IDD: Y
OUTGOING CODE: Must be made through the operator.

 442 959 (Embassy)

 No embassy in the UK. Europe: Embassy of the Republic of Guinea, 51 rue de la Faisanderie, 75016 Paris, France. Tel: (1) 47 04 81 48 or 45 53 85 45. Fax: (1) 47 04 57 65.

 British Consulate, BP 834, Conakry, Guinea. Tel: 442 959. Fax: 414 215.

 Refer to the Embassy in Paris.

 Secrétariat d'Etat au Tourisme at a Hôtellerie, BP1304, place des Martyrs, Conakry, Guinea. Tel: 442 606.

 Return Ticket Required. Requirements may be subject to change at short notice. Consult embassy before departure.
VALID PASSPORT REQUIRED BY ALL

 Visa Required. Tourist, Transit and Business are granted.

 Narcotics

 Departure tax FG9000 or US$5.

 Journalists may visit by government invitation only.

 POLIO, TYPHOID: R
MALARIA: Present in the Falciparum variety and resistance to chloroquine has been reported.
YELLOW FEVER: Vaccination is strongly recommended by to all visitors. Those arriving from infected areas over one year of age are required to have a vaccination certificate.
OTHER: Bilharzia, River Blindness, Hepatitis, Meningitis and rabies are present.

W1

Guinea Franc (FG) = 100 centimes. NOTE: Import and export of local currency is prohibited. Foreign currency must be declared on arrival. MasterCard has limited acceptance in the capital city. Travellers cheques can be changed at banks, French francs are the preferred currency.
ATM AVAILABILITY: Unavailable.

 MONEYGRAM: Unavailable.
WESTERN UNION: 45 11 10.

 AMEX: +44 1273 696933
DINERS CLUB: No local number.
MASTERCARD: 1 314 542 7111
VISA: No local number.
AMEX: No local number.
THOMAS COOK: +44 1733 318950
VISA: +4401733 318949

 0830–1230 and 1430–1630 Mon–Fri.

 Tourist areas tend to be more expensive.

 French and several local languages.

 Hot and Humid climate. Wet season: May–Oct. Dry season: Nov–Apr.

 Mostly Muslim with the remainder Christian and Animist.

 1998: Jan 1, 30*; Apr 3, 7, 13; May 1; July 6; Aug 15; Oct 2; Dec 25.
1999: Jan 1, 18*; Apr 3, 5, 7; May 1; July 6; Aug 15; Oct 2; Dec 25.

 220 Volts, 50 Hz

 Post will take over a week to reach Europe.

 BBC: 17.83 15.40 9.600 6.00
VOA: 21.49 15.58 9.575 6.035

 Due to the Muslim culture, patriarchal values exist.

 ROADS: Only 2/5 are suitable for all weather conditions. RAIL: A limited service exists which is generally not recommended.
DOCUMENTATION: IDP is required.

 Tourists should not venture out into Conakry at night due to a high level of street violence. Muslim traditions should be respected. Casual dress is acceptable. PHOTOGRAPHY: Permits are no longer required but taking photos of public buildings, bridges, ports or anything connected to the military is prohibited.

Guyana

CAPITAL: Georgetown

 GMT–3

 FROM UK: 592.
IDD: Y to main towns and cities.
OUTGOING CODE: 001

 Ambulance: 56900 (Georgetown only).

 High Commission for the Co operative
Republic of Guyana, 3 Palace Court,
Bayswater Road, London, W2 4LP. Tel:
(0171) 229 7684/8. Fax: (0171) 727 9809.
British High Commission, PO Box 10849, 44
Main Street, Georgetown, Guyana. Tel: (2)
65881/2/3/4. Fax: (0171) 873 8551.
Caribbean Tourism, Vigilant House 120
Wilton Road, London, SW1V 1JZ. Tel: (0171)
233 8382. Fax: (0171) 873 8551.
Tourist Association of Guyana, Tower Hotel,
74- 75 Main Street, Georgetown, Guyana.
Tel: (2) 72011/5. Fax: (2) 65691.

 Return Ticket Required. Requirements may
change at short notice. Contact the embassy
before departure.
VALID PASSPORT REQUIRED BY ALL

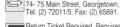 Visas not required for full nationals of Great
Britain. NOTE: Contact the High Commission
for an up-to-date list of nationals requiring
visas as requirements often change.

 Narcotics.

 GUY\$1500, payable in local currency.

 POLIO, TYPHOID: R.
MALARIA: Exists throughout the year in certain areas in the Falciparum variety. Resistance to chloroquine has been reported.
NOTE: Sleeping under a mosquito net and
using insect repellents is recommended.
YELLOW FEVER: A vaccination certificate is
required for travellers arriving from infected
countries (contact High Commission for list of
infected countries according to Guyana). Vaccination is strongly recommended to any traveller planning to travel outside urban areas.

 W2

 Guyana Dollar (Guy\$) = 100 cents. Limited
acceptance of credit cards. Travellers
cheques (in US\$) are accepted, but can take
a long time to exchange.
ATM AVAILABILITY: Unavailable.

 MONEYGRAM: 165 then 800 592 3688
WESTERN UNION: (2) 751 41.

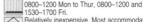 AMEX:+44 1273 696933
DINERS CLUB: No local number.
MASTERCARD: 1 314 542 7111
VISA: (1) 410 581 9091
AMEX: (1) 801 964 6665
THOMAS COOK: +44 1733 318950
VISA: +44 1733 318949

 0800–1200 Mon to Thur, 0800–1200 and
1530–1700 Fri.

 Relatively inexpensive. Most accommodation
is located in populated areas.

English. Hindi, Urdu, Creole and Amerindian
are also spoken.

 Hot tropical climate with the most rain
between Nov–Jan and Apr–July.

 Christian, Hindu and Muslim.

 1998: Jan 1; Feb 23; Mar 24; Apr 7*, 10, 13;
May 1; July 6, 7*; Aug 1; Oct 19*; Dec 25–26.
1999: Jan 1; Feb 23; Mar 24; Apr 7*, 2, 5;
May 1; July 6, 7*; Aug 1; Oct 19*; Dec 25–26.

 110 Volts AC, 60Hz

 7–10 days. Post services can be unreliable
so recorded delivery is recommended.

 BBC: 11.87 9.640 7.325 6.195
VOA: 15.12 11.58 9.775 5.995

A mixture of Latin, African and Caribbean
ensure that society is diverse and sometimes
volatile. Women in the interior are influenced
by Myan traditions, whilst on the coastal populated areas women's roles tend to diversify.

FLIGHTS: The only reliable means of travelling into the interior is by air. ROAD: All
weather roads are concentrated in the
Eastern coastal strip. Most journeys will
involve crossing waterways with ferries,
which may create delays. BUS: Regular but
crowded services operate in Georgetown.
TAXI: Recommended as a method of transport at night. A supplement is added to
evening fares and for long journeys it is recommended that fares are agreed in advance.

 Guyana, Georgetown in particular, is
notorious for street crime. Do not expose
valuable possessions at any time and avoid
showing signs of wealth. Travel with caution
after dark. Men should not wear shorts.

CAPITAL: Port-au-Prince

GMT – 5.

FROM UK: 509   IDD: Y
OUTGOING CODE: 00

Police: 114; Ambulance: 118.

No Embassy in the UK. EUROPE: Embassy of the Republic of Haiti, BP25, 160a avenue Louise, B-1050 Brussels, Belgium. Tel: (2) 649 7381. Fax: (2) 640 6080.
British Consulate, PO Box 1302 Hotel Montana, rue F cardoza, Bourchon, Port-a-Prince, Haiti. Tel: 573 969. Fax: 574 048.
Caribbean Tourism, Vigilant House, 120 Wilton Road, London, SW1V 1JZ. Tel: (0171) 233 8382. Fax: (0171) 873 8551.
Office National du Tourisme d'Haiti, avenue Marie Jeanne, Port-a-Prince, Haiti. Tel: 221 729.

Return Ticket required. Requirements may be subject to short-term change. Contact embassy before departure.
VALID PASSPORT REQUIRED BY ALL

Visa not required by Nationals of the UK.

Coffee, matches, methylated spirits, pork, all meat products from Brazil and the Dominican Republic.

US$25. Transit passengers and children under 2 years of age are exempt.

POLIO, TYPHOID: R.
MALARIA: Exists throughout the year on the Falciparum variety below 300 m.
YELLOW FEVER: Recommended. A vaccination certificate s required from all passengers coming from infected areas.
OTHER: Bancroftian filariasis, Rabies.

W1

Gourde (Gde) = 100 centimes. Exch: US$ accepted and exchanged everywhere. Amex is widely accepted, but other credit cards less so. Travellers cheques are accepted in banks and major shops. US dollars are the preferred currency.
ATM AVAILABILITY: Unavailable.

MONEYGRAM: 183 then 800 592 3688.
WESTERN UNION: 22 7876.

AMEX: +44 1273 696933
DINERS CLUB: No local number.
MASTERCARD: 1 214 542 7111
VISA: (1) 410 581 9091

AMEX: (1) 801 964 6665
THOMAS COOK: 1 800 223 7373
VISA: 1 800 732 1322

0900–1300 Mon to Fri.

Accommodation is limited in Haiti, varying form luxury hotels to modest small inns and guesthouses.

French and Creole. English is widely spoken in tourist areas.

Tropical climate with high humidity. Intermittent rain throughout the year. Hill resorts are much cooler.

Roman Catholic. Protestant minorities.

1998: Jan 1, 2; Feb 24; Apr 10, 14; May 1, 8, 18, 29; Aug 15; Oct 17, 24; Nov 1, 2, 18; Dec 25.
1999: Jan 1, 2; Feb 24; Apr 2, 14; May 1, 8, 18, 29; Aug 15; Oct 17, 24; Nov 1, 2, 18; Dec 25.

110 volts AC, 60 Hz.

Up to 1 week.

BBC: 17.84 15.22 7.325 5.975
VOA: 15.12 11.91 9.590 5.995.

A multi-cultural heritage ranging from Christianity, Roman catholicism and Voodoo play a major part in the roles of women in society.

ROADS: All weather roads have been constructed. BUS: Operate on an unscheduled basis. TAXI: Station wagons run between the capital and the large towns. CAR HIRE: Available independently or through the hotels. NOTE: Petrol can be scarce outside the capital. DOCUMENTATION: Some national licences are accepted but IDP is recommended.

RISK of personal crime and violence, especially for tourists due to their relative affluence. It is estimated that 85% of the population live below the poverty line. Do not leave your accommodation after dark and do not travel to rural areas.

Honduras

CAPITAL: Tegucigalpa

 GMT – 6

 FROM UK: 504   IDD: Y
OUTGOING CODE: 00

 Police: 119; Fire: 198; Ambulance: 37 8654.

 Embassy of the Republic of Honduras and
Consulate General, 115 Gloucester Place,
London, W1H 3PJ. Tel (0171) 486 4880. Fax:
(0171) 486 64550.

 British Embassy, Apartado Postal 290,
Edificio Palmira, 3º Piso, Colonia Palmira,
Tegucigalpa, Honduras, CA. Tel: 325 429 or
320 612. Fax: 325 480.

 Refer to the Embassy.

 Instituto Hondureño De Turismo, Apartado
Postal 3261, Centro Guanacaste, Barrio
Guanacaste, Tegucigalpa, Honduras. Tel:
383 975. Fax: 382 102

 Return Ticket Required. Requirements may
change at short notice. Contact the embassy
before departure.
VALID PASSPORT REQUIRED BY ALL

 Visa not required

 Narcotics.

 US$10 is levied on all passengers over 12
years of age.

 POLIO, TYPHOID: R.
MALARIA: Exists throughout the year in the
Vivax variety within certain regions.
YELLOW FEVER: A vaccination certificate is
required from all travellers arriving from
infected areas.
OTHER: Cholera, Rabies

 W1

Lempira (L) = 100 centavos. All credit cards
are accepted. Travellers cheques in US dollars are recommended.
ATM AVAILABILITY: Over 20 locations.

MONEYGRAM: 123 then 800 592 5755
(Spanish).
WESTERN UNION: 39 0037.

 AMEX: +44 1273 696933
DINERS CLUB: 504 37 4251
MASTERCARD: 1 314 542 7111
VISA: (1) 410 581 9091
AMEX: (1) 801 964 6665
THOMAS COOK: 1 800 223 7373
VISA: 1 800 732 1322

 0900–1500 Mon to Fri, some open
0900–1100 Sat.

 Relatively inexpensive. Accommodation is
graded. Food and transport are also
inexpensive.

 Spanish. English is also spoken.

 Tropical climate which is cooler in the mountains. Rainy season is May–Oct. The North
coast is usually very hot with rain all year.

 Roman Catholic, Evangelist and Mormon.

 1998: Jan 1; Apr 9, 10, 14; May 1; Sept 15;
Oct 3, 12, 21; Dec 25.
1999: Jan 1; Apr 1, 2, 14; May 1; Sept 15;
Oct 3, 12, 21; Dec 25.

 110/220 Volts AC, 60Hz

 7 days.

BBC: 17.84 15.26 9.590 5.975
VOA: 15.21 11.74 9.815 6.030

 There are strong Spanish influences but the
majority of the population are Mestizo, leading mainly an agricultural way of life. Many
rural communities can still be found leading a
relatively unchanged traditional lifestyle.
Usual precautions should be taken by
women travellers.
FLIGHTS: Local airlines operate services
between principle towns, which is much
more convenient for business visitors.
ROAD: Over half the roads are suitable for
all weather conditions. BUS: Services operate to most large towns but they are well
used and booking in advance is essential.
TAXI: Usually unmetered so agree the fare in
advance. CAR HIRE: Available at the airport.
DOCUMENTATION: Foreign and international licences are accepted.

Exercise caution – beware of bag slashing,
and muggings. Beware of poisonous snakes,
alligators, scorpions, wasps and other stinging insects. Beachwear should not be worn
in towns. Visitors should register with the
Embassy or consulate on arrival.

GMT + 8.

 FROM UK: 852   IDD: Y
OUTGOING CODE: 00

 All services: 999 (subject to change).

 Hong Kong Government Office, 6 Grafton Street, London W1X 3LB. Tel: (0171) 499 9821. Fax: (0171) 495 5033 or 493 1964.

 Not present.

 Hong Kong Tourist Association, 125 Pall Mall, London SW1Y 5EA. Tel: (0171) 930 4775. Fax: (0171) 930 4777.

 Hong Kong Tourist Association, 9–11th floor, Citicorp Centre, 18 Whitfield Road, North Point, Hong Kong. Tel: 28 07 65 43. Fax: 28 06 03 03.

 VALID PASSPORT REQUIRED BY ALL

 Visa requirements for all nationals are issued subject to duration of stay. Visitors are advised to check for current information.

 Non-prescribed drugs without a doctor's certificate.

 Adults pay HK$ 50 in local currency.

 POLIO, TYPHOID: R.
MALARIA: There may occasionally be a risk in rural areas.

 Hong Kong Dollar (HK$) = 100 cents. All credit cards and travellers cheques are widely accepted. Pound sterling and US dollars are the preferred currency.
ATM AVAILABILITY: Over 1,000 locations.

 MONEYGRAM: 001 800 66639472.
WESTERN UNION: 2528 5631.

 AMEX: +44 1273 696933
DINERS CLUB: (852) 2529 9223
MASTERCARD: 800 966677
VISA: 800 96 42 18

AMEX: (852) 885 9331
THOMAS COOK: 800 2505
VISA: 800 2495

0900–1630 Mon to Fri and 0900–1330 Sat.

 Although Hong Kong is a tax haven, commodities and accommodation can be expensive. However, transport is cheap and some luxury items are often cheaper than in Europe.

 Chinese and English, Cantonese is most widely spoken.

 Winter: influenced by the North–Northeast monsoon. Summer: is influenced by the Southwest monsoon. Summers are very hot with the rainy season June–Aug. Spring and autumn are warm with occasional rain and cooler evenings. Winters can be cold.

 Buddhist, Confucian, Taoist with Christian and Muslim minorities, but there are also places of worship for most other religious groups.

 1998: Jan 1, 28; Apr 6, 10, 11, 13; May 30; Aug 17; Oct 1, 2, 6, 28; Dec 25, 26.
1999: Jan 1, 28; Apr 2, 4, 5, 6; May 29; Aug 17; Oct 1, 2, 6, 28; Dec 25, 26.

 220 volts AC, 50.

 Airmail to Europe takes 3- 5 days.

 BBC: 21.75 17.83 15.36 9.740
VOA: 17.74 15.29 15.16 9.760

 Hong Kong has a unique a cultural mix, of Chinese, Cantonese and western ideologies. Women, depending on their heritage, will conform accordingly. Generally all customs co-exist. There are no particular dangers for foreign female travellers.

 RAIL: More expensive than the ferry, but quicker. BUS: Services are often very crowded. DOCUMENTATION: IDP is recommended but not legally required.

Hong Kong has reverted to Chinese rule as a Special Administrative Region of the People's Republic. Contact the Embassy or tourist office prior to travelling for up-to-date information on passport and visa requirements. Usual social courtesies should be applied. When addressing a national of Hong Kong the family name comes first, for example, Wong Man Ying is Mr Wong. Casual dress is acceptable.

CAPITAL: Budapest

GMT + 1 (GMT + 2 in the summer)

FROM UK: 36   IDD: Y
OUTGOING CODE: 00

Police: 107; Ambulance: 104; Fire: 105.

Embassy of the Hungarian Republic, 35 Eaton Place, London SW1X 8BY. Tel: (0171) 235 4048. Fax: (0171) 823 1348. Consulate Tel: (0171) 235 2664 or (0891) 171 204 (visa enquiries).
British Embassy, Harmincad UCTA 6, Budapest V, Hungary. Tel: (1) 266 2888 or 266 1430. Fax: (1) 266 0907.

Hungarian Tourist Board, PO Box 4336, London SW18 4XE. Tel/Fax: (0181) 871 4009 (administration) or (0891) 171 200 (recorded message).
Tourinform (Hungarian Tourist Board), H 1052 Budapest, Sütö2, Hungary. Tel: (1) 117 9800. Fax: (1) 117 9578.

Requirements may be subject to short term change. Contact embassy before departure. Valid Passport Required. All passports must be valid for at least 6 months.

Visa not required by Nationals of the UK for a stay of up to 6 months.

Narcotics and firearms.

Rabies

Hungarian Forint (HUF) = 100 fillér. Exchange: banks, hotels, airports, railway stations, some businesses. NOTE: Import and export of local currency is limited to HUF 10,000. Retain all exchange receipts. All major credit cards and travellers cheques are widely accepted. German DM is the preferred currency.
ATM AVAILABILITY: Over 1000 locations.

MONEYGRAM: 00 800 12249.
WESTERN UNION: (1) 267 4282.

AMEX: +44 1273 696933
DINERS CLUB: 36 1 268 8888
MASTERCARD: 00 800 12517
VISA: (1) 410 581 9091

AMEX: +44 1273 571 600
THOMAS COOK: 00 800 11501
VISA: 00 800 11117

0900–1400 Mon to Fri.

Westerners will not experience great disparity in local and Western prices.

Hungarian (Magyar). German is widely spoken. Some English and French may also be spoken, mainly in the West.

June–Aug. is usually very warm. Spring and autumn are mild and winters are very cold. There is rainfall throughout the year and snow in winter.

Mostly Roman Catholic with some Protestant. Eastern Orthodox and Jewish minorities are also present.

1998: Jan 1; Mar 15; Apr 13; May 1; June 1; Aug 20; Oct 23; Dec 25, 26.
1999: Jan 1; Mar 15; Apr 5; May 1; 31; Aug 20; Oct 23; Dec 25, 26.

220 volts Ac, 50 Hz.

3–7 days to other European destinations.

BBC: 15.07 12.09 9.410 6.195
VOA: 9.670 6.040 5.995 1.197

Traditional roles persist in rural areas. However, modern influences developing in urban regions.

RAIL: All main cities are connected by regular services but facilities are often inadequate. Concessions are available to groups of six or more and the young and elderly. ROAD: Generally the road system is good. BUS: Services link Budapest with the major provincial towns. CAR HIRE: Available at large hotels and the main airports. DOCUMENTATION: Pink, national UK licence is accepted, but IDP is required if a green licence is held.

Petty crime is rife in Budapest, especially in tourist areas. Very few people speak English outside of large hotels and restaurants. A knowledge of German is very useful. Usual social courtesies apply. Both Christian and surname should be used in introductions. PHOTOGRAPHY: Do not take photographs of anything connected with the military. Other restrictions will be sign posted.

Iceland

CAPITAL: Reykjavik

 GMT

 FROM UK: 354   IDD: Y
OUTGOING CODE: 90.

 Embassy of the Republic of Iceland, 1 Eaton Terrace, London, SW1W 8EY. Tel: 0171 730 5132. Fax: 0171 730 1683.

 British Embassy, PO Box 460, Laufasvegur 49, 121 Reykjavik, Iceland. Tel 551 5883/4. Fax 552 7940.

 Iceland Tourist Bureau, 3rd Floor, 172 Tottenham Court Road, London W1P 0LY.

Iceland Tourist Board, Laekjargata 3, 101 Reykjavik, Iceland. Tel 552 7488. Fax: 562 4749.

 Regulations may change at short notice and you are advised to contact the relevant consular authority before finalising travel arrangements.
Passports with at least 3 months validity are required.

 Visa required.

 Uncooked meat

 Icelandic Krona (1Kr) = 100 aurar. The major credit cards are widely accepted. Traveller's cheques are also widely used and the preferred currency is US Dollars.
ATM Availability: over 500 locations at main banks.

 MONEYGRAM: 800 9001 then 800 592 3688
WESTERN UNION: no local number

 AMEX: +44 1273 696933
DINERS CLUB: No local number.
MASTERCARD: 1 341 542 7111
VISA: (1) 410 581 9091

AMEX: +44 1273 571 600
THOMAS COOK: 44 1733 318950
VISA: 44 171 937 8091

 0915–1600 Mon to Fri.

 Can be very expensive, as with other Scandinavian countries.Icelandic. English and Danish are also widely spoken.

 Icelandic. English and Danish are also widely spoken.

 Summers are mild and winters are rather cold. From the end of May to the beginning of August there are nearly 24 hours of perpetual daylight in Reykjavik, whilst in the Northern part of the country the sun rarely sets at all. The weather is highly changeable at all times of the year.

 Lutheran with a catholic minority.

 1998: Jan 1; Apr 9, 10, 12, 13, 23; May 1,21; June 1, 17; Aug 3; Dec 24, 25, 26, 31.
1999: Jan 1; Apr 9, 10, 12, 13, 23; May 1,21; June 1, 17; Aug 3; Dec 24, 25, 26, 31.

 220 volts AC, 50 Hz.

 Efficient airmail service to Europe.

 BBC: 9.410 6.195 3.955 0.198
VOA: 11.97 9.760 6.040 0.792

 Men and women are considered equal.

 ROAD: serve all settlements. Studded tyres are compulsory on vehicles between October and April. RAIL: There is no rail system. FLIGHTS: connect 12 local airports.

 People who wish to travel off road during winter are should contact local authorities. Visitors who wish to tour the Skeithararsandur sands icebergs are advised to do so only in the company of a local guide because of quicksands in the area. Casual wear is not suitable for social functions.

India

CAPITAL: New Delhi

 GMT +5.30.

 FROM UK: 91   IDD: Y
OUTGOING CODE: 00

 Contact the hotel reception.

 Officer of the High Commissioner for India, India House, Aldwych, London WC2B 4NA. Tel: (0171) 836 8484. Fax: (0171) 836 4331. Visas Tel: (0171) 836 0990 or (0171) 240 2084 or (0891) 880 800.

 British High Commission, Shanti Path, Chanakyapuri, New Delhi 110021, India. Tel: (11) 687 2161. Fax: (11) 687 2161. or (11) 687 2882. Deputy High Commissions in Bombay, Calcutta and Madras.

 Government of India Tourist Office, 7 Cork Street, London W1X 2LN. Tel: (0171) 437 3677 or (01233) 211 999 (brochure request line). Fax: (0171) 494 1048.

 Refer to the Office of the High Commissioner for India.

 Requirements may be subject to short-term change. Contact the relevant authority before departure.
VALID PASSPORT REQUIRED BY ALL

 Visa required by all. Ensure your visa is valid for the areas you wish to travel.

 Plants, gold and silver bullion and coins not in current use are prohibited.

 RS750 payable, in local currency, on departure.

 Entry is refused to nationals of a) Afghanistan if their passport or ticket shows evidence of transit or boarding in Pakistan and b) British passport holders, including those of Indian origin, who are being deported to India without their consent.

 POLIO, TYPHOID: R.
MALARIA: Exists in the vivax variety throughout the year in the whole country excluding parts of Himachal Pradesh, Jammu and Kashmir and Sikkim. High resistance to chloroquine has been reported in the falciparum variety.

YELLOW FEVER: A vaccination certificate is required from everyone coming or who have transited through infected areas.
OTHER: Bubonic plague, meningitis, tick-borne relapsing fever, dengue fever, visceral leishmaniasis, filariasis and Hepatitis B.

 W1

 Rupee = 100 paise. Exchange: At banks or authorised exchangers. NOTE: Import and export of local currency is prohibited. All major credit cards are accepted. Traveller's cheques can be widely exchanged. Pound sterling and US dollars are the preferred currencies.
ATM AVAILABILITY: Over 150 locations.

 MONEYGRAM: 000 117 then 800 592 3688.
WESTERN UNION: (022) 838 2038.

 AMEX: +44 1273 696933
DINERS CLUB: 91 44 8522833
MASTERCARD: 1 314 542 7111
VISA: (1) 410 581 9091

 AMEX: (11) 687 5930
THOMAS COOK: +44 1733 318950
VISA: +44 1733 318949

 1000–1400 Mon to Fri,
1000–1200 Sat.

 Caters for all visitors and budgets. Accommodation ranges from international standard to youth hostels. All commodities are inexpensive, in comparison with other countries.

The universal national language is English. There are 14 official languages in India. About 50% of the population are Hindi speakers. The Muslim population generally speak Urdu.

Hot tropical weather with variations from region to region. Coolest weather lasts from November to mid March, with cool fresh mornings and evenings and dry sunny days. Really hot weather occurs between April and June. Monsoon rains occur in most regions during the summer.

 Most of the population is Hindu. The remainder being Muslim, Sikh, Christian, Buddhist and a minority of others.

India

1998: Jan 1, 26, 30; Mar 31; May 1; Aug 15;
Sept 30; Oct 2, 11, 19; Dec 25.
1999: Jan 1, 26, 30; Mar 31; May 1; Aug 15;
Sept 30; Oct 2, 11, 19; Dec 25.

Usually 220 volts AC, 50 Hz. Plugs are of the
round 2 and 3 pin type.

Airmail to Western Europe takes up to 1
week. Stamps are sold in hotels.

BBC: 17.79 15.31 11.75 9.740
VOA: 21.55 15.42 9.760 6.070.

Women should dress conservatively and
respect the religious customs, which are practised in the different regions. Usual precautions should be taken and it is inadvisable to
walk alone at night. Indian women prefer not
to shake hands. Many do not drink alcohol.

AIR: The domestic airline connects over 70
cities. Special fares are available throughout
the year. SEA/RIVER: Services are often
seasonal and suspended during the monsoon
period. One particularly attractive route is the
'backwaters' excursion in the vicinity of
Cochin. RAIL: The network covers much of
the country and is relatively inexpensive.

NOTE: The Travel Advice Unit of the Foreign
and Commonwealth Office advises against
travelling to Jammu and Kashmir and athe
north east because of civil unrest. Major
tourist destinations are quiet. However there
is a serious risk of kidnapping in the state of
Jammu and Kashmir. Foreigners have been
held at gun-point and therefore visitors are
advised against travelling to this area. Ignore
touts who claim this area is safe.

Check with local tourist offices before venturing away from tourist areas, as foreigners as
forbidden entry to some parts of the country.
Severe penalties exist for the possession of
drugs.

Footwear should be removed when entering
houses or places of worship. Many Hindus
are vegetarian. Religion plays a large role in
everyday life and visitors are expected to
respect the customs followed by Indian
people.

CAPITAL: Jakarta

 GMT + 7 (West); +8 (Central); +9 (East).

 FROM UK: 62   IDD: Y to main cities.
OUTGOING CODE: 00

 Police:110; Fire: 113; Ambulance: 118.

Embassy of the Republic of Indonesia, Consular Section, 38a Adams Row, London W1X 9AD. Tel: (0171) 499 7661 or (0891) 171 210 (recorded message). Fax: (0171) 491 4993.
British Embassy, Jalan M. H. Thamrin 75, Jakarta 10310, Indonesia. Tel: (21) 330 904. Fax: (21) 314 1824 or 390 2726.
Indonesian Tourist Office, 3–4 Hanover Street, London, W1R 9HH. Tel: (0171) 493 0030. Fax (0171) 493 1747.
Directorate – General of Tourism, 16/19 Jalan Merdeka-Barat, Jakarta 10110, Indonesia. Tel: (21) 386 0822. Fax: (21) 386 7589.

 Return Ticket required. Requirements may change at short notice. Contact the embassy before departure.
VALID PASSPORT REQUIRED BY ALL
 Tourist visas not required providing your stay does not exceed 60 days.

 Television sets, Chinese publications, medicines and pornography. Cameras and jewellery must be declared on arrival.
Varies according to airport Rp25,000, payable in local currency, from Denpassar.

 Portuguese nationals will be refused admission under all circumstances. Nationals of Israel will require special approval.

 POLIO, TYPHOID: R. MALARIA: Exists in the Falciparum variety everywhere except the main tourist resorts of Bali, Java and large cities. YELLOW FEVER: A vaccination certificate is required if arriving from infected areas. OTHER: Bilharzia, Rabies.

 W1

 Rupiah (Rp) = 100 sen. Exch.: Not a problem in tourist areas, may be more difficult in less commercialised areas. NOTE: Import and export of local currency is limited to Rp 50,000. Traveller's cheques are easily exchanged in large hotels and banks. Preferred cheque currency is US dollars. Visa, MasterCard and Amex are all accepted, Diners Club has a more limited use.
ATM AVAILABILITY: Over 1300 locations.

 MONEYGRAM: 001 800 011 0945.
WESTERN UNION: (21) 230 0888.

 AMEX: +44 1273 696933
DINERS CLUB: (62) (21) 5701255
MASTERCARD: 001803 1 887 0623
VISA: (1) 410 581 9091

AMEX: 001 800 6105
THOMAS COOK: +44 1733 318950
VISA: +44 1733 318949

 0800–1500 Mon to Fri.

 Tourist resorts are more expensive although cheap accommodation can be found in the form of bungalows in the main resorts. Provisions may be difficult to find in rural areas.

Bahasa Indonesian and 250 local dialects. Dutch and English are also spoken.

 The climate is tropical and varies from area to area. June–Sept is the Easter Monsoon which brings the driest weather. The Western monsoon brings the main rains from Dec–Mar. However, rainstorms can occur all year round.

 Mainly Muslim. Christian, Hindu, Buddhism and Animist beliefs.

 1998: Jan 1, 30*; Mar 29; Apr 7, 10, 28; May 11, 21; July 6; Aug 17; Nov 17; Dec 25.
1999: Jan 1, 30*; Mar 29; Apr 7, 10, 28; May 11, 21; July 6; Aug 17; Nov 17; Dec 25.

 110 Volts AC 50Hz, but may vary between areas,

 Up to 10 days.

 BBC: 15.36 11.95 9.740 6.195
VOA: 15.42 11.72 9.770 6.110

 Women should dress modestly although dress in tourist areas is likely to be more relaxed. This is a male orientated country.

 FLIGHTS: Good internal air system. ROADS: Good roads within Java but less so in Bali and Sumatra. The other islands have poor road systems. TAXI: Available in all main cities, all are metered. DOCUMENTATION: IDP is required.

 Never pass or accept anything with your left hand. Foreigners are regarded as walking bank accounts. There is very little violent crime but pick-pockets are common.

Iran

CAPITAL: Tehran

 GMT + 3.5 (GMT + 4.5 during the summer).

 FROM UK : 98   IDD: Y
OUTGOING CODE: 00

 Not present.

 Iranian Consulate, 50 Kensington Court, Kensington High Street, London W8 5DB. Tel: (0171) 937 5225 or 795 4901 (for visa enquiries). Fax: (0171) 938 1615.

British Embassy, PO Box 11365-4474, 143 Ferdowsi Avenue, Tehran 11344, Iran. Tel: (21) 675 01. Fax: (21) 678 021.

 Refer to Consulate.

 Information unavailable.

 Return Ticket required. Requirements may be subject to short-term change. Contact the relevant authority before departure.
VALID PASSPORT REQUIRED BY ALL

 Visa required

 Alcohol, aerial photographic equipment, transmitter and receiver apparatus, indecent photos, films, records and any fashion magazines.

 RL 70,000, payable in local currency. Transit passengers remaining in the airport and those under visitors under 7 years of age are exempt.

 Nationals of Israel. Women dressed immodestly will be refused entry.

 POLIO, TYPHOID: R.
MALARIA: Exists in the vivax variety in certain provinces. Resistance to chloroquine has been reported in the falciparum variety.
OTHER: Cutaneous leishmaniasis, Tick-borne relapsing fever and Bilharzia.

 W2

 Iranian Rial (RL) = 100 Dinars. Foreign visitors must convert the equivalent of US$ 300 into Iranian Rials. Declare all currency on arrival. Credit cards and traveller's cheques are not accepted.
ATM AVAILABILITY: Unavailable.

 MONEYGRAM: Unavailable.
WESTERN UNION: Unavailable.

 AMEX: +44 1273 696933
DINERS CLUB: No local number.
MASTERCARD: No local number.
VISA: No local number.
AMEX: No local number.
THOMAS COOK: No local number.
VISA: No local number.

 0900–1600 Sat to Wed, 0900–1200 Thur. Closed Fri.

 Commodities are quite limited outside the main city of Tehran. The economy is in a state of transition following the war with Iraq and the US embargo on Iranian oil.

 Persian (Farsi). Arabic in Khuzestan and Turkish in the Northwest. English, French and German are often spoken by businessmen and officials.

 Summers are hot and dry and winters are harsh.

 Predominantly Islamic (Shia) with a minority of Sunnis. Also Zoroastrians, Bahais, Armenian and Assyrsian Christians.

 1998: Jan 20*, 30; Feb 11, 23; Mar 10, 20, 21; Apr 1, 2, 8*, 16*; May 6*, 8; June 4, 5, 15, 23; July 6; Nov 13, 17; Dec 5.
1999: Jan 20*, 30; Feb 10, 23; Mar 10, 20, 21; Apr 1, 2, 8*, 16*; May 6*, 8; June 4, 5, 15, 23; July 6; Nov 13, 17; Dec 5.

 220 volts AC, 50 Hz.

 At least 2 weeks to Western Europe.

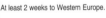 BBC: 15.57 11.769.410 15.07
VOA: 15.21 11.83 9.700 9.530

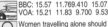 Women travelling alone should be prepared to adjust to the local code if they want to avoid problems. Dress should be discreet and conservative. It is advisable to befriend local women.

 ROAD: There is an extensive road network but the quality is unreliable. BUS: Cheap and comfortable although may be erratic. TAXIS: Available in all cities. CAR HIRE: Available in all cities and airports. DOCUMENTATION: IDP and personal insurance is required. All motorists must possess a carnet de passage or pay a large deposit.

 Western influences are discouraged. Violent crime is almost unheard of but the usual precautions should still be taken. Particular care should be taken not to offend against the Islamic religion. PHOTOGRAPHY near military installations is strictly prohibited.

CAPITAL: Baghdad

 GMT + 3 (GMT + 4 during the summer).

 FROM UK: 964   IDD: Y
OUTGOING CODE: 00.

 Not present.

 Iraqi Interests Section, 21 Queen's Gate, London SW7 5JG. Tel: (0171) 585 7141/6. Fax: (0171) 584 7716.

 Not present.

 Tourists are not permitted to entry to Iraq at the present time.

 Return Ticket required. Requirements may be subject to short-term change. Contact the relevant authority before departure.
VALID PASSPORT REQUIRED BY ALL.

 Visa required.

 Holders of Israeli passports or other passports containing Israeli visas. US passports are not currently valid for travel to or in Iraq without special validation being required

 Many types of fruits and plants, souvenirs in amounts considered to be of commercial value and electrical items other than personal effects.

 Departure tax ID 2000, payable in local currency.

 POLIO, TYPHOID: R.
MALARIA: Exists entirely in the vivax variety between May and November.
YELLOW FEVER: A vaccination certificate is required from travellers arriving from infected areas.
OTHER: Visceral leishmaniasis, Bilharzia, Crimean-Congo fever, Rabies.

 W1

 Iraqi Dinar (ID) = 20 dirhams = 1000 fils.
NOTE: Import of local currency is allowed up to ID 25. Export of local currency is limited to ID 5. Credit cards and traveller's cheques are not accepted.
ATM AVAILABILITY: Unavailable.

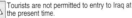 MONEYGRAM: Unavailable.
WESTERN UNION: Unavailable.

 AMEX: +44 1273 696933
DINERS CLUB: No local number.
MASTERCARD: No local number.
VISA: No local number.

 AMEX: No local number.
THOMAS COOK: No local number.
VISA: No local number.

 0800–1200 Sat to Wed, 0800–1100 Thur. Banks close at 1000 during Ramadan.

 Since the Gulf War and the imposition of United Nations sanctions, Iraq's economy has become hyper-inflated.

 Mostly Arabic. Some Kurdish, Turkish and Aramaic.

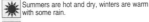 Summers are hot and dry, winters are warm with some rain.

 Sunni Muslim and Shia Muslim with Druze and Christian minorities.

 1998: Jan 1, 6, 30; Feb 8; Mar 21; Apr 7, 17; May 1, 7; July 6, 14, 17; Aug 8.
1999: Jan 1, 6, 30; Feb 8; Mar 20; Apr 7, 17; May 1, 7; July 6, 14, 17; Aug 8.

 220 volts AC, 50 Hz.

 Usually takes 5–10 days between Europe and Iraq but can take much longer.

 BBC: 15.58 15.07 11.76 9.410
VOA: 9.670 6.040 5.995 1.260

 Women are greatly influenced by the Muslim religion and are often veiled.

 ROAD: BUS: Services run between Baghdad and other main cities. TAXI: Available in the cities. Fares should be agreed in advance. Metered taxies charge twice the amount shown on the meter. CAR HIRE: Available at the airport and in Baghdad. DOCUMENTATION: IDP is required and third party insurance is necessary.

 EXTREME RISK. Travelling to Iraq is strongly discouraged by virtually all governments. Visitors should respect the Islamic religion and act accordingly. Avoid taking photographs.

CAPITAL: Dublin

GMT

FROM UK: 353   IDD: Y
OUTGOING CODE: 16

All services: 999.

Embassy of the Republic of Ireland, 17 Grosvenor Place, London SW1X 7HR. Tel: (0171) 235 2171. Fax: (0171) 245 6961. Passports – Tel: (0171) 245 9033. Fax: (0171) 493 9065.
British Embassy, 31–33 Merrion Road, Dublin 4, Ireland. Tel: (1) 269 5211. Fax: (1) 283 8423.

Irish Tourist Board, 150–151 New Bond Street, London W1Y 0AQ. Tel: (0171) 493 3201. Fax: (0171) 493 9065.
Bord Fáilte Eireann, Baggot Street Bridge, Dublin 2, Ireland. Tel: (1) 676 5871. Fax: (1) 602 4100.

Return Ticket required. Requirements may be subject to short term change. Contact the relevant authority before departure.
VALID PASSPORT REQUIRED BY ALL: except Nationals of EU countries providing they carry a national ID card; persons born in the United Kingdom travelling directly from the United Kingdom.

Visa not required

Narcotics.

IR£ 5, payable on all departures.

Irish Punt = 100 pence. NOTE: Export of local currency is limited to 150 Irish Punts and of foreign currency to the amount imported. All major credit cards and traveller's cheques are accepted throughout Ireland. Pound sterling is the preferred currency.
ATM AVAILABILITY: Approx. 1000 locations.

MONEYGRAM: 00 800 66639472.
WESTERN UNION: 1 800 395 395.

AMEX: +44 1273 696933
DINERS CLUB: +44 (252) 275252
MASTERCARD: 1 800 55 7378
VISA: 1 800 55 9345

AMEX: 1 800 6260000
THOMAS COOK: +44 1733 318950
VISA: +44 1733 318949

1000–1600 Mon to Fri. Banks may stay open longer in Dublin (till 1700 on Thur) in other parts of the country.

Food and drink can be quite expensive. However 'Bed and Breakfast', or camp sites offer cheaper accommodation.

Irish (Gaelic) is the official language and is mainly spoken in the west. English is more widely spoken.

Rain falls all year. Spring and autumn are very mild. Summers are warm, winters are much cooler.

Roman Catholic. Protestant minority.

1998: Jan 1; Mar 17; Apr 10, 13; May 1, 4; June 1; Aug 3; Oct 25; Dec 25, 26, 28, 29.
1999: Jan 1; Mar 17; Apr 2, 5; May 1, 3, 31; Aug 2; Oct 25; Dec 25, 26, 27, 28.

220 volts AC, 50 Hz.

Irish postage stamps must be used on all mail. Poste Restante correspondence is available.

BBC: 12.10 9.410 6.195 0.648
VOA: 9.760 6.040 1.197 0.792

Usual precautions should be followed. No additional problems should be encountered.

RAIL: Extensive network between the main cities. ROAD: The network links all parts of Ireland. TAXI: Services available in the main cities. BUS: A nation-wide network of buses serves all the main cities but services to remote areas will be infrequent. CAR HIRE: Available from the major air and sea ports and large hotels. DOCUMENTATION: Owners taking their own cars into Ireland require the vehicles registration book, nationality plates, insurance for the Republic and a full EU licence or IDP. A 'green card' is strongly recommended.

The Irish are a very gregarious people and usually have very close community bonds. Visitors will find people very friendly. Casual wear is acceptable.

Israel

CAPITAL: Jerusalem

 GMT + 2 (GMT + 1 during the summer).

 FROM UK: 972   IDD: Y
OUTGOING CODE: 00

 Fire / Police: 100; Ambulance: 101.

 Embassy of Israel, 2 Palace Green, London W8 4QB. Tel: (0171) 957 9500. Fax: (0171) 957 9577. Consular Section: 15A Old Court Place, London W8 4QB. Tel: (0171) 957 9516. Fax: (0171) 957 9577.
British Embassy, 192 Rehov Hayarkon, Tel Aviv 63405, Israel. Tel: (3) 524 9171/8. Fax: (3) 524 3313.

 Refer to Consulate.

 Ministry of Tourism, PO Box 1018, 24 King George Street, Jerusalem 91009, Israel. Tel: (2) 675 4811. Fax: (2) 56 25 34 07 or 56 25 08 90.

 Return Ticket required. Requirements may be subject to short-term change. Contact the relevant authority before departure.
VALID PASSPORT REQUIRED BY ALL: Passports must be valid for 6 months after the intended date of arrival.
All nationals require a stamp on arrival.
Visa not required by Nationals of EU countries

 Flowers, plants and seeds may not be imported without prior permission. Fresh meat may not be imported.

 Approximately £9.

 POLIO, TYPHOID: R
OTHER: Rabies

 W2

 New Israeli Shekel (NIS) = 100 new agorot. Exch: Foreign currency can only be exchanged at authorised banks and hotels. Payment in foreign currency exempts tourists from VAT on certain purchases. All major credit cards and traveller's cheques are accepted.
ATM AVAILABILITY: Over 1000 locations.

 MONEYGRAM: 177 101 2939.
WESTERN UNION: 1 770 222 131.

 AMEX: +44 1273 696933
DINERS CLUB: (972) (3) 5726333
MASTERCARD: 177 101 8873
VISA: (1) 410 581 9091
AMEX: 1678 72000
THOMAS COOK: 177 440 8424
VISA: 177 440 8338

 0830–1230 and 1600– 1730 Mon, Tues, and Thur. 0830–1230 Wed, 0830–1200 Fri.
Relatively expensive compared with other middle Eastern countries, excluding Kibbutz.

 Hebrew and Arabic. English is spoken in most major centres. French, Spanish, German, Yiddish, Russian, Polish and Hungarian may also be spoken.

 Summers are hot with winds from the Mediterranean. Winters can be cool in the North. Spring and autumn are usually pleasant.

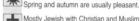 Mostly Jewish with Christian and Muslim minorities.

 1998: Jan 1, 8; Feb 11; Mar 11–13; Apr 11, 17, 23 29, 30; May 14, 24, 31; July 12; Aug 2; Sept 21, 23, 30; Oct 5, 12; Dec 13, 20.
1999: Jan 1, 8; Feb 11; Mar 10–12; Apr 11, 17, 23 29, 30; May 14, 24, 31; July 12; Aug 2; Sept 21, 23, 30; Oct 5, 12; Dec 13, 20.

 220 volts Ac, 50 Hz. 3 pin plugs are standard.

 Airmail to Europe takes up to a week.

 BBC: 15.07   12.09   9.410   1.323
VOA: 9.700   9.530   7.205   6.060

 Certain areas within religious buildings can only be entered by men.

 RAIL: Regular services provided between Tel Aviv and other major centres. All services are closed between sunset on Fri and sunset on Sat and during religious holidays. ROAD: There is a good road network. BUS: Services are cheap, quick and efficient. DOCUMENTATION: Full national driving licence and insurance is required. IDP is recommended.

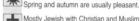 MODERATE RISK: Recent terrorist attacks require visitors to Israel to be extremely vigilant. There are restrictions on movement in and out of the Gaza strip. Dress is casual except in holy places. In many restaurants and hotels it is considered an insult to smoke. SPECIAL PRECAUTIONS: Do not drive through the occupied territories.

CAPITAL: Rome

GMT + 1 (GMT + 2 in summer)

FROM UK: 39 (followed by 6 for Rome, 2 for Milan, 11 for Turin, 81 for Naples, 41 for Venice and 55 for Florence).
IDD: Y   OUTGOING CODE: 00

Police: 112; Ambulance: 113; Fire: 115.

Embassy of the Italian Republic, 14 The Kings Yard, Davies Street, London W1Y 2EH. Tel: (0171) 312 2200. Fax: (0171) 312 2230.
British Embassy, Via XX Settembre 80A, 00187 Rome, Italy. Tel: (6) 482 5551 or 482 5441. Fax (6) 487 3324. Consulates in Bari, Brindisi, Cagliari, Florence, Messina, Milan, Turin, Trieste, Genoa, Venice, Naples and Palermo.

Italian Sate Tourist Office (ENIT), 1 Princes Street, London W1R 8AY. Tel: (0171) 408 1254. Fax: (0171) 493 6695.
Ente Nazionale Italiano per il Turismo (ENIT), Via Parigi 11, 00185 Rome, Italy. Tel: (6) 488 991. Fax: (6) 481 9316.

Requirements may be subject to change at short notice. Contact the relevant authority before travelling.
VALID PASSPORT REQUIRED

Visa not required by Nationals of the EU.

Although there are no legal limits for tobacco and alcohol, travellers may be questioned.

Included in ticket price.

Rabies.

W3

Italian Lira (Lit). Exch: banks, railway stations, airports and in some hotels. NOTE: Import and export of local currency is limited to Lit20,000,000, otherwise it must be validated on form V2 on arrival. MasterCard, Visa and Diners Club are widely accepted. US dollars are the preferred travellers cheque currency.
ATM AVAILABILITY: Over 20,000 locations.

MONEYGRAM: 167 8 76580.
WESTERN UNION: 1670 16840.

AMEX: +44 1273 696933
DINERS CLUB: 39 6 3213841
MASTERCARD: 1678 70866
VISA: 1678 75617

AMEX: 1678 72000
THOMAS COOK: 1678 72050
VISA: 1678 70987

They vary from city to city but in general, 0830–1330 and 1530–1930 Mon to Fri.
Cities and tourist centres can be very expensive, especially at centres of historical or religious importance.

Italian with dialects in different regions. French in border areas from the Riviera to the area North of Milan. Slovenian spoken in provinces. German, French and English may be spoken in cities and resorts.

Summer is hot, especially in the South. Spring and Autumn are mild. Winter is much drier in the South. Mountain regions are colder with heavy snowfalls.

Roman Catholic with Protestant minorities.

1998: Jan 1, 6; Apr 13; May 1; June 29; Aug 14, 15; Nov 1; Dec 7, 8, 24, 25, 26, 31.
1999: Jan 1, 6; Apr 5; May 1; June 29; Aug 14, 15; Nov 1; Dec 7, 8, 25, 26, 31.

220 volts Ac, 50 Hz.

7–10 days but may be subject to delays. Letters for Poste Restante should be addressed to 'Fermo Post' and the Town. When sending mail, underline the destined country and write the person's surname in capitals.

BBC: 17.64 12.09 9.410 6.195
VOA: 15.20 9.760 6.040 5.995

Society is multi-cultural. Religion does influence the behaviour of women, especially in the Southern, rural areas, where more traditional values apply. Extra care should be taken if travelling alone in the South.

RAIL: Simple, but cheap and efficient.
ROADS: BUS: Services connect main towns and local services also operate. CAR HIRE: Available in all the main towns. DOCUMENTATION: A 'Green Card' must be carried or other insurance. A UK licence is valid but 'Green' licences will need to be translated.

The Roman Catholic church holds a high position in Italian society. Visitors must dress conservatively when visiting religious buildings and smaller traditional communities. Theft is quite common, especially in the cities. It is advisable to remain extremely alert at all times.

CAPITAL: Kingston

 GMT – 5

 FROM UK: 1809   IDD: Y
OUTGOING CODE: 011

 Police: 119; Fire/Ambulance: 110.

 Jamaica High Commission, 1-2 Prince Consort Road, London, SW7 2BZ. Tel: (0171) 823 9911. Fax: (0171) 589 5154.

 British High Commission, PO Box 575, Trafalgar Road, Kingston 10, Jamaica. Tel: 926 9050. Fax: 929 7869.

 Jamaica Tourist Board (at High Commission in London). Tel: (0171) 224 0505. Fax: (0171) 224 0551.

 Jamaican Tourist Board, 2 St Lucia Avenue, Kingston 5, Jamaica. Tel: 929 9200. Fax: 929 9375.

 Return Ticket required. Requirements may be subject to short-term change. Contact embassy before departure.
VALID PASSPORT REQUIRED

 Visa not required by Nationals of EU countries. (For varying lengths of stay, see the High Commission.)

 Fruit, meat coffee, honey, rum, vegetables.

 J$500 payable in local currency for all passengers over 2 years of age. Transit passengers are exempt.

 Evidence of sufficient funds must be available to finance stay.

 POLIO, TYPHOID: R.
YELLOW FEVER: A vaccination certificate is required from travellers over one year of age coming from infected areas.

 W2

 Jamaican Dollar (J$) = 100 cents. Exchange: Visitors should only change money at airport bureaux, banks or hotels. All major credit cards are accepted. US dollar travellers cheques are recommended.
ATM AVAILABILITY: Over 45 locations.

 MONEYGRAM: 0 800 543 4080.
WESTERN UNION: 926 2454.

 AMEX: +44 1273 696933
DINERS CLUB: No local number.
MASTERCARD: 0800 307 7309
VISA: 0800 847 2399

 AMEX: (1) 801 964 6665
TC: 1 800 223 7373
VISA: 1 800 732 1322

 0900–1400 Mon to Thur and 0900–1500 Fri.

 Expensive in the tourist centres.

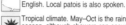 English. Local patois is also spoken.

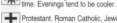 Tropical climate. May–Oct is the rainy season, although showers can occur at any time. Evenings tend to be cooler.

 Protestant. Roman Catholic, Jewish, Muslim, Hindu and Bahai minorities.

 1998: Jan 1; Feb 25; Apr 10, 13; May 23; Aug 1, 6; Oct 20; Dec 25, 26.
1999: Jan 1; Feb 25; Apr 2, 5; May 23; Aug 1, 6; Oct 20; Dec 25, 26.

 110 volts AC, 50 Hz. American 2 pin plugs are mainly used.

 4–5 days.

 BBC: 17.84 9.915 6.195 5.975
VOA: 15.21 11.70 6.130 5.995

 Extra care should be taken. It is inadvisable to travel alone at night. A multi-cultural society influenced by colonial rule and Rastafarianism, with its origins in Ethiopia, means that women have a diverse role.

 ROAD: One third of the 17,000 km network is tarred. BUS: Reliable in Kingston and Montego bay less so for trans island travel. TAXI: Not all taxis are metered. CAR HIRE: Most major towns and airport have hire facilities. DOCUMENTATION: A full UK licence is valid for up to 1 year.

Over the past few years there has been an increase in violence against tourists, especially in the downtown Kingston area. Possession of Marijuana may lead to imprisonment or deportation.

Japan

CAPITAL: Tokyo

 GMT + 9

 FROM UK: 81   IDD: Y
OUTGOING CODE: 001

 Tokyo English Life Line (TELL): 3403 7106; Japan Helpline: 0120 461 997 (operator service).

 Embassy of Japan, 101 Piccadilly, London, W1V 9FN. Tel: (0171) 465 6500. Fax: (0171) 491 9348.

 British Embassy, No 1 Ichiban-Cho, Chiyoda-Ku, Tokyo 102, Japan. Tel: (3) 32 65 55 11. Fax: (3) 52 75 31 64.

 Japan National Tourist Organisation, Heathcote, House, 20 Saville Row, London, W1X 1AE. Tel: (0171) 734 9638. Fax: (0171) 734 4290.

 Japan National Tourist Association, Tokyo Kotsu Kaikan Building, 2-10-1 Yuraku-cho, Chiyoda-ku, Tokyo, Japan. Tel: (3) 32 16 19 01. Fax: (3) 32 14 76 80.

 Return ticket required. Requirements may change at short notice. Contact the embassy before departure.
VALID PASSPORT REQUIRED BY ALL
Visa not required by Nationals of the Republic of Ireland and the UK for a stay not exceeding 6 months. Requirements may change at short notice, check with embassy for an up to date list of requirements.

 Items which infringe upon copyright, trade marks, patents. Obscene material, some plants, meats and animals without relevant health certificates.

 Vary between 2040–2650 ¥, payable in local currency, depending on airport.

 POLIO, TYPHOID: R.

 Japanese Yen (¥). Exch: At authorised banks and money-changers. NOTE: Import of local currency is limited to ¥5,000,000. All major credit cards are accepted. Travellers cheques, preferably in US dollars, can be exchanged in banks and large hotels.
ATM AVAILABILITY: Over 700 locations.

MONEYGRAM: 001 800 66639472.
WESTERN UNION: Available.

 AMEX: +44 1273 696933
DINERS CLUB: (81) (3) 34991181
MASTERCARD: 0031 11 3886
VISA: 0031 11 3794

 AMEX: 0120 030130
TC: +44 1733 318950
VISA: +44 1733 318949

 0900–1500 Mon to Fri.

 Japan can be extremely expensive in comparison with other Asian countries.

 Japanese. English may also be spoken in main cities.

 Winter: Cold and sunny in the South and around Tokyo. Very cold around Hokkaido. Summer (June–Sept) can be warm to very hot. Spring and Autumn are generally mild. Sept–Oct typhoons may occur.

 Shintoist and Buddhist. Christian minority.

 1998: Jan 1–3, 15; Feb 11; Mar 21; Apr 29; May 3, 4; July 20; Sept 15, 23; Oct 10; Nov 3, 23; Dec 23, 31.
1999: Jan 1–3, 15; Feb 11; Mar 21; Apr 29; May 3, 4; July 20; Sept 15, 23; Oct 10; Nov 3, 23; Dec 23, 31.

 100 Volts AC 60 HZ in the west. 50 Hz in Eastern Japan and Tokyo.

 4–6 Days.

BBC: 17.83 15.28 11.96 9.740
VOA: 17.74 15.43 11.72 6.110

 Most women still behave in accordance with traditional culture and etiquette in the home, but are influenced by western culture in the workplace. Strict traditional customs are less apparent in major cities. Usual precautions should be taken by women travellers, although the crime rate is comparatively low.

 RAIL: Network is one of the best in the world. ROAD: Driving in Japan is not recommended. DOCUMENTATION: IDP is required. Public transport is well developed and efficient.

Bowing is the customary form of greeting although handshaking is becoming more common. Remove shoes when entering a host's home. Public toilets are often unsegregated. Blowing your nose in public is frowned upon. Japanese etiquette is very complex but foreign 'ignorance' is tolerated.

Jersey

CAPITAL: St Helier

 GMT (+1 in Summer)

 FROM UK: 01534, elsewhere use the UK code followed by 1534.
IDD: Y   OUTGOING CODE: 00

 All services: 999.

 Jersey is an English Channel Island.

 Jersey Tourism (Information and Public Relations Office), Wordsmith Marketing and Public Relations, 38 Dover Street, London W1X 3RB. Tel: (0171) 493 5278. Fax: (0171) 491 1565.

 Jersey Tourism, Liberation Square, St Helier, Jersey JE1 1BB. Tel: 500 800. Fax: 500 808.

 See UK entry.

 The regulations for tourist and business visas are the same as those for the UK. See UK entry.

 See entry for the UK.

 £20, payable in local currency.

 Pound Sterling (£) = 100 pence. Exch: Bureaux de change, banks and many hotels. NOTE: Channel Island notes and coins are not accepted in the UK. Notes can be changed at parity in UK banks. All major credit cards and travellers cheques are accepted. Pound sterling is the preferred currency.
ATM AVAILABILITY: Over 10 locations.

 MONEYGRAM: Limited to capital city
WESTERN UNION: Available.

 AMEX: +44 1273 696933
DINERS CLUB: No local number.
MASTERCARD: 0800 96 4767
VISA: 0800 96 3833

 AMEX: 0800 521313
TC: 0800 622101
VISA: 0800 515884

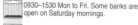 0930–1530 Mon to Fri. Some banks are open on Saturday mornings.

 The Channel Islands are a low duty zone.

 English. A dialect of Norman/French is still spoken by some.

 Most popular holiday season is May until the end of September with temperatures averaging 20–21ºC. Most rain falls during the cooler months.

 Each parish has its own Anglican church.

 1998: Jan 1. Apr 10, 13. Mar 17. May 4, 25. Aug 3, 31. Dec 25, 26, 28.
1999: Jan 1. Apr 2, 5. Mar 17. May 3, 24. Aug 2, 30. Dec 25, 26, 27.

 240 volts AC, 50 Hz.

 UK stamps are not valid in Jersey. Generally a very good postal service operates.

 BBC: No local number
VOA: No local number

 There is little inequality between men and women. Usual precautions should, however, be taken.

 BUS: Services operate throughout the island.
CAR HIRE: Generally very cheap as is the petrol. DOCUMENTATION: Visitors who take their own car must have a 'Green Card' or valid certificate of insurance. Nationality plates must be displayed.

 Similar to the UK but with French influences.

Jordan

CAPITAL: Amman

 GMT + 2 (GMT + 3 during the summer).

 FROM UK: 962.
IDD: Available within cities, with direct dialling to most countries.
OUTGOING CODE: 00

 Police: 192; Fire / Ambulance: 193.
All services: 62111 (Jerusalem only).

 Embassy of the Hasemite Kingdom of Jordan, 6 Upper Phillimore Gardens, London W8 7HB. Tel: (0171) 937 3685. Fax: (0171) 937 8795. For Visa enquiries Tel: (0891) 171 261.
British Embassy, PO Box 87, Abdoun, Amman, Jordan. Tel: (6) 823 100. Fax: (6) 813 759.

 Jordan Tourist Information Office, 211 Regent Street, London W1R 7DD. Tel: (0171) 437 9465. Fax: (0171) 494 0433.
Ministry of Tourism, PO Box 224, Amman, Jordan. Tel: (6) 642 311. Fax: (6) 648 465.

 Requirements may be subject to short-term change. Contact the relevant authority before departure.
VALID PASSPORT REQUIRED BY ALL

 Visa required. Visas can be obtained on arrival at the airport in Jordan.

 JD 10 for individual tourists, payable in local currency. Transit passengers are exempt.

 Nationals of Bahamas, Bangladesh, India, Pakistan, Sri Lanka and all African countries with the exception of Egypt and South Africa if they have not obtained prior permission from the ministry of Interior in Amman.

 POLIO, TYPHOID: R.
YELLOW FEVER: A vaccination certificate is required from all travellers over 1 year of age coming from infected areas.
OTHER: Rabies.

 W1

 Dinar (JD) = 1000 fils. Amex and Visa are accepted widely, but MasterCard and Diners Club have more limited use. Traveller's cheques issued by British banks are accepted in authorised bureaux de change. US dollars are the preferred currency.
ATM AVAILABILITY: Over 50 locations.

 MONEYGRAM: 18 800 000 then 800 592 3688.
WESTERN UNION: 616 910.

 AMEX: +44 1273 696933
DINERS CLUB: (962) (6) 601878
MASTERCARD: 1 314 542 7111
VISA: (1) 410 581 9091
AMEX: (973) 256 834
TC: +44 1733 318950
VISA: +44 1733 318949

 0830–1230 and 1530–1730 Sat to Thur.
Hours during Ramadam are 0830–1000, although some banks open in the afternoon.

 Jordan is one of the smallest countries in the Middle East. It is also one of the most expensive, since most of the accommodation is in Amman.

 Arabic. English and French are also spoken.

 Summers are hot and dry with cool evenings. Nov–Mar are the cooler months with rainfall.

 Sunni Muslim. Shiite Muslim and Christian minorities.

 1998: Jan 1, 30*; Apr 7, 19, 28; May 1, 25; June 10; July 6*; Aug 11; Nov 14, 17; Dec 25.
1999: Jan 1, 30*; Apr 7, 19, 28; May 1, 25; June 10; July 6*; Aug 11; Nov 14, 17; Dec 25.

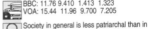 220 volts Ac, 50 Hz.

 Packages should be left open for customs officials. Airmail to Western Europe takes 3 to 5 days.

BBC: 11.76 9.410 1.413 1.323
VOA: 15.44 11.96 9.700 7.205

Society in general is less patriarchal than in other Middle Eastern countries. However women should still dress and act modestly.

ROAD: Good network of roads exists but vehicle needs to be in good working order and plenty of water and supplies should be taken on journeys. BUS: Services are efficient and cheap. TAXIS: Shared taxi service to all towns on fixed routes, also available for private hire. CAR HIRE: International companies are available from hotels.

 Jordan is safe to travel in. The military keep a low profile and you are unlikely to experience anything but friendliness and hospitality. It is very important that Muslim beliefs and local customs are respected. Beach wear should be confined to the beach/pool.

CAPITAL: Almaty

 GMT + 6 (GMT + 7 during the summer).

 FROM UK: 7 (3272 for Almaty).
IDD: No. Certain hotels have IDD by satellite for residents.
OUTGOING CODE: International calls are made at reduced rate 2000–0800 local time.

 All services: 03.

Embassy of the Republic of Kazakhstan, 4th Floor, 114A Cromwell Road, London SW7 4ES. Tel: (0171) 244 0011 or 244 6572 (visa enquiries). Fax: (0171) 244 0129 or 244 0022 (consulate).
British Embassy, 173 Furmanov Street, Almaty 480110, Kazakhstan. Tel: (3372) 506 192. Fax: (3272) 506 260.

 See Consulate.

 'Proftour' Association (former Kazakh Council for Tourism), 5 Mitina Street, Almaty, Kazakhstan. Tel: (3272) 640 567. Fax: (3272) 531 928.

 Valid passport and return ticket required. As regulations are expected to change at short notice, visitors are advised to contact the consulate for current requirements. Carry your passport at all times.

 Travellers are advised to contact the consulate for current visa requirements.

 Pornography, loose pearls and couriering. Works of art and antiques, lottery and state loan tickets can not be exported. Contact the Consulate for a full list.

 Diphtheria, Rabies.

 W1

 1 Tenge = 100 tigin. Exchange: must be made at authorised bureaux and receipts should be retained for all transactions. US Dollars are preferred. Major credit cards are accepted in large hotels. US Dollar traveller's cheques are preferred.
ATM AVAILABILITY: 3 locations.

 MONEYGRAM: Unavailable.
WESTERN UNION: 327 2507 106.

 AMEX: 1273 696933
DINERS CLUB: No local number.
MASTERCARD: 1 314 542 7111
VISA: (1) 410 581 9091
AMEX: (973) 256 834
THOMAS COOK: +44 1733 318950
VISA: +44 1733 318949

 0930–1730 Mon to Fri. All banks close Sat–Sun and for lunch 1300–1400.

 Generally inexpensive.

 Kazakh, Russian.

 Continental climate: Summers are hot and winters are cold. Hottest period: July–Aug.

 Mainly Sunni Muslim. Russian Orthodox and Jewish minorities.

 1998: Jan 1, 2; Mar 8, 21; May 1, 9; Aug 30; Oct 25; Dec 16.
1999: Jan 1, 2; Mar 8, 20; May 1, 9; Aug 30; Oct 25; Dec 16.

 220 volts Ac, 50 Hz. Plugs are the 2 pin continental type.

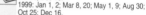 2–3 weeks. Addresses should be laid out from top to bottom: country, postcode, city, street, house number/name, and finally name.

 BBC: 17.64 15.07 9.410 6.195
VOA: 15.20 9.760 6.040 5.995

 Inside mosques, women observe their own ritual and are separated from the men. Arms and legs must be covered at religious sites.

 RAIL: Cost is minimal to Western fares. Regular connections between all major centres. NOTE: There has been an increase in robberies on rail and road. Passengers should travel in groups and compartments should be locked on overnight trains. ROAD: A reasonable network connects all towns. BUS: Reliable connections between all main towns. CAR HIRE: Hertz has agencies at the airport and the large hotels in the centre. DOCUMENTATION: IDP required.

 NOTE: Robberies and personal attacks have increased, especially in the larger cities. Do not walk alone on the streets at night or travel in unmarked taxis. Keep expensive items out of site. Kazakh's are very hospitable. Shorts should not be worn except for sports. Formal dress is often required for evening engagements.

Kenya

CAPITAL: Nairobi

GMT + 3

FROM UK: 254   IDD: Y to main cities
OUTGOING CODE: 000

All services: 336886 / 501280.

Kenya High Commission, 45 Portland Place, London W1N 4AS. Tel: (0171) 636 2371/5. Fax: (0171) 323 6717.
British High Commission, PO Box 30465, Bruce House, Standard Street, Nairobi, Kenya. Tel: (2) 335 944. Fax: (2) 333 196. Consulates in Mombassa and Malindi.
Kenya Tourist Office, 25 Brooks Mews, off Davies Street, Mayfair, London, W1Y 1LG. Tel: (0171) 355 3144. Fax: (0171) 495 8656.
Kenya Tourist Development Corporation, PO Box 42013, Utaliib House, Uhuru Highway, Nairobi, Kenya. Tel (2) 330 820.

Return Ticket required. Requirements may be subject to change at short notice. Consult embassy before departure.
VALID PASSPORT REQUIRED BY ALL: valid from 6 months from the date of entry.

Visa not required

Gold, diamonds, wildlife skins and game trophies.

US$20 is levied on international flights.

POLIO, TYPHOID: R.
MALARIA: Prevails throughout the year. Falciparum variety is present and high resistance to Chloroquine has been reported.
YELLOW FEVER: Vaccination is strongly recommended to all visitors travelling outside urban areas. A vaccination certificate is required by anyone arriving from infected areas.
OTHER: Bilharzia, rabies, AIDS – take sterilised needles if injections are required

W1

Kenyan Shilling (Ksh) = 100 cents. NOTE: Import and export of local currency is prohibited. Black market transactions are inadvisable. Diners Club and Visa are accepted. Traveller's cheques can be changed at banks. Pound sterling is the preferred currency.
ATM AVAILABILITY: 40 locations.

MONEYGRAM: Unavailable

WESTERN UNION: 2 251 696.

AMEX: No local number.
DINERS CLUB: (254) (02) 449 100
MASTERCARD: No local number.
VISA: (1) 410 581 9091
AMEX: +44 1273 571 600
THOMAS COOK: +44 1733 318950
VISA: +44 1733 318949

0900–1500 Mon to Fri 0900–1100 on the first and last Saturday of each month. The airport bank is open until midnight every day.
Kenya is greatly influenced by Western European standards of living.

English and Kiswahili.

Coastal areas are tropical and the lowlands are hot and dry. the rainfall can be heavy.

Mostly traditional with Christian and Muslim minorities.

1998: Jan 1, 30*; Apr 10, 13; May 1; June 1; Oct 10, 20; Dec 12, 25, 26.
1999: Jan 1, 18*; Apr 2, 5; May 1; June 1; Oct 10, 20; Dec 12, 25, 26.

220/240 Volts AC 50Hz Plugs = UK type 3 pin.
About 4 days to Europe. Letters can be sent c/o Poste Restante in any town. Poste Restante is well organised in Nairobi and free to collect.

BBC: 17.88 15.42 11.86 9.630
VOA: 21.49 15.60 9.525 6.035

Sexual harassment is far less prevalent in Kenya, though this essentially relates to white women. It is frowned upon for native women to walk alone at night.

ROADS: All major roads are now tarred.
TRAIN: Overnight to Mombassa and Nairobi.
BUS: Matatus (normally mini buses) are notorious for their involvement with accidents.
BEWARE: Bandits are common on the roads leading to the Somali border. Walking alone at night can be dangerous. DOCUMENTATION: British licence is valid for 90 days but must be endorsed by the police.

Western European habits prevail. Be alert for muggings and armed attacks if travelling in Nairobi or Mombasa. Avoid travelling after dark and isolated places. Game reserves and tourist areas on the coast are generally very safe.

CAPITAL: Bairiki

 GMT + 12 except Canton Island. Enderbury Island +11 and Christmas Island + 10.

 FROM UK: 686
IDD: Available throughout urban Tarawa.
OUTGOING CODE: All international calls must go through the operator.

 All calls are via the operator.

 Consulate of Kiribati, Faith House, 7 Tufton Street, London, SW1P 3QN. Tel: (0171) 222 6952. Fax: (0171) 976 7180.

 The British High Commission in Suva (Fiji) deals with enquiries – see Fiji.

 Refer to Consulate.

 Kiribati Visitors Bureau, PO Box 261, Bikenibeu, Bairiki, Tarawa, Kiribati. Tel: 28287. Fax: 26193.

 Return Ticket required. May be subject to change at short notice. Contact the Consular authority before departure.
VALID PASSPORT REQUIRED BY ALL

 Visa not required by Nationals of the UK (excluding Northern Island) for a 28 day stay maximum.

 Dogs and cats can only be imported from Fiji, Australia and New Zealand, with an import permit. See the Consulate for an up-to-date list.

 A$ 10.

 POLIO, TYPHOID: R.
YELLOW FEVER: A vaccination certificate is required from travellers over 1 year of age arriving from infected areas.
OTHER: Filariasis, Dengue Fever, Diarrhoel diseases and helminthic infections are common. Hepatitis A and B are reported.

 W1

 Australian Dollar (A$) = 100 cents. US $ can be exchanged for local currency at banks and some shops. Credit cards are not accepted. Traveller's cheques are accepted at some hotels and the bank of Kiribati. Australian dollar cheques are preferred, but US dollar cheques can also be exchanged.
ATM AVAILABILITY: Over 10 locations.

 MONEYGRAM: Unavailable.
WESTERN UNION: Unavailable.

 AMEX: No local number.
DINERS CLUB: No local number.
MASTERCARD: No local number.
VISA: No local number.

 AMEX: (61) 2 886 0689
THOMAS COOK: 1 800 127 495
VISA: 1 800 127 477

 0930–1500 Mon to Fri.

 There are four hotels in Kiribati on each major island. These tend to be more expensive than the rest houses found on all the other islands. Local products can be purchased cheaply, such as imported canned food, which the locals regard as a luxury.

 Kiribati and English.

 Mar–Oct is the most comfortable time to visit. Dec–Mar has the highest rainfall. Nov–Feb is very hot and humid.

 Gilbert Islands Protestant and Roman Catholic.

 1998: Jan 1; Apr 10, 13, 18; July 11, 13, 14; Aug 5; Dec 10, 25–26.
1999 Jan 1; Apr 2, 5, 18; July 11, 13, 14; Aug 5; Dec 10, 25–26.

 240 Volts Ac 50 Hz.

 Up to 2 weeks.

 BBC: 15.34 11.95 9.740 9.660
VOA: 15.18 11.72 9.525 5.985

 Like other Pacific Islands people are friendly and hospitable, yet retain their own traditions. Equal status between men and women is considered the norm.

 FLIGHTS: Air Tungaru operates an internal scheduled service to nearly all outer islands linking them with Tarawa.

 Tourism is largely undeveloped. If travelling to remote islands it is advisable to bring adequate supplies of essential items. Traditional culture should be respected and beachwear should not be worn away from the beach/pool.

Korea (The Democratic People's Republic of)

CAPITAL: Pyongyang

 GMT + 9

 FROM UK: 850.
IDD: Y (but is a sparse network).
OUTGOING CODE: Calls go through the operator.

 Not present.

 No embassy in the UK. EUROPE: General Delegation of the DPRK, 104 boulevard Bineau, 92200 Neuilly-sur-Seine, France. Tel: (1) 47 45 17 97. Fax: (1) 47 38 12 50.

 There is currently no British representation.

 Not present.

 National Directorate of Tourism, Central District, Pyongyang, DPR Korea. Tel: (2) 381 7201. Fax: (2) 381 7607.

 Return ticket required. Requirements may change at short notice. Contact the embassy before departure.
VALID PASSPORT REQUIRED BY ALL

 Required by all. NOTE: Tourism in North Korea is currently permitted only in officially organised groups of 10 persons only.

 Binoculars, Wireless sets, plants and seeds, groceries without authorisation.

 POLIO, TYPHOID: R.
OTHER: Rabies

 W1

 Won (NKW) = 100 jon. NOTE: Import and export of local currency is prohibited. Credit cards and Traveller's cheques are not accepted.
ATM AVAILABILITY: Unavailable.

 MONEYGRAM: Unavailable.
WESTERN UNION: Unavailable.

 AMEX: No local number.
DINERS CLUB: No local number.
MASTERCARD: No local number.
VISA: No local number.

 AMEX: No local number.
THOMAS COOK: No local number.
VISA: No local number.

 Economic crisis and the loss of several valuable trading partners has resulted in a shortage of commodities and an increase in prices.

 Korean.

 Hottest: July–Aug, which is also the rainy season. Dec–Jan is the coldest time. Spring and Autumn are usually dry and mild

 Buddhism. Christian and Chundo Kyo.

 1998: Jan 1; Mar 8; June 6; July 27; Sept 9; Oct 10;. Dec 27.
1999: Jan 1; Mar 8; June 6; July 27; Sept 9; Oct 10; Dec 27.

 110/220 Volts AC 60 Hz.

 Approx. 10 days. Outside the capital services are slow and unlimited.

 BBC: 17.83 15.28 9.740 7.110
VOA: 17.73 15.43 11.72 5.985

 A communist regime remains in DPR Korea isolating itself from outside influences. Society subsequently is totalitarian with no discrimination between gender.

 ROAD: Quality is good. RAIL: Extensive rail network.

 Independent travel is prohibited, however there are official tours available, via Regent Holidays, UK. Concessions are made for specific business trips.

CAPITAL: Seoul

 GMT + 9

 FROM UK: 82
IDD: Y in Seoul and other major cities.
OUTGOING CODE: 001

 Not present.

 Embassy of the Republic of Korea, 4 Palace Gate, London W8 5NF. Tel: (0171) 581 0247 or 581 3330 (visas). Fax: (0171) 581 8076.
British Embassy, 4 Chung-dong, Chung-Ku, Seoul 100, Republic of Korea. Tel: (2) 735 7341/3. Fax: (2) 733 8368 or 736 6241.

 Korean National Tourism Corporation, 20 St George Street, London W1R 9RD. Tel: (0171) 409 2100. Fax: (0171) 491 2302.
Korea Tourist Association, Saman Building, 945 Taechi-dong, Kangnam-ku, Seoul, Republic of Korea. Tel: (2) 556 2356. Fax: (2) 556 3818.

 Requirements may change at short notice. Contact the embassy before departure.
VALID PASSPORT REQUIRED BY ALL
For full details contact the embassy for an up to date list of requirements.

 Any printed material, films or phonographic material which is regarded to be harmful to national security or public interests. Textile fabrics larger than 5 m² or more than 5 foreign phonograph records.

 SKW9000, payable in local currency, at the airport.

 Those wishing to stay for more than one month may be required to provide a certificate proving they are HIV negative, issued within one month of their arrival.

 POLIO, TYPHOID: R.
OTHER: Cholera, Japanese Encephalitis.

 W1

 Won (SKW). NOTE: if the amount of foreign currency is greater than US$ 10,000 in value it must be registered on arrival. Export of local currency is limited to SKW 500,000. All credit cards are widely accepted. Traveller's cheques are accepted, but may be difficult to cash in smaller towns. US dollars are the preferred currency.
ATM AVAILABILITY: Over 1000 locations.

 MONEYGRAM: Unavailable.
WESTERN UNION: Unavailable.
AMEX: +44 1273 696933
DINERS CLUB: (82) (2) 222 611
MASTERCARD: 0078 11 887 0823
VISA: 0038 11 0165
AMEX: 0800 230060
THOMAS COOK: +44 1733 318950
VISA: +44 1733 318949

 0930–1630 Mon to Fri, 0930–1330 Sat.

 Caters for all types of budget. Hotels are government registered. Traveller's usually opt to stay in Yogwans, a traditional Korean inn, which are reasonably priced, self-catering is available. Internal travel is inexpensive and reliable.

 Korean.

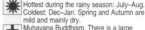 Hottest during the rainy season: July–Aug. Coldest: Dec–Jan. Spring and Autumn are mild and mainly dry.

 Muhayana Buddhism. There is a large Christian minority and also Confucian, Daoism and Chundo Kyo.

 1998: Jan 1–2, 27–29; Mar 1; Apr 5; May 1, 3, 5; June 6; July 17; Aug 15; Oct 3–6; Dec 25.
1999: Jan 1–2, 27–29; Mar 1; Apr 5; May 1, 3, 5; June 6; July 17; Aug 15; Oct 3–6; Dec 25.

 110/220 Volts Ac 60 Hz.

 Up to 10 days.

 BBC :17.83 15.28 9.740 7.110
VOA: 17.73 15.42 11.76 6.110

 Traditional custom and practice is more prevalent in rural areas. Women wear traditional costume and perform mainly agrarian tasks.
FLIGHTS: Frequent domestic services operate between main centres. ROAD: Excellent motorways link all major cities but minor roads may be poorer quality. BUS: Inexpensive and frequent services operate but are often overcrowded and make no allowances for English speakers. DOCUMENTATION: IDP is required.

 Korean culture is unique, incorporating a vivid portrayal of self-identity. Traditional agrarian culture persists in rural areas whilst the cities are a blend of history and technology. Shoes must be removed when entering someone's house. Use the right hand for passing and receiving.

CAPITAL: Kuwait City

GMT + 3

FROM UK: 965   IDD: Y
OUTGOING CODE: 00

Not present.

Embassy of the Sate of Kuwait, 2 Albert Gate, Knightsbridge, London SW1X 7JU. Tel: (0171) 590 3400. Fax: (0171) 259 5042.

British Embassy, PO Box 2, Arabian Gulf Street, 13001 Safat, Kuwait City, Kuwait. Tel: 240 3334/5/6. Fax: 240 7395.

Kuwait Information Centre, 8th Floor 30 Old Burlington Street, London W1X 1LB. Tel: (0171) 734 0017. Fax: (0171) 734 4763.

Department of Tourism, Ministry of Information, PO Box 193, 13002 Safat, as-Sour St, Kuwait City, Kuwait. Tel: 243 6644. Fax: 242 9758.

Requirements may be subject to change at short notice. Contact the relevant authority before travelling.
VALID PASSPORT REQUIRED BY ALL.

Visa required

Alcohol, pork products, goods from Israel. Penalties are severe and almost everyone's bag is searched at customs.

KWD 2 for international departures. Children under 12 are exempt.

POLIO, TYPHOID: R
OTHER: Cholera

W2

Kuwait Dinar (KWD) = 1000 fils. All credit cards and traveller's cards are accepted. US dollars are the preferred currency. ATM AVAILABILITY: 180 locations.

MONEYGRAM: 800 288.
WESTERN UNION: 245 0852.

AMEX: +44 1273 696933
DINERS CLUB: 965 5755588
MASTERCARD: 1 314 542 7111
VISA: (1) 410 581 9091

AMEX: (973) 256 834
THOMAS COOK: +44 1733 318950
VISA: +44 1733 318949

0800–1200 Sun to Thur.

Expensive and may be difficult for the budget traveller.

Arabic. English is generally widely understood.

Similar to Europe but hotter and dryer. Summer: (Apr–Oct) is hot and humid with little rain. Winter: (Nov–Mar) is cool with limited rainfall.

Mostly Muslim with Christian and Hindu minorities.

1998: Jan 1, 30*; Feb 25, 26; Apr 7, 28; July 6*; Nov 17*.
1999: Jan 1, 31*; Feb 26–27; Apr 7, 28; July 6*; Nov 17*.

240 volts AC, 50 Hz single phase. UK-type flat 3 pin plugs are used.

Airmail to Western Europe takes about 5 days.

BBC: 17.64 15.58 11.76 9.410
VOA: 15.21 11.83 9.740 6.070

Harassment of women travellers has been increasing. Do not travel alone in secluded places.

ROAD: A good network exists between cities. BUS: Reliable and inexpensive service operates between main cities. TAXI: Popular and reliable service, but fares should always be agreed in advance. CAR HIRE: Available. DOCUMENTATION: IDP required. Temporary licence available on presentation of a valid British licence.

NOTE: British nationals should not attempt to travel anywhere near the border with Iraq. British nationals should register with their Embassy on arrival. All Islamic laws should be respected. Women should dress modestly. Men should not wear shorts or go topless in public. It is greatly appreciated if visitors learn a few words of Arabic. SPECIAL PRECAUTIONS: There is a danger of unexploded land mines throughout the country. Seek advice before using beaches and venturing out of the city. PHOTOGRAPHY: In theory a photography permit is required.

CAPITAL: Bishkek

 GMT + 5 (GMT + 6 during the summer).

 FROM UK: 7 (3312 for Bishkek).
IDD: International calls are made from a telephone office, usually attached to a post office.
OUTGOING CODE: 062

 All services: 03.

No representation in the UK. EUROPE: Embassy of the Republic of Kyrgyzstan, 32 rue Denbosch, 1050 Brussels, Belgium. Tel (2) 534 6502. Fax: (2) 534 2325.
British Embassy in Almaty deals with enquiries relating to Kyrgyzstan. (See Kazakhstan entry).

 Not present.

State Committee for Tourism and Sport, Togolok Moldo 17, 720033 Bishkek, Kyrgyzstan Tel: (3312) 220 657 Fax: (3312) 212 845.

 Requirements may be subject to short-term change. Contact the relevant authority before departure.
VALID PASSPORT REQUIRED BY ALL: must be valid for 1 year after period of stay. As Visa requirements are liable to change visitors are advised to contact the Kyrgyz embassies in Brussels.

 Pornography, loose pearls and anything owned by a third party to be carried for that third party. Works of art and antiques, lottery and state loan tickets can not be exported. Contact the relevant authority for a full list.

 POLIO, TYPHOID: R.
OTHER: Rabies, Diphtheria.

 W2. It may be difficult to obtain a balanced diet and it may therefore be wise to take vitamin supplements.

 1 Som = 100 Tyn. Exch: All bills are normally settled in tax. Due to the shortage of change travellers advised to take small notes. NOTE: The import and export of foreign currency is prohibited. Credit cards are accepted in some of the large hotels in the capital. Take US Dollars in cash in preference to traveller's cheques.
ATM AVAILABILITY: Unavailable.

 MONEYGRAM: Unavailable.
WESTERN UNION: Unavailable.

 AMEX: +44 1273 696933
DINERS CLUB: No local number.
MASTERCARD: 1 314 542 7111
VISA: (1) 410 581 9091

AMEX: (973) 256 834
THOMAS COOK: +44 1733 318950
VISA: +44 1733 318949

 Usually 0930–1730 Mon to Fri.

 Relatively inexpensive.

 Kyrghz and Russian. English may be spoken by those involved with tourism.

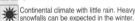 Continental climate with little rain. Heavy snowfalls can be expected in the winter.

 Sunni Muslim with a Russian Orthodox minority.

 1998: Jan 1, 7; Mar 8; 21. May 1, 5, 9; Aug 31.
1999: Jan 1, 7; Mar 8, 21; May 1, 5, 9; Aug 31.

 220 volts AC, 50 Hz. Round 2 pin continental plugs are standard.

 Anything from 2 weeks and 2 months.

 BBC: 15.07 12.10 9.410 6.195
VOA: 15.16 9.760 6.045 5.990

 Muslim culture prevails, influenced by Northern Asia and the Former Soviet Union. Women tend to be conservative. A patriarchal society exists. Usual precautions should be taken. Modest dress is advised.

 ROAD: Travel by road is difficult because of the terrain. BUS: There are regular services to many parts of the country but they are often crowded. TAXI: Can be found in all major towns. Many are unlicensed and fares should be agreed in advance. Many street names have changed so it is wise to ask for directions with the old and new street names. DOCUMENTATION: IDP and 2 photos.

 Mugging and theft is increasing in cities and rural areas, some thought to be committed by uniformed police. Exercise caution at all times and keep valuable items out of sight. Do not walk at night.

Laos

CAPITAL: Vientiane

 GMT + 7

 FROM UK: 856   IDD: Y, limited.
OUTGOING CODE: Telephone link exists with Bangkok.

 Not present.

 No embassy in the UK. EUROPE: Embassy of the Lao People's Democratic Republic, 74 Avenue Raymond Poincare, 75116 Paris, France. Tel: (1) 45 53 02 98. Fax: (1) 47 27 57 89.

 The British embassy in Bangkok deals with enquiries relating to Laos.

 Not present.

 National Tourism Authority of Laos People's Democratic Republic, BP 3556, Vientiane, Laos. Tel: (21) 212 248. Fax: (21) 212 769.

 Return ticket required. Requirements may change at short notice. Contact the embassy before departure.
VALID PASSPORT REQUIRED BY ALL

 Visa required. Transit passengers are exempt.

 US$ 5, children under 2 years are exempt.

 POLIO, TYPHOID: R. MALARIA: Exists all year throughout the country in the Falciparum variety, which has been reported as being highly resistant to chloroquine. YELLOW FEVER: A vaccination certificate is required for travellers arriving from infected areas. OTHER: Rabies.

 W1

 Laotian New Kip (Kp) = 100 cents. Exchange: Banks and hotels in Vientiane and Luang Prabang. NOTE: Import and export of local currency is prohibited. Both credit cards and traveller's cheques are not accepted.
ATM AVAILABILITY: Unavailable.

 MONEYGRAM: Unavailable.
WESTERN: UNION: Unavailable.

AMEX: +44 1273 696933
DINERS CLUB: No local number.
MASTERCARD: No local number.
VISA: No local number.

 AMEX: No local number.
THOMAS COOK: No local number.
VISA: No local number.

 0900–1630 Mon to Fri.

 Laos is one of the poorest countries in the world. The foreign traveller can expect to pay very little for local items. As hotels are only located in the capital prices may fluctuate.
Laotian, French, Vietnamese and some English may be spoken.

 Cooler weather in the highlands. Most of the country is hot and tropical, May–Oct has the highest temperatures and is the rainy season. Nov–Apr is the dry season.

Laos-Lum (Valley Laos) people follow the Hinayana (Theravada) form of Buddhism. The religion of the Laos Theung ranges from traditional Confucianism to Animism and Christianity.

1998: Jan 1, 20; Mar 8; May 1; Oct 17; Dec 2.
1999: Jan 1, 20; Mar 8; May 1; Oct 17; Dec 2

 220 Volts AC 50 Hz.

Restricted to Vientiane.

 BBC: 15.28 11.96 9.740 6.195
VOA: 15.43 11.96 6.110 1.575

 A subsistence economy prevails. Traditional roles for women exist. Sexual harassment is much less common here than in any other Asian country. Long trousers, skirts, or walking trousers are acceptable attire. Tank-tops, sleeveless blouses and short skirts are not.

 FLIGHTS: Domestic air services run from Vientiane to Luang Prabang, Pakse and Savannakhet. ROAD: Few roads are suitable for all-weather driving. BUS: Services link only a few major towns. CAR HIRE: Arrangements can be made through hotels. DOCUMENTATION : IDP is recommended although not legally required.

 Laos has only been accessible to foreign visitors since 1988. Tourists should avoid travelling outside the capital independently as bandits are likely to attack. Religious beliefs must be respected. Avoid all topics relating to politics. Laos nationals should not be touched on the head. Dress neatly and remove shoes when entering religious buildings. Buddha objects are religious images so do not pose in front of them and do not drink or sit on them. Common sense precautions should be followed with regard to personal safety.

Latvia

CAPITAL: Riga

 GMT + 2 (GMT + 3 in summer).

 FROM UK: 371   IDD: Y
OUTGOING CODE: 810

 Ambulance: 03; Police: 02; Fire: 01.

Embassy of Latvia, 45 Nottingham Place, London W1M 3FE. Tel: (0171) 312 0040. Fax: (0171) 312 0042.

 British Embassy, Alunana iela 5, LV – 1010 Riga, Latvia. Tel: 733 8126. Fax: 733 8132.

 Not present.

National Tourism Board of Latvia, Pils laukums 4, Riga LV 1050, Latvia. Tel: 722 9945. Fax: 722 9945.

Return Ticket required. Requirements may be subject to short term change. Contact the relevant authority before departure.
VALID PASSPORT REQUIRED BY ALL:
Must be valid for 2 months after period of stay.

 Visa not required by Holders of British passports.

 Narcotics, guns and ammunition.

 US$12.

 Rabies, Diphtheria and Hepatitis.

 1 Latvian Lat (Ls) = 100 santims. Exchange: the banking system is still being developed but there are bureaux de change in most post offices, hotels and railway stations. Credit cards and traveller's cheques are only accepted on a limited basis. The preferred foreign currencies are US dollars and the German Deutschemark.
ATM AVAILABILITY: Over 10 locations.

 MONEYGRAM: Riga: 700 7007 then 800 592 3688; outside Riga: 8 2700 7007 then 800 592 3688.
WESTERN UNION: 700 7007

 AMEX: +44 1273 696933
DINERS CLUB: No local number.
MASTERCARD: 1 314 542 7111
VISA: (1) 410 581 9091

 AMEX: +44 1273 571 600
THOMAS COOK: +44 1733 318950
VISA: +44 1733 318949

 1000–1800 Mon to Fri.

 Generally less expensive than Western Europe.

 Latvian. Russian is increasing. English, German and Swedish may also be spoken.

 Temperate climate but with considerable temperature fluctuations. The Summer is warm with relatively mild weather in spring and autumn. Winters can be very cold.

 Protestant (Lutheran), Roman Catholic and a Russian Orthodox minority.

 1998: Jan 1; Apr 10, 13; May 1, 10; June 23, 24; Nov 18; Dec 25, 26, 31.
1999: Jan 1; Apr 2, 5; May 1, 9; June 23, 24; Nov 18; Dec 25, 26, 31.

 220 volts AC, 50 Hz. European style 2 pin plugs are used.

 Airmail to Western Europe takes 3 – 4 days.

 BBC: 15.07 12.10 9.410
VOA: 9.760 6.040 1.197

 Traditionally, a patriarchal society has prevailed, but gender roles are slowly changing.

RAIL: Reasonably developed network connects Riga with the other main towns.
ROAD: There are good connections from Riga to all other parts of the country. BUS: A better form of transport than trains in Latvia.
CAR HIRE: Available through hotels. Reservations are recommended.

 Latvians can appear rather reserved and formal, but very welcoming to foreign visitors. Tourists should exercise caution as petty crime is a problem. Carry a copy of your passport as ID.

Lebanon

CAPITAL: Beirut

 GMT + 2 (GMT + 3 during the summer).

 FROM UK: 961   IDD:Y
OUTGOING CODE: 00

 Police: 386 440 425 (Emergency police: 16); Fire: 310 105; Ambulance: 386 675.

 Embassy of the Republic of Lebanon, 21 Kensington Palace Gardens, London W8 4QM. Tel: (0171) 229 7265. Fax: (0171) 243 1699. Consular Section: 15 Palace Gardens Mews, London W8 4RA. Tel: (0171) 727 6696. Fax: (0171) 243 1699.
British Embassy, Rabieh, rue 8, Beirut, Lebanon. Tel: (1) 405 070 or 403 640. Fax: (1) 402 032.

 Lebanon Tourist and Information Office, 21 Piccadilly, London W1V 9HB. Tel: (0171) 409 2031. Fax: (0171) 493 4929.
Ministry of Tourism, PO Box 11-5344, 5500 Central Bank Street, Beirut, Lebanon. Tel: (1) 343 196 or 340 940/4. Fax: (1) 340 945.

 Return Ticket required. Requirements may be subject to short term change. Contact the relevant authority before departure.
VALID PASSPORT REQUIRED: must be valid for at least 6 months beyond the estimated duration of stay.

 Visa required. Do not enter with Israeli stamps on your passport.

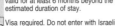 Firearms and ammunitions require a valid import licence.

 POLIO, TYPHOID: R.
YELLOW FEVER: A vaccination certificate is required if coming from infected areas.
OTHER: Cholera, Rabies.

 W2

 Lebanese Pound (L£) = 100 piastres. Credit cards and traveller's cheques have limited acceptance.
ATM AVAILABILITY: Over 30 locations.

 MONEYGRAM: 426 801 then 800 592 3688.
WESTERN UNION: (01) 601 315.

 AMEX: +44 1273 696933
DINERS CLUB: 491 576
MASTERCARD: 1 314 542 7111
VISA: (1) 410 581 9091

 AMEX: (973) 256 834
THOMAS COOK: +44 1733 318950
VISA: +44 1733 318949

 0830–1200 Mon to Sat.

 Relatively expensive. Accommodation can be especially expensive for the traveller looking for a cheap place to stay. Food, however can be cheap if purchased from sandwich and snack bars.

 Arabic. French and English are spoken. Kurdish and Armenian are spoken by a small minority.

 Summer (June–Sept) is hot along the coast and cooler in the mountains. Winter (Dec–mid Mar) is mostly rainy with snow in the mountains. Spring and Autumn are cool and pleasant.

 Muslim (mainly Shia) and Christian (mostly Roman Catholic).

 1998: Jan 1, 30; Feb 9; Apr 7, 10, 13, 17, 20, 28. May 1, 6, 7; July 6*; Aug 15; Nov 1, 22; Dec 25.
1999: Jan 1, 30*; Feb 9; Apr 2, 7, 5, 17, 20, 28; May 1, 6, 7; July 5*; Aug 15; Nov 1, 22; Dec 25.

 110/220 volts, AC 50 Hz.

 Usually 5- 6 days to Europe, up to 8 days to the USA.

 BBC: 15.07 12.09 9.410 1.323
VOA: 15.44 11.90 9.700 7.205

 Women are likely to encounter rude remarks and leers. The dress code should be obeyed and revealing clothes should not be worn.

 BUS: Intercity buses are cheap and efficient but may be uncomfortable. TAXI: Fares should be agreed in advance. They are usually shared and a 50% surcharge will be added after 2200 hours. CAR HIRE: chauffeur-driven cars are recommended although self drive cars are available. DOCUMENTATION: IDP is recommended although not legally required.

 Muslim traditions and practices should be respected. Casual dress is suitable for daytime clothing. The main danger spots are in the south, which can be subject to Israeli shelling or air raids.

Lesotho

CAPITAL: Maseru

 GMT + 2

 FROM UK: 266   IDD: Y to some cities
OUTGOING CODE: 00

 Police: 123 / 124; Ambulance: 121; Fire: 122

 High Commission for the Kingdom of Lesotho, 7 Chesham Place, Belgravia, London SW1 8HN. Tel: (0171) 235 5686. Fax: (0171) 235 5023.

 British High Commission, PO Box Ms 521, Maseru 100, Lesotho. Tel: 323 961. Fax: 310 120.

 Refer to the High Commission.

 Lesotho Tourist Board, PO Box 1378 Masseru 100, Lesotho. Tel: 313 760 or 312 896 (information). Fax 310 108.

 Return Ticket required. Requirements may be subject to change at short notice. Consult embassy before departure.
VALID PASSPORT REQUIRED BY ALL

 Required by all non-Commonwealth members

 Departure tax is Lo 20, in local currency only, transit passengers and children are exempt.

 POLIO, TYPHOID: R.
YELLOW FEVER: A vaccination certificate is required by travellers arriving from infected areas.
OTHER: Bilharzia and Rabies are present.

 W1

 Loti (Lo) = 100 Lisente. Limited acceptance of Visa, MasterCard. Traveller's cheques are widely accepted. US dollars are the preferred currency.
ATM AVAILABILITY: Unavailable.

 MONEYGRAM: Unavailable.
WESTERN UNION: Unavailable.

AMEX: +44 1273 696933
DINERS CLUB: No local number.
MASTERCARD: 1 314 542 711
VISA: (1) 410 581 9091

 AMEX: +44 1273 571 600
THOMAS COOK: +44 1733 318950
VISA: +44 1733 318949

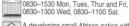 0830–1530 Mon, Tues, Thur and Fri, 0830–1300 Wed, 0830–1100 Sat.

 A developing small African nation with a growing economy.

 Sesotho and English.

 The climate is temperate. Rain falls mostly between Oct–Apr. The hottest period is between Jan and Feb.

 Catholic with Lesotho Evangelical and Anglican.

 1998: Jan 1; Mar 11; Apr 4, 10, 13; May 1, 21; July 17; Oct 4; Dec 25, 26.
1999: Jan 1, 2; Mar 11; Apr 2, 4, 5; May 1, 20; July 17; Oct 4; Dec 25, 26.

 220 Volts AC.

 7 days.

 BBC: 11.97 90.2
VOA: 21.49 15.60 9.525 6.035

 Women should dress modestly in accordance with the Muslim faith.

ROADS: Few roads are tarred and are impassable during the rainy season. DOCUMENTATION: IDP is recommended.

Inform the head chief if you intend to spend a short stay in a rural village. Dress is casual although stricter in the Muslim areas.
Religion plays an important part in traditional life. PHOTOGRAPHY: Do not take photos of the palace, police establishments, government offices or anything connected with the military.

CAPITAL: Monrovia

 GMT

FROM UK: 231   IDD: Y, to some cities.
OUTGOING CODE: 00

Not present.

Embassy of the Republic of Liberia, 2 Pembridge Place, London W2 4XB. Tel: (0171) 221 1036.

The British High Commission in Abidjan deals with enquiries relating to Liberia (see Côte d'Ivoire).

Refer to the Embassy.

Bureau of Tourism, Sinkor, Monrovia, Liberia. Tel: 222 229.

Return Ticket required. Requirements may be subject to change at short notice. Consult embassy before departure.
VALID PASSPORT REQUIRED BY ALL.

Visa required.

Import of safety matches.

Departure Tax of L$20, except those under 12 years and those transiting within 24 hours. Tax is payable in local currency.

POLIO, TYPHOID: R.
MALARIA: R. Falciparum variety present. High resistance to choloroquine has been reported.
YELLOW FEVER: A vaccination certificate must be presented with all visa applications.
OTHER: Bilharzia, Rabies, Cholera and Meningitis.

W1

Liberian Dollar (L$) = 100 Cents. Limited acceptance of MasterCard and Visa. Traveller's cheques are not accepted.
ATM AVAILABILITY: Unavailable.

MONEYGRAM: Unavailable.
WESTERN UNION: Unavailable.

AMEX: +44 1273 696933
DINERS CLUB: No local number.
MASTERCARD: 1 314 542 7111
VISA: (1) 410 581 9091

AMEX: No local number.
THOMAS COOK: No local number.
VISA: No local number.

0900–1200 Mon to Thur, 0800–1400 Fri. The Bank of Monrovia, Tubman Boulevard, Sinkor, is open 0800–1100 Sat.

Unpredictable due to an unstructured economy and civil unrest.

English and various African languages.

The climate is hot and tropical. Oct–May is wet season. Winds prevail from Dec–Mar.

Mostly Christian, but Islam is practised in the North and traditional beliefs elsewhere.

1998: Jan 1; Feb 11; Mar 12, 15; Apr 10, 11; July 26; Aug 24; Nov 6, 29; Dec 25.
1999: Jan 1; Feb 11; Mar 12, 15; Apr 2, 3; July 26; Aug 24; Nov 6, 29; Dec 25.

110 Volts AC, 60 Hz

Airmail takes 5–12 days to Europe.

BBC: 17.83 15.40 11.84 6.005
VOA: 21.49 13.71 9.575 6.035

Women should respect Muslim dress codes.

RAIL: Limited services. ROADS: Many of the smaller roads are untarred. Difficulty in bridging river estuaries along the coast.

Visitors are advised by the FCO not to travel to Liberia unless essential. Food and dress laws should be respected.

Libya

CAPITAL: Tripoli

 GMT + 1

 FROM UK: 218   IDD: Y
OUTGOING CODE: 00

 Not present.

 Libyan Interests Section, c/o Royal Embassy of Saudi Arabia, 119 Harley Street, London W1. Tel: (0171) 486 8387. Fax: (0171) 224 6349.

 British Interests Section, c/o Embassy of Italian Republic, PO Box 4206, Sharia Uahran 1, Tripoli, Libya. Tel: (21) 333 1191. Telex 20296.

 Refer to the Libyan Interests Section.

 Department of Tourism and Fairs, PO Box 891, Sharia Omar Mukhtar, Tripoli, Libya. Tel: (21) 333 2255.

 Return Ticket required. Requirements may be subject to change at short notice. Consult embassy before departure.
VALID PASSPORT REQUIRED

 Visa required. NOTE: It is very difficult to obtain tourist visas.

 All alcohol is prohibited. Goods made in Israel or manufactured by companies who deal with Israel are prohibited as is the import of any kind of food. Contact the nearest Libyan Diplomatic Rep. for further information.

 Departure tax = LYD3, payable in local currency, except children under 2 years.

 Holders of Israeli and South African passports containing a valid or expired visa for Israel or South Africa, will be refused entry or transit. Women married to, and children of, Arab league countries will be refused entry if they are travelling alone, unless they are met at the airport by their husband/father.

 POLIO, TYPHOID: R. MALARIA: A small risk exists in certain areas. YELLOW FEVER: A vaccination certificate is required for visitors arriving from infected areas. OTHER: Bilharzia, Cholera and Rabies are present.

 W2

 Libyan Dinar (LD) = 100 Dirhams. NOTE: Import and export of local currency is prohibited. Visa and Diners Club have a limited acceptance. Traveller's cheques in US dollars are widely accepted.
ATM AVAILABILITY: Unavailable.

 MONEYGRAM: Unavailable.
WESTERN UNION: Unavailable.

 AMEX: +44 1273 696933
DINERS CLUB: No local number.
MASTERCARD: No local number.
VISA: (1) 410 581 9091
AMEX: +44 1273 571 600
THOMAS COOK: +44 1733 318950
VISA: +44 1733 318949

 0800–1200 Sat to Wed (winter), 0800–1200 Sat to Thur and 1600–1700 Sat and Wed (summer).

 Libya has great internal wealth, but due to its foreign policy can not form constructive trade links with U.N. states.

 Arabic, some English and Italian.

 The climate is warm all year round. It can be cool in the evenings. Some rainfall Nov–Feb.

 Muslim (sunni).

 1998: Jan 30; Mar 2; Apr 7; June 11; July 6*, 23; Sept 1.
1999: Jan 18; Mar 2; Apr 7; June 11; July 6*, 23; Sept 1.

 150/220 Volts AC, 50 Hz. There are many power cuts.

 Takes approximately 2 weeks to Europe, can be erratic and unreliable.

 BBC: 17.64 15.07 9.410 6.195
VOA: 15.44 11.90 9.700 7.205

 Women do not attend Arab gatherings and should dress modestly in religious buildings and small towns. Many people advise against women travelling alone in Libya.

 ROAD: Petrol is available but spare parts are difficult to obtain. Driving standards are poor.
TAXI: Fares should be agreed in advance.
CAR HIRE: Available in Tripoli and Benghazi.

 NOTE: Since 1992 United Nations' sanctions has prohibited all flights to and from Libya.

Liechtenstein

224

CAPITAL: Vaduz

GMT + 1 (GMT + 2 during the summer).

FROM UK: 41 75   IDD: Y
OUTGOING CODE: 00

Ambulance: 144; Fire: 118; Police: 117.

 Liechtenstein represents very few overseas missions and is generally represented by Switzerland.

British Consulate General, Dufourstrasse 56, CH-8008 Zürich, Switzerland. Tel: (91) 261 1520 – 6. Fax (1) 252 8351.

Swiss National Tourist Office (SNTO), Swiss Centre, Swiss Court, London W1V 8EE. Tel: (0171) 734 1921 (general enquiries) or (0171) 734 4577 (trade). Fax: (0171) 437 4577.

Liechtenstein National Tourist Office, Postfach 139, Kirchstrasse 10, FL-9490 Vaduz, Liechtenstein. Tel: 232 1443. Fax: 392 1618.

 See Switzerland.
VALID PASSPORT REQUIRED BY ALL

 See Switzerland.

 See Switzerland.

 See Switzerland

 Swiss Franc (SFr) = 100 centimes. All major credit cards and traveller's cheques are accepted.
ATM AVAILABILITY: Over 50 locations.

 MONEYGRAM: Available in large towns.
WESTERN UNION: Available.

 AMEX: +44 1273 696933
DINERS CLUB: (41) (1) 8333738
MASTERCARD: 0800 89 7092
VISA: 0800 89 6046

 AMEX: 155 0100
THOMAS COOK: 0800 55 0130
VISA: 0800 55 7262

 0800–1630 Mon to Fri.

 Moderate to expensive.

 German. A dialect of Alemannish is widely spoken. English may also be spoken.

 Temperate climate with wet, warm summers and cool to cold winters.

 Christian, mainly Roman Catholic.

 1998: Jan 1, 6; Feb 24; Mar 19; Apr 10, 13; May 1, 8, 21; Aug 15; Nov 1; Dec 25, 26.
1999: Jan 1, 6; Feb 16; Mar 19; Apr 2, 5; May 1, 8, 20; Aug 15; Nov 1; Dec 25, 26.

 220 volts AC, 50 Hz.

 3–4 days.

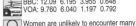 BBC: 12.09 6.195 3.955 0.648
VOA: 9.760 6.040 1.197 0.792

 Women are unlikely to encounter many problems while travelling in Liechtenstein.

 RAIL: The best rail access is via the Swiss border stations at Buchs or Sargans or Feldkirch. BUS: Local buses operate between the local villages. ROAD: A national driving licence is sufficient.

 Same as the rest of Northwest Europe.

Lithuania

CAPITAL: Vilnius

 GMT + 2 (GMT + 3 during the summer).

 FROM UK: 370 (2 for Vilnius, 5 for Kaunas, 6 for Klaipeda)
IDD: Y   OUTGOING CODE: 810

 Ambulance: 03; Fire: 01; Police: 02.

 Embassy of the Republic of Lithuania, 84 Gloucester Place, London W1H 3HN. Tel: (0171) 486 6401/2. Fax: (0171) 486 4603.

 British Embassy, PO Box 863, Antakalnio 2, 2600 Vilnius, Lithuania. Tel: (2) 222 070/1. Fax: (2) 727 579.

 Refer to the Embassy.

 Lithuanian Tourist Board, Ukmeriges 20, 2600 Vilnius, Lithuania. Tel (2) 622 610. Fax (2) 226 819.

 Requirements may be subject to short term change. Contact the relevant authority before departure.
VALID PASSPORT REQUIRED BY ALL

 Visa Regulations are in a state of change. Contact the Embassy for an up to date list.

 Narcotics.

 US$7.

 Rabies, Hepatitis A and B and Diphtheria are present.

 The Litas = 100 centas. Exchange: Currency can be exchanged at banks and exchange bureaux. NOTE: The import of local and foreign currency is unlimited but must be declared on arrival. All major credit cards are accepted in large hotels, shops and restaurants. Most banks will cash traveller's cheques, but commission rates are high. US dollars are the preferred currency.
ATM AVAILABILITY: Over 10 locations.

 MONEYGRAM: Unavailable.
WESTERN UNION: 22 232 613.

AMEX: +44 1273 696933
DINERS CLUB: No local number.
MASTERCARD: 1 314 542 7111
VISA: (1) 410 581 9091

 AMEX: +44 1273 571 600
THOMAS COOK: +44 1733 318950
VISA: +44 1733 318949

 0900–1700 Mon. to Fri.

 Tourists can expect to pay higher prices than the locals.

 Lithuanian and a large number of dialects.

 Temperate climate but with considerable temperature variations. Summers are warm and spring and autumn are usually mild. Winters can be very cold.

 Roman Catholic. Minority of Evangelical Lutheran, Evangelical Reformism and Russian Orthodox.

 1998: Jan 1; Feb 16; Mar 11; Apr 12, 13; July 6; Nov 1; Dec 25, 26.
1999: Jan 1; Feb 16; Mar 11; Apr 2, 5; July 6; Nov 1; Dec 25, 26.

 220 volts Ac, 50 Hz. European 2 pin plugs are used.

 To Western Europe takes up to 6 days.

 BBC: 15.07 12.10 9.410 6.195
VOA: 11.97 9.760 6.040 5.995

 Traditionally a patriarchal society, but gender roles are slowly changing.

 RAIL: There are good connections from Vilnius to the other main cities. ROAD: There is a good network of roads. BUS: Generally more frequent and quicker than domestic trains and serve almost every town and village. CAR HIRE: Several local firms provide car hire services. DOCUMENTATION: European nationals should e in possession of the new European driving licence. Otherwise, a national driving licence is sufficient.

 Lithuanians appreciate a show of respect for their culture and national heritage. Do not accept food and drink from strangers. Petty crime is rife on public transport.

Luxembourg

CAPITAL: Luxembourg-Ville

 GMT + 1 (GMT + 2 during the summer).

 FROM UK: 352   IDD: Y
OUTGOING CODE: 00

 Ambulance / Fire: 112; Police: 113.

 Embassy of the Grand Duchy of Luxembourg, 27 Wilton Crescent, London SW1X 8SD. Tel: (0171) 235 6961. Fax: (0171) 235 9735.

 British Embassy, 14 boulevard Roosevelt, L-2450 Luxembourg-Ville, Luxembourg. Tel 229 864/5/6. Fax: 229 867.

 Luxembourg Tourist Office, 122 Regent Street, London W1R 5FE. Tel: (0171) 434 2800. Fax: (0171) 734 1205.

 Office National du Tourisme BP 1001, 77 rue d'Anvers, L-1010 Luxembourg-Ville, Luxembourg. Tel: 400 8081. Fax 404 748.

 Requirements may be subject to short-term change. Contact the relevant authority before departure.
VALID PASSPORT REQUIRED

 Visa not required by nationals of EU member states.

 Narcotics and firearms.

 US$ 10 is levied on all foreign departures.

 Rabies

Luxembourg Franc (Luxfr) = 100 centimes. Both credit cards and traveller's cheques are widely accepted.
ATM AVAILABILITY: Over 250 locations.

MONEYGRAM: Available at single American Express location.
WESTERN UNION: 0800 40 40.

AMEX: +44 1273 696933
DINERS CLUB: (352) 400321
MASTERCARD: 0800 4533
VISA: (1) 410 581 9091

 AMEX: +44 1273 571 600
 THOMAS COOK: 0800 2123
VISA: 0800 2119

 Generally 0900–1200 and 1330–1630 Mon to Fri, but may vary greatly.

 Similar to other Western European countries.

Letzeburgesch, a German – Moselle – Frankish dialect. French and German are usually used for administrative purposes. Many also speak English.

 May–Sept is warm. Snow is common during the winter months.

 Mostly Roman Catholic with Protestant, Anglican and Jewish minorities.

 1998: Jan 1; Apr 13; May 1, 21; June 1, 23; Aug 15; Nov 1; Dec 24–26.
1999: Jan 1; Apr 5; May 1, 20, 31; June 23; Aug 15; Nov 1; Dec 24–26.

 220 volts AC, 50 Hz.

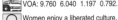 2–4 days to other European destinations.

BBC: 12.10 6.195 3.995 0.648
VOA: 9.760 6.040 1.197 0.792.

 Women enjoy a liberated culture, similar to the rest of Western Europe. Usual precautions apply. No additional problems should be encountered.

 RAIL: Efficient service and fully integrated with the bus service. Reductions can often be found. ROAD: Excellent network. BUS: Cross-country buses are punctual and operate between all major towns. TAXI: Metered, but cannot be hailed in the street – a 15% tip is usual. CAR HIRE: All the main agencies operate. DOCUMENTATION: 3rd party insurance is necessary. A 'green card' is strongly recommended. A valid national licence is sufficient.

 Western European social courtesies should be followed. Casual dress is widely acceptable, but formal clothing is required by some restaurants and social functions.

CAPITAL: Macau

GMT + 8

FROM UK: 853   IDD: Y
OUTGOING CODE: 00

Fire, Police and Ambulance: 999.

Embassy of the Portuguese Republic, 11 Belgrave Square, London, SW1X 8PP. Tel: (0171) 235 5331/4. Fax: (0171) 245 1287.

The British Trade Commission in Hong Kong, 9th Floor, Bank of Armenia Tower, 12 Harcourt Road, Hong Kong. Tel: 523 0176. Fax: 845 2870.

Macau Tourist Information Bureau, 6 Sherlock Mews, Paddington Street, London W1M 3RH. Tel: (0171) 224 3390. Fax: (0171) 224 0601.

Direção dos Serviços de Turismo, CP 3006, Edifício Ritz, Largo do Senado 9, Macau. Tel: 3155 156. Fax: 510 104.

Requirements may change at short notice. Contact the embassy before departure.
VALID PASSPORT REQUIRED BY ALL

Visa not required by nationals of Great Britain for stays of less than 20 days. Visas may be obtained on arrival in Macau.

Narcotics, firearms, endangered species of animal and plants and pesticides.

Departure tax of MOP130 per person, payable in local currency.

Diarrhoel diseases, hepatitis A and B, Oriental liver and oriental lung fluke and haemorrhagic fever with renal syndrome may occur in this area.

W1

Pataca (MOP) = 100 avos. MasterCard is accepted. Traveller's cheques may be changed at hotels, banks and bureau de change. Cheques in US dollars are the preferred currenc.y
ATM AVAILABILITY: Over 20 locations.

MONEYGRAM: 0800 111 then 800 592 3688.
WESTERN UNION: Unavailable.

AMEX: No local number.
DINERS CLUB: No local number.
MASTERCARD:1 314 542 7111
VISA: No local number.

AMEX: (852) 885 9331
THOMAS COOK: +44 1733 318950
VISA: +44 1733 318949

0930–1600 Mon to Fri, 0930–1200 Sat.

Visitors may expect to pick up a variety of bargains since Macau is a free port. A wide range of accommodation, suitable for all budgets, is available.

Portuguese and Chinese (Cantonese). English may be spoken by those involved in tourism.

Sub-tropical climate with very hot summers. There is a rainy period during the summer months. Winds can reach gale force and typhoons are not unheard of.

Roman Catholic, Buddhism, Daoism and Confucianism.

1998: Jan 1, 28–30; Apr 6, 10, 11, 13, 25; May 1, 30; June 10; July 1; Aug 17; Oct 1, 2, 5, 6, 28; Nov 2; Dec 1, 8, 24, 25, 26.
1999: Jan 1, 28–30; Apr 2, 5, 6, 25; May 1, 30; June 10; July 1; Aug 17;Oct 1, 2, 5, 6, 28; Nov 2; Dec 1, 8, 24, 25, 26.

Usually 220 Volts AC 50 Hz.

3–5 days.

BBC: 15.36 11.95 9.740 6.195
VOA: 17.73 15.15 11.76 6.110

Travel is as safe as in any Western country. Revealing beach-wear, however is likely to arouse attention.

ROAD: There are 5 bus routes in he city. CAR HIRE: Available. TAXI: Fares should be agreed in advance. DOCUMENTATION: IDP not required for drivers from the UK.

Macau is a mixture of Portuguese, Chinese and Western culture, the visitor can experience all of these in one location. Violent crime is quite rare although residential burglaries and pick-pocketing is a problem.

CAPITAL: Skopje

 GMT +1 (GMT + 2 during the summer).

 FROM UK: 389   IDD: Y
OUTGOING CODE: 99

 Police: 92; Fire: 93; Ambulance: 94.

Embassy of the Former Yugoslav Republic of Macedonia, 10 Harcourt House, 19A Cavendish Square, London W1M 9AD. Tel: (0171) 499 5152. Fax: (0171) 499 2804.

British Embassy, ul. Veljko Vlahovic 26, 91000 Skopje, Former Yugoslav Republic of Macedonia. Tel: (91) 116 772. Fax: (91) 117 005.

 See Embassy or the Foreign and Commonwealth Travel Advice Unit (0171 270 3000 – switchboard).

 Not present.

 Requirements may be subject to short-term change. Contact embassy before departure. VALID PASSPORT REQUIRED BY ALL

 Visa not required by nationals of EU countries.

 Narcotics and firearms.

 Rabies, Tick-borne encephalitis.

 Macedonian Denar = 100 deni. Credit cards are accepted on a limited basis, in the capital only. Traveller's cheques, preferably in German Deutschmarks or US Dollars, are easily exchanged.
ATM AVAILABILITY: 7 locations.

 MONEYGRAM: Unavailable.
WESTERN UNION: Unavailable.

AMEX: +44 1273 696933
DINERS CLUB: No local number.
MASTERCARD: 1 314 542 7111
VISA: (1) 410 581 9091

 AMEX: +44 1273 571 600
THOMAS COOK: +44 1733 318950
VISA: +44 1733 318949

 0730–1530 Mon–Fri.

 Macedonia is the poorest of the former Yugoslav republics. Tourists can expect to pay more for goods than the locals.

 Macedonian. Albanian, Turkish, Roma and Serbo-Croat are also used by ethnic groups.

 Continental climate with hot summers and very cold winters.

 Eastern Orthodox Macedonians, Muslim Albanians, Muslim Turks, Serbian Orthodox Serbs.

 1998: Jan 1; May 1; Aug 2; Sept 8; Oct 11.
1999: Jan 1; May 1; Aug 2; Sept 8; Oct 11.

 220 volts AC, 50 Hz.

 2–3 days within Europe, except for Serbia and Greece, with which communications are currently uncertain.

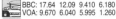 BBC: 17.64 12.09 9.410 6.180
VOA: 9.670 6.040 5.995 1.260

 Due to religious restrictions, women play fairly traditional roles within society. Muslim dress is worn by about 20% of women.

 The situation is subject to change at short notice due to political uncertainty. Contact the Foreign and Commonwealth Travel Advice Unit for up-to-date information. RAIL ROAD: are currently operating normally.

 Due to the recent socio-economic collapse of the republic day-to-day business often moves very slowly or not at all due to the local bureaucracy.

Madagascar

CAPITAL: Antananarivo

GMT + 3

FROM UK: 261   IDD:Y to major towns.
OUTGOING CODE: 16

Not present.

Consulate of the Republic of Madagascar, 16 Lanark Mansions, Pennard Road, London W12 8DT. Tel: (0181) 746 0133. Fax: (0181) 746 0134.

British Embassy, BP 167, Première Etage, Immeuble 'Ny Havana', Cité de 67 Ha, 101 Antananarivo, Madagascar. Tel: (2) 222 7749. Fax: (2) 222 6690.

Not present.

Direction du Tourisme de Madagascar, Ministry of Tourism, BP 610, Tsimbazaza, 101 Antananarivo, Madagascar. Tel: (2) 26298. Fax: (2) 26710.

Return Ticket required. Requirements may be subject to short-term change. Contact the relevant authority before departure.
VALID PASSPORT REQUIRED BY ALL

Visa Required.

All vegetables must be declared and animals require a detailed veterinary certificate and must be vaccinated against rabies.
FRF 100, or US$ 2, on most international flights.

POLIO, TYPHOID: R. MALARIA: Exists in the falciparum variety all year. The highest risk is along the coast. Resistance to chloroquine has been reported. YELLOW FEVER: A vaccination certificate is required from everyone arriving from areas considered by the Malagasy authorities to be infected. OTHER: Bilharzia, Cholera, Rabies, Hepatitis A, B and E are endemic. Dysenteries and many viral diseases have been reported.

W1

Malagasy Franc (MGFr) = 100 centimes.
NOTE: Non-residents cannot export local currency. Credit cards are accepted in the capital's major hotels. Traveller's cheques can be exchanged at banks and major hotels, French francs preferred.
ATM AVAILABILITY: Unavailable.

MONEYGRAM: Unavailable.
WESTERN UNION: Unavailable.

AMEX: +44 1273 696933
DINERS CLUB: No local number.
MASTERCARD: 1 314 542 7111
VISA: (1) 410 581 9091
AMEX: (1) 801 964 6665
THOMAS COOK: +44 1733 318950
VISA: +44 1733 318949

0800–1300 Mon to Fri.

Relatively inexpensive. Hotels vary from international prices to cheaper guesthouses. Malagasy and French. Local dialects are also spoken. Very little English is spoken.

Generally hot and sub-tropical. Nov–Mar: rainy season; Apr–Oct: dry season. The South and West are hot and dry. Dec–Mar: the monsoon may cause storms and cyclones. Mountainous regions are hot and thundery Nov–Apr, dry, cool and windy the rest of the year.

Mostly Animist and Christian with the remainder Muslim.

1998: Jan 1; Apr 10, 13; May 1, 21, 25; June 1, 26; Aug 15; Dec 25, 31.
1999: Jan 1; Apr 2, 5; May 1, 21, 25; June 1, 26; Aug 15; Dec 25, 31.

Mostly 220 volts AC, 50 Hz. Plugs are generally 2 pin.

Poste Restante at the main post office is the most reliable option. Airmail to Europe takes at least 7 days, surface mail 3 to 4 months.

BBC: 17.89 11.94 6.190 3.255
VOA: 17.90 15.58 13.71 7.495

A liberal, friendly society exists.

FLIGHTS: Most places can be reached by air. Air Madagascar's 'Air Tourist Pass' allows unlimited travel for certain periods. SEA/RIVER/CANAL: Many coastal transport services. RAIL: Services operate in the East, North and South. ROAD: The road network is need of repair. Many are impassable during rainy season. BUS: Services are often unreliable. A flat rate is charged. TAXI/RICK-SHAW/STAGECOACH: Available.

The locals are very welcoming and have a very relaxed attitude towards time. To offer money for board and lodging could be considered an insult, tact is required. Respect should always be paid to local taboos. PHOTOGRAPHY: Do not take photographs of military establishments or the police.

Malawi

CAPITAL: Lilongwe

 GMT + 2

 FROM UK: 265   IDD: Y
OUTGOING CODE: 101

 Not present.

 High Commission for the Republic of Malawi, 33 Grosvenor Street, London W1X 0DE. Tel: (0171) 491 4172/7. Fax: (0171) 491 9916.

 British High Commission, PO Box 30042, Lingadzi House, Lilongwe 3, Malawi. Tel: 782 400. Fax: 782 657.

 Refer to the High Commission.

 Department of Tourism, PO Box 402, Blantyre, Malawi. Tel: 620 300. Fax: 620 947.

 Return Ticket Required. Requirements may be subject to change at short notice. Consult embassy before departure.
VALID PASSPORT REQUIRED BY ALL

 Visa not required. On arrival a 3 month Visa will be issued. Extensions will not normally be granted in Malawi.

 Departure tax US$20 payable in US currency unless a holder of a national passport when local currency will be accepted.

 POLIO, TYPHOID: R
MALARIA: Exists throughout the year in the Falciparum variety. Resistance to chloroquine has been reported.
YELLOW FEVER: A vaccination certificate is required by visitors travelling from infected areas within the last 6 days.
OTHER: Bilharzia and Rabies

 W1

 Kwacha (Mk) = 100 Tambala. Exch: Less well known currencies are difficult to exchange. There is limited acceptance of credit cards. American Express, MasterCard and Diners Club are accepted in the capital city and main hotels. US dollars and Pound sterling are the preferred currency in traveller's cheques.
ATM AVAILABILITY: Unavailable.

 MONEYGRAM: Unavailable.
WESTERN UNION: Unavailable.

 AMEX:+44 1273 696933
DINERS CLUB:No local number.
MASTERCARD:1 314 542 7111
VISA:No local number

 AMEX:+44 1273 571 600
THOMAS COOK:+44 1733 318950
VISA:+44 1733 318949

 0800–1300 Mon to Fri

 Malawi's economy fluctuates with developments in the climate. Currently the cost of living is reasonable due to the country's heavy borrowing.

 English, Chichewa and various other African languages.

 Winter: May–July and gets cold at night. Nov–Mar is the rainy season.

 Animist with Christian, Hindu and Muslim minorities.

 1998: Jan 1, 15; Mar 3; Apr 10, 13; May 1; June 15; July 6; Oct 14; Dec 25, 26, 28.
1999: Jan 1, 15; Mar 3; Apr 2, 5; May 1; June 15; July 6; Oct 14; Dec 25, 26, 27.

 220/240 Volts AC, 50 Hz Plugs = Various types used. Most modern buildings use square 3 pin.

 10 Days to Europe.

 BBC: 21.66 11.94 6.190 3.255
VOA: 21.49 15.38 9.530 6.035

 Women should cover their knees with appropriate clothing.

 RAIL: Regular but slow and expensive services. ROAD: All major and most secondary are all weather roads. DOCUMENTATION: UK licence is sufficient.

 Dress laws should be observed and respected. Long hair for men is disliked. Bag snatching is a problem in the main towns and cities. Be cautious of people who offer to act as guides.

Malaysia

CAPITAL: Kuala Lumpur

GMT + 8

FROM UK: 60   IDD: Y
OUTGOING CODE:00

All services: 999.

Malaysian High Commission, 45 Belgrave Square, London SW1X 8QT. Tel: (0171) 235 8033. Fax: (0171) 235 5161.

British High Commission, 185 Jalan Ampang, 50450 Kuala Lumpar, Malaysia. Tel: (03) 248 2122 or 248 7122 (consular section). Fax: (03) 248 0880.

Tourism Malaysia, 57 Trafalgar Square, London WC2N 5DU. Tel (0171) 930 7932. Fax: (0171) 930 9015.

Tourism Development Corporation of Malaysia, 24–27th Floors, Menara Dato'Onn, Putra World Trade Centre, 45 Jalan Tun Ismail, 50480 Kuala Lumpur, Malaysia. Tel: (3) 293 5188. Fax: (3) 293 5884.

Return ticket required. Requirements may change at short notice. Contact the embassy.

Valid Passport Required: must be valid for 6 months beyond the intended stay. All visitors must have proof of adequate funds for stay.

Most nationals do not require a visa providing the stay is less than a month and for social, business purposes. A visit pass is required which will be issued at the point of entry.

Visitors must declare valuables and may be required to pay a deposit. It is prohibited to import goods from Israel, pornography or any material including verses from the Koran.

R 40 for international departures, payable in local currency.

Women in an advanced state of pregnancy and those of a scruffy appearance will not be allowed entry.

POLIO, TYPHOID: R. MALARIA: Exists in certain inland regions e.g. Sabah where there is a risk in the Falciparum variety which has been reported as being highly resistant to chloroquine. YELLOW FEVER: A vaccination certificate is required if arriving from infected areas. OTHER: Cholera, Rabies.

W1

Ringgit (R) = 100 sen. All credit cards are accepted. Traveller's cheques are accepted by all banks, hotels and department stores. US dollar cheques are the preferable currency. ATM AVAILABILITY: Over 2000 locations.

MONEYGRAM: Unavailable
WESTERN UNION: Unavailable.
AMEX: +44 1273 696933
DINERS CLUB: (60) (3) 2611266
MASTERCARD: 800 804594
VISA: 800 80 2640
AMEX: (65) 7383383
THOMAS COOK: +44 1733 318950
VISA: +44 1733 318949

1000–1500 Mon to Fri, 0930–1130 Sat. Banks in Sabah usually open 0800 and close for lunch 1200–1400.

Can be reasonably inexpensive. Wide range of accommodation available. Goods and luxury items vary in price depending on location.

Bahasa Malaysian. English is also widely spoken.

Tropical without extremely high temperatures. Days are very warm whilst nights are fairly cool. Aug is the wettest time on the West coast. East Malaysia has heavy rains Nov–Feb. Rainfall differs in the East and West coast according to the Monsoon wind.

Muslim majority. Buddhist, Taoist, Confucianists, Hindu and Animist.

1998: Jan 1, 16, 28, 30*; Feb 1, 10, 15; Mar 14, 21, 30; Apr 7, 8, 10, 15, 19, 28, 29; May 1, 7*, 10, 28, 30–1; June 1, 6; July 6, 11, 19; Aug 31; Sept 12, 16; Oct 10*, 19, 24, 27; Nov 17; Dec 20, 25.
1999: Jan 1, 16, 28, 30*; Feb 1, 10, 15; Mar 14, 21, 30; Apr 7, 8, 10, 15, 19, 28, 29; May 1, 7*, 10, 28, 29–31; June 1, 6; July 6, 11, 19; Aug 31; Sept 12, 16; Oct 10*, 19, 24, 27; Nov 17; Dec 20, 25.

220 Volts Ac 50 Hz. Square 3 pin plugs are used.

There are post offices in the commercial centres of all towns.

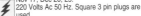

BBC:15.36   11.95   7.110   6.195
VOA:15.42   11.76   9.770   7.120

Malaysia is a multi-racial society. Although predominantly Muslim other cultures influence women's stature in society. Women travellers must respect the Muslim dress code where this applies. Do not walk alone at night on empty streets or beaches.

ROAD: Most roads are paved. BUS: Services are extensive. TAXI: There is a surcharge after 2400–0600 of 50%.

Respect religious beliefs – take off your shoes at the door and wear the appropriate clothing. Smoking is prohibited in a number of public places. Malaysia prides itself on an expansive range of cuisine. There are severe penalties for driving offences.

Maldives Republic

CAPITAL: Malé

 GMT + 5

 FROM UK: 960   IDD: Y
OUTGOING CODE: 00

 Police: 119; Fire: 118; Ambulance: 102.

Maldives High Commission, Nottingham Place, London W1M 3FB. Tel: (0171) 224 2135. Fax: (0171) 224 2157.

The British High Commission in Colombo deals with enquiries relating to the Maldives (see the entry for Sri Lanka).

Refer to the High Commission.

Ministry of Tourism, Boduthakurufaanu Magu, Malé 20 – 05, Maldives Republic. Tel: 323 224. Fax: 322 512.

 Return Ticket required. Requirements may be subject to short-term change. Contact the relevant authority before departure.
VALID PASSPORT REQUIRED BY ALL

 Tourist visas for 30 days will be issued to all visitors in possession of valid travel documents. NOTE: Visitors must be in possession of US$10 per day of stay.

 Alcoholic beverages, pornographic literature, idols of worship, pork products and certain other animal products may not be imported.

 US$10 is levied on all international departures.

 POLIO, TYPHOID: R
MALARIA: Malaria is disappearing. The last two incidents reported were in 1983.
YELLOW FEVER: A vaccination certificate is required from travellers coming from infected areas.
OTHER: Rabies, Hepatitis A, B and E can occur.

 W2 (the water in resort areas is generally safe).

 Maldivian Rufiya (Rf) = 100 laari. Most major island resorts will accept Amex, Visa, MasterCard, and Diners Club. Traveller's cheques are generally accepted in US Dollars.
ATM AVAILABILITY:Unavailable.

 MONEYGRAM: Unavailable.
WESTERN UNION: Unavailable.

 AMEX: +44 1273 696933
DINERS CLUB: No local number.
MASTERCARD: 1 314 542 7111
VISA: (1) 410 581 9091

 AMEX: (1) 801 964 6665
THOMAS COOK: +44 1733 318950
VISA: +44 1733 318949

 0900–1300 Sun to Thur.

As a luxury holiday destination the Maldives can be very expensive in the tourist centres.

 Dhivehi. English spoken in Malé and resorts.

 The climate is hot and tropical. There are two monsoons, the Southwest monsoon from May to Oct and the Northeast monsoon from Nov to Apr. The temperature rarely falls below 25ºC, even during the night. The best time to visit is November to Easter.

 Sunni Muslim.

 1998: Jan 1, 30*; Apr 7, 28; July 6, 26, 27; Nov 11, 12; 13.
1999: Jan 1, 30*; Apr 7, 28; July 6, 26, 27; Nov 11, 12; 13.

 220 volts Ac, 50 Hz. Round 2 pin plugs are used, although square pin plugs are becoming more common.

 Airmail to Western Europe takes about 1 week.

 BBC: 17.79 15.31 11.96 9.740
VOA: 17.74 15.37 9.760 6.110

 Women who are not involved in the tourist industry live in isolated communities on remote islands. The government enforces a strict Muslim code.

 SEA: Island hopping ferry services are available. ROAD: Travel on individual islands creates few problems since few of them take longer than half an hour to cross foot.

 Tourist resorts are self-contained, catering for the visitors' needs. Backpacking is prohibited. The government enforces standards restricting beach-wear outside the resorts. There are severe penalties for drug offences.

CAPITAL: Bamako

GMT

FROM UK: 223   IDD: Limited
OUTGOING CODE: 00

Not present.

No Embassy in the UK. EUROPE: Embassy of the Republic of Mali, 487 Ave Molière, B – 1060 Brussels, Belgium. Tel: (2) 345 7432. Fax: (2) 344 5700.

British Consulate BP 1598, Plan International, Bamako, Mali. Tel: 230 583. Fax: 228 143.

Refer to the Embassy in Belgium.

Ministry of Industry, Handicrafts and Tourism BP 1759, Bemako, Mali. Tel: 228 058. Fax: 230 261.

Return Ticket required. Requirements may be subject to change at short notice. Consult embassy before departure.
VALID PASSPORT REQUIRED

Visa required.

Cameras and film must be declared on arrival.

XOF 6000, for destinations in Africa. XOF 4500 or US$ 12 for international flights. Children under two years are exempt.

POLIO, TYPHOID: R.
MALARIA: Exists throughout the year in the falciparum variety. Resistance to chloroquine has been reported.
YELLOW FEVER: A vaccination certificate is required by travellers over one year of age arriving from all countries.
OTHER: Bilharzia, Cholera and Rabies.

W1

XOF Franc (XOF Fr) = 100 centimes Exch: should be available from most banks, however sufficient time must be allowed. French Franc notes are sometimes accepted in cash transactions. Limited use of MasterCard and Visa – they are accepted in the capital city only. Traveller's cheques: French francs are the preferred currency.
ATM AVAILABILITY: Unavailable.

MONEYGRAM: Unavailable.
WESTERN UNION: 22 50 89.

AMEX: No local number.
DINERS CLUB: No local number.
MASTERCARD: 1 314 542 7111
VISA: (1) 410 581 9091

AMEX: +44 1273 571 600
THOMAS COOK: +44 1733 318959
VISA: +44 1733 318949

0730–1200 and 1315–1500 Mon to Thur, 0730–1230 Fri.

Mali is one of the poorest countries in the world and is looking to develop a tourist industry.

French and some African languages are also spoken.

June–Oct is the rainy season. Oct–Feb is the cool season. Mar–May is the hot season.

Muslim with Christian and Animist minorities.

1998: Jan 1, 20, 30*; Mar 26; Apr 7*, 20; May 1, 25; July 6*, 21; Sept 22; Dec 25;
1999: Jan 1, 20, 18*; Apr 7*, 12; May 1, 25. July 6*, 21; Sept 22; Dec 25.

220 Volts Ac, 50 Hz. Larger towns in Mali have their own locally generated supply.

Airmail takes approximately two weeks to Europe. International post is limited to main towns and central post offices.

BBC: 17.79 15.07 12.09 9.410
VOA: 21.49 15.60 9.525 6.035

Women must dress modestly. Women travelling alone will arouse the attention of locals, even if visiting with a guide.

FLIGHTS: Limited provision. ROADS: Range from moderate to very bad. Driving can be difficult during the rainy season. Police check points frequently interrupt journeys.

Religious customs should be respected. The people are very proud of their traditions. Discussion of politics should be avoided. Travel to the north of the country should be avoided, and in some cases visitors should only travel in groups.

CAPITAL: Valletta

GMT + 1 (GMT + 2 during the summer).

FROM UK: 356   IDD: Y
OUTGOING CODE: 00

Police: 191; Ambulance: 196; Fire: 199.

High Commission of Malta, Malta House, 36–38 Piccadilly, London W1V 0PP. Tel: (0171) 292 4800. Fax (0171) 734 1832.
British High Commission, PO Box 506, 7 St Anne Street, Floriana, Valletta VLT 15, Malta. Tel: 233 134. Fax: 242 001.
Malta National Tourist Office, Malta House, 36–38 Piccadilly, London W1V 0PP. Tel: (0171) 292 4900. Fax: (0171) 734 1880.
National Tourism Organisation – (NTOM), 280 Republic Street, Valetta CMR 02, Malta. Tel: 224 444. Fax: 224 401.

Return Ticket required. Requirements may be subject to short-term change. Contact the relevant authority before departure.
VALID PASSPORT REQUIRED

Visa not required by nationals of the EU.

Pets are not allowed into Malta without prior approval from the director of Agriculture and Fisheries.

It is advisable to declare any large electronic equipment (e.g. video cameras, portable televisions) on arrival as this will prevent duty being levied on them on departure.

YELLOW FEVER: A vaccination certificate is required from travellers over 9 months of age arriving from infected areas.
OTHER: A cholera vaccination certificate may be required from travellers arriving from infected areas.

Maltese Lira (MTL) = 100 cents = 100 mils. Exch: Money can be exchanged at banks, some hotels and shops. NOTE: The import of local currency is limited to MTL 50. The export of local currency is limited to MTL 25. Credit cards and Traveller's cheques are accepted. The preferred currency for cheques is Pound sterling.
ATM AVAILABILITY: Over 100 locations.

MONEYGRAM: 0800 890 110.
WESTERN UNION: 235 751.

AMEX: +44 1273 696933
DINERS CLUB:N ot present.
MASTERCARD: 1 314 542 7111
VISA: (1) 410 581 9091

AMEX: +44 1273 571 600
THOMAS COOK: +44 1733 318950
VISA: +44 1733 318949

0800–1200 Mon to Thur, 0800–1200 and 1430–1600 Fri, 0800–1130 Sat.

Relatively inexpensive.

Maltese. English and Italian may also be spoken.

Mediterranean climate. Hot summers especially July–Sept, although there are cool breezes. Rain falls for very short periods. Winters are mild.

Roman Catholic.

1998: Jan 1; Feb 10; Mar 19; Apr 10; May 1; June 7, 29; Aug 15; Sept 8, 21; Dec 8, 13, 25.
1999: Jan 1; Feb 10; Mar 19; Apr 5; May 1; June 7, 29; Aug 15; Sept 8, 21; Dec 8, 13, 25.

240 volts AC, 50 Hz.

Good postal services exist within the island.

BBC: 17.64 15.07 12.09 9.410
VOA: 11.97 9.670 6.040 5.995

Revealing clothes should not be worn away from the beach / pool.

ROAD: BUS: Good local services operate from Luqa, Valletta, Sa Maison and Victoria (Gozo) to all towns. TAXI: Meter operated under governmental control. CAR HIRE: A number of firms are present and rates on Malta are amongst the cheapest in Europe. DOCUMENTATION: Full national driving licence is required.

Visitors should note the importance of the Roman Catholic church, i.e. modest dress should be adopted (legs and shoulders covered) when visiting churches.

CAPITAL: Fort-de-France

GMT –4.

FROM UK: 596 IDD: Y
OUTGOING CODE: 19

Police: 17; Fire/Ambulance: 18.

Martinique is an overseas territory of France therefore see the French Embassy in London.

British Consulate, Route du Phare, 97200 Fort-de-France, Martinique. Tel: 615 630. Fax: 613 389.

French West Indies Tourist Office, 178 Piccadilly, London, W1V 0AL. Tel: (0171) 629 2869. Fax: (0171) 493 6594.

Office du Tourisme, BP 520, Pavillon du Tourism, boulevard Alfasse, 97206 Forte-de-France, Martinique. Tel: 637960. Fax: 736693.

Return Ticket required. Requirements may be subject to short-term change. Contact embassy before departure.
VALID PASSPORT REQUIRED: As for France.

As for France.

Same as for France.

FFr 75 payable in local currency is levied on all foreign nationals.

As for France.

POLIO, TYPHOID: R
YELLOW FEVER: A vaccination certificate is required from travellers over 1 year of age coming from infected areas.
OTHER: Bilharzia, Tuberculosis.

W2

French Franc (FFr) = 100 centimes. Exch: US and Canadian Dollars are widely accepted. All major credit cards are accepted, as are Traveller's cheques, preferably in French francs or US dollars.
ATM AVAILABILITY: Unavailable.

MONEYGRAM: Unavailable.
WESTERN UNION: Unavailable.

AMEX: +44 1273 696933
DINERS CLUB: No local number.
MASTERCARD: 1 314 542 7111
VISA: (1) 410 581 9091
AMEX: (1) 801 964 6665
THOMAS COOK: 1 800 223 7373
VISA: 1 800 732 1322

0800–1600 Mon to Fri.

Expensive, especially in the tourist centres.

French (Creole dialect).

Warm all year round with most rain falling during the Autumn, although showers can occur all year round. Upland areas are cooler.

Roman Catholic.

1998: Jan 1; Feb 23–25; Apr 13; May 1, 8, 19. June 1; July 14, 21; Aug 15; Nov 1, 11; Dec 25.
1999: Jan 1; Feb 22–24; Apr 5; May 1, 8, 19, 31; July 14, 21; Aug 15; Nov 1, 11; Dec 25.

220/380 volts AC, 50 Hz.

1 Week. Airmail must be sent from post offices.

BBC: 17.84 15.22 6.195 5.975
VOA: 15.21 11.70 6.130 5.995

Usual precautions should be taken. Do not travel alone at night.

SEA: Scheduled ferries operate between the main ports. ROAD: The system is well developed and surfaced. BUS: A limited service operates. TAXI: Government controlled, plentiful and reasonably cheap if shared. CAR HIRE: Excellent car hire facilities are available. Bicycles can also be hired. DOCUMENTATION: An IDP is recommended, but a national driving licence is sufficient providing the driver has at least one year's experience.

The French influence is clearly evident. The usual social courtesies should be applied.

Mauritania

CAPITAL: Nouakchott

 GMT

 FROM UK: 222
IDD: Y in Nouakchott and Nouadhibou
OUTGOING CODE: International calls go through the operator

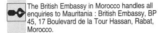 Not present.

Honorary Consulate of the Islamic Republic of Mauritania, 140 Bow Common Lane, London E3 4BH. Tel: (0181) 980 4382. Fax: (0181) 980 2232.

The British Embassy in Morocco handles all enquiries to Mauritania : British Embassy, BP 45, 17 Boulevard de la Tour Hassan, Rabat, Morocco.

Refer to the Honorary Consulate.

Société Mauritanienne de Tourisme et d'Hôtellerie (SMTH), BP 552, Nouakchott, Mauritania. Tel: 53351.

Return Ticket required. Requirements may change at short notice. Contact the embassy before departure
VALID PASSPORT REQUIRED

Visa required

Alcohol can not be imported.

US$ 2, payable on all international departures.

POLIO, TYPHOID: R.
MALARIA: Risk exists throughout the year in the falciparum variety.
YELLOW FEVER: A vaccination certificate is required for all travellers above one year of age, except travellers arriving from non-infected areas and staying less than two weeks in the country.
OTHER: Bilharzia, Cholera, Rabies.

 W1

Mauritanian Ougiya (U) = 5 Khoums. NOTE: Import and export of local currency is prohibited. Credit cards and Traveller's cheques (in French francs) have limited acceptance.
ATM AVAILABILITY: Unavailable.

 MONEYGRAM: Unavailable
WESTERN UNION: 25 36 36.

 AMEX: No local number.
DINERS CLUB: No local number.
MASTERCARD: No local number.
VISA: No local number.

AMEX: No local number.
THOMAS COOK: No local number.
VISA: No local number.

 0700–1500 Sun to Thur.

 Very inexpensive.

 Arabic and French. English is rarely spoken.

 Most of the country is dry and hot with little rain. South – Rainy season is July to Sept. The deserts are cool and windy in March and April.

 Islam.

1998: Jan 1, 30*; Apr 7*, 28*; May 1, 25; July 6*; Nov 28.
1999: Jan 1, 18*; Apr 7*, 28*; May 1, 25; July 6*; Nov 28.

127/220 Volts AC, 50Hz. Plugs = round 2 pin usually used.

2 weeks to Europe. Postal facilities limited to main cities.

 BBC: 17.83 15.40 9.600 6.005
VOA: 21.49 15.60 9.525 6.035

 Women should dress modestly due to the Islamic Influence.

RAIL: 1 line operates between Nouadhibou and Nouakchott which serves passengers for free, however this is not recommended as journeys are often long and arduous.
ROADS: Adequate but require 4 wheel drives. Sand storms may obscure vision in the dry season and may be impassable in the wet season.

 Respect should be paid to the Islamic traditions.

CAPITAL: Port Louis

 GMT + 4.

 FROM UK: 230   IDD: Y
OUTGOING CODE: 00

 Not present.

 Mauritius High Commission, 32 Elvaston Place, London SW7 5NW. Tel: (0171) 581 0294. Fax: (0171) 823 8437.

 British High Commission, Les Cascades Building, Edith Cavell Street, Port Louis, Mauritius. Tel: 211 1361. Fax: 211 1369.

 Mauritius Tourism Promotion Authority. At High Commission. Tel: (0171) 584 3666. Fax: (0171) 225 1135.

 Mauritius Tourism Promotion Authority, Emmanuel Anquetil Building, Sir Seewoosagur Ramgoolam Street, Port Louis, Mauritius. Tel: 201 1703. Fax: 212 5142.

 Return Ticket required. Requirements may be subject to short-term change. Contact the relevant authority before departure.
VALID PASSPORT REQUIRED BY ALL: The passport must be valid for 6 months.

 Visa not required by nationals of EU countries for stays up to 3 months.

 Narcotics and firearms.

 Mre300, or US$7. Transit passengers departing within 48 hours and those under 2 years of age are exempt.

 MALARIA: Exists in the vivax variety in the Northern rural areas, except on Rodrigues Island.
YELLOW FEVER: A vaccination certificate will be required from travellers over 1 year of age coming from infected areas.
OTHER: Bilharzia

 W1

 Mauritian Rupee (Mre) = 100 cents. All major credit cards are accepted. Traveller's cheques, preferably in US dollars or pound sterling, can be exchanged at banks and hotels.
ATM AVAILABILITY: Over 125 locations.

MONEYGRAM: Unavailable.
WESTERN UNION: Unavailable.

 AMEX: +44 1273 696933
DINERS CLUB: No local number.
MASTERCARD: 1 314 542 7111
VISA: (1) 410 581 9091

 AMEX: (1) 801 964 6665
THOMAS COOK: +44 1733 318950
VISA: +44 1733 318949

 0930–1430 Mon to Fri, 0930–1130 Sat (except for the Bank of Mauritius.

 It is possible to live relatively inexpensively by shopping away from the main tourist centres.

 English is the official language. The most widely spoken languages are Creole, Hindi, and Bhojpuri. French, Urdu and Chinese are also spoken.

 Warm coastal climate, especially from January to Apr. Tropical storms are likely to occur in the cyclone season (Dec–Mar). Sea breezes occur throughout the year.

 Hindu with Christian and Muslim minorities.

 1998: Jan 1–2, 28, 30; Feb 10, 25; Mar 12, 29; May 1; Aug 15, 27; Oct 19; Dec 25;
1999: Jan 1–2, 28, 30; Feb 10, 25; Mar 12, 29; May 1; Aug 15, 27; Oct 19; Dec 25.

 220 volts AC, 50 Hz. UK 3 pin type plugs are often used in hotels.

 Airmail to Western Europe takes approx. 5 days. Surface mail takes 4 to 6 weeks.

 BBC: 11.94 9.600 6.190 3.255
VOA: 17.89 15.60 9.575 6.035

 Women's roles are defined by whichever religion they follow. The usual precautions should be taken.

 ROAD: There is a good network of paved roads covering the island. BUS: There are excellent and numerous bus services to all parts of the island. CAR HIRE: There are numerous car hire firms. DOCUMENTATION: IDP is recommended, although a foreign licence is accepted.

 Visitors should always respect local customs and traditions. The hospitality received by visitors will be dependent on the religion and social customs of the host.

Mexico

CAPITAL: Mexico City

Spans 3 time zones from GMT – 6 to – 8

FROM UK: 52   IDD: Y
OUTGOING CODE: 98

All services 08.

Embassy of the United Mexican States, 42 Hertford Street, Mayfair, London W1Y 7TF. Tel: (0171) 499 8586. Fax: (0171) 495 4035.
British Embassy, Apartado 96 bis, Rio Lerma 71, Colonia Cuauhtemoc, 06500 Mexico DF, Mexico. Tel: (5) 207 2089. Fax: (5) 207 7672.
Mexican Ministry of Tourism, 3rd Floor, 60 – 61 Trafalgar Square, London WC2N 5DS. Tel: (0171) 734 1058. Fax: (0171) 930 9202.
Fondo Nacional de Fomento al Turismo (FONATUR), 17th Floor, Insurgentes Sur 800, Colonia de Valle, 03100 México DF, Mexico. Tel: (5) 687 2697.

Return Ticket required. Requirements may change at short notice. Contact the embassy before departure.
VALID PASSPORT REQUIRED BY ALL: must be valid for at least 6 months from the date of entry.

Visa usually required. Check the requirements with the appropriate consular authority.

Any uncanned foods, pork or pork products, plants, fruits, vegetables and their products. Firearms and ammunition and all pets and birds require an import permit.

US$ 13.37 for international departures. Children under 2 years of age are exempt.

POLIO, TYPHOID: R.
MALARIA: Exists in the Vivax variety in rural areas of certain states.
YELLOW FEVER: A vaccination certificate is required for travellers over 6 months of age arriving from infected areas.
OTHER: Rabies, Cholera – is a serious risk, precaution is strongly recommended. Travellers arriving within 2 weeks of having visited an infected area are required to have a vaccination certificate.

W1

Nuevo Peso (MXN) = 100 cents. All credit cards are accepted. US dollar Traveller's cheques are preferred.
ATM AVAILABILITY: Over 9,000 locations.

MONEYGRAM: 001 800 824 2220.
WESTERN UNION: 5 721 3080.

AMEX: +44 1273 696933
DINERS CLUB: (52) (5) 5801677
MASTERCARD: 95 800 307 7309
VISA: 95 800 847 2399
AMEX: (525) 326 3625
THOMAS COOK: 95 800 223 7373
VISA: 95 800 010 0588

0900–1330 Mon to Fri, some banks are open Sat afternoon.

Relatively inexpensive. Caters for all travellers and budgets.

Spanish is the official language. English is widely spoken.

Climate varies according to altitude. Lowland are hot and humid whilst higher areas have a more temperate climate.

Roman Catholic.

1998: Jan 1; Feb 5; Mar 21; Apr 8–10; May 1, 5; Sept 1, 16; Nov 2, 20; Dec 12, 24, 25, 31.
1999: Jan 1; Feb 5; Mar 21, 31; Apr 1, 2; May 1, 5; Sept 1, 16; Nov 2, 20; Dec 12, 24, 25, 31.

110 Volts AC, 60 Hz, US 2 pin, flat plugs are standard.

5–7 days to Europe, surface mail is slow.

BBC: 17.84 15.22 9.590 5.975
VOA: 15.20 11.91 9.775 6.130

There is inequality between men and women.

FLIGHTS: There is an excellent network of daily scheduled flights between commercial centres. RAIL: Mexico has a good rail network, which connects the major towns. ROAD: Slightly less than half is paved. BUS: Mexico is linked by an excellent and very economical bus service. CAR HIRE: Available at airports, city centres and resorts. DOCUMENTATION: IDP or nationals driving licence is acceptable.

Violent robbery is increasing. Exercise caution on public transport. Use taxis from ranks.

CAPITAL: Chisinau

 GMT + 2

 FROM UK: 373 IDD: Y (to major towns).
OUTGOING CODE: International calls go through the operator.

 Consult hotel on arrival.

 No Embassy in the UK. EUROPE: Embassy of the Republic of Moldova, 175 avenue Emile Max, 1040 Brussels, Belgium. Tel: (2) 732 9659. Fax: (2) 732 9660.
The British Embassy in Moscow deals with enquiries relating to Moldova. See the Russian Federation entry.

 Not present.

 Moldova – Tur, 4 Stefan cel Mare, 2058 Chisinău, Moldova. Tel: (2) 262 569. Fax: (2) 262 586.

 Requirements may be subject to short-term change. Contact the relevant authority before departure.
VALID PASSPORT REQUIRED BY ALL: must be valid for 6 months from date of arrival. In certain cases additional documentation may be required.

 Visa required.

 The import of local currency is prohibited by all foreign visitors.

 US$8 is levied on all foreign travel.

 Rabies, Hepatitis B.

 1 Leu (l) = 100 bani. Foreign currencies can be exchanged in hotels or bureaux de change. Moldova is essentially a-cash only economy. Credit cards and Traveller's cheques (US$) are accepted on a limited basis.
ATM AVAILABILITY: Unavailable.

 MONEYGRAM: Unavailable.
WESTERN UNION: 095 119 8250.

 AMEX: +44 1273 696933
DINERS CLUB: No local number.
MASTERCARD: 1 314 542 711
VISA: (1) 410 581 9091

 AMEX: +44 1273 571 600
THOMAS COOK: +44 1733 318950
VISA: +44 1733 318949

 0900–1200, Mon to Fri.

 Reasonably inexpensive.

 Russian. Romanian.

 The climate is pleasant and mild. The autumns are crisp and sunny and there is sometimes snow in the winter.

 Eastern Orthodox Christian and other Christian denominations. Some Jews are also present.

 1998: Jan 1, 7, 8; Mar 8; Apr 19, 20, 26–27; May 1, 9; Aug 27, 31.
1999: Jan 1, 7, 8; Mar 8; Apr 4, 5, 25–26; May 1, 9; Aug 27, 30.

 220 volts AC, 50 Hz.

 All mail to and from Moldova is subjected to long delays of up to 6 weeks. It is advisable to send recorded delivery to avoid loss.

 BBC: 17.64 15.58 12.10
VOA: No local number.

 Women enjoy equal status with men.

 ROAD: the road network covers 10,000km. TAXI: These can be found in front of the main hotels housing foreigners. Fares should be negotiated in advance although drivers prefer to charge per hour. Taxis run mostly on liquid gas hence the bottles, which are stored in the boot leave little room for luggage. CAR HIRE: Is available. DOCUMENTATION: IDP is required.

 Dress should be casual but conservative. Expensive jewellery and cameras should be kept out of sight. Travel to Transdniestria should be avoided, since it is not under Moldovan government control and the security situation is not under control. Do not share taxis with strangers.

CAPITAL: Monaco-Ville

GMT + 1 (GMT + 2 during the summer)

FROM UK: 377 IDD: Y
OUTGOING CODE: 00

Police: 17; Fire/Ambulance: 18.

Monaco Embassy and Consulate General, 4 Cromwell Place, London SW7 2JE. Tel: (0171) 225 2679. Fax: (0171) 581 8161.

British Consulate, BP 265, 33 boulevard Princess Charlotte, MC-98005 Monaco, Cedex. Tel: 93 50 99 66. Fax: 93 50 14 47.

Monaco Government Tourist and Convention Office, 3–18 Chelsea Garden Market, Chelsea Harbour, London SW10 0XE. Tel: (0171) 352 9962. Fax: (0171) 352 2103.

Direction du Tourisme et des Congrès de la Principauté de Monaco 2a boulevard des Moulins, M-C 98030 Monaco, Cedex. Tel: 92 16 61 16 (admin.) or 92 16 61 66 (information). Fax: 92 16 60 00.

See France.
VALID PASSPORT REQUIRED: See France.

See France.

See France.

Rabies

French Franc. See France for more details. All major credit cards are widely accepted. Traveller's cheques in French francs are preferred.
ATM AVAILABILITY: Over 40 locations.

MONEYGRAM: Single location in Monte Carlo.
WESTERN UNION: (05) 5542 5396.

AMEX: +44 1273 696933
DINERS CLUB: (33) (1) 47627575
MASTERCARD: 0 800 90 1387
VISA: 0 800 9 01235

AMEX: 0 590 8600
THOMAS COOK: +44 1733 318950
VISA: +44 1733 318949

0900–1200 and 1400–1630 Mon to Fri.

Very expensive, especially around the fashionable coast and social areas. .

French. Monegasque (mixture of French Provencal and Italian Lingurian). English and Italian may also be spoken.

Mild climate throughout the year. The hottest months are July–Aug and the coolest Jan–Feb. There is an average of only 60 days rain a year, usually during winter.

Roman Catholic with Anglican minorities..

1998: Jan 1, 27; Feb 24; Mar 17; Apr 13; May 1, 8, 21; June 1, 11; July 14; Sept 3; Nov 1, 2, 11, 19; Dec 8, 24–25.
1999: Jan 1, 27; Feb 24, Mar 9; Apr 5; May 1, 8, 20, 31; June 10; July 14; Sept 3; Nov 1, 19; Dec 8, 24–25.

220 volts AC, 50 Hz. Round 2 pin plugs are in use.

2–3 days.

BBC: 12.10 9.410 6.195
VOA: 9.760 6.040 1.195 5.995

Similar culture to the rest of Western Europe. However, usual precautions should be taken, by women travellers

RAIL: An extensive network runs through the principality connecting all the major towns. ROAD: COACH: There is a direct service connecting Nice airport with Monaco. BUS: There are good connections with the surrounding areas. DOCUMENTATION: As for France a national driving licence will suffice.

Kissing on both cheeks is the usual form of greeting. Formal wear is expected in restaurants, clubs and casinos, but casual clothing is acceptable elsewhere.

Mongolia

CAPITAL: Ulan Bator

 GMT + 9 (GMT + 8 during the summer).

 FROM UK: 976 (Followed by 1 for Ulan Bator).
IDD: N   OUTGOING CODE: 00

 Not present.

Embassy of Mongolia, 7 Kensington Court, London W8 5DL. Tel: (0171) 937 0150 or 937 5238. Fax: (0171) 937 1117. Visa section: (0171) 937 5238 ext. 29.

British Embassy PO Box 703, 30 Enkh Taivny Gudamzh, Ulan Bator 13, Mongolia. Tel: (1) 358 133. Fax: (1) 358 036.

 Refer to the Embassy.

Mongolian Tourism Association PO Box 10/195, Ulan Bator, Mongolia. Tel: (1) 323 363 or 320 219. Fax: (1) 323 363 or 320 219.

 Requirements may be subject to short-term change. Contact the relevant authority before departure.
VALID PASSPORT REQUIRED BY ALL

 Visa required

 Contact the Embassy as there is a long list of prohibited items. A customs declaration form must be completed on arrival and retained until departure.

 US$8.

 POLIO, TYPHOID: R.
OTHER: Rabies.

 W1

 Tugrik (MNT) = 100 mongos. Exch: Commercial banks in Ulan Bator and bureau de change at certain hotels. Credit cards are accepted by main commercial banks and large hotels. US dollars are the preferred currency in travellers cheques.
ATM AVAILABILITY: Unavailable.

MONEYGRAM: Unavailable.
WESTERN UNION: Unavailable.

 AMEX: +44 1273 696933
DINERS CLUB: No local number.
MASTERCARD: 1 314 542 7111
VISA: (1) 410 581 9091

 AMEX: (1) 801 964 6665
THOMAS COOK: +44 1733 318950
VISA: +44 1733 318949

 1000–1500 Mon to Fri.

 Very cheap for Mongolians although visitors are expected to pay ten times the prices charged to locals. Ask the price before you eat. Independent travel can be relatively cheap although tour groups may be charged very high prices.

 Khalkha Mongolian. Many dialects are spoken.

 Cool climate with short, mild summers and longer severe winters.

 Buddhist Lamaism is the main religion. Shamanism is also widespread.

 1998: Jan 1, 28; June 1; July 10; Nov 26.
1999: Jan 1, 27; June 1; July 9; Nov 26.

 220 volts AC, 50 Hz.

 Airmail to Europe takes up to 2 weeks.

 BBC: 21.71 15.36 9.740
VOA: 17.74 15.29 11.72

 Women have a minor role in society but this does not apply to foreigners.

 FLIGHTS: Internal flights are operated by Air Mongol. NOTE: It is not known whether maintenance procedures are properly carried out on internal flights. RAIL: The main route runs from North to South. ROAD: Paved roads can only be found in or near major cities. Most of the roads are unpaved. BUS: Services run between towns. CAR HIRE: Available through tourism companies.

 NOTE: As communications within Mongolia are poor, providing consular assistance can be difficult. Visitors may only enter Mongolia by air or train. Entry overland by other means is not permitted. Religious customs should be respected. Do not talk about death, divorce or accidents as mentioning this is considered a bad omen and will be taken seriously. SPECIAL PRECAUTIONS: Street crime is on the increase in Ulan Bator and visitors should exercise caution; do not go out on foot after dark.

Montserrat

CAPITAL: Plymouth

 GMT – 4

 FROM UK: 1809 followed by 491.
IDD: Y   OUTGOING CODE: 011

 Police: 999; Ambulance: 911.

 UK Passport Agency, Visas to British Dependant Territories, Room 203, Clive House, Petty France, London SW1H 9HD. Tel: (0990 210 410).

No Embassy present.

Montserrat Tourist Board, Suite 433, High Holborn House, 52–54 High Holborn, London WC1V 6RB. Tel: (0171) 242 3131. Fax: (0171) 242 2838.

Montserrat Tourist Board, PO Box 7, Marine Road, Plymouth, Montserrat. Tel: 2230 or 8730. Fax: 7430.

 Return Ticket required. Requirements may be subject to short-term change. Contact embassy before departure.
Valid Passport not required by Nationals of the UK and its colonies, who may enter as tourists with a form of identity for a maximum stay of 6 months.

 Visa not required

 Firearms. Cats and dogs require a veterinary certificate.

 US$ 6 or equivalent in any international currency.

 Visitors must have sufficient funds to finance stay and be in possession of onward or return tickets.

 POLIO, TYPHOID: R
OTHER: Bilharzia, Dengue Fever, Dysentery and Hepatitis A are present.

W2

East Caribbean Dollar (EC$) = 100 cents. Visa is widely accepted. Traveller's cheques are accepted in tourist areas. Pound sterling or US $ are the preferred currencies. ATM AVAILABILITY: 1 location only.

 MONEYGRAM: Unavailable.
WESTERN UNION: 491 2361.

 AMEX: No local number.
DINERS CLUB: No local number.
MASTERCARD: No local number.
VISA: (1) 410 581 9091
AMEX: (1) 801 964 6665
THOMAS COOK: 1 800 223 7373
VISA: 1 800 732 1322

 0800–1500 Mon, Tues and Thur, 0800–1300 Wed, 0800–1700 Fri.

 Following the volcanic eruption in 1996, the economy and the tourist industry have suffered.

 English.

 Subtropical climate and warm all year round. Most rain falls between Sept and Nov. The heavy cloud-bursts refresh the climate and once cleared the sun re-appears.

 Roman Catholic, Anglican, Methodist, other Christian denominations.

 1998: Jan 1; Mar 17; Apr 10, 13; May 4; June 1; Aug 3; Dec 25, 26, 31.
1999: Jan 1; Mar 17; Apr 2, 5; May 3, 31; Aug 2; Dec 25, 26, 31.

 120/220 volts AC, 60 Hz.

 1 Week.

BBC: 17.84 15.22 9.640 5.975
VOA: 15.21 11.70 9.590 6.130

 A blend of West Indian and British culture has resulted in a pleasant relaxed society.

 ROAD: A good network exists connecting all towns, but driving can be difficult for those not use to winding mountain roads. BUS: Scheduled buses run hourly. CAR HIRE: Available at the airport and hotels and is often included in the price of accommodation. DOCUMENTATION: A valid foreign licence can be used to purchase a temporary licence either at the airport or Plymouth police station.

 Access to some parts of the island is forbidden because of volcanic activity. Volcanic ash poses health problems. Consult the British Embassy for further information.

CAPITAL: Rabat

GMT

FROM UK: 212   IDD: Y
OUTGOING CODE: 00

Police: 19; Fire and Ambulance: 15.

Embassy of the Kingdom of Morocco, 49 Queens Gate Gardens, London, SW7 5NE. Tel: (0171) 581 5001. Fax: (0171) 225 3862.
British Embassy, BP 45, 17 Boulevard de la Tour Hassan, Rabat, Morocco. Tel: (7) 720 905/6 or 731 403/4. Fax: (7) 704 531. Consulates in Casablanca, Tangier, Agadir.
Moroccan National Tourist Office, 205 Regent Street, London, W1R 7DE. Tel: (0171) 437 0073/4. Fax: (0171) 734 8172.
Office Nationale Marocain de Tourisme, 31 angle rue Oued Fès, Avenue Al Abtal, Agdal, Rabat, Morocco. Tel: (7) 775 171. Fax: (7) 777 437.

Return Ticket required. Requirement may change at short notice. Contact the embassy before departure.
VALID PASSPORT REQUIRED

Visa not required. Contact embassy for the most recent list. Single entry, multiple entry and transit visas are granted

A permit is required for sporting guns and ammunition. This is obtainable from Police authorities, when a permit is already held in the passenger's country of residence.

Israeli passport holders are prohibited from entering as are those of 'scruffy' appearance.

POLIO, TYPHOID: R. MALARIA: A minimal risk of becoming infected exists at certain times of the year, in rural areas. OTHER: Bilharzia and Rabies.

W2

Moroccan Dirham (DH) = 100 Centimes.
NOTE: Import and Export of local currency is prohibited. It is advisable to bring sufficient money as bank transfers can take up to 6 weeks. Traveller's cheques and all major credit cards are accepted.
ATM AVAILABILITY: Over 250 locations.

MONEYGRAM: 002 11 0011 then 800 592 3688.
WESTERN UNION: (2) 20 8080.

AMEX: +44 1273 696933
DINERS CLUB: (212) (2) 299 455
MASTERCARD: 1 314 542 7111
VISA: (1) 410 581 9091
AMEX: +44 1273 571 600
THOMAS COOK: +44 1733 318950
VISA: +44 1733 318949

0830–1130 and 1430–1700 Mon to Fri (winter), 0800–1530 Mon to Fri (summer). These hours may vary during Ramadan.
Savings can be made at Souks. Bargaining is essential and can lead to purchases costing 1/3 of the original asking price.

Arabic with some Berber. French is widely spoken with Spanish in the North. English is understood in the North.

Mostly dry with high temperatures. The mountains are cooler. Inland is cooler than the coast.

Mainly Muslim with Jewish and Christian minorities.

1998: Jan 1, 11, 30*; Mar 3; Apr 7–28; May 1, 23; July 6*, 9; Aug 14, 20; Nov 6, 18.
1999: Jan 1, 11, 18*; Mar 3; Apr 7–28; May 1, 23; July 6*, 9; Aug 14, 20; Nov 6, 18.

110–120 Volts AC 50Hz is also common.

Up to 1 week, but can be unreliable

BBC: 17.70 15.07 12.09 9.410
VOA: 11.86 9.670 6.040 5.995

Muslim religious beliefs require women to dress modestly, covering arms and legs. Visitors often find themselves pestered by the local men. It is advisable to take a low profile and continue on your way if approached.

RAIL: Limited but cheap. Most have air conditioning, sleepers and restaurant cars.
ROADS: Major roads are all weather. Travelling in the mountains is difficult. CAR HIRE: available but expensive. DOCUMENTATION: 3rd party insurance is required and a green card. A UK licence is sufficient.

Mainly French social customs. Be courteous but wary of young boys selling goods or acting as guides. Beachwear should be confined to the beach and pool side. PHOTOGRAPHY: Ask permission before taking photos.

Mozambique

CAPITAL: Maputo

 GMT + 2

 FROM UK :258   IDD: Y
OUTGOING CODE: Outgoing International calls must go through the operator.

 All services: 493924 (Maputo only); Police: 119; Ambulance: 117; Fire: 198

 Embassy of the Republic of Mozambique, 21 Fitzroy Square, London W1P 5HJ. Tel: (0171) 383 3800. Fax: (0171) 383 3801.

 British Embassy, Caixa Postal 55, Avenida Vladimir I Lénine 310, Maputo, Mozambique. Tel: (1) 420 111/1/2/5/6/7. Fax: (1) 421 666.

 Refer to the Embassy.

 Empresa Nacionale de Tourismo (ENT) CP 2446, Avda 25 de Setembro 1203, Maputo, Mozambique. Tel: 421 794.

 Return Ticket required. Requirements may change at short notice. Contact the embassy before departure
VALID PASSPORT REQUIRED BY ALL: with a minimum validity of 6 months.

 Visa required.

 Narcotics.

 US$20, or US$10 if travelling within Africa.

 POLIO, TYPHOID: R.
MALARIA: Risk exists throughout the years across the whole country in the Falciparum variety. Reported as being highly resistant to chloroquine.
YELLOW FEVER: A vaccination certificate is required by all travellers over one year of age arriving from infected areas.
OTHER: Bilharzia, Cholera and Rabies.

 W1

Mozambique Metical (M) = 100 Centavos.
NOTE: import and export of local currency is prohibited. No credit cards or travellers cheques are accepted currently.
ATM AVAILABILITY: Unavailable

MONEYGRAM: Unavailable.
WESTERN UNION: 1 455 155.

 AMEX: No local number.
DINERS CLUB: No local number.
MASTERCARD: No local number.
VISA: No local number.

 AMEX: No local number.
THOMAS COOK: No local number.
VISA: No local number.

 0745–1115 Mon to Fri.

 Although civil war has ended, economy remains unstable.

 Portuguese in addition to many African languages.

 The climate varies according to the area. Inland is cooler with most rain between Jan and March. The coast is warm and dry Apr–Sept. Hottest and wettest between Oct–Mar.

 Christian (mainly Roman Catholic) with Muslim, Hindu and traditional beliefs.

 1998: Jan 1; Feb 3; Apr 7; June 25; Sept 7, 25; Nov 10; Dec 25.
1999: Jan 1; Feb 3; Apr 7; June 25; Sept 7, 25; Nov 10; Dec 25.

 220 Volts AC, 50Hz.

 Approximately 1 week by air to Europe. Available from main cities.

 BBC: 17.89 11.94 6.190 3.255
VOA: 21.49 15.60 9.525 6.035

 A higher population of women than men exists due to civil war.

 FLIGHTS: Air taxi services are available and are the safest means of travel outside the main cities due to the internal fighting. RAIL: All rail services are liable to disruption at present. BUS: Buses are available but plenty of food and water should be taken since journeys are frequently interrupted by check points to examine documents. DOCUMENTATION: IDP is required.

 NOTE: Armed robbery and other violent crimes are prevalent. There is also the risk of unexploded mines. Travel between major cities should only be undertaken in daylight. Casual wear is acceptable. Formal dress is seldom required.

CAPITAL: Yangoon (Rangoon)

 GMT + 6.30

 FROM UK: 95   IDD: Y to main cities.
OUTGOING CODE: 0

 Not present.

 Embassy of the Union of Myanmar, 19a Charles Street, Berkeley Square, London, W1X 8ER. Tel: (0171) 629 6966. Fax: (0171) 629 4169.

British Embassy, PO Box 638, 80 Strand Road, Yangoon, Myanmar. Tel: (1) 95300. Fax (1) 89566.

 No tourist office.

 No tourist office.

 Return ticket required. Requirements may change at short notice. Contact the embassy before departure.
VALID PASSPORT REQUIRED BY ALL

 Visa required

 Playing cards, gambling antiques, archaeological equipment and pornography. Jewellery must be declared and must obtain a permit from the Exchange Control Department to take jewellery totalling more than MMK 250 in value.

 US$8. Passengers in transit are exempt.

 POLIO, TYPHOID: R.
MALARIA: Exists in certain areas especially below 1000 m in the Falciparum variety, which is reported as being highly resistant to chloroquine.
YELLOW FEVER: A vaccination certificate is required if arriving from an infected area.
OTHER: Cholera, Japanese Encephalitis, Plague, Rabies.

 W1

 Kyat (MMK) = 100 pyas. Import and export of local currency is prohibited. Only 25% of foreign currency changed to Kyats can be re converted on exit. Keep receipt for customs checks on exit. Credit cards are not accepted, but travellers cheques can be exchanged.
ATM AVAILABILITY:Unavailable.

 MONEYGRAM: Unavailable.
WESTERN UNION: Unavailable.

 AMEX: No local number.
DINERS CLUB: No local number.
MASTERCARD: No local number.
VISA: No local number.
AMEX: (852) 885 9331
THOMAS COOK: +44 1733318950
VISA: +44 1733318949

 1000–1400 Mon to Fri.

 Can be high when compared with South East Asian countries standards especially when considering the low cost tourism facilities Myanmar has to offer.

 Burmese. Over 100 district languages are spoken. English is often spoken in business.

 Monsoon climate with 3 main seasons: Feb–May = hottest season with little or no rain. May–Oct = Rainy season. Oct–Feb = cooler.

 Mostly Therevada Buddhist. Hindu, Muslim, Christian and Animist minorities.

 1998: Jan 1, 4; Feb 10; Mar 2, 15, 27; July 30; Oct 27–31*; Dec 5, 21*, 25.
1999: Jan 1, 4; Feb 10; Mar 2, 15, 27; July 30; Oct 27–31*; Dec 5, 21*, 25.

 220/230 Volts Ac 50 Hz.

 Up to 1 week to Europe. It is recommended that correspondence is taken to the post office and registered for which a small fee will be charged.

 BBC: 15.36 11.95 9.740 3.915
VOA: 17.74 15.42 11.76 6.11

 Women must cover shoulders in religious buildings and should not wear shorts and short skirts.

 FLIGHTS: The most efficient way to move around Myanmar, but delays are frequent and scheduled flights are limited. SEA/RIVER: Regarded as the best way to see Myanmar but as delays are frequent allow plenty of time. DOCUMENTATION: IDP is required. BUS: There are long distance buses but they are not recommended due to their condition and the condition of the roads. RAIL: Several good services operate. Tickets should be purchased 2 hours in advance.

Keep to officially designated tourist areas. All internal travel must be by train, road or air. Cycling is strongly discouraged. Avoid discussion of politics. Political tension is high causing risk of sectarian violence. Avoid discussion of politics. Respect towards religious beliefs should be shown.

Namibia

CAPITAL: Windhoek

 GMT +2

 FROM UK: 264   IDD: Y
OUTGOING CODE: 09

 Police: 1011; Ambulance: 2032276;
Fire: 2032270.

 High Commission for the Republic of
Namibia, 6 Chandos Street, London, W1M
0LQ. Tel: (0171) 636 624. Fax: (0171) 637
5694.

 British High Commission, 116 Leutwein
Street, Windhoek, Namibia. Tel: (61) 223
022. Fax: (61) 228 895.

 Refer to the Embassy.

 Namibia Tourism, Private Bag 13346,
Windhoek, Namibia. Tel: (61) 284 2111. Fax:
(61) 221 930.

 Return Ticket required. Requirement may
change at short notice. Contact the embassy
before departure.
VALID PASSPORT REQUIRED BY ALL:
must be valid for 6 months after the date of
leaving Namibia.
Visa not required by nationals of EU
countries for stays of up to 3 months.

 Hunting Rifles need a permit. The import of
obscene literature, 2nd hand military clothing
is prohibited without special authorisation.

 POLIO, TYPHOID: R.
MALARIA: Exists in certain areas during periods of the year in the Falciparum variety.
YELLOW FEVER: A vaccination certificate is
required by those arriving from infected areas
excluding those under 1 year of age. If arriving by scheduled flights and are in transit a
certificate will not be required if passengers
do not leave the airport.
OTHER: Bilharzia, Cholera, Rabies.

 W2

 South African Rand (R) = 100 cents.
Namibian Dollar (N$) has also been intro-
duced. All currency must be declared at the
point of entry. Import and export of local currency is limited to N$500. Credit cards are
widely accepted. Traveller's cheques in
German DM currency are widely accepted.
ATM AVAILABILITY: 34 locations.

 MONEYGRAM: Unavailable.
WESTERN UNION: 461 246 970.

 AMEX: +44 1273 696933
DINERS CLUB: No local number.
MASTERCARD: 1 314 542 7111
VISA: (1) 410 581 9091

 AMEX: +44 1273 571 600
THOMAS COOK: +44 1733 318950
VISA: +44 1733 318949

 0900–1530 Mon to Fri, 0830–1100 Sat.

 Moderately expensive in urban areas, but
reasonably inexpensive in rural locations.

 English, Afrikaan, German and African
languages are spoken.

 The coast is cool and rain free most of the
year. Inland rain falls between Oct–Apr.
Summer temperatures are high.

 Christian majority.

 1998: Jan 1; Mar 21; Apr 10, 13; May 1, 4,
21, 25; Aug 26; Dec 10, 25, 26.
1999: Jan 1; Mar 21; Apr 2, 5; May 1, 4, 20,
25; Aug 26; Dec 10, 25, 26.

 220/240 Volts AC, Plugs are of the 3 pin
type.

 4 days to 2 weeks. Good airmail service
available.

 BBC: 17.88 15.42 6.190 3.255
VOA: 21.49 15.60 9.525 6.035

 Equal or higher social standing exists for
women in Namibia.

 ROADS: Are well maintained. FLIGHTS: Are
often the most economic way to travel. The
national airline links all the major cities. RAIL:
Trains operate between the main cities, and
offer first class and sleeping facilities. DOCU-
MENTATION: IDP is required.

 Western customs prevail. Do not enter the
Sperrgebiet (prohibited diamond area). Take
advice locally on which areas to avoid. Do
not enter the townships at night.

Nauru

CAPITAL: Yaren

 GMT + 12

 FROM UK: 674　　　　　　IDD: Y
OUTGOING CODE: Calls must be made through the international operator.

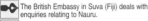 Contact local operator.

Nauru Government Office, 3 Chesham Street. London, SW1X 8ND. Tel (0171) 235 6911. Fax: (0171) 235 7423.

 The British Embassy in Suva (Fiji) deals with enquiries relating to Nauru.

 Refer to government office.

 Not present.

 Return Ticket required. Regulations may be subject to short-term change. Contact the embassy before departure.
VALID PASSPORT REQUIRED BY ALL

 Visa required, apart from those in transit providing they hold tickets for immediate travel to a third country.

 Nauruan artefacts may not be exported without a licence.

 A$ 10 per person over 12 years, on departure.

 POLIO, TYPHOID: R.
YELLOW FEVER: A vaccination certificate is required from travellers over 1 year of age arriving from infected areas.

W2

Australian Dollar (A$) = 100 cents. Credit cards are widely accepted. Traveller's cheques, preferably in Australian dollars, can be exchanged.
ATM AVAILABILITY: Unavailable.

 MONEYGRAM: Unavailable.
WESTERN UNION: Unavailable.

AMEX: +44 1273 696933
DINERS CLUB: No local number.
MASTERCARD: 1 314 542 7111
VISA: (1) 410 581 9091

 AMEX: (61) 2 886 0689
TC: +44 1733 318950
VISA: +44 1733 318949

 0900–1500 Mon to Thur, 0900–1630 Fri.

 The absence of taxes means some goods are cheaper e.g. electrical goods, cigarettes and alcohol. Visitors should buy essential goods in advance as shops are rather limited.

 Nauruan and English.

 A maritime, equatorial climate tempered by Northeast trade winds from Mar to Oct. The wettest period is from Mar to Oct. Hot all year round, wettest period – Dec to Mar.

 Christian, most Nauruan Protestant Church.

 1998: Jan 1, 31; Apr 10, 13–14; May 17; Oct 26; Dec 25, 26.
1999: Jan 1, 30; Apr 2, 5–6; May 17; Oct 26; Dec 25, 26.

 110/240 Volts Ac 50 Hz.

 Up to 1 week.

 BBC: 15.28　11.95　9.740　6.195
VOA: 15.43　15.18　9.525　1.143

 Western and Nauru culture co-exist.

 ROAD: A sealed road 19 km long circles the island and there are several miles of road running inland to Buada and the phosphate areas. Buses provide public transport. CAR HIRE: Available. DOCUMENTATION: A national driving licence is sufficient.

The island has a casual atmosphere in which diplomacy and tact are preferable to confrontation. Tourism is non-existent due to the environmental condition of the island following extensive phosphate mining throughout the 1990s.

Nepal

CAPITAL: Kathmandu

 GMT + 5.45.

 FROM UK: 977
IDD: Available in Kathmandu only.
OUTGOING CODE: 00

 Not present.

 Royal Nepalese Embassy, 12a Kensington Palace Gardens, London W8 4QU. Tel: (0171) 229 1594. Fax: (0171) 792 9861.

 British Embassy, PO Box 106, Lainchaur, Kathmandu, Nepal. Tel: (1) 410 583. Fax: (1) 411 789.

 Refer to Embassy.

 Ministry of Tourism, Tripureshnawar, Kathmandu, Nepal. Tel: (1) 211 286. Fax: (1) 227 758.

 Requirements may be subject to short-term change. Contact the relevant authority before departure.
VALID PASSPORT REQUIRED

 Visa required

 All baggage must be declared on arrival. Restrictions on the import of goods such as cameras, videos and electronic goods. Objects of archaeological or historical interest cannot be exported.

 NPR 700, or US$ 8, for international flights.

 POLIO, TYPHOID: R.
MALARIA: Exists in the vivax variety in many rural areas. The falciparum variety has also been reported and is highly resistant to chloroquine.
YELLOW FEVER: A vaccination certificate is required from travellers coming from infected areas.
OTHER: Cholera. High Altitude sickness. Japanese encephalitis. Hepatitis A and B. Meningitis.

 W1

 Nepalese Rupee (Rs) = 100 paisa. Exch: Obtain 'Foreign Exchange Encashment' receipts when changing currency – they may be needed when making transactions. Import of local and Indian currency is prohibited. Export of local currency is prohibited. Import

of foreign currency must be declared. Amex is widely accepted. MasterCard has a more limited acceptance. Traveller's cheques are accepted at banks and major hotels. US dollars are the preferred currency.
ATM AVAILABILITY: Unavailable.

 MONEYGRAM: Unavailable.
WESTERN UNION: (1) 223 530.

 AMEX: +44 1273 696933
DINERS CLUB: No local number.
MASTERCARD: 1 314 542 7111
VISA: No local number.

 AMEX: (1) 801 964 6665
THOMAS COOK: +44 1733 318950
VISA: +44 1733 318949

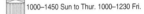 1000–1450 Sun to Thur. 1000–1230 Fri.

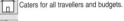 Caters for all travellers and budgets.

 Nepali, with Maithir and Bhojpuri.

 June–Oct: Summer and monsoon. Rest of the year is dry. Spring and autumn is the most pleasant time. Temperatures drop dramatically in the winter.

 Mostly Hindu and Buddhist with a small Muslim minority.

 1998: Jan 11, 29; Feb 12, 18; Mar 7, 8, 9, 24; Apr 7, 13, 16, 17; May 15; Sept 8; Nov 8; Dec 29.
1999: Jan 11, 29; Feb 12, 18; Mar 6, 8, 9, 24; Apr 7, 13, 16, 17; May 15; Sept 8; Nov 8; Dec 29.

 220 volts Ac, 50 Hz.

 Services are available at most centres. Post boxes should not be used for important communications.

 BBC: 17.79 15.31 11.75 9.740
VOA: 21.55 15.40 9.645 7.120

 An unspoilt country, where women play a traditional role.

FLIGHTS: A network of domestic flights links major towns. ROAD: The road system is of unpredictable quality. BUS: Services operate, but poor state of roads and high incidence of accidents make long-distance bus travel inadvisable. CAR HIRE: Hertz and Avis are present. NOTE: Driving and vehicle maintenance is poor and the cause of frequent accidents. DOCUMENTATION: An IDP is valid in Nepal for 15 days. A temporary licence can be obtained on presentation of a national licence.

 NOTE: The political situation is generally calm but demonstrations may occur and should be avoided. There have been recent outbreaks of political violence in the mid-west region.

The locals are superstitious and religious. Visitors are considered to be 'polluted' and are likely to be treated by the locals accordingly. Shoes should be removed before entering a local's home.

SPECIAL PRECAUTIONS: Do not trek on your own without a professional guide. Comprehensive travel insurance is essential and should cover all physical activities. Beware of the dangers of high altitude sickness. Travellers should register their presence with the British Embassy in Kathmandu.

The Netherlands

CAPITAL: Amsterdam

 GMT + 1 (GMT + 2 during the summer).

 FROM UK: 31 (followed by 20 for Amsterdam, 10 for Rotterdam, and 70 for the Hague)
IDD: Y   OUTGOING CODE: 00

 All services: 0611.

 Royal Netherlands Embassy, 30 Hyde Park Gate, London, SW7 5DP. Tel: (0171) 590 3200. Fax: (0171) 581 3458. Visa information line (0891) 171 217.

 British Embassy, Lange Voorhout 10, 2514 ED The Hague, The Netherlands. Tel: (70) 364 5800 or 427 0427. Fax(70) 427 0345.

 Netherlands Board of Tourism, PO Box 523, London SW1E 6NT. Tel: (0891) 717 777.

 Nederlands Bureau voor Toerisme PO Box 458, 2260 MG Leidschendam, The Nederlands. Tel: (70) 370 5705. Fax: (70) 320 1654.

 VALID PASSPORT REQUIRED: must be valid for at least 3 months after the last day of the intended visit.

 Visa not required by EU nationals.

 Cats and dogs cannot be imported, unless from Luxembourg or Belgium, without a health certificate and a rabies certificate. Firearms and ammunition can only be imported with a licence.

 Guilder (Gld) = 100 cents. Exch: Offices are indicated with the letters GWK. All major credit cards are accepted. Traveller's cheques, in any major international currency, are easily exchanged.
ATM AVAILABILITY: Over 6000 locations.

 MONEYGRAM: 0 800 022 3392.
WESTERN UNION: 06 0566.

AMEX:+44 1273 696933
DINERS CLUB:(32) (2) 5125793
MASTERCARD:0800 022 5821
VISA:0800 022 8498

AMEX:+44 1273 571 600
THOMAS COOK:0800 022 8630
VISA:0800 022 2431

 0900–1600 Mon to Fri.

 Similar to other Western European countries.

 Dutch. English, French and German are also spoken.

 Mild, maritime climate. Summers are generally warm with changeable periods but excessively hot weather is rare. Winters can be fairly cold with the possibility of some snow. Rainfall is prevalent all year.

 Roman Catholic and Protestant. Approx. 26% do not profess any religion.

 1998: Jan 1; Apr 10, 13, 30; May 21; June 1; Dec 25, 26.
1999: Jan 1; Apr 2, 5, 30; May 20; June 1; Dec 25, 26.

 220 volts AC, 50 Hz.

 Approx. 5 days within Europe.

 BBC: 9.410 6.195 3.955 0.648
VOA: 9.760 6.040 5.995 1.197

The women's movement is strong and has a firm foothold in society.

RAIL: The highly developed rail network is efficient and cheap. ROAD: Excellent road system. BUS: Extensive regional bus services exist. Long distance coach services operate between cities. TAXI: It is less usual to hail a taxi in the street in Holland. They are usually metered. CAR HIRE: Available from airports and main hotels. DOCUMENTATION: An international driving licence is not required as long as the licence from the country of origin is held. A 'green card' is advisable but not compulsory.

English is widely spoken and many locals will willingly use it. Casual clothes are acceptable everywhere. Possession of more than 30 grams of marijuana could lead to a hefty fine or even a jail sentence. Possession of hard drugs will result in immediate imprisonment.

CAPITAL: Noumea

 GMT + 11

 FROM UK: 687   IDD: Y
OUTGOING CODE: 00

 Emergency medical treatment: 15; Police: 17; Ambulance and Fire: 18.

 Refer to the French Embassy

 Refer to British Embassy in Paris.

 Refer to French Tourist Office.

 GIE Destination Nouvelle-Calédonie, BP 688, Immeuble Manhattten, 39–41 rue de Verdun, Nouméa, New Caledonia. Tel: 272 632 Fax: 274 623

 Return Ticket required. Regulations may be subject to short-term change. Contact the embassy before departure.
VALID PASSPORT REQUIRED

Visa not required by nationals of EU countries for a maximum of 3 months.

Contact the French Embassy for an up to date list.

POLIO, TYPHOID: R
YELLOW FEVER: A vaccination certificate is required from those over 1 year of age arriving from infected areas.

W2

French Pacific Franc (CFP Fr) = 100 centimes. Foreign exchange facilities available at the airport and trade bank. Credit cards are widely accepted. Australian dollar travellers cheques are accepted.
ATM AVAILABILITY: 8 locations.

MONEYGRAM: Unavailable.
WESTERN UNION: Unavailable.

AMEX: +44 1273 696933
DINERS CLUB: No local number.
MASTERCARD: 0 800 90 1387
VISA: (1) 410 581 9091

AMEX: (61) 2 886 0689
THOMAS COOK: 0800 90 8330
VISA: 0800 91 5617

 0730–1545 Mon to Fri.

 Accommodation varies from moderate to expensive. There is a youth hostel situated outside the city. Locally made food and other commodities are sold cheaply, but imported goods are expensive to buy.

 French. Polynesian, Melanesian and English are also spoken.

 Warm sub-tropical climate. Cool season is from June to Sept and the hottest period from Oct to May. The main rains are between Jan and March. Climate is tempered by trade winds.

 Roman Catholic and Protestant.

 1998: Jan 1, 2; Apr 13; May 1, 8, 21, 22; June 1; July 13–14; Aug 15; Sept 24; Nov 1, 11; Dec 24–25.
1999: Jan 1, 2; Apr 5; May 1, 8, 20, 22; June 1; July 13–14; Aug 15; Sept 24; Nov 1, 11; Dec 24–25.

 220 Volts AC 50 Hz

 Up to 1 week to Western Europe.

 BBC: 17.83 15.34 11.95 9.740
VOA: 18.82 15.18 9.525 1.735

 Local traditions and European culture co-exist. Usual precautions should be followed. Beach-wear should be confined to the beach.

 FLIGHTS: Services are operated by the national airline from the capital to various airfields on the island. SEA: There are regular sea links to the other smaller islands from Grande Terre. ROAD: Limited BUS: Available throughout the island. CAR HIRE: Major and smaller companies have agencies in the capital. DOCUMENTATION: IDP is required.

 New Caledonia houses the only casino in the South Pacific, situated at Anse Beach. Local traditions should be respected.

CAPITAL: Wellington

 GMT + 12 (GMT + 13 from the last week in March to the first week in Oct.)

 FROM UK: 64   IDD: Y
OUTGOING CODE: 00

 All services: 111.

New Zealand High Commission, New Zealand House, 80 Haymarket, London, SW1Y 4TQ. Tel: (0171) 930 8422. Fax: (0171) 839 4580.

British High Commission, PO Box 1812, 44 Hill Street Wellington 1, New Zealand. Tel (4) 472 6049. Fax: (4) 471 1974. Consulate in Auckland and Christchurch.

New Zealand High Commission, New Zealand House, 80 Haymarket, London, SW1Y 4TQ. Tel: (0839) 300 900 (recorded information).

New Zealand Tourism Board PO Box 95, 256 Lambton Quay, Wellington, New Zealand. Tel: (4) 472 8860. Fax: (4) 478 1736.

 Return Ticket required (except for nationals of Australia). Regulations may be subject to short term change. Contact the embassy before departure.
VALID PASSPORT REQUIRED
Visa not required by Nationals of the UK and other British Passport holders for visits of up to 6 months providing they have proof of the right of abode

 Visitors are advised not to take fruit or plant material with them. The New Zealand Government produces a full list of personal items which may be imported.

 NZ\$ 20, payable in local currency, on all departures. Transit passengers and children under 2 years are exempt.

 New Zealand Dollar (NZ\$) = 100 cents. All major credit cards accepted. Traveller's cheques in any international currencies, are widely accepted.
ATM AVAILABILITY: Over 1,500 locations.

 MONEYGRAM: 00 800 66639474.
WESTERN UNION: 0800 27 0000.

 AMEX: +44 1273 696933
DINERS CLUB: (64) (9) 3095465
MASTERCARD: 0800 44 9140
VISA: 0800 449 149

 AMEX: 0800 441068
THOMAS COOK: 0800 44 0112
VISA: 0800 44 0110

 0900–1630 Mon to Fri.

 It is possible to travel relatively cheaply in New Zealand.

English and Maori.

 Subtropical in the North island, temperate in the South Island. The North has no extremes of heat or cold, but winter can be quite cool in the South with snow in the mountains. Rainfall is distributed throughout the year.

 Anglican and Roman Catholic. Other Christian denominations are present.

1998: Jan 1, 2, 19, 26; Feb 2, 6; Mar 9, 23; Apr 10, 13, 25; June 1; Sept 22; Oct 23, 26; Nov 2, 13, 30; Dec 25, 26.
1999: Jan 1, 2, 19, 26; Feb 2, 6; Mar 9, 23; Apr 2, 5, 25; June 1; Sept 22; Oct 23, 26; Nov 2, 13, 30; Dec 25, 26.

 230 Volts AC 50 Hz. Most hotels provide 110 volt sockets AC for electric razors.

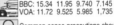 4–5 days to Western Europe, slightly less to the USA.

BBC: 15.34 11.95 9.740 7.145
VOA: 11.72 9.525 5.985 1,735

 Common sense precautions should be followed (e.g. not walking alone at night).

 FLIGHTS: The national airline operates flights between the main airports. RAIL: Reliable but limited. TRAVEL PASSES: allow unlimited travel on New Zealand Railways' train, coach and ferry services. ROAD: COACH: Modern coaches operate scheduled services throughout the country. It is advisable to make reservations for seats. – Contact the tourism board for details. BUS: Regional bus services serve most parts of the country. TAXI: Metered taxis operate throughout the country. CAR HIRE: Major international and local firms have agencies at airports and most major cities. Minimum age for driving a rental car is 21 years.

Should a visitor be invited to a Maori occasion the pressing of noses is common.

Nicaragua

CAPITAL: Managua

 GMT -6

FROM UK: 505   IDD: Y
OUTGOING CODE: 00

Police: 118, Fire: 265 0162, Ambulance: 265 1761.

Consulate General of Nicaragua, Vicarage House, 58–60 Kensington Church Street, London W8 4DB. Tel: (0171) 938 2373. Fax: (0171) 937 0952.

British Embassy, Apartado A – 169, El Reparto "Los Robles", Primera Etapa, Entrada principal de la Carretera a Masaya, 4a Casa a Mano Derecha, Mangua, Nicaragua. Tel: (2) 780 014 or 780 887 Fax: (2) 784 085.

Not present.

Instituto Nicaragüense de Turismo (Inturismo), Hotel Intercontinental, 1 cuadra al Oeste y L cuadra al Sur, Managua, Nicaragua. Tel: (2) 281 137 or 227 185 Fax: (2) 281 187.

 Return Ticket Required. Requirements may change at short notice. Contact the embassy before departure.
VALID PASSPORT REQUIRED: must be valid for a further 6 months (minimum).
Visa not required by Nationals of Ireland. Not required by Nationals of the UK for up to 90 days.

  Canned meats, dairy products, medicines without prescriptions and military uniforms.

US$ 18 on all departures, children under 2 years are exempt.

 POLIO, TYPHOID: R
MALARIA: Exists in the Vivax variety from June to Dec in the rural areas and the out-skirts of towns.
YELLOW FEVER: A vaccination certificate is required by travellers over one year of age arriving from infected areas.
OTHER: Rabies

 W1

Nicaraguan Gold Córdobe (NIO) = 100 centavos. Credit cards have limited use.
Traveller's cheques are accepted, preferably in US dollars.
ATM AVAILABILITY: Unavailable.

MONEYGRAM: 001 800 220 0038.
WESTERN UNION: (02) 668 126.

AMEX:+44 1273696933
DINERS CLUB:No local number.
MASTERCARD:1 314 542 7111
VISA:(1) 410 581 9091
AMEX:(1) 801 964 6665
THOMAS COOK:1 800 223 7373
VISA:1 800 732 1322

0800–1600 Mon to Fri, 0840–1130 Sat.

Relatively inexpensive but accommodation is in short supply.

Spanish. English is also spoken along the Mosquito Coast.

 Tropical climate. Rainy season: June–Nov. The mountains in the North are much cooler.

Roman Catholic.

1998: Jan 1; Apr 9, 10; May 1, 30; July 19; Aug 1, 10; Sept 14, 15; Nov 2; Dec 8, 25.
1999: Jan 1; Apr 1,2; May 1, 29; July 19; Aug 1, 10; Sept 14, 15; Nov 2; Dec 8, 25.

110 Volts AC, 60 Hz

Up to 2 weeks. Poste Restante is available in Managua.

BBC: 17.84 15.22 9.640 5.975
VOA: 15.21 11.91 9.590 6.130

 Some towns and cities run women's centres (casa de mujer), mainly consisting of women's clinics. There are no specific dangers facing women travellers in Nicaragua but the normal precautions should be taken.

ROADS: Tarred roads exist to San Juan del Sur and Corinto. CAR HIRE: Available in Managua or at the airport. This is the most convenient way of travelling because public transport is often over crowded. DOCUMENTATION: National licences are only valid for 30 days. BUS: There is a service to the main towns, booking seats in advance is recommended. TAXI: Fares should be agreed in advance.

 Violent outbursts and bandit like activities do take place preceding major political events. Be prepared for pick pocketing during your stay. PHOTOGRAPHY: Avoid taking photos of military installations. Do not walk alone at night.

Niger

CAPITAL: Niamey

GMT + 1

FROM UK: 227   IDD: Y
OUTGOING CODE: 00

Not present.

No Embassy in the UK. Europe: Embassy of the Republic of Niger, 154 rue du Longchamp, 75116 Paris, France. Tel: (1) 45 04 80 60. Fax: (1) 45 04 62 26.

Honorary British Vice – Consulate, BP 11168, Niamey, Niger. Tel: 732 015, 732 539 or 722 052.

Not present.

Office Nationale du Tourisme, Bp 612, avenue du Président H Luebke, Niamey, Niger. Tel: 732 447.

Return Ticket required. Requirement may change at short notice. Contact the embassy before departure.
VALID PASSPORT REQUIRED

Visa required.

Pornography is prohibited. A licence is required for sporting guns.

US$ 9, levied on all international flights.

POLIO, TYPHOID: R.
MALARIA: Exists throughout the country in the Falciparum variety. Resistance to chloroquine has been reported.
YELLOW FEVER: A vaccination certificate is required by all travellers arriving from all countries, over one year of age.
OTHER: Bilharzia, Cholera and Rabies

W1

CFA Franc. (CFA Fr) = 100 centimes. Access and Mastercard are accepted on a limited basis. Hotels, restaurants and most shops exchange travellers cheques. French francs are the preferred currency.
ATM AVAILABILITY: Unavailable.

MONEYGRAM: Unavailable.
WESTERN UNION: 73 31 01.

AMEX:No local number
DINERS CLUB:No local number
MASTERCARD:1 314 542 7111
VISA:(1) 410 581 9091

AMEX:+44 1273 571 600
THOMAS COOK:+44 1733 318950
VISA:+44 1733 318949

0800–1100 and 1600–1700 Mon to Fri.

Moderately expensive for tourists.

French, Hausa – spoken widely in addition to other African languages.

Summers are very hot from Oct–May. Heavy rains and high temperatures are common from July to Aug.

Mostly Muslim, the remainder Christian or Animist.

1998: Jan 1, 30*; Apr 7, 13, 24; May 1; July 6*; Aug 3; Dec 18, 25.
1999: Jan 1, 18*; Apr 5, 24; May 1; July 6*; Aug 3; Dec 18, 25.

220/380 Volts Ac, 50 Hz

Up to 2 weeks. Poste Restante operates.

BBC: 17.79 15.40 15.07 9.410
VOA: 21.49 15.60 9.525 6.035

Women are advised not to wear revealing clothes.

ROAD: Many are impassable during the rainy season. It is prohibited to travel on any other route than the one entered on your passport by the police in the previous town.
BUS: Daily buses operate between the cities although can be unreliable. DOCUMENTATION: IDP, Carnet de Passage and 2 photos are required. The min age to drive is 23.

HIGH RISK. Contact the FCO Travel Advice Unit for up to date information. Niger remains politically unstable and travellers should be careful when visiting rural areas. Traditional Muslim beliefs prevail and should be respected. Those travelling outside the capital should contact the Embassy first.
PHOTOGRAPHY : Permits are required from the police.

CAPITAL: Lagos

GMT + 1

FROM UK: 234   IDD: Y
OUTGOING CODE: 009

Not present.

High Commission for the Federal Republic of Nigeria, Nigeria House, 9 Northumberland Avenue, London, WC2N 5BX. Tel: (0171) 839 1244. Fax: (0171) 839 8746.

British High Commission, Private Mail Bag 12136, 11 Eleke Crescent, Victoria Island, Lagos Nigeria. Tel: (1) 619551 or 619531 or 619 537. Fax: (1) 666 909. Deputy High Commission – Kaduna.

Refer to the High Commission.

Nigerian Tourist Board, PO Box 2944, Trade Fair Complex, Badagry Expressway, Lagos, Nigeria. Tel: (1) 618 665.

Return Ticket required. Requirements may change at short notice. Contact the embassy before departure.
VALID PASSPORT REQUIRED

Visa required.

The import of champagne or sparkling wine will result in a heavy fine or imprisonment. US$20. Transit passengers and those under two years old are exempt.

POLIO, TYPHOID: R.
MALARIA: Exists throughout the year mainly in the Falciparum variety. Resistance to chloroquine has been reported.
YELLOW FEVER: A vaccination certificate is required from passengers over one year of age arriving from infected areas. Travellers are advised to have the vaccination if travelling outside the urban areas.
OTHER: Bilharzia, Cholera and Rabies.

W1

Naira (N) = 100 Kobo. NOTE: Import and export of local currency is limited to N50 in notes. Credit cards have a limited acceptance, and due to a prevalence of credit card fraud, their use is ill advised. Traveller's cheques are accepted but expect to pay a high commission. US dollars and pound sterling are the preferred currency.
ATM AVAILABILITY: Unavailable.

MONEYGRAM: Available.
WESTERN UNION: 1 266 35 62.

AMEX:+44 1273 696933
DINERS CLUB:(234) (1) 665 142
MASTERCARD:1 314 542 7111
VISA:(1) 410 581 9091

AMEX:+44 1273 571 600
THOMAS COOK:+44 1733 318950
VISA:+44 1733 318949

0800–1500 Mon, 0800–1330 Tues–Fri.

Local produce can be bought inexpensively, but accommodation and foreign imports, such as spirits, are very expensive.

English. There are over 250 local languages.

The Southern coast is hot and humid with rainy season Mar–Nov. The North's rainy season Apr–Sept. Nights are cold between Dec and Jan.

Islamic majority with Christian minority and many local religions.

1998: Jan 1, 29, 30; Apr 7, 10, 13; May 1; July 6; Oct 1; Dec 25, 26.
1999: Jan 1, 29, 30; Apr 7, 2. 5; May 1; July 6; Oct 1; Dec 25, 26.

210/250 Volts AC, 50Hz.

Unreliable and takes about 3 weeks.

BBC: 17.79 15.40 15.07 9.410
VOA: 21.49 15.60 9.525 6035.

Women should dress modestly and should not wear trousers.

FLIGHTS: Operate between the main cities. It is advisable to book in advance and account for delays which frequently occur.
ROADS: Secondary roads are often impassable during the rainy season. Caution is required when travelling in the South. DOCUMENTATION: IDP is required.

Armed robberies are prevalent in Lagos. Visitors are advised not to travel after dark outside the main tourist areas. Casual wear is suitable. Smoking in public places is illegal.

Niue

CAPITAL: Alofi

 GMT –11

 FROM UK: 683   IDD: Y
OUTGOING CODE: International calls go through the operator.

 Police: 999, Fire: 4133, Hospital: 998

 Contact the New Zealand High Commission in London.

 Not present.

 Refer to the New Zealand Tourism Board, New Zealand House, 80 Haymarket, London SW1Y 4TQ. Tel: (0171) 973 0363. Fax: (0171) 839 8929.

 Niue Tourism Office, PO Box 42, Alofi, Niue Tel: 4224 Fax 4225.

 Return Ticket required. Regulations may be subject to short-term change. Contact the embassy before departure.
VALID PASSPORT REQUIRED

 Visa not required by bone fide tourist staying less than 30 days with return or onward tickets and sufficient funds to finance stay. An entry permit is granted on arrival. Visas are required for all nationals staying over 30 years except those from New Zealand.

 Visitors are allowed to import 1 radio cassette player, 1 radio, I record player, 1 typewriter, 1 pair of binoculars, 1 camera, 1 movie camera or video.

 NZ$ 20, payable in local currency. Children under 5 year of age are exempt

 POLIO, TYPHOID: R
YELLOW FEVER: A vaccination-certificate is required from all travellers over 1 year of age arriving from an infected area.

 New Zealand Dollar (NZ$) Exch: The Westpac bank in Alofi can exchange currency. Credit cards are accepted in most restaurants and tour agencies. Traveller's cheques are not accepted.
ATM AVAILABILITY: Unavailable.

 MONEYGRAM: Unavailable.
WESTERN UNION: Unavailable.

 AMEX: +44 1273 696933
DINERS CLUB: No local number.
MASTERCARD: 1 314 542 7111
VISA: (1) 410 581 9091
AMEX: No local number
THOMAS COOK: No local number
VISA: No local number

 0900–1400 Mon to Thur. 0830–1400 Fri.

 Moderate to expensive. Accommodation, ranging from modern hotels to guest houses, is affordable to the budget traveller

 Niuean and English.

 Tropical climate bathed tempered by trade winds. Warm days and pleasantly cool nights.

 Mostly Ekalesai Niue, Latter day Saints, Roman Catholics, Seventh Day Adventists and Jehovas Witnesses.

 1998: Jan 1. Feb 6; Apr 10, 13, 25; June 14; Oct 19, 26; Dec 25, 26.
1999: Jan 1; Feb 6; Apr 2, 5, 25; June 14; Oct 19, 26; Dec 25, 26.

 230 Volts AC 50 Hz. Plugs are the standard 3 pin type.

 1–2 weeks.

 BBC: 15.36 11.95 9.740 7.145
VOA: 17.74 15.18 11.87 9.525

 Niuean women are regarded for their quality weaving, of hats, baskets, handbags and mats produced from indigenous plants, such as pandanus. Children are bestowed with gifts of money or handmade mats from their relatives upon coming of age. Girls also have their ears pierced, and boys receive their first haircut.

 There is no organised public transport.
ROAD: Badly damaged by a cyclone in 1990, some of the roads are paved. CAR HIRE: Can be hired on arrival although it is better to arrange it in advance. BIKES: Mountain bikes, motor bikes and motor scooters can also be hired on the island. DOCUMENTATION: As well as a national driving licence visitors will have to obtain a local licence from the Niue police station.

 Sunday is taken seriously as a day of rest and activities such as boating and fishing are not allowed.

CAPITAL: Oslo

GMT + 1 (GMT + 2 during the summer).

FROM UK: 47   IDD: Y
OUTGOING CODE: 095

Oslo Police: 002, Ambulance: 003.

Royal Norwegian Embassy, 25 Belgrave Square, London SW1X 8QD. Tel: (0171) 235 7151. Fax (0171) 245 6993. Consulates are in Edinburgh and Newcastle upon Tyne.

British Embassy, Thomas Heftyesgate 8, 0244 Oslo, Norway. Tel (22) 552 400. Fax: (22) 551 041. Consulates in Ålesund, Bergen, Harstad, Haugesund, Kristiansund (N), Kristiansand (S), Stavanger, Tronsø and Trondhiem.

Norwegian Tourist Board, Charles House, 5 Lower Regent Street, London SW1Y 4LR. Tel: (0171) 839 6255. Fax: (0171) 839 6014.

NORTRA (Norwegian Tourist Board) PO Box 2893 Solle, Drammensveien 40, 0230 Oslo, Norway. Tel (22) 925 200. Fax: (22) 560 505.

Requirements may be subject to change at short notice. Contact the relevant authority before travelling.
VALID PASSPORT REQUIRED. NOTE: Expired passports can not be considered as valid travel documents.

Visa not required by Nationals of the EU.

Spirits over 60% volume and wine over 22% volume alcohol. Certain food stuffs. Birds and animals.

Rabies is present on the island of Savlbard.

Norwegian Krone (Nkr) = 100 øre. NOTE: Import and export of local currency is limited to Nkr 25,000. All major credit cards are accepted. Traveller's cheques, preferably in US dollars, can be exchanged in banks, hotels and shops.
ATM AVAILABILITY: Over 2000 locations.

MONEYGRAM: 800 12419.
WESTERN UNION: Unavailable.

AMEX: +44 1273 696933
DINERS CLUB: (45) 36737373
MASTERCARD: 800 12697
VISA: (1) 410 581 9091

AMEX: 800 11 000
THOMAS COOK: 800 11 005
VISA: 800 11 815

0900–1700 Mon to Thur in major cities and 0900–1530 Fri.

Relatively expensive as in the other Scandinavian countries.

Norwegian. Lappish is spoken by Sami people in the North. The majority of people also speak English.

Coastal areas have a moderate climate. Inland areas are more extreme with hot summers and cold winters.

Mostly Evangelical Lutherans with other Christian denominations.

1998: Jan 1; Apr 8, 9, 10, 12, 13; May 1, 17, 21; June 1; Dec 24–26, 31.
1999: Jan 1; Apr 2, 4, 5, 7, 8; May 1, 17, 20, 31; Dec 24–26, 31.

220 volts AC 50 Hz. Plugs are the continental 2 pin type.

2–4 days within Europe.

BBC: 9.410 6.195 3.955 0.198
VOA: 9.760 6.040 1.197 0.792.

There is very little inequality between men and women in Norway.

RAIL: Connects main cities and Sweden. Substantial reductions can be gained through a 'Scanrail' pass. ROAD: The road system is of variable quality especially in the North during freezing conditions. BUS: Efficient service. DOCUMENTATION: IDP or national driving licence is required along with the vehicles log book. A 'green card' is strongly recommended.

Punctuality is very important especially if invited to someone's home. Lunch is the main meal of the day, but it is often eaten as late as 1700. Casual dress is acceptable everywhere during the day.

Oman

CAPITAL: Muscat

 GMT + 4.

 FROM UK: 698   IDD: Y
OUTGOING CODE: 00

 All services: 999

 Embassy of the Sultanate of Oman, 167 Queen's Gate London SW7 5HE. Tel: (0171) 225 0001. Fax: (0171) 589 2505.

 British Embassy, PO Box 300, 113 Muscat, Oman. Tel: 693 077. Fax: 693 087.

 Not present.

 Directorate General of Tourism , PO Box 550, 113 Muscat, Oman. Tel: 774 253. Fax: 794 238.

 Return Ticket required. Requirements may be subject to short-term change. Contact the relevant authority before departure.
VALID PASSPORT REQUIRED

 Tourist and Business Visas are required.

 Fresh foods, pornography, all animals need an import licence.

 OMR3 for all departures, payable in local currency. Transit passengers and those under 12 years of age are exempt.

 Holders of Israeli passports will be refused entry and transit.

 POLIO, TYPHOID: R
MALARIA: Exists in the falciparum variety throughout the country. Resistance to chloroquine has been reported.
YELLOW FEVER: A vaccination certificate is required from travellers arriving from infected areas.
OTHER: Cholera, Rabies.

 W1

 Omani Rail (OR) = 100 baiza. Amex and Diners Club are accepted. Traveller's cheques, preferably in US dollars or pound sterling, are easily exchanged.
ATM AVAILABILITY: 50 locations.

MONEYGRAM: Unavailable.
WESTERN UNION: 714 609.

 AMEX: +44 1273 696933
DINERS CLUB: (968) 706 007
MASTERCARD: No local number
VISA: No local number
AMEX: (973) 256 834
THOMAS COOK: +44 1733 318950
VISA: +44 1733 318949

 0800–1200 Sat–Wed and 0800–1130 Thur.

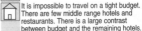 It is impossible to travel on a tight budget. There are few middle range hotels and restaurants. There is a large contrast between budget and the remaining hotels.

 Arabic and English.

 June–July are very hot. Rainfall varies according to the region.

 Ibadi Muslim with Sunni and Shia Muslim minorities.

 1998: Jan 30; Apr 7*, 28; July 6*; Nov 17–18; Dec 31.
1999: Jan 30; Apr 7*, 28; July 6*; Nov 16–17; Dec 31.

 220/240 volts Ac, 50 Hz.

 Up to 2 weeks to Western Europe.

 BBC: 15.57 12.10 11.76 9.410
VOA: 15.21 11.83 9.700 7.205.

 Although Oman displays a more tolerant attitude than it's neighbouring state, women should still dress modestly, in accordance with religious traditions.

 BUS: Services exist in Muscat and North Oman. TAXI: Prices are high and should be agreed in advance. NOTE: Visitors are not allowed to travel into the interior further up the coast than Seeb. DOCUMENTATION: Those who have a tourist visa can use their driving licence for up to 7 days. After 7 days a local licence is required and is available from the police station.

! Oman has only been open to the outside world for a short period therefore visitors should be sensitive to this. PHOTOGRAPHY: Signs will indicate areas where photography is prohibited. Collecting seashells, abalones corals, crayfish and turtle eggs is also forbidden. Avoid wearing shorts and tight-fitting clothes.

CAPITAL: Islamabad

 GMT + 5.

FROM UK: 92   IDD: Y
OUTGOING CODE: 00

Not present.

High Commission of the Islamic Republic of Pakistan, 35–36 Lowndes Square, London SW1X 9JN. Tel: (0171) 235 2044.

British High Commission, PO Box 1122, Diplomatic Enclave, Ramna 5, Islamabad Pakistan. Tel: (51) 822 131/5. Fax: (51) 823 439. Consulates in Karachi and Lahore.

Refer to the High Commission.

Ministry of Culture, Sport and Tourism, Block D, Pakistan Secretariat, Islamabad, Pakistan. Tel: (51) 214 697. Fax: (51) 815 767.
Return Ticket required. Requirements may be subject to short term change. Contact the relevant authority before departure.
VALID PASSPORT REQUIRED

Visa required.

Import of alcohol, matches, plants, fruit and vegetables and export of antiques is prohibited.
Rs 200 for economy class, payable in local currency (Rs 300 and 400 respectively for club and first class). There is an additional Foreign Travel Tax of Rs 700 on tickets issued within Pakistan. Transit passengers and those under 2 years of age are exempt.

POLIO, TYPHOID: R. MALARIA: Exists in the falciparum variety in all areas below 2000 m. It has been reported as being highly resistant to chloroquine. YELLOW FEVER: A vaccination certificate is required from all travellers coming from an infected area. Children under 6 months of age are exempt if the mother has proof of vaccination before the child was born. OTHER: Cholera, Rabies.

W1

Pakistani Rupee (Rs) = 100 paisa. Amex and Diners Club are widely accepted. Traveller's cheques are generally accepted at most banks, 4 and 5 star hotels and major shops. US dollars are the preferred currency.
ATM AVAILABILITY: 3 locations.

MONEYGRAM: Available in major cities.
WESTERN UNION: (21) 586 8261.

AMEX: +44 1273 696933
DINERS CLUB: (9221) 5868271 3
MASTERCARD: No local number
VISA: No local number
AMEX: (1) 801 964 6665
THOMAS COOK: +44 1733 318950
VISA: +44 1733 318949

0900–1300 and 1500–2000 Sun to Thur, closed Fri. Some banks open on Sat.

Staying in Pakistan can be relatively cheap if you are willing to shop at the markets and sacrifice luxuries.

Urdu and English. There are regional languages of Sindhi, Baluchi, Punjabi and Pashtu. There are numerous local dialects.

Three seasons: Winter (Nov–Mar) – warm but cooled by sea breezes. Summer (Apr–July) – extreme temperatures. Monsoon (July–Sept) – the highest rainfall on the hills.

Mostly Muslim with Christian and Hindi minorities.

1998: Jan 11, 30*; Feb 7; Mar 23; Apr 7, 28; July 1, 6*; Aug 14; Sept 6, 11; Nov 9; Dec 25, 31.
1999: Jan 11, 30*; Feb 7; Mar 23; Apr 7, 28; July 1, 6*; Aug 14; Sept 6, 11; Nov 9; Dec 25, 31.

220 volts Ac, 50 Hz. Round 2 or 3 pin plugs are in use.

Airmail takes 4 to 5 days to reach Western Europe.

BBC: 17.79   15.31   9.605   7.205
VOA: 21.55   15.43   9.760   6.070

Women should not wear tight or revealing clothing and should make sure arms and legs are covered. Strict Muslim rules always apply.

FLIGHTS: Many daily flights from Karachi to commercial centres. The quickest and most efficient means of travel. RAIL: Extensive rail network. Travel in air-conditioned coaches is advised along with reservations for longer journeys. ROAD: The highway network between cities is well made and maintained. BUS: Regular services between most towns and villages. Air-conditioned coaches are recommended for longer journeys. Advance booking is advised. TAXI: By far the most efficient mean of urban travel, being reasonably priced and widely available. CAR HIRE: Available in major cities. DOCUMENTATION: An IDP will be issued on presentation of a national driving licence.

Punjab region should be avoided as tourists are often targeted for political reasons. Muslim traditions and beliefs should be respected at all times. Mutual hospitality and courtesy are of great importance.

CAPITAL: Panama City

GMT – 5

UK: 507   IDD: Y
OUTGOING CODE: 00
Police: 104, Fire: 103, Ambulance: 225 1436/
228 2187.

Embassy of the Republic of Panama, 48 Park Street, London W1Y 3PD. Tel: (0171) 493 4646. Fax: (0171) 493 43333.

British Embassy, Apartado 889, Zona 1 4th and 5th Floor, Torre Banco Sur, Calle 53 Este, Panama 1, Republic of Panama. Tel: 690 866. Fax: 230 730.

Refer to the Embassy.

Instituto Panameño de Turismo (IPAT), Apartado, 4421, Centro de Convenciones ATLAPA, Via Israel, Panamá 5, Republic of Panama. Tel: 226 3167 or 226 4614. Fax: 226 3483.

Return Ticket required. Requirements may change at short notice. Contact the embassy before departure.
VALID PASSPORT REQUIRED

Visa Regulations are expected to change at short notice. Contact the consular authority before finalising arrangements. Panamanian immigration procedures are rigidly enforced. Non-compliance will result in transportation at the visitors expense to their country of origin.

Fruit, vegetables and animal products.

US$ 20 except for children under 2 years who are exempt.

Refer to the relevant Consular authority.

TYPHOID: R. MALARIA: Exists in the Vivax variety in certain areas. The Falciparum variety is also present in certain areas and is reported to be highly resistant to chloroquine.
YELLOW FEVER: Vaccination is strongly recommended for those planning to travel outside the urban areas. A vaccination certificate is recommended for those planning to visit the province of Darien. OTHER: Rabies

W2

Balboa (Ba) = 100 centesimos. Exch: Banks and Gambios. All major credit cards are accepted. Only US dollar travellers cheques are accepted.
ATM AVAILABILITY: Over 150 locations.

MONEYGRAM: 001 800 543 4080.
WESTERN UNION: 2 69 1055.

AMEX: +44 1273 696933
DINERS CLUB: 507 263 7922
MASTERCARD: 001 800 307 7309
VISA: (1) 410 581 9091

AMEX: (1) 801 964 6665
THOMAS COOK: 1 800 223 7373
VISA: 1 800 732 1322

0800–1330 Mon–Fri, 0830–1200 Sat.

Caters for all travellers and budgets.

Spanish. English is also spoken.

Hot all year with rains from May–Sept especially on the Pacific coast.

Roman Catholic.

1998: Jan 1, 9; Feb 23–25; Apr 9–11; May 1; Aug 15; Nov 3, 4, 10, 28; Dec 8, 24, 25, 31.
1999: Jan 1, 9; Feb 22–24; Apr 1–3; May 1; Aug 15; Nov 3, 4, 10, 28; Dec 8, 24, 25, 31.

120 Volts AC, 60 Hz. Plugs are flat 2 pin American type.

5–10 days.

BBC: 17.84 15.22 9.590 5.975
VOA: 15.12 11.58 9.775 5.995

A vibrant mixture of Spanish and American lifestyles dictates much of the culture. Inequality can still be a problem between men and women.

FLIGHTS: Internal air services are operated by local companies which Panama City share with all centres in the Interior. ROAD: BUS: Services between most large towns although they are very slow. TAXI: Fares are often not metered so agree fare in advance. CAR HIRE: Available in city centres and airports. DOCUMENTATION: A national driving licence will be sufficient.

Crime is rife in areas of the city. In the San Felipe district most of the cheap accommodation can be found, but it is not safe to venture out at night in this area. Colon is renowned for danger. Common sense precautions should be taken; deposit valuables in the hotel safe..

CAPITAL: Port Moresby

GMT + 10

FROM UK: 675   IDD: Y
OUTGOING CODE: 05
Police, Fire and Ambulance = 000. (NOTE : this is not accessible in some areas)

Papua New Guinea High Commission, 14 Waterloo Place, London, SW1Y 4AR. Tel: (0171) 930 0922. Fax: (0171) 930 0828.
British High Commission, PO Box 4778, Kiroki Street, Waigani, Boroko, Port Moresby, Papua New Guinea. Tel: 325 1677 or 325 1643 or 325 1645. Fax 325 3547.

Refer to High Commission.

Tourism Promotion Authority, PO Box 7144, Boroko, Papua New Guinea. Tel: 272 310 Fax: 259 119.

Return Ticket required. Contact the embassy before departure.
VALID PASSPORT REQUIRED: Passports should be valid for one year after entry.
Visa required. May change at short notice, contact the High Commission, who, on receipt of a stamped addressed envelope. can supply information sheets on how to apply for visas for Papua New Guinea.

Plants and soil, uncanned food of animal origin, unless from Australia or New Zealand, and all pig meat from New Zealand. Animals cannot be imported except for cats and dogs, which may be subject to lengthy quarantine.
PGK 15, in local currency, on all international flights. Children under 2 years and passengers not leaving the airport are exempt.

POLIO, TYPHOID: R. MALARIA: Exists all year throughout the country below 1800m. Falciparum is the dominant variety and reported to b highly resistant to chloroquine.
YELLOW FEVER: A vaccination certificate is required from travellers over one year of age arriving from infected areas. OTHER: Cholera – serious risk. Hepatitis A and B are endemic.

W1

Kina (PGK). Export of local currency is prohibited. Amex is widely accepted. Traveller's cheques are widely accepted in shops and hotels. Australian dollar cheques are preferred.
ATM AVAILABILITY: Unavailable.

MONEYGRAM: Unavailable.
WESTERN UNION: Unavailable.
AMEX: +44 1273 696933
DINERS CLUB: No local number
MASTERCARD: No local number
VISA: No local number
AMEX: (61) 2 886 0689
THOMAS COOK: +44 1733 318950
VISA: +44 1733 318949

0900–1500 Mon to Thur, 0900–1700 Fri.

Although accommodation varies from international hotels to basic huts, everything is very expensive.

English. 700 local dialects are also spoken.

Tropical climate which cools with increases in altitude. Most rain falls Dec–Mar.

Christian.

1998: Jan 1; Apr 10, 11, 13; June 15; July 18, 23; Sept 16; Dec 25, 26.
1999: Jan 1; Apr 2, 4, 5; June 15; July 18, 23; Sept 16; Dec 25, 26.

240 Volts AC 50 Hz. Australian style 3 pin plugs are in use.

7–10 days.

BBC: 15.36 12.28 9.740 6.195
VOA: 15.42 15.18 9.770 1.143.

The anthropological diversity found in Papua New Guinea is wide. Indigenous tribes inhabit the interior, whilst modern and cultural tolerance is found in the main cities. Women dress conservatively. It is unsafe for women to venture out alone in Papua New Guinea since there is a serious risk of sexual assaults near the main towns.

FLIGHTS: Services which operate are expensive. Internal services should be booked between November and February. ROAD: Limited. Public motor vehicles (PMV) are very efficient and provide a good way of meeting the locals. DOCUMENTATION: A national driving licence is sufficient. RIVERS: Commonly used as a thoroughfare.

Law and order remains poor. Incidents of rioting, looting and shooting occur without warning in major towns. Increase in violent crime requires extra care to be taken. Do not use public transport. Travellers should be met at Port Moresby upon arrival.

Paraguay

CAPITAL: Asuncion

GMT + 5

FROM UK: 595   IDD: Y

All services: 00.

Embassy of the Republic of Paraguay, Braemar Lodge, Cornwall Gardens, London, SW7 4AQ. Tel: (0171) 937 1253 or 937 6629. Fax: (0171) 937 5687.

British Embassy, Casilla 404, Calle Presidente Franco 706, Asuncion, Paraguay. Tel: (21) 44472 or 49146. Fax: (21) 446385.

Refer to Embassy.

Direccion General de Turismo, Ministerio de Obas, Pulicas Y Communicacions, Palma 468, Asuncion, Paraguay. Tel: (21) 441530. Fax: (21) 491230.

Return Ticket required. Requirements may change at short notice. Contact the embassy before departure.
VALID PASSPORT REQUIRED

Visa not required by Nationals of EU countries entering as tourists for stays up to 90 days.

Narcotics.

US$15 levied on all international departures excluding transit and those passengers who are under 2 years of age.

POLIO, TYPHOID: R.
MALARIA: Exists in the Vivax variety in some rural areas from Oct–May.
YELLOW FEVER: A vaccination certificate is required for visitors arriving from endemic areas. A certificate is also required for travellers leaving Paraguay to Endemic areas.
OTHER: Rabies.

W2

Guarani (G). Many of the expensive hotels will accept credit cards and exchange travellers cheques. US$ are preferred to sterling travellers cheques. Major credit cards are widely accepted, although Diners Club has a more limited acceptance.
ATM AVAILABILITY: Over 26 locations.

MONEYGRAM: 008 11 800 then 800 592 5755 (Spanish).
WESTERN UNION: (21) 211 060.

AMEX: +44 1273 696933
DINERS CLUB: 595 21 440706
MASTERCARD: 1 314 542 7111
VISA: (1) 410 581 9091

AMEX: (1) 801 964 6665
THOMAS COOK: 1 800 223 7373
VISA: 1 800 732 1322

0845–1215 Mon to Fri.

Accommodation is limited to the city and needs to be booked, in writing, well in advance. Other commodities tend to be moderately expensive.

Spanish. Guarani.

Sub-tropical climate. Hottest and wettest period is Dec–Mar.

Roman Catholic.

1998: Jan 1; Mar 1; Apr 9–10; May 1, 15; June 12; Aug 15; Sept 29; Dec 8, 25.
1999: Jan 1; Mar 1; Apr 1–2; May 1, 15; June 12; Aug 15; Sept 29; Dec 8, 25.

220 Volts AC, 50 Hz

5 days by airmail.

BBC: 17.82 15.22 11.75 9.590
VOA: 15.12 11.58 9.775 5.995

Culture is dominated by Roman catholicism.

FLIGHTS: Several visitor flights operate providing a popular view of local sites. RAIL : Services are unreliable and irregular. ROAD: Roads serving the main centres are in good condition. Approx. 10% of roads are unsurfaced and therefore impassable in poor weather. DOCUMENTATION: IDP and national driving licences are all accepted. BUS: The cheapest method of transport NOTE: for longer distances advance booking is necessary. Express links to major cities operate.

Beware of poisonous snakes. Paraguay is generally safer than its neighbours but common sense precautions should be followed.

CAPITAL: Lima

GMT – 5

FROM UK: 51   IDD: Y
OUTGOING CODE: 00

All services: 011 / 5114.

Embassy of the Republic of Peru, 52 Sloane Street, London, SW1X 9SP. Tel: (0171) 235 1917 or 235 6867 (visa section). Fax: (0171) 235 4463.

British Embassy, PO Box 854, Natalio Sanchez 125, Edificio El Pacifico, Pisos, 11 y 12, Plaza Washington, Lima 100, Peru. Tel: (1) 433 5032. Fax (1) 433 4738.

Refer to the Embassy.

Fondo de Promoción Turística (FOPTUR) Calle Uno, s/n Urb, Corpac, Lima 27, Peru. Tel: (1) 224 3142 or 224 3408. Fax: (1) 224 3133 or 224 3396. E-mail: postmaster@foptur.gob.peru

Return Ticket required. Requirements may change at short notice. Contact the embassy before departure.

VALID PASSPORT REQUIRED

Refer to the embassy for the latest visa information.

Seek up to date information from the relevant Consular authority.

US$ 17.70 is levied on all international departures except transit and those passengers under 2 years of age.

POLIO, TYPHOID: R. MALARIA: Exists in rural areas below 1500m in the Vivax variety. The Falciparum variety exists sporadically near national borders and where petroleum is being exploited and resistance to chloroquine has been reported. YELLOW FEVER: A vaccination certificate is required by visitors over 6 months travelling from infected areas. Vaccination is strongly recommended to all travellers who plan to journey out of the urban areas. OTHER: Cholera, Rabies.

W2. Street vendor food is not recommended

Nuevo Sol = 100 centimos Exch: Changing currency other than US$ can be difficult. Credit cards have limited acceptance outside Lima. Exchanging travellers cheques can prove a complex process outside of Lima. US dollar cheques are recommended. ATM AVAILABILITY: Over 430 locations.

MONEYGRAM: 001 800 824 2220.
WESTERN UNION: (1) 422 9723.

AMEX: +44 1273 696933
DINERS CLUB: (51 1) 221 2050
MASTERCARD: 1 314 542 7111
VISA: (1) 410 581 9091
AMEX: (1) 801 964 6665
THOMAS COOK: 1 800 223 7373
VISA: 1 800 732 1322

0930–1600 Mon to Fri. (Some banks open 0930–1230 Sat.)

Costs have increased dramatically in the last few years. Budget travellers can still find cheap accommodation, although the cities are much more expensive than rural areas.

Spanish and Quechua. English may also be spoken.

Coastal areas: Summer is Oct–Apr which is the rainy season in the mountainous regions. May–Sept is regarded as the best time to visit the mountains.

Roman Catholic.

1998: Jan 1; Apr 9–10; May 1; June 29; July 28–29; Aug 30; Oct 8; Nov 1; Dec 8, 25.
1999: Jan 1; Apr 1–2; May 1; June 29; July 28–29; Aug 30; Oct 8; Nov 1; Dec 8, 25.

200 Volts AC 60 Hz

Up to 2 weeks. Postal facilities are limited outside Lima.

BBC: 17.84 15.26 15.22 9.915
VOA: 15.21 11.58 9.775 5.995

Inequality exists between men and women.

RAIL: Can provide a scenic view of the landscape and sections are of the highest railway in the world. Connections are limited. ROAD: A recently built highway connects Lima with other cities. NOTE: Landslides are common in the rainy season making for slow travel. A 'Customs Duty Payment' badge must be displayed at all times. BUS: 'Greyhound' type buses operate along the Pan-American highway. TAXIS: Do not use meters so agree fare in advance. CAR HIRE: International companies have outlets in the major cities and airport. DOCUMENTATION: IDP is required.

Register with your Embassy when you arrive in Lima. Terrorist action may occur. Travel in groups is recommended. Street crime is common.

CAPITAL: Manila

 GMT + 8

 FROM UK: 63   IDD: Y to main towns.
OUTGOING CODE: International calls to smaller towns must go through the operator.

 Not present.

 Embassy of the Republic of the Philippines, 9a Palace Green, London W8 4QE. Tel: (0171) 937 1600. Fax: (0171) 937 2925.
British Embassy, 15th – 17th Floors, L V Locsin Building, 6752 Ayala Avenue Makati, Metro Manila 3116, Philippines. Tel (2) 8167116. Fax: (2) 819 7206.
Philippine Department of Tourism, 17 Albermarle Street, London W1X 7HA. Tel: (0171) 499 5443 (general enquiries) or (0171) 499 5652 (incentive travel). Fax: (0171) 499 5772.
Philippine Department of Tourism, Department of Tourism Building, Teodoro Valencia Circle, Rizal Park, Ermita, Manila, Philippines. Tel: (2) 599 031. Fax: (2) 501 567.

 Return Ticket required. Requirements may change at short notice. Contact the embassy before departure.
VALID PASSPORT REQUIRED
Visa not required by transit passengers.
Tourists and business travellers will not require visas if they have a valid passport for at least one year and onward tickets, providing their stay does not exceed 21 days.
NOTE: Certain nationalities will require pre arrival approval by the authorities in Manila before visas can be issued. Check with the embassy before making travel arrangements.

 Pornographic material, seditious or subversive material.

 PP500 for international departures, payable in local currency. Children under 2 years of age and transit passengers are exempt.

 POLIO, TYPHOID: R. MALARIA: Exists in certain areas below 600 m in the Falciparum variety, which has been reported as being highly resistant to chloroquine. OTHER: Bilharzia, Cholera and Rabies.

 W1

Philippine Peso (PP) = 100 centavos. Exch: Large commercial and central bank dealers in Manila. Always use authorised money changers or banks in Manila Metro area. Credit cards are accepted in larger cities. Traveller's cheques are widely accepted. US dollar cheques are the preferred currency.
ATM AVAILABILITY: Over 800 locations.

 MONEYGRAM: 1 800 111 0223
WESTERN UNION: (02) 811 1687.
AMEX: +44 1273696933
DINERS CLUB: (63) (2) 8190161 70
MASTERCARD: 1 800 1 111 0061
VISA: 1 800 1 111 0248
AMEX: (852) 885 9331
THOMAS COOK: +44 1733 318950
VISA: +44 1733 318949

 0900–1600 Mon to Fri.

 Can be relatively inexpensive in comparison with Northern and Western Europe. The Philippines is a haven for shoppers with bargains in all shops, but especially markets. Hotels range from the deluxe to small guest houses and prices vary accordingly.

Filipino. English is widely spoken and Spanish may also be spoken.

 Tropical climate with constant sea breezes. Rainy season: June–Sept. Oct–Feb is the cool dry season. Mar–May is usually hot and dry. Occasional typhoons June–Sept.

 Mainly Roman Catholic. Muslims, Christians, Buddhism and Taoists are also present.

 1998: Jan 1; Apr 9, 10; May 1; June 12; Aug 30; Nov 1, 30; Dec 25, 30, 31.
1999: Jan 1; Apr 8, 10; May 1; June 12; Aug 30; Nov 1, 30; Dec 25, 30, 31.

220 Volts AC 60 Hz. 110 Volts is available in most hotels. Plugs: flat and round 2- and 3-pin.

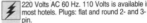 At least 5 days.

BBC:17.83 15.36 11.96 9.740
VOA:15.43 11.76 9.770 7.120

 Filipino women tend to be fairly conservative, in accordance with the general culture. Filipino men may make persistent advances to western women.

 FLIGHTS: Internal services are operated by several companies. Reservations should be confirmed prior to departure date due to high demand. BUS: Widely available and cheap. ROAD: Travel off national highways and paved roads, especially at night, is particularly dangerous.

 Tourists from the West are considered wealthy by the host population. Stick to the main tourist areas. Casual dress is acceptable in most areas, excluding Muslim areas where visitors will be required to cover up. The Philippines consist of over 7,000 islands. Charter planes may be hired to visit the most remote.

Poland

CAPITAL: Warsaw

GMT + 1 (GMT + 2 during the summer).

FROM UK: 48   IDD: Y
OUTGOING CODE: 00

Police: 997, Fire: 998, Ambulance: 999.

Embassy of the Republic of Poland, 47 Portland Place, London W1N 4GH. Tel: (0171) 580 4324/9. Fax: (0171) 323 4018. Consulate General of the Republic of Poland, 73 New Cavendish Street, London W1M 8LS. Tel: (0171) 580 0476 or (0891) 600358 (recorded information). Fax: (0171) 323 2320.

British Embassy, Aleja Roz 1, 00-556 Warsaw, Poland. Tel: (22) 628 1001/2/3/4/5. Fax: (22) 621 7161.

Polish National Tourist Office, First Floor, Remo House, 310–312 Regent Street, London W1R 5AJ. Tel: (0171) 580 8811. Fax: (0171) 580 8866.

Warsawfie Centrum Informacji Gurwstycznej (Warsaw Information Centre), Zankovu Square 1/13, 00-26 Warsaw. Tel: (22) 635 1881. Fax: (22) 310 464.

Requirements may be subject to short-term change. Contact the relevant authority before departure.
VALID PASSPORT REQUIRED
Visa not required by UK Nationals for tourist or business visits not exceeding 6 months.

Works of art and antiques cannot be exported.

US$ 10 levied on all international travel.

Rabies. Tick-borne encephalitis.

Zloty (Zl) = 100 grozy. Exch: border crossing points, hotels. NOTE: Import and export of local currency by non-residents is prohibited. All major credit cards and travellers cheques are accepted. Traveller's cheques in German Deutschmarks are preferred.
ATM AVAILABILITY: Over 500 locations.

MONEYGRAM: Single location in the capital.
WESTERN UNION: (22) 636 5688.

AMEX: +44 1273 696933
DINERS CLUB: (48) (22) 274513
MASTERCARD: 0 0800 111 1211
VISA: (1) 410 581 9091

AMEX: 00 44 0800 9591
THOMAS COOK: +44 1733 318950
VISA: +44 1733 318949

0800–1800 Mon to Fri.

Prices are no longer as cheap as they once were.

Polish. There is a German-speaking minority. English and French may also be spoken.

Temperate climate with warm summers and cold winters. Rain falls throughout the year.

Mainly Roman Catholic. The remaining are mainly Polish Orthodox.

1998: Jan 1; Apr 13; May 1, 3; Aug 15; Nov 1, 11; Dec 25, 26.
1999: Jan 1; Apr 5; May 1, 3; June 10; Aug 15; Nov 1, 11; Dec 25, 26.

220 volts AC, 50 Hz. Continental sockets are used.

4 days. Poste Restante facilities are available throughout the country.

BBC:15.07   12.09   6.195   3.955
VOA:9.670   6.040   5.995   1.197

Conservatism prevails among older women, but younger women have a broader liberal outlook on society. If travelling alone, foreign women may attract curiosity from local men. Take the usual safety precautions.

BUS: There are good regional bus and coach services. CAR HIRE: Various car rental agencies operate and rental also available at the airport. DOCUMENTATION: Travellers using their own cars should have car registration cards, a 'green card' for insurance purposes an valid insurance. An IDP is recommended though not compulsory.

Visitors are made welcome by the Poles, who are very hospitable. Roman Catholicism plays an important role in daily rural life. Conservative casual wear is acceptable for the day. More formal attire is suitable for social evenings out.
Visitors are advised to register with a hotel or local authorities within 48 hours of arrival. There is a serious risk of personal robbery on trains and at main rail stations. Passengers are at most risk when boarding trains. Never leave property unattended.

CAPITAL: Lisbon

GMT + 1 (GMT + 2 during the summer).

FROM UK: 351   IDD: Y
OUTGOING CODE: 00

All services: 115.

Embassy of the Portuguese Republic, Belgrave Square, London SW1X 8PP. Tel (0171) 235 5331/4. Fax: (0171) 245 1287. Portuguese Consulate, Silver City House, 62 Brompton Road, London SW3 1BJ. Tel: (0171) 581 8722/4 or (0891 600 202.

British Embassy, Rua de São Bernardo 33, 1200 Lisbon, Portugal. Tel (1) 396 1191 or 396 1147 or 396 3181. Fax (1) 397 6768. Consulates in Funchal (Madeira), Oporto, Ribeira Grande (Azores) and Portimão.

Refer to the Embassy.

ICEP/Turismo Placio Foz, Praça dos Restauradores, 1200 Lisbon, Portugal. Tel (1) 346 3643. Fax (1) 342 5231.

Requirements may be subject to short term change. Contact the relevant authority before departure.
VALID PASSPORT REQUIRED: Not required by Nationals of Ireland holding national ID cards.
Visa not required by Nationals of EU countries for stays up to 3 months.

Narcotics.

YELLOW FEVER: A yellow fever vaccination certificate is required from travellers over 1 year of age arriving in or destined for the Azores or Madeira if coming from infected areas.

W2

Escudo (Esc) = 100 centavos. NOTE: The personal export allowance is the equivalent of Esc 1,000,000 in foreign currency. The export of gold and other valuable is subject to special conditions. All credit cards are accepted and travellers cheques are easily exchanged. ATM AVAILABILITY: Over 5000 locations.

MONEYGRAM: 0501 8 11 435.
WESTERN UNION: (02) 207 2102.

AMEX: +44 1273 696933
DINERS CLUB: (351) (1) 3554011
MASTERCARD: 0501 11 272
VISA:0501 11 426

AMEX: 0505 449080
THOMAS COOK: 0505 44 9095
VISA: 0505 44 8307

Generally 0830–1500 Mon to Fri. Certain banks in Lisbon are open 1800–2300 Mon to Fri.

Relatively inexpensive and offers excellent value in transport, accommodation and food.

Portuguese.

Northwest: mild winters with a high rainfall and fairly short summers. Northeast: longer winters and hot summers. South: Summers are hot with little rain, high temperatures are moderated by a permanent breeze.

Roman Catholic.

1998: Jan 1; Feb 24; Apr 9, 10, 25; May 1, 18, 21; June 1, 10, 11, 13, 24; July 1; Aug 15, 21; Oct 5; Nov 1; Dec 1, 8, 24, 25.
1999: Jan 1; Feb 24; Apr 1, 2, 25; May 1, 18, 20; June 1, 10, 13, 24; July 1; Aug 15, 21; Oct 5; Nov 1; Dec 1, 8, 24, 25.

220 volts AC, 50 Hz, may vary in other areas. Continental 2 pin plugs are used.

3–5 days to the rest of Europe.

BBC:15.07 12.09 9.410 6.195
VOA:11.96 9.760 6.040 5.995.

Women who are travelling alone should not encounter many problems.

RAIL: Services are provided in every town. Cheap fares are available on 'blue' days – usually Monday afternoon to Thursday. Tourist tickets providing a period of unlimited travel are also available. ROAD: Every town can be reached by an adequate system of roads. TAXI: Charged according to distance and are metered. CAR HIRE: Available from main towns and airports. DOCUMENTATION: IDP or Foreign licence are accepted. Third party insurance is compulsory and a 'green card' must be obtained.

Politeness is essential. Beach wear should not be worn in towns. It is offensive to smoke during meal times.

Puerto Rico

CAPITAL: San Juan

 GMT – 4

 FROM UK: 1809   IDD: Y
OUTGOING CODE: 135 or 011, depending on the area.

 Police: 787 343 2020, Fire: 787 343 2330, All services: 911.

 As Puerto Rico is a commonwealth state of the USA, it is represented abroad by US Embassies and Consulates.

 British Consulate, American Airline Buildings 1101, 1509 Lopez Landron Street, Santurce 00911, Puerto Rico. Tel: 721 5193 or 728 6366.

 See USA TO address in the UK.

 Puerto Rico Hotel and Tourism Association, Suit 702, Plaza Centre, 954 Ponce de León Avenue, Miramar, Sancture 00907, Puerto Rico. Tel: 721 2400. Fax 725 2913.

 See USA.
VALID PASSPORT REQUIRED: Same as the USA.

 Same as the USA

 Same as for the USA.

 POLIO, TYPHOID: R
OTHER: Bilharzia and Rabies

 US Dollar (US$) = 100 cents. All major credit cards accepted. US dollars are preferred for travellers cheques.
ATM AVAILABILITY: Over 630 locations.

 MONEYGRAM: Unavailable.
WESTERN UNION: Unavailable.

 AMEX: +44 1273 696933
DINERS CLUB: 1 800 525 9040
MASTERCARD: 1 800 307 7309
VISA: 1 800 847 2399

AMEX: 1 800 221 7282
THOMAS COOK: 1 800 223 7373
VISA: 1 800 732 1322

 0900–1430 Mon to Thur, 0900–1430 and 1530–1700 Fri.

 Accommodates all types of travellers.

 Spanish. English is widely spoken.

 Hot tropical climate. The temperature varies little throughout the year. Cooler in upland areas.

 Roman Catholic, other Christian denominations and a Jewish minority.

 1998: Jan 1, 6, 13, 19; Feb 17; Mar 22; Apr 10, 12, 21; May 25; July 4, 25, 28; Sept 7; Oct 12; Nov 11, 19, 26; Dec 25.
1999: Jan 1, 6, 13, 19; Feb 17; Mar 22; Apr 2, 5, 21; May 25; July 4, 25, 28; Sept 7; Oct 12; Nov 11, 19, 26; Dec 25.

 120 volts AC, 60 Hz.

 Up to 1 week

 BBC:17.84 15.22 9.915 5.975
VOA:15.21 11.70 6.130 0.930

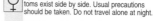 Spanish and American manners and customs exist side by side. Usual precautions should be taken. Do not travel alone at night.

 TAXI: A special service called a 'Linea' will pick up and drop off passengers where they wish. They operate between San Juan and most towns at a fixed rate. CAR HIRE: Available at the airport and city agencies. DOCUMENTATION: An IDP is required. BUS: Services operate in the cities although usually stop at 2100.

As well as offering lavish entertainment, notably casinos and a variety of nightlife, in the interior there are anthropological sights of interest, such as a replica of a Taino Indian village, near Guayama.

Qatar

CAPITAL: Doha

GMT + 3

FROM UK: 974   IDD: Y
OUTGOING CODE: 0

All services: 999

Embassy of the Sate of Qatar, 1 South Audley Street, London W1Y 5DQ. Tel: (0171) 493 2200. Fax: (0171) 493 2819.

British Embassy, PO Box 3, Doha, Qatar. Tel: 421 991. Fax: 438 692.

Not present.

Ministry of Tourism and Culture, PO Box 1836, Doha, Qatar. Tel: 831 333. Fax: 831 518.

Return Ticket and sufficient funds for stay are required. Requirements may be subject to short term change. Contact the relevant authority before departure.
VALID PASSPORT REQUIRED

Visa required.

All alcohol is prohibited. Animals can not be imported.

QR20, payable in local currency.

Those with passports containing a visa for Israel or holders of Israeli passports.

POLIO, TYPHOID: R.
YELLOW FEVER: A vaccination certificate will be required from travellers over 1 year of age arriving from infected areas. OTHER: Cholera, Rabies.

W1

Qatar Riyal (QR) = 100 dirhams. All credit cards and travellers cheques are widely accepted. US dollars and pound sterling are the preferred currency in traveller's cheques. ATM AVAILABILITY: Over 30 locations.

MONEYGRAM: Unavailable.
WESTERN UNION: 424 373.

AMEX: +44 1273 696933
DINERS CLUB: 974 439 596
MASTERCARD: 1 314 542 7111
VISA: (1) 410 581 9091

AMEX: (973) 256 834
THOMAS COOK: +44 1733 318950
VISA: +44 1733 318949

0730–1130 Sat–Thur.

Qatar is one of the richest countries in the world. Accommodation is hotel-based only, ranging from international to standard.

Arabic. Some English may be spoken.

Summers (June–Sept) are very hot with low rainfall. Spring and autumn are warm and pleasant.

Muslim

1998: Jan 30*; Apr 7–12; Sept 3; Dec 31.
1999: Jan 30*; Apr 7–12; Sept 3; Dec 31.

240/415 volts AC, 50 Hz.

Up to a week to Europe.

BBC: 15.57 12.10 11.76 9.140
VOA: 15.21 9.740 7.205 6.070.

Strict Muslim rules apply to all women. Single women may find they are unwelcome in some restaurants and hotels. Women should dress conservatively and only travel in the back seat when taking a taxi.

ROAD: Conditions can be poor when it rains. TAXI: Have black and yellow number-plates and are metered. CAR HIRE: Available from hotels and at the airport. DOCUMENTATION: A 90 day temporary driving permit will be granted on presentation of a national driving licence or IDP.

Qatar is more liberal than Saudi Arabia but not as liberal as Dubai or Bahrain. Extra care has to be taken on the roads. It is important to respect Muslim traditions and local customs – dress modestly and behave courteously

CAPITAL: St Denis

GMT + 4.

FROM UK: 262   IDD: Y
OUTGOING CODE: 19

Police: 17, Fire: 18, Ambulance: 15.

Réunion is an overseas Département of the Republic of France. See the entry for France to find the address of the French Embassy.

British Consulate, Kohjenta, 94B avenue Leconte de Lisle, 97490 Sante-Clotide, Réunion. Tel: 291 491. Fax: 293 991.

Refer to the French Consulate General in London or Comité du Tourisme de la Réunion, 90 rue la Boétie, 75008 Paris, France. Tel: (1) 40 75 02 79. Fax: (1) 40 75 02 73.

Office du Tourisme, 48 rue Saint-Marie, 97400 Saint-Denis, Réunion. Tel: 418 300. Fax: 213 776.

Contact the French Consular authority for up to date information as passport/visa requirements are subjected to constant change.
VALID PASSPORT REQUIRED: See France.

Visa requirements are constantly changing. It is advisable to contact the French Consular authority for current information.

See France.

Ffr10.

POLIO, TYPHOID: There is a risk of Typhoid.
YELLOW FEVER: A vaccination certificate is required from travellers over 1 year of age coming from infected areas.
OTHER: Rabies.

W1

French Franc (Ffr) = 100 centimes. Major cards are widely accepted although MasterCard has a more limited acceptance. Traveller's cheques in French francs are the preferred currency.
ATM AVAILABILITY: Unavailable.

MONEYGRAM: Unavailable.
WESTERN UNION: Unavailable.

AMEX: +44 1273 696933
DINERS CLUB: No local number.
MASTERCARD: 0 800 90 1387
VISA: (1) 410 581 9091

AMEX: (1) 801 964 6665
THOMAS COOK: 0800 90 8330
VISA: 0800 91 5617

0800–1600 Mon to Fri.

Wide range of hotels, inns and guest-houses, all of which are expensive.

French. Local Creole is also spoken.

The climate is hot and tropical but temperatures are cooler in the hills. The cyclone season is from Jan to Mar and brings hot but wet weather.

1998: As for France, with the addition of Dec 20.
1999: As for France, with the addition of Dec 20.

220 volts AC, 50 Hz.

Airmail to Western Europe takes up to 3 weeks.

BBC: 17.89 11.94 6.190 3.255
VOA: 17.76 15.60 9.575 6.035

Similar to Western Europe.

SEA: Four shipping lines run services around the island. ROADS: Fair and many of the highways are tarred. The island can be crossed easily by bus, taxi, or hired car. CAR HIRE: Available from the airport and Saint-Denis.

The locals follow French fashion. Licensing laws are unrestricted.

Romania

CAPITAL: Bucharest

GMT + 2 (GMT + 3 during the summer).

FROM UK: 40   IDD: Y
OUTGOING CODE: Dial 971 for international operator assistance.

Ambulance: 961, Police: 955, Fire: 981.

Embassy of Romania, Arundel House, 4 Palace Green, London W8 4QD. Tel: (0171) 937 9666/8. Fax: (0171) 937 8069. Visa section, Tel: (0891) 880 828.

British Embassy, Strada Jules Michelet 24, 70154 Bucharest, Romania. Tel: (1) 312 0303/4/5/6. Fax: (1) 312 0229, (1) 312 2594 or 312 3907.

Romanian National Tourist Office (Carpati), 83A Marylebone High Street, London W1M 3DE. Tel: (0171) 224 3692.

Nationals Tourist Office (Carpati) Boulevard Magheru 7, Bucharest 1, Romania. Tel: (1) 614 5160.

Return Ticket required. Requirements may be subject to short-term change. Contact the relevant authority before departure.
VALID PASSPORT REQUIRED BY ALL: Passports must have a minimum validity of 3 months after return.

Visa required.

Ammunition, explosives, narcotics, pornographic material, uncanned meat and animal and dairy products.

POLIO, TYPHOID: R. OTHER: A number of cases of cholera have been reported and travellers may want to take precautions. An epidemic of viral meningitis is currently affecting some parts of Bucharest. The ministry of health does not consider visitors to be at risk.

W2

Leu (plural Lei) = 100 bani. Exch: Visitors are advised to take hard currency, particularly US Dollars. Sterling can be easily exchanged in most resorts. Visitors are advised to shop around for the best rates of exchange. Do not use the black market. NOTE: The import and export of local currency is prohibited. Major credit cards are accepted in large hotels only. Traveller's cheques can only be used at the tourist office and for paying hotel bills. US dollar cheques are preferable.
ATM AVAILABILITY: Over 60 locations.

MONEYGRAM: 01 800 4288 then 800 592 3688.
WESTERN UNION: (1) 321 1609.

AMEX: +44 1273 696933
DINERS CLUB: 40 0 145160
MASTERCARD: 1 314 542 7111
VISA: (1) 410 581 9091
AMEX: +44 1273 571 600
THOMAS COOK: +44 1733 318950
VISA: +44 1733 318949

0900–1200 Mon to Fri. 1300–1500 Mon to Fri (currency exchange only).

Romania remains relatively inexpensive, since the move to modernise the economy following the 1989 revolution.

Romanian. Hungarian and German in border areas. English and French may be spoken by those involved with tourism.

Summer: inland is hot but the exterior is cooled by a sea breeze. Snow can fall throughout the country. Winters are mildest along the coast.

Romanian Orthodox, Roman Catholic. Lutheran, Muslim and Jewish minorities.

1998: Jan 1. Apr 19, 20. Dec 1, 25, 26.
1999: Jan 1. Apr 19, 20. Dec 1, 25, 26.

220 volts AC, 50 Hz. Plugs are of the 2-pin type.

Airmail to Western Europe takes up to 2 weeks.

BBC: 17.64 15.57 9.410 6.180
VOA: 9.760 6.040 1.197 0.792.

Women tend to be conservative in their behaviour in rural areas.

RAIL: 'Romanian State Railways' run efficient and cheap services. Seats must be reserved in advance for express and rapid trains. COACH: Local services operate to most towns and villages. TAXI: Can be hailed in the street or called from hotels. Prices are relatively low but drivers expect a tip. CAR HIRE: Available at hotels and the airport. Driving is very erratic so it may be wise to hire a driver. DOCUMENTATION: National driving licence or IDP and 'green card' insurance is required.

Petty crime is on the increase in Romania, particularly in Bucharest. PHOTOGRAPHY: Some tourist attractions charge visitors for photographs. Dress tends to quite conservative but casual clothes are usually suitable.

CAPITAL: Moscow

Moscow and St Petersburg + 3 (GMT + 4 during the summer). Other regions vary.

FROM UK: 7. When dialling from abroad the 0 of the area code must not be omitted. IDD: Y.
OUTGOING CODE: 810, in smaller cities international calls may go through the operator.

Fire: 01, Police: 02, Ambulance: 03.

Embassy of the Russian Federation, 13 Kensington Gardens, London W8 4QX. Tel: (0171) 229 3628. Fax: (0171) 727 8625. Consular Section: 5 Kensington Palace Gardens, London W8 4QS. Tel: (0171) 229 8027. Fax: (0171) 229 3215.

British Embassy, Soffiyskaya Naberezhnaya 14, Moscow 72, Russian Federation. Tel: (095) 956 7200. Fax: (095) 956 7420 or 956 7440 (visa section).

Intourist Travel Limited, Intourist House, 219 Marsh Wall, London E14 9PD. Tel: (0171) 538 8600. Fax: (0171) 538 5967.

Intourist, ulitsa Mokhovaya 13, 103009 Moscow, Russian Federation. Tel: (095) 292 3786 or 292 2300. Fax (095) 292 2034.

Return Ticket required. Requirements may be subject to short-term change. All travellers are advised to contact the nearest Russian Embassy or Consulate for up to date details.
VALID PASSPORT REQUIRED

Visa required.

Military weapons and ammunition, narcotics and drug paraphernalia. Pornography, loose pearls, fruit, vegetables and live animals. An information sheet is available from Intourist.

US$ 10 payable on international departures.

POLIO, TYPHOID: R.
OTHER: Cholera has been reported in Daghestan. Rabies is present.

W1

Rouble (Rub) = 100 Kopeks. Exch: Only at official bureaux. All transactions must be recorded on the currency declaration form issued on arrival. Keep your receipts. NOTE: Import and export of local currency is prohibited. All major credit cards are accepted. Traveller's cheques are preferred to cash but you should also take some hard currency. US dollar cheques are recommended.
ATM AVAILABILITY: Over 350 locations.

MONEYGRAM: Unavailable.
WESTERN UNION: (095) 119 8250.

AMEX: +44 1273 696933
DINERS CLUB: (095) 2843955
MASTERCARD: 1 314 542 7111
VISA: (1) 410 581 9091
AMEX: +44 1273 571 600
THOMAS COOK: +44 1733 318950
VISA: +44 1733 318949

0930–1730 Mon to Fri.

Moderate to expensive, since the change to free-market economy.

Russian. English, French or German are spoken by some people.

North and Central European Russia – variable climate. Winters can be very cold. Siberia – very cold winter. Considerable seasonal temperature variation. Summers are usually short and wet. Southern European Russia – winters are shorter than in the North.

Mainly Christian with the Russian Orthodox church being the largest Christian community. Muslim, Buddhist and Jewish minorities.

1998: Jan 2, 7; Mar 8, 9; May 1, 2, 4, 9; June 12; Nov 7, 9; Dec 12, 14.
1999: Jan 2, 7; Mar 8; May 1, 2, 3, 9; June 12; Nov 7, 9; Dec 12, 13.

220 volts AC, 50 Hz.

Airmail to Western Europe takes over 10 days.

BBC: 17.64 15.07 9.415 6.195
VOA: 15.20 9.765 6.040 5.995.

A mix of modern and traditional ideologies affect the way women are perceived. Since the move to democracy, old communist ideas persist especially amongst the older generation.

AIR: Aeroflot runs services from Moscow to major cities. RIVER: Many companies offer cruises along several rivers. RAIL: The rail system is vital due to the poor road system. Only a few long distance routes are open to use by visitors and reservations must be made on all journeys. NOTE: Do not leave possessions unattended. ROAD: The European part of the Russian Federation depends heavily on it's road network. The few roads in Siberia and further East are impassable in winter. It is worth planning your route in advance and arranging motoring holidays through Intourist or another reputable agency.

Each specific region has its own code of dress and traditions, which may be very different from those in the West. NOTE: Carry ID at all times. Incidents of violent mugging, theft and pick pocketing in all cities continue to occur. Keep all valuables out of sight.

Rwanda

CAPITAL: Kigali

 GMT + 2

 FROM UK: 250   IDD: N
OUTGOING CODE: All calls must go through the operator.

 All travellers should consult the foreign office in their country of residence regarding emergency assistance.

 Embassy of the republic of Rwanda, 42 Aylmer Road, London N2. Tel/Fax: (0181) 347 6967.

 British Consulate, BP 356, avenue Paul VI, Kigali, Rwanda. Tel: 75219 (office) 75905 (home).

 Travel for tourist purposes is not advised.

 Office Rwandais du tourisme et des parcs nationaux (ORTPN), BP 905, Kigali, Rwanda. Tel: 76514. Fax: 76512.

 Return Ticket required. Requirements may be subject to change at short notice. Contact the embassy before departure.
VALID PASSPORT REQUIRED

 Visa required by all nationalities, generally valid for 3 months.

 Departure tax US$20.

 POLIO, TYPHOID: R.
MALARIA: Exists throughout the year. Resistance to chloroquine has been reported.
YELLOW FEVER: A vaccination certificate is required by all travellers arriving over one year of age.
OTHER: Bilharzia, Rabies

 W1

Rwandese Franc (RwFr) = 100 centimes.
NOTE: Import and Export of local currency is limited to RwFr5000. There is limited acceptance of MasterCard. Traveller's cheques have limited acceptance. French francs are the preferred currency.
ATM AVAILABILITY: Unavailable

 MONEYGRAM: Unavailable
WESTERN UNION: Unavailable

 AMEX: No local number
DINERS CLUB: No local number
MASTERCARD: 1 314 542 7111
VISA: No local number

 AMEX: +44 1273 571 600
THOMAS COOK: +44 1733 318950
VISA: +44 1733 318949

 0800–1200 and 1400–1800 Mon to Fri, 0800–1300 Sat.

 Due to recent civil unrest, the economy has been decimated.

 Kinyarwanda and French. Kiswahili is also spoken.

 Rwanda is cool due to its high latitude, but warmer in the lowlands. Mid Jan–Apr and mid Oct–Dec are the rainy seasons.

 Christian (mainly Roman Catholic) with Islam and Animist minorities.

 1998: Jan 1, 30*; Apr 7; May 1; July 1, 4; Aug 15; Sept 25; Oct 1; Nov 1; Dec 25.
1999: Jan 1, 30*; Apr 7; May 1; July 1, 4; Aug 15; Sept 25; Oct 1; Nov 1; Dec 25.

 220 Volts AC 50Hz. There is no electricity supply at present but some hotels have their own generators.

 Approximately 2 weeks.

 BBC: 17.88 15.42 9.630 6.005
VOA: 21.49 15.60 9.525 6.035

 A volatile and patriarchal tribal culture exists.

 FLIGHTS: Internal flights are operated by the national airline to the main towns. ROADS: Most roads are unsealed and in bad condition. BUS: Services operate and a timetable is available. DOCUMENTATION: An IDP is required.

 NOTE: The FCO Travel Advice Unit advises against travelling to Rwanda unless on essential business. Supplies of water, fuel and power and accommodation are hard to find. Normal social courtesies apply. The traditional way of life is based on agriculture and cattle.

Saba

CAPITAL: The Bottom

 GMT – 4

 FROM UK: 599   IDD: Y
OUTGOING CODE: 00

 Police: 5994 63237

 No representation in the UK. EUROPE: Office of the Plenipotentiary of the Netherlands Antilles, Heiengiacht 19, 2511 EG The Hague, The Netherlands. Tel: (70) 362 4301. Fax: (70) 365 2679.

 British Consulate in Willemstad (See Curaçao entry) deals with enquiries relating to Saba.

 Not present.

 Saba Tourist Bureau, PO Box 527, Windwardside, Saba. Tel: (4) 62231. Fax (4) 62350.

 Return Ticket required. Requirements may be subject to short-term change. Contact embassy before departure.
VALID PASSPORT REQUIRED

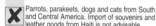 Up to date visa requirements can be obtained from the Office of the Minister Plenipotentiary of the Netherlands Antilles (address above).

 Parrots, parakeets, dogs and cats from South and Central America. Import of souvenirs and leather goods from Haiti is not advisable.

 US$ 2 to other Netherlands Antilles destinations, US$ 5 to other destinations.

 POLIO, TYPHOID: R.
YELLOW FEVER: A vaccination certificate is required from all travellers over 6 months of age coming from infected areas.

 Netherlands Antilles Guilder of Florin (NAG) = 100 cents. NOTE: Import and export of local currency is restricted to NAG 200. Mastercard and Visa are accepted in large establishments. Traveller's cheques in US dollars are preferred.
ATM AVAILABILITY: 10 locations approximately.

 MONEYGRAM: Unavailable.
WESTERN UNION: Unavailable.

 AMEX: No local number
DINERS CLUB: No local number
MASTERCARD: 1 800 307 7309
VISA: (1) 410 581 9091

 AMEX: (1) 801 964 6665
THOMAS COOK: 1 800 223 7373
VISA: 1 800 732 1322

 0830–1130 and 1330–1630 Mon to Fri.

 Accommodation on the island, ranges from guest houses around the area called The Bottom, to the more expensive at the coast.

 English is usually used. Dutch, the official language of the Netherlands Antilles is used for legal documents.

 Hot with cool sea breezes. Temperatures vary little throughout the year.

 Roman Catholic. Anglican and Wesleyan minorities.

 1998: Jan 1; Feb 23; Apr 10–13, 30; May 1, 21; Dec 25, 26.
1999: Jan 1; Feb 22; Apr 2, 5, 30; May 1, 21; Dec 25, 26.

 110 volts AC 60 Hz.

 4–6 days.

 BBC: 17.84 15.22 6.195 5.975
VOA: 15.21 11.58 9.590 5.995

 ROAD: Saba has one road 15 km long.
TAXIS: Are available. CAR HIRE: May be hired at Douglas Johnson's The Square Nickel.

 Saba has few tourists. Visitors tend to have a specific scientific interest.

St Eustatius

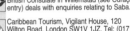

CAPITAL: Oranjestad

GMT – 4

FROM UK: 599   IDD:Y
OUTGOING CODE: 00

All services: 599 382211

Office of the Minister Plenipotentiary of the Netherlands Antilles, Heiengiacht 19, 2511 EG The Hague, The Netherlands. Tel: (70) 362 4301. Fax (70) 365 2679.

British Consulate in Willemstad (see Curaçao entry) deals with enquiries relating to Saba.

Caribbean Tourism, Vigilant House, 120 Wilton Road, London SW1V 1JZ. Tel: (0171) 233 8382. Fax: (0171) 873 8551.

St Eustatius Tourist Bureau, Fort Oranjestad z/n. Orangestad z/n, Oranjestad, St Eustatius, No local number. Tel/Fax (3) 82433.

Return Ticket required. Requirements may be subject to short-term change. Contact embassy before departure.
VALID PASSPORT REQUIRED

Up to date visa requirements can be obtained from the Office of the Minister Plenipotentiary of the Netherlands Antilles (address above).

Parrots, parakeets, dogs and cats from South and Central America. Import of souvenirs and leather goods from Haiti is not advisable.

US$ 3 to other Netherlands Antilles, US$ 4 for other international departures.

POLIO, TYPHOID: R.
YELLOW FEVER: A vaccination certificate is required from all travellers over 6 months of age coming from infected areas.

Netherlands Antilles Guilder of Florin (NAG) = 100 cents. NOTE: Import and export of local currency is restricted to NAG 200. Visa and Mastercard are accepted in large establishments. Traveller's cheques, preferably in US dollars are accepted.
ATM AVAILABILITY: 10 locations approximately.

MONEYGRAM: 001 800 872 2881 then 800 592 3688
WESTERN UNION: Unavailable.

AMEX: No local number
DINERS CLUB: No local number
MASTERCARD: 1 800 307 7309
VISA: (1) 410 581 9091

AMEX: (1) 801 964 6665
THOMAS COOK: 1 800 223 7373
VISA: 1 800 732 1322

0830–1130 and 1330–1630 Mon to Fri.

Despite the island's small size it has a variety of restaurants and accommodation at moderate prices.

English is the official language. Papiamento, French and Spanish are also spoken.

Hot climate with cooling sea breezes.

Protestant. Roman Catholic minority.

1998: Jan 1; Feb 23; Apr 10–13, 30; May 1, 21; Dec 25, 26.
1999: Jan 1; Feb 22; Apr 2, 5, 30; May 1, 21; Dec 25, 26.

110/220 volts AC 60 Hz.

4–6 days.

BBC: 17.84 15.22 6.195 5.975
VOA: 15.21 11.58 9.590 5.995

ROAD: A very small island with very few roads. The whole island can be walked around in a few hours. CAR HIRE and TAXI: Companies operate in Oranjestad. DOCUMENTATION: National licence is sufficient.

Twice a year sea turtles clamber onto the volcanic black sand to lay their eggs, and giant land crabs hunt on the beaches every night.

St Kitts & Nevis

CAPITAL: Basseterre

 GMT – 4

 FROM UK: 1 809   IDD:Y
OUTGOING CODE: 1 (Caribbean, Canada
and USA), 011 elsewhere.

 911

High Commission for Eastern Caribbean
States, 10 Kensington Court, London W8
5DL Tel: (0171) 937 9522 Fax: (0171) 937
5514.

The British High Commission in St Johns
(Antigua) deals with enquiries relating to St
Kitts and Nevis. See Antigua entry.

Refer to High Commission.

St Kitts & Nevis Department of Tourism

Return Ticket required. Requirements may be
subject to short-term change. Contact
embassy before departure.
VALID PASSPORT REQUIRED

Visa not required

 EC$ 27 (US$ 10). Children under 12 are
exempt.

 POLIO, TYPHOID: R
YELLOW FEVER: A vaccination certificate is
required from travellers over 1 year of age
coming from infected areas.

W2

Easter Caribbean Dollar (EC$) = 100 cents.
Amex and Visa are the only credit cards
accepted. Traveller's cheques in US dollars
are preferred.
ATM AVAILABILITY: 2 locations.

MONEYGRAM: 1 800 543 4080
WESTERN UNION: 465 8758

AMEX: +44 1273 696933
DINERS CLUB: No local number
MASTERCARD: No local number
VISA: (1) 410 581 9091
AMEX:(1) 801 964 6665
THOMAS COOK:1 800 223 7373
VISA:1 800732 1322

0800–1500 Mon to Thur, 0800–1500/1700
Fri, 0830–1100 Sat.

Very expensive, especially accommodation
although this is reduced in the low season.

English.

Hot tropical climate with cooling sea breezes.
Possibility of hurricanes Aug–Oct. Most rainfall during the summer May–Oct. Showers
may occur throughout the year.

Anglican Communion Church. Other
Christian Denominations.

1998: Jan 1, 2; Apr 10, 13; May 5, 19; Aug 3,
8; Sept 19; Dec 25, 26.
1999 Jan 1, 2; Apr 2, 5; May 5, 19; Aug 2, 8;
Sept 19; Dec 25, 26.

230 volts Ac, 60 Hz.

5–7 days.

BBC: 17.84 15.22 9.640 5.975
VOA: 15.21 11.70 6.130 5.995

 A fairly relaxed culture prevails. Usual precautions should be taken. Do not walk alone
at night.

SEA: There is a regular ferry service
between St Kitts and Nevis. ROAD: A good
road network on both island makes anywhere accessible within minutes. BUS: There
are private, regular but unscheduled buses,
which provide a comfortable service. TAXIS:
Services on both islands have set fares.
CAR & MOPED HIRE: Several agencies provide hire services. It is best to book cars
through the airline well in advance. DOCU-
MENTATION: A local temporary licence must
be obtained from the Police Traffic
Department before driving any vehicle. This
is readily issued on presentation of a valid
national licence and a fee of EC$ 30.

 Tourism is on the increase, especially on
Nevis. The islands are now commercialised
and all visitors are readily welcomed.
Suitable clothes should be worn for towns
and hotel/restaurants.

St Lucia

CAPITAL: Castries

 GMT – 4

 FROM UK: 1 809   IDD: Y
OUTGOING CODE: 011

 999

High Commission for Eastern Caribbean States, 10 Kensington Court, London W8 5DL. Tel: (0171) 937 9522. Fax: (0171) 937 5514.

 British High Commission, PO Box 227, Derek Walcott Square, Castries, St Lucia. Tel: 452 2484. Fax 453 1543.

 St Lucia Tourist Board, 421A Finchely Road, London NW3 6HJ. Tel: (0171) 431 3675. Fax: (071) 431 7920.

St Lucia Tourist Board, PO Box 221, Pointe Seraphine, Castries, St Lucia. Tel: 452 4094. Fax: 453 1121.

 Return Ticket required. Requirements may be subject to short term change. Contact embassy before departure.
VALID PASSPORT REQUIRED

 Visa not required by nationals of Great Britain.

 Narcotics and firearms.

 EC$20 or US$10. Transit passengers and children under 12 years of age are exempt.

 POLIO, TYPHOID: R.
YELLOW FEVER: A vaccination certificate is required from travellers over 1 year of age coming from infected areas.

 W2

Eastern Caribbean Dollar (EC$) = 100 cents. Exch: US$ gain a better rate. All major credit cards are accepted. Traveller's cheques in US dollars are preferred.
ATM AVAILABILITY: 3 locations.

MONEYGRAM: 1 800 872 2881 then 800 592 3688
WESTERN UNION: 452 4191.

 AMEX: +44 1273 696933
DINERS CLUB: No local number.
MASTERCARD: 1 800 307 7309
VISA: (1) 410 581 9091

 AMEX: (1) 801 964 6665
THOMAS COOK: 1 800 223 7373
VISA: 1 800 732 1322

 Generally 0800–1500 Mon to Thur, 0800–1700 Fri, 0800–1200 Sat.

 Caters for all types of budgets, with deluxe to self-catering accommodation.

 English. Local French patois is spoken.

 Hot tropical climate with cool sea breezes. Most rainfall occurs during the summer.

 Roman Catholic, Anglican, Methodist, Seventh Day Adventist, Baptist minorities.

 1998: Jan 1, 2; Feb 23–24; Apr 10, 13; May 1; June 1, 11; Aug 3; Oct 5; Dec 13, 25, 26.
1999: Jan 1, 2; Feb 22–23; Apr 2, 5; May 1, 11, 31; Aug 3; Oct 4; Dec 13, 25, 26.

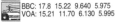 220 volts AC 50 Hz.

 Up to 1 week.

BBC: 17.8 15.22 9.640 5.975
VOA: 15.21 11.70 6.130 5.995

A multi-cultural society with colonial heritage exists. Usual precautions should be taken. Do not walk alone at night.

 ROAD: All major centres are served by a reasonably good road network. BUS: Services connect rural areas with the capital. TAXI: Cheap and easy to use – tipping is unnecessary. CAR HIRE: Available in the towns and at the airport. DOCUMENTATION: On presentation of a national or IDP a local licence will be issued.

St. Lucia is an island of contrasts with lush, green, volcanic vegetation in the interior, and long, unspoilt, white, sandy beaches. Beach wear should not be worn in towns.

St Maarten

CAPITAL: Philipsburg

 GMT – 4

 FROM UK: 599   IDD: Y
OUTGOING CODE:00

 Police: 599/5/222222
Ambulance: 599/5/22111.

 No representation in the UK. EUROPE:
Office of the Plenipotentiary of the
Netherlands Antilles, Heiengiacht 19, 2511
EG The Hague, The Netherlands. Tel: (70)
362 4301 Fax: (70) 365 2679.

 British Consulate in Willemstad (See Curaçao
entry) deals with enquiries relating to St
Maarten.

 Caribbean Tourism, Vigilant House, 120
Wilton Road, London SW1V 1JZ. Tel: (0171)
233 8382 Fax: (0171) 873 8551.

 St Maarten Tourist Board, 23 Walter Nisbeth
Road, Imperial Building, Philipsburg, St
Maarten. Tel: (5) 22337 Fax: (5) 22734.

 Return Ticket required. Requirements may be
subject to short-term change. Contact
embassy before departure.
VALID PASSPORT REQUIRED

 Up to date visa requirements can be obtained
from the Office of the Minister Plenipotentiary
of the Netherlands Antilles (address above).

 Parrots, parakeets, dogs and cats from South
and Central America. Import of souvenirs and
leather goods from Haiti is not advisable.

 US$ 10 for all international departures. US$ 5
for departures to other Caribbean islands.
Transit passengers and those under 2 years
of age are exempt.

 POLIO, TYPHOID: R
YELLOW FEVER: A vaccination certificate is
required from travellers over 1 year of age
coming from infected areas.

 Netherlands Antilles Guilder of Florin (NAG) =
100 cents. NOTE: Import and export of local
currency is restricted to NAG 200.
Mastercard and Visa are accepted in large
establishments. Traveller's cheques are
accepted, US dollars and French francs are
the most welcome.
ATM AVAILABILITY: 10 locations.

 MONEYGRAM: 001 800 872 2881 then 800
592 3688
WESTERN UNION: 5995 22403.

 AMEX: +44 1273 696933
DINERS CLUB: No local number.
MASTERCARD: 1 800 307 7309
VISA: (1) 410 581 9091

 AMEX: (1) 801 964 6665
THOMAS COOK: 1 800223 7373
VISA: 1 800 732 1322

 0830–1530 Mon to Fri.

 Good variety of duty free shops especially in
Philisburg offering cheap spirits and imported
luxury goods..

 English. Dutch is the official language for
legal documents. French is also spoken.

 Hot tropical climate with cool sea breezes.

 Protestant. Roman Catholic and Jewish
minorities.

 1998: Jan 1; Apr 10–13, 30; Apr 30; May 1,
8, 19; Nov 11; Dec 25–26.
1999: Jan 1; Apr 2–5, 30; Apr 30; May 1, 8,
19; Nov 11; Dec 25–26.

 110/220 volts AC 60 Hz.

 4–6 days.

 BBC: 17.84 15.22 6.195 5.975
VOA: 15.21 11.58 9.590 5.995

 Usual precautions should be taken.

 SEA: Small boats may be chartered for fishing trips and scuba diving. ROAD: Most
roads are good. CAR HIRE: Plenty of agencies at the airport and in the city.
DOCUMENTATION: A national licence is
acceptable.

 St. Maarten is the most popular of the
Netherlands Antilles with an estimated
900,000 tourists visiting each year. Usual
social courtesies should be applied.

St Vincent and the Grenadines

CAPITAL: Kingstown

GMT – 4

FROM UK: 1 809   IDD: Y
OUTGOING CODE: 0

All services: 999

High Commission for Eastern Caribbean States, 10 Kensington Court, London W8 5DL. Tel: (0171) 937 9522. Fax: (0171) 937 5514.

British High Commission, PO Box 132, Granby Street, Kingstown, St Vincent. Tel: 457 1701/2. Fax: 456 2750.

Refer to the High Commission.

St Vincent and the Grenadines Department of Tourism, PO Box 834, Bay Street, Kingstown, St Vincent. Tel: 457 1502. Fax: 456 2610.

Return Ticket required. Requirements may be subject to short-term change. Contact embassy before departure.
VALID PASSPORT REQUIRED: Not required by Nationals of the UK holding a driver's licence or birth certificate.

Visa not required. Length of stay decided by immigration authority on arrival. If necessary, check with Consulate or High Commission before finalising travel arrangements.

Firearms and narcotics.

EC$ 20 or US$ 10. Children under 12 are exempt.

POLIO, TYPHOID: R.
YELLOW FEVER: A vaccination certificate is required from travellers over 1 year of age coming from infected areas.

W2

Eastern Caribbean Dollar (EC$) = 100 cents. All major credit cards are widely accepted. All major currencies are accepted in travellers cheques.
ATM AVAILABILITY: Unavailable.

MONEYGRAM: Available in St Vincent only.
WESTERN UNION: Available.

AMEX: +44 1273 696933
DINERS CLUB: No local number.
MASTERCARD: 1 800 307 7309
VISA: (1) 410 581 9091

AMEX: (1) 801 964 6665
THOMAS COOK: 1 800 223 7373
VISA: 1 800 732 1322

0800–1500 Mon to Thur, 0800–1700 Fri.

Caters or all types of budget. Accommodation varies from luxury hotels to rugged log cabins in the interior.

English.

Tropical climate with trade winds cooling the hottest months, which are June and July.

Roman Catholic. Anglican, Methodist and other Christian minorities.

1998: Jan 1, 22; Apr 10, 13; May 5, 19; July 7, 8; Aug 4; Oct 27; Dec 25, 26.

220/240 volts AC, 50 Hz.

Up to 2 weeks .

BBC: 17.84 15.22 9.640 5.975
VOA: 15.12 11.58 9.455 6.130

The culture, generally, is of English and West Indian, and is very relaxed.

SEA: Yacht chartering is easily arranged and one of the bet ways to explore the Grenadines. BUS: Services run regularly throughout St Vincent. TAXI: These are shared and charge standard rates (fixed by the government) CAR HIRE: Easily arranged by a number of national and international firms. DOCUMENTATION: A local licence is required and can be obtained on presentation of a local licence at the airport or the police station in Bay Street, Kingstown.

Good West Indian cuisine is found on St Vincent.

CAPITAL: Apia

GMT – 11

FROM UK: 685   IDD: Y
OUTGOING CODE: Calls must be made through the international operator.

All services: 999.

No Embassy in the UK. EUROPE: Embassy of Samoa, avenue Franklin D Roosevelt 123, B-1050 Brussels, Belgium. Tel: (2) 220 8454. Fax: (2) 675 0336.
Office of the Honorary British Representative, c/o Apia Kruse Va'ai and Barlow, PO Box 2029, Apia, Samoa. Tel: 21895. Fax: 21407.

Tourism council of the South Pacific, 375 Upper Richmond Road West, London SW14 7NX. Tel: (0181) 392 1838.

Samoa Visitor Bureau, PO Box 2272. Apia, Samoa. Tel: 20878. Fax: 20886.

Return Ticket required. Regulations may be subject to change at short notice. Contact the embassy before departure.
VALID PASSPORT REQUIRED: must be valid for 6 months beyond the intended stay in Samoa.
Visa not required by tourists for stays of up to 30 days providing they have confirmed onward travel documentation and a valid passport. For longer stays visas should be obtained before arrival.

Live animals and plants required prior approval.

S$20, payable in local currency, for adults.

POLIO, TYPHOID: R.
YELLOW FEVER: A vaccination certificate is required from those travellers over 1 year of age arriving from infected areas.

W2

Samoan Dollar (WS$) or Tala (WS$) = 100 sene. Foreign exchange available at airport or through trade banks. Limited acceptance of all credit cards. Traveller's cheques are accepted in major hotels and tourist shops. Australian dollar cheques are preferred.
ATM AVAILABILITY: Unavailable.

MONEYGRAM: Unavailable.
WESTERN UNION: Unavailable.

AMEX: +44 1273 696933
DINERS CLUB: No local number.
MASTERCARD: 1 314 542 7111
VISA: (1) 410 581 9091
AMEX: (61) 2 886 0689
THOMAS COOK: +44 1733 318950
VISA: +44 1733 318949

0900–1500 Mon to Fri. Some open 0830–1130 Sat.

Hotel accommodation is expensive, whilst self-catering beach pensions are moderately priced.

Samoan, English.

Warm, tropical climate with cool nights. Rainfall heaviest Dec–Apr.

Congregational Church, Roman Catholic, Methodist and Latter Day Saints.

1998: Jan 1, 2; Apr 10, 11, 13, 25; May 11; June 1, 2; Aug 3; Oct 12; Nov 6; Dec 25, 26.
1999: Jan 1, 2; Apr 2, 4, 5, 25; May 11; June 1, 2; Aug 2; Oct 11; Nov 6; Dec 25, 26.

250 volts AC, 50 Hz.

Up to 3 weeks.

BBC: 15.36 11.95 9.740 7.145
VOA: 15.18 11.72 9.525 5.985

Samoans adhere to moral and traditional codes of behaviour, more than their neighbours, the American Samoans. Life in each village is still regulated by a council of chiefs, consisting of mostly men. This extended family social system is inclusive of all society. Outside resorts it is preferable for women to wear dresses.

FLIGHTS: Polynesian airlines operate domestic flights between main centres. SEA: Passenger/vehicle ferries operate. BUS: Public transport covers most of the island TAXI: Cheap and readily available in the capital. CAR HIRE: Available from several agencies, deposit and insurance is required. DOCUMENTATION: IDP is required for persons over 21 years or a valid national licence. A local licence will be issued by the transport ministry, for a small fee.

Traditional moral and religious codes are very important. Beachwear should be kept for the beaches.

San Marino

CAPITAL: San Marino

GMT + 1 (GMT + 2 during the summer).

FROM UK: 378   IDD: Y
OUTGOING CODE: 00

Police: 112, Fire: 116, Ambulance: 113.

Currently no Embassy in the UK.

British Consulate, Lungarno Corsini 2, 50123 Florence, Italy. Tel: (55) 284 133. Fax: (55) 219 112.

Not present.

Ufficio di Stato per il Turismo, Palazzo del Turismo, Contrada Omagnano 20, 47031, Republic of San Marino. Tel: 882 412. Fax: 882 575.

You must comply with Italian passport / visa requirements as entry is via Italy. See entry for Italy.
VALID PASSPORT REQUIRED: See Italy.

See Italy.

See Italy.

See Italy.

Health regulations and recommendations are the same as those for Italy.

Italian Lira (L). All major credit cards are accepted. Traveller's cheques, preferably in US dollars, are widely accepted.
ATM AVAILABILITY: Over 20 locations.

MONEYGRAM: Unavailable.
WESTERN UNION: Unavailable.

AMEX: +44 1273 696933
DINERS CLUB: 39 6 3213841
MASTERCARD: 1678 70866
VISA: 1678 75617

AMEX: 1678 72000
THOMAS COOK: 1678 72050
VISA: 1678 70987

0830–1300/1320 and 1430–1530 Mon to Fri

Accommodation varies from international to budget class.

Italian.

Climate is temperate. Moderate snow in winter, some brief rain showers in the summer.

Roman Catholic.

1998: Jan 1, 6; Feb 5; Mar 25; Apr 1, 13; May 1; June 1; July 28; Aug 15; Sept 3; Oct 1; Nov 1, 2; Dec 8, 24, 25, 26; 31.
1999: Jan 1, 6; Feb 5; Mar 25; Apr 1, 5; May 1; June 10; July 28; Aug 15; Sept 3; Oct 1; Nov 1, 2; Dec 8, 24, 25, 26; 31.

220 volts AC, 50 Hz.

Good postal service. Airmail to Western Europe takes approx. 4 days.

BBC: 15.58 12.10 9.410 6.195
VOA: 9.760 6.040 1.197 0.792.

Similar to Italy. Usual safety precautions should be observed.

RAIL: The nearest railway station is Rimini.

Normal European courtesies and codes of conduct should be observed.

CAPITAL: São Tomé

 GMT

 FROM UK: 239　　　　IDD: Very limited
OUTGOING CODE: All international calls must go through the operator.

 Not present.

 Honorary Consulate of the Democratic Republic of São Tomé and Principe, 42 North Audley Street, W1A 4PY. Tel: (0171) 499 1995. Fax: (0171) 629 6460.

 British Consulate, c/o Hull Blythe (Angola) Ltd, BP 15 São Tomé, São Tomé and Principe.

 Refer to the Consulate.

 Not present.

 Return Ticket required. Requirements may be subject to change at short notice. Contact the embassy before departure.
VALID PASSPORT REQUIRED

 Visa required. Transit visas are not required by those with tickets for onward journeys on the same day.

 US$20 adults, US$10 children except those under two years of age, who are exempt.

 POLIO, TYPHOID: R.
MALARIA: Exists throughout the year in the Falciparum variety. Resistance to chloroquine has been reported.
YELLOW FEVER: Vaccination is strongly recommended to all travellers. A certificate is required for travellers arriving from infected areas.
OTHER: Bilharzia, Rabies

 W1

Dobra (Db) = 100 centimes. Credit cards are not accepted. US dollar traveller's cheques preferred.
ATM AVAILABILITY: Unavailable.

 MONEYGRAM: Unavailable.
WESTERN UNION: Unavailable.

 AMEX: No local number
DINERS CLUB: No local number
MASTERCARD: No local number
VISA: No local number

 AMEX: No local number
THOMAS COOK: No local number
VISA: No local number

 0730–1130 Mon to Fri.

 Very inexpensive, without a tourist industry and unspoilt by external influences.

 Portuguese and native dialects are most widely spoken. French and English are also spoken.

 Dry Season: June to Sept and Dec to beginning of Feb. The South is wetter than the North.

 Roman Catholic majority.

 1998: Jan 1; Feb 3; May 1; July 12; Sept 6, 30; Dec 21, 25.
1999: Jan 1; Feb 3; May 1; July 12; Sept 6, 30; Dec 21, 26.

 220 Volts AC.

 Up to 2 weeks.

 BBC: 17.83　15.40　15.07　9.600
VOA: 21.49　15.58　9.575　6.035

 A patriarchal tribal society prevails.

 FLIGHTS: There are 3 flights a week from São Tomé to Principe. ROADS: Generally deteriorating therefore a 4 wheel drive is required to get around. BUSES: A bus service is in operation. TAXIS: operate.

Usual social courtesies should be shown. Portuguese influence is still dominant.

Saudi Arabia

CAPITAL: Riyadh

 GMT + 3

 FROM UK: 966   IDD: Y
OUTGOING CODE: 00

Not present.

Royal Embassy of Saudi Arabia, 30 Charles Street, London W1X 8LP. Tel: (0171) 917 3000. Fax: (0171) 917 3255.

British Embassy, PO Box 94351, Riyadh 11693, Saudi Arabia. Tel: (1) 488 0077. Fax: (1) 488 2373. Consulates in Jeddah and Al Khobar.

Saudi Arabia Information Centre, Cavendish House, 18, Cavendish Square, London W1M 0AQ. Tel: (0171) 629 8803. Fax: (0171) 629 0374.

Saudi Hotels and Resort Areas Co (SHARA-CO) PO Box 5500, Riyadh 11422, Saudi Arabia. Tel: (1) 465 7177. Fax: (1) 465 7172.

Return Ticket required. Requirements may be subject to short-term change. Contact the relevant authority before departure.
VALID PASSPORT REQUIRED: valid for 6 months beyond the intended period of stay.

Visa required.

Pork, pornography, contraceptives, pearls, children's dolls, jewellery, statues in the form of an animal or human, musical instruments. Duty is levied on cameras and typewriters.

Those with passports with Israeli stamps in them. Passengers not complying with Saudi conventions of dress and behaviour, including. those who appear to be in a state of intoxication. Those of the Jewish faith.

POLIO, TYPHOID: R.
MALARIA: Exists in the falciparum variety throughout the year within certain areas.
YELLOW FEVER: A vaccination certificate is required from all travellers arriving from countries where any parts are infected.
OTHER: Rabies, Bilharzia, Meningococcal Meningitis.

 W1

Saudi Arabian Rial (SAR) = 100 halalan. All major credit cards accepted. Traveller's cheques in, preferably, US dollars accepted. ATM AVAILABILITY: Over 1,000 locations.

 MONEYGRAM: Unavailable.
WESTERN UNION: (2) 667 2468.

AMEX: +44 1273 696933
DINERS CLUB: (966) (2) 652 0020
MASTERCARD: 1 314 542 7111
VISA: (1) 410 581 9091

AMEX: (973) 256 834
THOMAS COOK: +44 1733 318950
VISA: +44 1733 318949

0830–1200 and 1700–1900 Sat to Wed, 0830–1200 Thur.

Generally expensive. Prices increase by 25% during the summer and hotel charges double in Medina and Mecca during the pilgrimage season. Cheap accommodation and food can be found by the budget traveller.

Arabic. English is spoken in business circles.

 Desert climate. Jeddah is warm most of he year. Riyadh is hot in the summer and cooler during the winter. This is one of the driest countries in the world.

Sunni Muslim is the majority. Shiites predominated in the Eastern province.

 1998: Jan 30*. Apr 7*.
1999: Jan 30*. Apr 7*.

 125/215 volts AC, 50/60 Hz.

 Airmail to Europe takes up to 1 week.

BBC: 15.57 11.76 1.413 1.323
VOA: 15.44 11.96 9.700 6.060.

Saudi culture is based on the fundamentalist aspects of the Muslim religion, subsequently strict rules apply. Men and women are segregated. Unaccompanied women cannot check into a hotel without a letter from a sponsor. Unaccompanied women must be met at the airport by their husband or sponsor. There are restrictions on women travelling by car with men who are not related by blood. Women are not permitted to drive.

FLIGHTS: 19 domestic airports. Flying is the most convenient method of travelling. ROAD: The system is continually being updated and expanded, however standards of driving are erratic and many driving offences carry an automatic prison sentence. TAXI: Available in all centres but very expensive. Few have meters and fares should be agreed in advance. CAR HIRE: The major international companies have agencies in Saudi Arabia. Minimum driving age is 25. DOCUMENTATION: A national driving licence is valid for up to 3 months. An IDP with translation is recommended.

Dress codes and behavioural codes are strictly adhered to. Penalties for drug offences are severe. Non-political criminal activity is minimal, mainly due to the strict implementation of Saudi law. Extreme care must be taken when driving as the blame for accidents may be apportioned wrongly. Visitors should be aware that innocent contact with veiled women can be misinterpreted.

Senegal

CAPITAL: Dakar

GMT

FROM UK: 221   IDD: Y
OUTGOING CODE: 00

237 392 (Embassy)

Embassy of the Republic of Senegal, 11 Phillmore Gardens, London W8 7QG. Tel: (0171) 937 0925/6. Fax: (0171) 937 8130.

British Embassy, BP 6025, rue du Docteur Guillet, Dakar, Senegal. Tel: (8) 237 392 or (8) 239 971. Fax: (8) 232 76.

Refer to the Embassy.

Ministry of Tourism and Air Transport, BP 4049, 23 rue Calmette, Dakar, Senegal. Tel: (8) 236 502. Fax: (8) 229 413.

Return Ticket required. Requirements may be subject to change at short notice. Contact the embassy before departure.
VALID PASSPORT REQUIRED

Visa not required by Nationals of Great Britain.

There is no free import of alcoholic beverages.

CFA Fr5000 or US$ 7.

POLIO, TYPHOID: R.
MALARIA: Exists throughout the country in Falciparum variety. Resistance to chloroquine has been reported.
YELLOW FEVER: A vaccination certificate is required by travellers arriving from endemic areas.
OTHER: Bilharzia, Cholera, Meningitis, Rabies

W1

CFA Franc (CFA Fr) = 100 centimes. Amex and Mastercard are accepted, but other credit cards are not. Traveller's cheques, preferably in French francs, are accepted.
ATM AVAILABILITY: 9 locations.

MONEYGRAM: Unavailable.
WESTERN UNION: 23 10 00.

AMEX: +44 1273 696933
DINERS CLUB:No local number
MASTERCARD: 1 314 542 7111
VISA: No local number

AMEX: +44 1273 571 600
THOMAS COOK: +44 1733 318950
VISA: +44 1733 318 949

0800–1115 and 1430–1630 Mon to Fri

Accommodation is expensive, especially in the capital city and surrounding areas.

French. Many local languages are also spoken.

Dry season = Dec–May. Rainy season = June–Nov.

90% Muslim, 5% Catholic and Protestant and a minority of other beliefs.

1998: Jan 1, 30*; Apr 4, 7, 12,13; May 1, 11, 21; June 1; July 6*; Aug 15; Nov 1; Dec 25.
1999: Jan 1, 30*; Apr 4, 5, 7; May 1, 11, 20; June 1; July 6*; Aug 15; Nov 1; Dec 25.

220 Volts AC 50 Hz

7–10 days to Europe.

BBC: 17.83 15.40 9.660 6.005
VOA: 21.49 15.58 9.530 6.035

Beachwear should be confined to the beach.

ROADS: many are impassable during the rainy season. There are frequent check points and speed restrictions are strict.
DOCUMENTATION: IDP is required.

Avoid travel to the CAsamance region. It is polite to pay respect to the headman or school-teacher of any village you visit. Tipping is not always deemed courteous.

CAPITAL: Victoria

 GMT + 4.

 FROM UK: 248   IDD: Y
OUTGOING CODE: Calls must go through the operator.

 Not present.

 High Commission for the Republic of the Seychelles, 2nd Floor, Eros House, 111 Baker Street, London W1M 1FE. Tel: (0171) 224 1660. Fax: (0171) 487 5756.

 British High Commission, PO Box 161, 3rd Floor, Victoria House, Victoria, Mahé, Seychelles. Tel: 225 225 or 225 356. Fax: 225 127.

 As for the High Commission. Tel: (0171) 224 1670. Fax: (0171) 486 1352.

 Seychelles Tourist Board, PO Box 92, Independence House, Victoria, Mahé, Seychelles. Tel: 225 313. Fax: 224 035.

 Return Ticket required. Requirements may be subject to short-term change. Contact the relevant authority before departure.
VALID PASSPORT REQUIRED

 Visa not required.

 The import of animals, food and other agricultural produce is controlled and subject to licensing.

 US$20.

 POLIO, TYPHOID: Y.
YELLOW FEVER: A visitors permit is required from visitors arriving within 6 days of leaving or transiting affected areas.
OTHER: Rabies

 Seychelles Rupee (Srs) = 100 cents. Exch: Airport and Banks. Amex and Visa are widely accepted. Traveller's cheques, preferably in US dollars, are accepted in hotels, guest houses and most shops.
ATM AVAILABILITY: 3 locations.

 MONEYGRAM: Unavailable.
WESTERN UNION: Unavailable.

 AMEX: +44 1273 696933
DINERS CLUB: No local number
MASTERCARD: No local number
VISA: (1) 410 581 9091
AMEX: (1) 801 964 6665
THOMAS COOK: +44 1733 318950
VISA: +44 1733 318949

 0830–1430 Mon to Fri, 0830–1100 Sat.

 The island is a luxurious getaway for affluent holiday makers. Prices are often very expensive.

 Creole. English and French.

 Monsoon: Nov–Feb, which brings hot and humid weather. The temperatures rarely fall below 24 ºC.

 Mostly Roman Catholic with Anglican. 7th Day Adventists, Muslim and other minorities are also present.

 1998: Jan 1, 2; Apr 10; May 1; June 5, 11, 18, 29; Aug 15; Nov 2; Dec 8, 25.
1999: Jan 1, 2; Apr 2; May 1; June 5, 11, 18, 29; Aug 15; Nov 2; Dec 8, 25.

 240 volts AC, 50 Hz. British 3-pin plugs are in use.

 Airmail to western Europe takes up to 1 week.

 BBC: 17.88 15.42 9.630 6.005
VOA: 21.49 15.60 9.525 6.035.

 Men and women enjoy equal status. Beach wear should be confined to the pool or beach.

  FLIGHTS: An efficient network of scheduled and chartered services operate. SEA: Privately owned schooners provide regular inter island connections. ROAD: There are paved roads only on the two largest islands. BUS: A regular service is operated on Mahé. Pries for buses and coaches are very reasonable. TAXIS: Government controlled. Rates on Praslin are 25% higher. CAR HIRE: Should be booked in advance. Minimum age is 21. DOCUMENTATION: A national licence is sufficient.

 Casual wear is acceptable. Tourism in the Seychelles is regulated to ensure that the character and natural beauty of the islands remain unspoilt.

CAPITAL: Freetown

GMT

FROM UK: 232   IDD: Y
OUTGOING CODE: International calls must be made through the operator.

223 961/5 (Embassy)

High Commission for the Republic of Sierra Leone, 33 Portland Place, London W1N 3AG. Tel: (0171) 636 6483/6. Fax: (0171) 323 3159.

British High Commission, Standard Chartered Bank Building of Sierra Leone Ltd, Lightfoot Boston Street, Freetown, Sierra Leone. Tel: 223 961/5.

Refer to the High Commission.

National Tourist Board of Sierra Leone, International Conference Centre, Aberdeen Hill, PO Box 1435, Freetown , Sierra Leone. Tel: 272 520 or 272 396. Fax: 272 197.

Return Ticket required. Requirements may be subject to change at short notice. Contact the Embassy before departure.
VALID PASSPORT REQUIRED

Visa required.

Narcotics.

Le5000 or US$20 on international departures. Transit passengers are exempt.

POLIO, TYPHOID: R.
MALARIA: Exists all year throughout the country in the Falciparum variety. Resistance to chloroquine has been reported.
YELLOW FEVER: Vaccination is strongly recommended to all visitors if planning to journey into rural areas. A vaccination certificate is required for travellers arriving from infected areas.
OTHER: Bilharzia, Cholera, Rabies

W1

Leone (Le) = 100 cents. NOTE: Import and export of local currency is limited to Le 50,000. Amex is accepted, but all other credit cards are unacceptable. Traveller's cheques are accepted, in US dollars or pound sterling, preferably.
ATM AVAILABILITY: Unavailable.

MONEYGRAM: 1100 then 800 592 3688.
WESTERN UNION: 22 22 27 92.

AMEX: +44 1273 696933
DINERS CLUB: No local number
MASTERCARD: No local number
VISA: No local number

AMEX: +44 1273 571 600
THOMAS COOK: +44 1733 318950
VISA: +44 1733 318949

0800–1330 Mon to Fri, 0800–1400 Fri.

Expensive.

English Krio (widely spoken) other local dialects.

Climate is tropical and humid all year round. May–Nov is the rainy season.

Animist with Muslim and Christian minorities.

1998: Jan 1, 30*; Apr 7*, 10, 13, 27; July 6*; Dec 25, 26.
1999: Jan 1, 30*; Apr 2, 5, 7*, 27; July 6*; Dec 25, 26.

220240 Volts AC 50 Hz Supply subject to variations.

5 days to Europe

BBC: 17.83 15.40 11.84 6.005
VOA: 21.49 15.60 9.525 6.035

A patriarchal, tribal culture still prevails in most of the country.

ROADS: Secondary roads are impassable during the rainy season. There are road blocks at night on major roads near the centres of populations. There is a major petrol shortage with up to 48 hour waits at petrol stations. DOCUMENTATION IDP is required.

The FCO advises against all travel to Sierra Leone.

GMT + 8

 FROM UK: 65   IDD: Y
OUTGOING CODE: 005

 All services: 999

 High Commission for the Republic of Singapore, 9 Wilton Crescent, London SW1X 8SA. Tel: (0171) 235 8315 or 235 5441 (visa). Fax: (0171) 245 6583.

British High Commission, Tabglin Road, Singapore 1024. Tel: 473 9333. Fax: 475 2320 or 474 0468.

Singapore Tourism Promotion Board, 1st Floor, Carrington House, 126–130 Regent Street, London W1R 5FE. Tel: (0171) 437 0033. Fax: (0171) 734 2191.

Singapore Tourism Promotion Board, Raffles City Tower #36 – 04, 250 North Bridge Road, Singapore 0617. Tel: 339 6622. Fax: 339 9423.

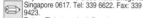 Return Ticket required. Requirements may change at short notice. Contact the Embassy before departure.

 VALID PASSPORT REQUIRED
Visa not required. All visitors require a 14-day social visit pass which is issued on arrival providing they have a valid passport and return tickets and sufficient funds to cover their expenses during their stay. This may be extended to 3 months on application to the Singapore immigration authorities at their discretion. For stays of 2 weeks or longer the passport must be valid for 6 months after departure from Singapore.

 Pornographic film and literature, and chewing gum.

SING $15 at Changi Airport, payable in local currency. Transit passengers and those under 2 years of age are exempt.

 Women more than 6 months pregnant must obtain a social visit pass prior to arrival.

 POLIO, TYPHOID: There may be a risk of Typhoid. OTHER: Cholera.

 W2

Singapore Dollar (Sing $) = 100 cents. The currency of Brunei is also legal tender. All credit cards are widely accepted. Traveller's cheques are accepted; US dollars are the preferred currency.
ATM AVAILABILITY: Over 1,000 locations.

 MONEYGRAM: 800 1100 560.
WESTERN UNION: Unavailable.

 AMEX: +44 1273 696933
DINERS CLUB: (65) 29 27055
MASTERCARD: 800 1100 113
VISA: 800 1100 806

 AMEX: (65) 7383383
THOMAS COOK: 800 4481 115
VISA: 800 4481 114

 1000–1500 Mon to Fri. 1100–1600 Sat. Certain banks are open on Sun on Orchard Road.

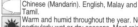 Much more expensive than other S E Asian countries. Hotels range from the new high-class to international standard. Prices start at US$ 100. Singapore is known as the shopping capital, where all types of luxury items can be purchased inexpensively.

 Chinese (Mandarin). English, Malay and Tamil.

 Warm and humid throughout the year. No particularly wet or dry seasons. Most rain falls during the Northeast monsoon (Nov–Jan) and showers can be sudden and heavy.

 Confucian, Taoist, Buddhism, Christian, Hindu and Muslim.

 1998: Jan 1, 28, 29*, 30; Apr 7, 10; May 1, 10, 11; Aug 9, 10; Oct 19*; Dec 25.
1999: Jan 1, 28, 29*, 30; Apr 2, 7; May 1, 10, 11; Aug 9, 10; Oct 19*; Dec 25.

 220/240 Volts AC 50 Hz. Plugs are flat 3 pin.

 Up to 1 week.

 BBC: 15.36 11.95 9.740 6.195
VOA: 15.43 15.18 9.770 7.120

 The crime rate is much lower than other countries and sexual harassment is very rare. Here, women enjoy much more freedom and sexual equality than in other parts of Asia.

SEA: Ferry runs frequent service. ROAD: DOCUMENTATION: IDP is required. BUS: Cheap and efficient. TAXI: Numerous and cheap. METRO: Cheap and efficient.

Singapore has a very low crime rate and very severe penalties for those who break the law. Smoking is widely discouraged and is illegal in public places. The death penalty is applied to some drug offences.

Slovak Republic

CAPITAL: Bratislava

 GMT + 1 (GMT + 2 during the summer).

 FROM UK: 42   IDD: Y
OUTGOING CODE: 00

 Fire: 150, Ambulance: 155, Police: 158.

 Embassy of the Slovak Republic, 25 Kensington Palace Gardens, London, W8 4QY. Tel: (0171) 243 0803. Passport section: (0171) 243 0803. Fax: (0171) 727 5824.

British Embassy, 35 Grösslingova, 811 09 Bratislava, Slovak Republic. Tel: (7) 364 420 or 364 431 or 364 363. Fax: (7) 364 396.

 Refer to Embassy.

Slovak Agency for Tourism, 2 Námestie slobody, PO Box 497, 974 01 Banská Bystrica, Námestie, Banská, Slovak Republic. Tel: (88) 746 626 or 45890. Fax: (88) 746 626.

 Requirements may be subject to short-term change. Contact the relevant authority before departure.
VALID PASSPORT REQUIRED: Passports must be valid for 8 months from the point of entry.

 Visa not required by Nationals of the UK for stays of up to 6 months.

 Materials which promote war, fascism, Nazism or racism. All forms of pornographic literature. All items of value must be declared on arrival to allow clearance on departure.

 US$7.40 is payable on all international departures.

 Rabies.

Koruna (Sk) or Slovak Crown = 100 halierov.
Exch: exchange offices, SATUR offices, main hotels, road border crossings as well as some post offices and some travel agencies.
NOTE: Import and export of local currency is prohibited. All major credit cards can be used to exchange currency and are also accepted in large hotels, restaurants and shops. Traveller's cheques are widely accepted, preferably in US dollars.
ATM AVAILABILITY: Over 650 locations.

 MONEYGRAM: Unavailable
WESTERN UNION: (17) 830 790.

 AMEX: (44) 1273 696933
DINERS CLUB: No local number.
MASTERCARD: 1 314 542 7111
VISA: (1) 410 581 9091

 AMEX: +44 1273 571 600
THOMAS COOK: +44 1733 318950
VISA: +44 1733 318949

 Generally 0800–1700 Mon to Fri.

 Since the Slovak Republic became an independent state in 1993, the transition to a western style economy has increased the standard of living greatly.

 Slovak, Czech, Hungarian, German and English may also be spoken.

 Cold winters and mild summers.

 Roman Catholic, with the remainder being Protestant; Reformed, Lutheran, Methodist and Jewish.

 1998: Jan 1, 6; Apr 10, 13; May 1, 8; July 5; Aug 29; Sept 1, 15; Nov 1; Dec 24, 25, 26.
1999: Jan 1, 6; Apr 2, 5; May 1, 8; July 5; Aug 29; Sept 1, 15; Nov 1; Dec 24, 25, 26.

 Generally 220 volts AC, 50 Hz.

 Poste Restante services are available.

BBC: 12.10 9.410 6.195
VOA: 9.760 6.040 1.197

 Traditional ideas and values persist in rural areas, especially amongst the older generation. Whilst the younger generation are more tolerant of new ideas and change.

RAIL: There are several daily express trains between Bratislava and main cities and resorts. Reservations should be made in advance on major routes. Fares are low but supplements are charged on express trains. BUS: The extensive network covers areas not accessible by train, and is efficient and comfortable. CAR HIRE: May be booked through the tourist office in main towns and resorts. DOCUMENTATION: A valid national driving licence is sufficient for car hire.

Dress should be casual but conservative. Tourism is on the increase and more accommodation is being built in remote regions.

CAPITAL: Ljubljana

 GMT + 1 (GMT + 2 during the summer).

 FROM UK: 386   IDD: Y
OUTGOING CODE: 00

 Ambulance: 94, Fire: 93, Police: 92

 Embassy of the Republic of Slovenia, Suite 1, Cavendish Court, 11–15 Wigmore Street, London W1H 9LA. Tel: (0171) 495 7775. Fax: (0171) 495 7776.
British Embassy, 4th Floor, Trg Republike 3, 1000 Ljubljana, Slovenia. Tel (61) 125 7191. Fax: (61) 125 0174.

 Slovenian Tourist Office, 2 Cranfield Place, London NW6 3BT. Tel: (0171) 372 3767. Fax: (0171) 372 3763.
Slovenian Tourist Board, Dunajska 156, 1000 Ljubljana, Slovenia. Tel: (61) 189 1840. Fax: (61) 189 1841.

 Return Ticket required. Requirements may be subject to short-term change. Contact the relevant authority before departure.
VALID PASSPORT REQUIRED: except for Nationals of EU countries with a valid ID card.

 Visa not required by Nationals of EU countries.

 Narcotics and firearms.

 US$ 16 or DM 25 is payable on international flights.

 POLIO, TYPHOID: R.
OTHER: Rabies.

 Slovene Tolar (SIT) = 100 stotins. Major credit cards are accepted in tourist hotels and restaurants. Traveller's cheques can be exchanged. Deutsche Mark or US dollar cheques are preferred.
ATM AVAILABILITY: Over 70 locations.

 MONEYGRAM: Unavailable.
WESTERN UNION: (061) 140 1223.

 AMEX: +44 1273 696933
DINERS CLUB: No local number.
MASTERCARD: 1 314 542 7111
VISA: (1) 410 581 9091

 AMEX: + 44 1273 571 600
THOMAS COOK: +44 1733 318950
VISA: +44 1733 318949

 0800–1800 Mon to Fri. Some branches are open 0800–1200 Sat.

 With the dissolution of Yugoslavia in 1991 and the change to a western type economy, Slovenia is marginally more expensive than the other former states.

 Slovene which is closely related to the Serb-Croat. Some Hungarian and Italian may be spoken.

 The climate is continental. Summers are warm and winters are cold. There is a Mediterranean climate along the coast.

 Mostly Roman Catholic. Eastern Orthodox with Muslim and Jewish minorities.

 1998: Jan 1, 2; Feb 8; Apr 13, 27; May 1–2; June 25; Aug 15; Oct 31; Nov 1; Dec 25–26.
1999: Jan 1, 2; Feb 8; Apr 5, 27; May 1–2; June 25; Aug 15; Oct 31; Nov 1; Dec 25–26.

 220 volts AC, 50 Hz.

 Reasonable internal service.

 BBC: 15.58 12.10 9.410 6.195
VOA: 9.760 6.040 5.995 1.260

 More traditional values persist among the older generation, particularly in the rural areas. The younger generation have adopted western ideologies.

 RAIL: Intercity trains operate and are relatively cheap. ROAD: There is a good network of high quality roads. However because of the civil war they now effectively end at Zagreb. DOCUMENTATION: Full national driving licences are accepted. International insurance is mandatory for all foreign vehicles with a small number of exceptions.

 Normal social conventions apply. Informal dress is acceptable. SPECIAL PRECAUTIONS: Travellers can become targets of pick pockets and purse snatchers, especially at railway stations and airports.

Solomon Islands

CAPITAL: Honiara

 GMT + 11

 FROM UK: 677   IDD: Y
OUTGOING CODE: 00

Not present.

Solomon Islands Honorary Consulate, 19 Springfield Road, London, SW19 7AL. Tel: (0181) 296 0232. Fax: (0181) 946 1744.

British High Commission, PO Box 676, Telekom House, Mendana Avenue, Honiaran, Solomon Islands. Tel: 21705/6. Fax: 20765.

Refer to the Consulate.

Solomon Island Tourist Authority, PO Box 321, Honiara, Solomon Islands. Tel: 22442. Fax 23986.

Return Ticket required. Regulations may be subject to change at short notice. Contact the embassy before departure.
VALID PASSPORT REQUIRED: Passport valid for at least 6 months required by all. Visa not required for stays of up to 3 months. A Visitors Permit is required and will be issued on arrival at the airport.

Plants and animals will be subject to restrictions.

SI$ 30, payable in local currency, for all departures. Transit passengers and children under 2 years are exempt.

Proof of sufficient funds for period of stay and onward or return tickets will be required to enter the country.

POLIO, TYPHOID: R.
MALARIA: Exists throughout the year in particular areas in the Falciparum variety, which is reported to be highly resistant to chloroquine.
YELLOW FEVER: A vaccination certificate is required from travellers arriving within 6 days of leaving or transiting infected areas,

W2

Solomon Islands Dollar (SI$) = 100 cents.
NOTE: Export of local currency is limited to SI$ 250. Credit cards are not accepted. Australian dollar Traveller's cheques can be exchanged at banks.
ATM AVAILABILITY: Unavailable.

 MONEYGRAM: Unavailable.
WESTERN UNION: Unavailable.

AMEX: No local number
DINERS CLUB: No local number
MASTERCARD: No local number
VISA: No local number
AMEX: (61) 2 886 0689
THOMAS COOK: +44 1733 318950
VISA: +44 1733 318949

0830–1500 Mon to Fri.

Accommodation can be quite expensive due to the small number of hotels. However, in the Reef accommodation is cheaper.

English and Pidgin English and over 87 local dialects are spoken.

Mainly Hot and Humid with little variation throughout the year.

More than 95% of the population are Christian.

1998: Jan 1; Apr 10, 11, 13; June 1, 12, 13; July 6, 7; Dec 25, 26.
1999: Jan 1; Apr 2, 4, 5; June 1, 12, 13; July 6, 7; Dec 25, 26.

240 Volts AC 50Hz, Australian-type, flat, 3-pin plugs are commonly used.

Approx. 7 days to Europe.

BBC: 15.34   11.95   9.740   6.195
VOA: 15.42   9.525   5.985   1.143

European and local traditions and customs co-exist.

FLIGHTS: National airline runs services between main islands and towns. SEA: Large and small ships provide the best means of travelling between the islands. Services are run by the government and a host of private operators. ROAD: General condition is poor resulting in limited use. TAXI: Available in main cities, advisable to agree the fare in advance.

Permission is required before use of beaches, footpaths etc. Beachwear should be kept for the beach. Swimming is not advised in the sea around Honiara, because of the presence of sharks, bristle-worms, stinging corals and sea urchins. PHOTOGRAPHY: Always seek permission before taking photographs of locals.

CAPITAL: Mogadishu

 GMT + 3

 FROM UK: 252   IDD: Y
OUTGOING CODE: International calls must go through the operator.

 All travellers are advised to consult the foreign office in their country of residence before departure regarding emergency assistance.

 There is no diplomatic representation in the UK at the moment because of civil war. Contact the Foreign and Commonwealth Office or Somalia Community Information Centre, 490 Harrow Road, London, W9 4QA. Tel/Fax (0181) 964 4540.

 British Embassy, PO Box 1036, Hassan Geedi Abtow, Mogadishu, Somalia. Tel (1) 20288/9. All staff are presently withdrawn.

 Not present.

 Not present.

 Return Ticket required. Requirements may be subject to change at short notice. Contact the embassy before departure.
VALID PASSPORT REQUIRED

 Visa required. Transit visas are not required by visitors with reserved onward travel.

 The equivalent of US$20 is levied on al international departures. Transit and passengers under two years are exempt.

 POLIO, TYPHOID: R.
MALARIA: Exists throughout the year in the Falciparum variety. Resistance to chloroquine has been reported.
YELLOW FEVER: Vaccination is strongly recommended to all travellers. A vaccination certificate is required by those arriving from infected areas.
OTHER: Bilharzia, Cholera (VACCINATION REQUIRED) and Rabies.

 W1

 Somali Shilling (SoSh) = 100 cents. NOTE: Import and export of local currency is limited to SoSh 200. Diners Club has limited acceptance. US dollars cash is preferred to traveller's cheques..
ATM AVAILABILITY: Unavailable

 MONEYGRAM: Unavailable.
WESTERN UNION: 1 215 036.

 AMEX: No local number
DINERS CLUB: No local number.
MASTERCARD: No local number
VISA: No local number

 AMEX: +44 1273 571 600
THOMAS COOK: +44 1733 318950
VISA: +44 1733 318949

 0800–1130 Sat to Thur.

 Economy decimated by political strife and drought, resulting in high inflation and a sparcity of products.

 Somali and Arabic.

 Jan–Feb Hot and Dry, Mar–June is the first rainy season, monsoon winds occur between July and Aug. The second rainy season occurs between Sept and Dec.

 Mostly Muslim with a Christian minority.

 1998: Jan 1, 30; Apr 7; May 1; June 26; July 1, 6; Oct 21.
1999: Jan 1, 30; Apr 7; May 1; June 26; July 1, 6; Oct 21.

 220 Volts AC 50 Hz

 Up to 2 weeks.

 BBC: 17.88 17.64 15.42 9.630
VOA: 21.49 15.60 9.525 6.035

 Women are advised to cover arms and legs in accordance with the Muslim religion.

 ROAD: It is difficult to travel outside of Mogadishu by car because of poor road conditions. DOCUMENTATION : IDP is required.

 The Travel Advice Unit of the Foreign and Commonwealth Office advises against all travel to Somalia. Informal wear is acceptable. PHOTOGRAPHY: People with cameras must have a permit.

CAPITAL: Pretoria

GMT + 2

FROM UK: 27   IDD: Y
OUTGOING CODE: 09
Police: 1011, ambulance: 10222, Fire: 1022

High Commission of the Republic of South Africa, South Africa House Trafalgar Square, London WC2N 5DP. Tel: (0171) 930 4488. Fax: (0171) 451 7284.
British High Commission, 255 Hill Street, Arcadia, Pretoria 0002, South Africa. Tel: (12) 483 1200. Fax: (12) 483 1302. Or 91 Parliament Street, Cape Town 8001, South Africa. Tel: (21) 461 7220. Fax: (21) 461 0017.

Refer to the High Commission.

South African Tourism Board (SATOUR), Private Bag, X164, 442 Rigel Avenue South, Frasmusrand, Pretoria 0001, South Africa. Tel: (12) 347 0600. Fax (12) 454 889 or 454 768.

Return Ticket required. Requirements may be subject to change at short notice. Contact the embassy before departure.
VALID PASSPORT REQUIRED: must be valid for 6 months after departure.

Visa not required.

Obscene literature and second hand military clothing is prohibited.

Rand 60, inclusive of international return fare.

POLIO, TYPHOID: R. MALARIA: Exists throughout the year in the falciparum variety. Resistance to chloroquine has been reported.
YELLOW FEVER: A vaccination certificate is required from all passengers over one year of age travelling from infected areas. Passengers arriving by unscheduled flights at airports other than those used by scheduled airlines must possess a certificate. OTHER: Bilharzia, Cholera and Rabies.

W2

South African Rand (R) = 100 cents NOTE: Import and export of local SA Reserve Bank notes is limited to R500. Foreign currency must be declared on arrival. All major credit cards are widely accepted. Traveller's cheques.in all currencies are accepted, including SARand.
ATM AVAILABILITY: Widely available.

MONEYGRAM: 0 800 996 048.
WESTERN UNION: 0800 126 000

AMEX: +44 1273 696933
DINERS CLUB: (27) (11) 482 2203
MASTERCARD: 0800 990418
VISA: (1) 410 581 9091
AMEX: 0800 99 1021
THOMAS COOK: 0800 99 8175
VISA: 0800 99 8174

0830–1530 Mon to Fri, 0800–1130 Sat.

Accommodation and other tourist facilities in the cities can be expensive. Avoid short trips in city taxis which are sometimes more expensive than long distance journeys.

English and Afrikaan with 9 other African languages.

Generally warm and sunny. Winds are usually mild.

Dutch Reform Church, Nededuitsch, Hervormde, C of E, Roman Catholic, Jews, Hindu, Muslim and many others.

1998: Jan 1; Mar 21; Apr 10–13, 27; May 1; June 16; Aug 9, 10; Sept 24; Dec 16, 25, 26.
1999: Jan 1; Apr 2–5, 27; May 1; June 16; Aug 9, 10; Sept 24; Dec 16, 25, 26.

250 Volts AC in Pretoria. 220/230 Volts AC elsewhere.

Up to 7 days for airmail to Europe.

BBC: 15.07 12.09 9.410 6.195
VOA: 21.49 15.60 9.525 6.035

Political reforms have redefined the role of women. Cultural sociological and economic differences continue to cause tension.

FLIGHTS: Regular domestic flights operate between main cities. SEA: 'Starlight' cruises operate between the major ports. ROADS: A well maintained network of roads exists. NOTE: Fines are imposed for speeding. It is illegal to carry petrol unless in built up petrol tanks DOCUMENTATION: IDP is required.

Casual remarks should not be made about the political situation, which is complex. Unwise for outsiders from any race to enter into a black township without a guide. Daylight muggings are not uncommon especially in parts of Johannesburg. There is a risk of car-jacking and armed robbery.

CAPITAL: Madrid

Mainland Spain and Balearics GMT + 1 (GMT + 2 during the summer).

FROM UK: 34   IDD: Y
OUTGOING CODE: 07

Police: 091, Fire/Ambulance: 085

Embassy of the Kingdom of Spain, 24 Belgrave Square, London SW1X 8QA. Tel: (0171) 235 5555. Fax: (0171) 259 5392.
British Embassy, Calle de Fernando el Santo 16, 28010 Madrid, Spain. Tel: (1) 319 0200. Fax: (1) 319 0423. Consulates in Seville, Alicante, Barcelona, Tarragona, Bilbao, Las Palmas, Santa Cruz de Tenerife, Malaga, Palma, Ibiza, Santander, Menorca and Vigo.

Spanish Tourist Office, 57–58 St James Street, London SW1A 1LD. Tel: (0171) 499 0901 (general information), 499 4593 (travel agents/promotion), 499 9237 (customer services), 0891 669 920 (brochure request).
Direccion General de Turespaña, Jose Lázaro Galdiano 6, 28036 Madrid, Spain. Tel: (1) 343 3500. Fax: (1) 343 3446.

Requirements may be subject to short term change. Contact the relevant authority before departure. It is advisable to have a return ticket, otherwise you may be asked of sufficient proof of funds to finance your stay.
Valid Passport not required by UK Nationals with passports expired less than 1 year.

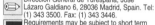

Narcotics and firearms.

W3

Peseta (Pta) Exch: Any banks and most travel agencies. NOTE: Import and export of local currency is subject to the amount of declaration if the amount exceeds Pta 1,000,000 and the amount exported must not exceed the amount declared on arrival. All major credit cards are accepted. Traveller's cheques in Sterling pounds can be easily exchanged.
ATM AVAILABILITY: Over 35, 000 locations.
MONEYGRAM: 900 96 1218.
WESTERN UNION: (95) 205 0219.
AMEX: +44 1273 696933
DINERS CLUB: (43) (1) 5474000
MASTERCARD: 900 97 1231
VISA: 900 95 1125
AMEX: 900 99 4426
THOMAS COOK: 900 99 4403
VISA: 900 97 4447

0900–1400 Mon to Fri, 0900–1300 Sat (except during the summer).

Similar prices to other Western European countries.

Spanish (Castilian), Catalan, Galician and Basque.

Varies from temperate in the North to hot and dry in the South. The best months are Apr–Oct, although it can be excessively hot July–Aug except at coastal regions. The central plateau can be very cold during winter.

Roman Catholic in the majority.

1998: Jan 1, 6, 22; Mar 19; Apr 9–11, 13; May 1, 2, 15; June 1, 24; July 25; 31; Aug 15; Sept 8, 11, 24; Oct 12; Nov 1, 2, 9; Dec 6, 8, 25, 26.
1999: Jan 1, 6, 22; Mar 19; Apr 1–3, 5; May 1, 2, 15, 31; June 24, July 25; 31; Aug 15; Sept 8, 11, 24; Oct 12; Nov 1, 2, 9; Dec 6, 8, 25, 26.

220 volts AC, 50 Hz.

5 days. Poste Restante facilities are available at main post offices.

BBC: 15.58 12.09 9.410 6.195
VOA: 9.760 6.040 5.995.

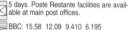

Spanish women retain traditional values in rural areas, but many of the formerly strict religious and social customs are becoming slightly more relaxed, particularly in urban and tourist regions. Spain is one of the safest countries for women to travel in.

RAIL: Most cities are well served. It is mainly a radial service with connections between Madrid and all major cities. It is one of the cheapest in Europe, with discounts and special concessions. ROAD: Motorways are well maintained and connect North and South. Trunk roads between major cities are general well maintained. BUS: Services are cheap and efficient. CAR HIRE: All major companies have agencies. DOCUMENTATION: IDP is required or a translation of national driving licence. Insurance is required and a 'green card' is strongly recommended.

Spaniards are a very hospitable, and value courtesy. Conservative casual dress is suitable, but some larger hotels may insist that men wear a jacket. Beach-wear should be confined to the beach/pool. Street crime can be a problem in some of the tourist areas and large cities.

Sri Lanka

CAPITAL: Colombo

 GMT + 5.30.

 FROM UK: 94   IDD: Y, in principal cities.
OUTGOING CODE: 00

 All services: 1 691095/699935.

 High Commission of Sri Lanka, 13 Hyde Park Gardens, London W2 2LU. Tel: (0171) 262 1841. Fax: (0171) 262 7970.
British Embassy, PO Box 1433, 190 Galle Road, Kollupitiya, Columbo 3, Sri Lanka. Tel: (1) 437 336. Fax: (1) 430 308.
Sri Lanka Tourist Board, 22 Regent Street, London SW1Y 4QD. Tel: (0171) 930 2627. Fax: (0171) 930 9070.
Sri Lanka Tourist Board, PO Box 1504, 78 Stewart Place, Colombo 3, Sri Lanka. Tel: (1) 437 059. Fax: (1) 437 953.

 Return Ticket required. Requirements may be subject to short-term change. Contact the relevant authority before departure.
VALID PASSPORT REQUIRED: Passport must be valid for 3 months.
For tourist visits, nationals of EU countries will be issued a visa free of charge on arrival at Colombo airport for a maximum stay of 30 days.

 Precious metals must be declared on arrival.

 SL Rs500, payable in local currency. Transit and passengers under 2 years are exempt.

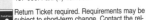 POLIO, TYPHOID: R.
MALARIA: R.
YELLOW FEVER: A vaccination certificate is required from travellers over 1 year of age coming from infected areas.
OTHER: Cholera, Rabies.

 W1

 Sri Lankan Rupee (SL Re, Rs (plural)) = 100 cents. Exch: An exchange form is issued on arrival, which must be stamped for all exchange transactions. Banks, hotels exchange currency. All major credit cards are widely accepted. Traveller's cheques are accepted, for a better exchange rate offered than cash. US dollars are the preferred cheque currency.
ATM AVAILABILITY: Over 12 locations.

 MONEYGRAM: 430 430 then 800 592 3688.
WESTERN UNION: (1) 320 671.

 AMEX: +44 1273 696933
DINERS CLUB: (94) (1) 33404
MASTERCARD: 1 314 542 7111
VISA: (1) 410 581 9091
AMEX: (11) 6875930

 THOMAS COOK: +44 1733 318950
VISA: +44 1733 318949

 0900–1300 Mon to Sat, 0900–1500 Tues to Fri.

 Suitable for all travellers and budgets.

 Sinahala, Tamil and English.

 Tropical climate. The coastal areas are cooled by the sea winds. The Monsoons are May–July and Dec–Jan.

 Buddhist with Hindu. Christian and Muslim minorities.

 1998: Jan 12, 14, 30*; Feb 4, 10, 25; Mar 12; Apr 7, 10, 11, 13, 14; May 1, 11, 12; June 9*; July 6, 7; Aug 7; Sept 8; Oct 5, 19; Nov 3; Dec 3, 25.
1999: Jan 12, 14, 30*; Feb 4, 10, 25; Mar 12; Apr 2, 7, 11, 13, 14; May 1, 11, 12; June 9*; July 6, 7; Aug 7; Sept 8; Oct 5, 19; Nov 3; Dec 3, 25.

 230/240 volts AC, 50 Hz. Round 3 pin plugs are usual.

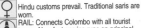 Airmail to western Europe takes up to 1 week.
BBC: 17.79 15.31 11.95 9.740
VOA: 15.42 15.19 9.770 9.760

 Hindu customs prevail. Traditional saris are worn.

RAIL: Connects Colombo with all tourist towns. New fast service runs on principal routes. Rail services to the northern area have been greatly reduced because of violent disruptions. ROAD: Most roads are tarred. BUS: An extensive network of reasonable quality. CAR HIRE: Available from several international agencies. DOCUMENTATION: Obtain an IDP before departure to avoid lengthy red tape in Sri Lanka.

NOTE: Whilst most of Sri Lanka remains unaffected, fighting between the security forces and the Tamil Tigers (LTTE) continues in the North and East. Do not visit these areas. There have been terrorist attacks resulting in fatalities in Colombo. It is considered impolite to refuse the offer of tea. Punctuality is considered important. Arms and legs should be covered when visiting religious sites and shoes and hats must be removed.

CAPITAL: Khartoum

 GMT + 2

 FROM UK: 249   IDD: Y
OUTGOING CODE: International calls must go through the operator.

 Not present.

 Embassy of the Democratic Republic of Sudan, 3 Cleveland Row, St James Street, London SW1A 1DD. Tel: (0171) 839 8080. Fax: (0171) 839 7560.
British Embassy, PO Box 801, Street 10, off Sharia Al Baladiya Khartoum East, Sudan. Tel: (11) 770 769 or 780 856.

 Refer to the Embassy.

 Public Corporation of Tourism and Hotels PO Box 7104, Khartoum, Sudan. Tel: (11) 781 764.

 Return Ticket required. Requirements may change at short notice. Contact the embassy before departure. Valid Passport required: valid for 6 months.

 Visa required (including transit passengers).

 Import of foodstuffs are prohibited.

 US$20 is levied on international departures. Transit passengers and those under two years of age are exempt.

 Holders of passports that contain visas for Israel either valid or expired.

 POLIO, TYPHOID: R. MALARIA: Exists in the Falciparum variety throughout the year. High resistance to chloroquine has been reported.
YELLOW FEVER: A vaccination certificate is required for passengers over 1 year of age arriving from infected areas and may be required from travellers leaving Sudan. Vaccination is strongly recommended to any-one planning to travel outside urban areas.
OTHER: Bilharzia, Cholera, Rabies and Visceral leishmaniasis.

W1

Sudanese Pound (Sud £) = 100 piastres and Sudanese Dinar. NOTE: Exchange rates are subject to great change and import and export of local currency is prohibited. Amex is widely accepted but all other major credit cards are not accepted. Traveller's cheques are accepted in sterling only.
ATM AVAILABILITY: Unavailable.

 MONEYGRAM: Unavailable.
WESTERN UNION: Unavailable.

 AMEX: +44 1273 696933
DINERS CLUB: No local number
MASTERCARD: No local number
VISA: No local number
AMEX: +44 1273 571 600
THOMAS COOK: +44 1733 318950
VISA: +44 1733 318949

 0830–1200 Sat to Thur.

 Inexpensive, apart from the larger hotels in Khartoum.

 Arabic, English, Local dialects are widely spoken.

 Extremely hot with sandstorms from Apr–Sept in the Sahara region. Wet season in the south from May–Oct.

 Muslim in the North, Christian and Animist in the south.

 1998: Jan 1, 7, 30*; Feb 12; Apr 7, 20, 28*; June 30; July 6*; Nov 17*; Dec 25.
1999: Jan 1, 7, 30*; Feb 12; Apr 7, 20, 28*; June 30; July 6*; Nov 17*; Dec 25.

 240 Volts AC, 50 Hz

Up to 1 week to Europe.

BBC: 17.64 15.07 12.09 9.410
VOA: 15.21 11.83 9.700 9.530

 Women should respect the Muslim dress code and not wear revealing clothes.
NOTE: Travellers must register with the Police headquarters within 3 days of arrival, and Police permission must be obtained before moving to another location within Sudan. FLIGHTS: Sudan Airways serves 20 national airports. ROADS: Outside the main towns roads are usually in very poor condition and unsuitable for travel during rainy season. Vehicles must be in good condition, with a supply of spare parts, water, food, fuel. RAIL: Extensive network but services are very slow and uncomfortable. DOCUMENTATION: Carnet de Passage, adequate finance, a road worthiness certificate (from embassy) required. IDP recommended. Trailers and cars less than 1500cc are refused entry.

! HIGH RISK. Contact the FCO Travel Advice Unit for latest information. The Arab culture predominates in the North. In the South the people belong to a number of tribes. It is inadvisable to travel to any of the southern provinces due to civil war.

Suriname

CAPITAL: Paramaribo

GMT – 3

FROM UK: 597   IDD: Y
OUTGOING CODE: 001

Contact hotel operator.

No representation within the UK. EUROPE: Embassy of the Republic of Suriname, Alexander Gogelweg 2, 2517 JH The Hague, The Netherlands. Tel: (70) 365 0844. Fax: (70) 361 7445.
British Honorary Consulate, c/o VSH Untied Buildings, PO Box 1860, Van't Hogerhuys-straat 9–11, Paramaribo, Suriname. Tel: 472 870 or 472 558. Fax: 475 515.

Refer to Embassy.

Suriname Tourism Department, Cornelis Jongbawstraat 2, Paramaribo, Suriname. Tel: 410 357.

Return Ticket required. Requirements may change at short notice. Contact the embassy before departure.
VALID PASSPORT REQUIRED: valid for 6 months after intended period of stay.

Visa not required by Nationals of the UK. A 60 day tourist card is required, which is offered on arrival for a fee to those able to present a valid passport. Transit visas are not required by those continuing their journey on the next aircraft.

Fruit, vegetables and meat products.

US$5, children under 2 are exempt.

POLIO, TYPHOID: R.
MALARIA: Exists throughout the country all year round in the Falciparum variety which has been reported as being highly resistant to chloroquine.
YELLOW FEVER: A vaccination certificate is required if arriving from infected areas.
OTHER: Bilharzia, Rabies.

W2

Suriname Guilder (S Gld) = 100 cents. Exch: Some banks and hotels are authorised to exchange money. Amex is widely accepted. Traveller's cheques in US dollars can be exchanged in banks.
ATM AVAILABILITY: Unavailable.

MONEYGRAM: Unavailable.
WESTERN UNION: 42 11 52.

AMEX: +44 1273 696933
DINERS CLUB: No local number
MASTERCARD: No local number
VISA: No local number
AMEX: (1) 801 964 6665
THOMAS COOK: 1 800 223 7373
VISA: 1 800 732 1322

0730–1400 Mon to Fri.

Hotels are generally located in the city and fairly expensive. A youth hostel and campsite are outside the city. Travellers are advised to bring their own hammock and food.

Dutch. Taki-Taki, Hindi, Javanese, English, Chinese French and Spanish.

Hottest and wettest: May–Oct. Dec–Apr is more comfortable .

Christian. Hindu and Muslim.

1998: Jan 1, 30*. Apr 10–13. May ., July 1. Nov 25; Dec 25.
1999: Jan 1, 30*; Apr 2–5; May 1; July 1; Nov 25; Dec 25.

110/220 Volts AC, 60 Hz European 2 pin plugs are used.

Usually takes about 1 week to and from Europe.

BBC: 11.86 9.915 9.640 6.195
VOA: 15.12 11.58 9.590 5.995

The diversity of ethnicity all cultures co-exist. Women should wear long trousers for trips to the interior.

FLIGHTS: Domestic flights to the interior are operated. ROAD: Reasonable road network with patches of poor quality. Drivers using their own cars should ensure they are carrying a full set of spares. BUS: Services operate from the main cities to most villages at low prices. TAXI: Agree fares in advance as these are not metered. DOCUMENTATION: IDP is not required but recommended.

Beach wear should not be worn away from beach/pool. PHOTOGRAPHY: Avoid public, police and military subjects. Seek permission before taking photos.

CAPITAL: Mbabane

 GMT + 2

 FROM UK: 268   IDD: Y
OUTGOING CODE: International calls must go through the operator.

 Not present.

 Kingdom of Swaziland High Commission, 20 Buckinghamgate, London SW1E 6LB. Tel: (0171) 630 6611. Fax: (0171) 630 6564.

 British High Commission, Alister Miller Street, Mbabane, Swaziland. Tel: 42581 Fax: 42585.

 Refer to the High Commission.

 Ministry of Broadcasting, Information and Tourism, PO Box 338, Mbabane, Swaziland. Tel: 42761 Fax: 42774.

 Return Ticket recommended though not essential. Requirements may change at short notice. Contact the embassy before departure. VALID PASSPORT REQUIRED

 Visa not required by nationals of Britain.

 Duty free for married couples is restricted to one quota.

 Departure Tax is E20, payable in local currency.

 POLIO, TYPHOID: R.
MALARIA: Exists throughout the year in certain areas in the Falciparum variety. resistance to chloroquine has been reported.
YELLOW FEVER: A vaccination certificate is required for travellers arriving from infected areas.
OTHER: Bilharzia, Meningitis (recommended), Rabies.

 W1

 Lilangeni (E) = 100 cents. South African Rand is also accepted as legal tender. Amex and MasterCard are widely accepted. Visa is accepted on a more limited basis. Traveller's cheques are accepted, preferably in Pound sterling.
ATM AVAILABILITY: Unavailable.

 MONEYGRAM: Unavailable.
WESTERN UNION: Unavailable

 AMEX: +44 1273 696933
DINERS CLUB: No local number
MASTERCARD: 1 314 542 7111
VISA: (1) 410 581 9091

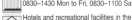 AMEX: +44 1273 571 600
THOMAS COOK: +44 1733 318950
VISA: +44 1733 318949

 0830–1430 Mon to Fri, 0830–1100 Sat.

 Hotels and recreational facilities in the Holiday Valley complex in Ezulwini is expensive.

 English and Siswati

 Weather can be changeable due to the high altitude. Lowlands are the hottest and the higher lands have the most rain between Oct–Mar.

 Christian and Animist minority.

 1998: Jan 1; Apr 10, 13, 19, 20, 25; May 1, 21; July 22; Sept 6; Dec 25, 26.
1999: Jan 1; Apr 2, 5, 19, 20, 25; May 1, 21; July 22; Sept 6; Dec 25, 26.

 20 Volts AC 50 Hz Plugs = 15amp round pin.

 Up to 2 weeks.

 BBC: 17.88 9.600 6.190 3.255
VOA: 21.49 15.60 9.525 6.035

 A patriarchal and tribal culture prevails.

ROADS: Generally in good condition. BUS: Numerous buses connect various parts of the country some of which are non-stop. CAR HIRE: A number of companies operate. DOCUMENTATION: National driving licences are valid for up to 6 months provided they are printed in English. IDP is recognised.

Those wanting to camp in villages should see the village chief. PHOTOGRAPHY: Permission should be asked. Photos of national buildings and the royal family are prohibited.
Do not camp near houses or graveyards without being granted permission.

Sweden

CAPITAL: Stockholm

GMT + 1 (GMT + 2 during the summer).

FROM UK: 46   IDD: Y
OUTGOING CODE: 009

All services : 90 000/112.

Royal Swedish Embassy, 11 Montagu Place, London W1H 2AL. Tel (0171) 917 6400. Fax (0171) 724 4174. Consular section: Tel: (0171) 917 6413 or 917 6418. Fax: 917 6475.

British Embassy, PO Box 27819, Skarpöga-tan 6–8, 115 93 Stockholm, Sweden. Tel (8) 671 9000. Fax: (8) 662 9989. Consulates in Gothenburg, Malmö, Luleå and Sundsvall.

Swedish Travel and Tourism Council, 11 Montagu Place, London W1H 2AL. Tel: (0171) 724 5868 or (01476) 578 811 (24 hour brochure request line). Fax: (0171) 724 5872.

Swedish Travel and Tourism Council, PO Box 3030, 103 61 Stockholm, Sweden. Tel: (8) 725 5500. Fax (8) 725 5531.

Requirements may be subject to short-term change. Contact the relevant authority before departure.
VALID PASSPORT REQUIRED: Not required by Nationals of Ireland holding a valid national ID card (for a stay of up to 3 months).

Visa not required by Nationals of EU countries.

Most meat and dairy products, plants, eggs and endangered species.

14 Skr is payable on international departures.

Swedish Krone (Skr) = 100 øre. Personal cheques can be cashed in Swedish banks through the Eurocheque system. All major credit cards are accepted. Traveller's cheques, preferably in US dollars, are widely accepted.
ATM AVAILABILITY: Over 2, 000 locations.

MONEYGRAM: 009 800 66639472.
WESTERN UNION: 020 741 742.

AMEX: +44 1273 696933
DINERS CLUB: (45) 3672
MASTERCARD: 020 791 324
VISA: (1) 410 581 9091

AMEX: 020 795 155
THOMAS COOK: 020 795 110
VISA: 020 792 221

Generally 0930–1500 Mon to Fri but in many large cities banks close at 1800.

Expensive – similar to other Scandinavian countries.

Swedish. Lapp and English are also spoken.

The climate is mild, which varies according to its great length. Summers can be very hot but get shorter further North. The midnight sun can be seen between mid- May and mid-June above the Arctic circle. Winters can be bitterly cold particularly in the North.

Swedish Sate Church (Evangelical Lutheran). Other Protestant minorities.

1998: Jan 1, 6; Apr 10, 13; May 1, 21; June 1,19; Oct 31; Nov 1; Dec 24, 25, 26, 31.
1999: Jan 1, 6; Apr 2, 5; May 1, 20 31; June 19; Oct 31; Nov 1; Dec 24, 25, 26, 31.

220 volts 3 phase AC, 50 Hz. 2 pin plugs are used.

3–4 days. Poste Restante is widely available.

BBC: 15.07 12.09 9.410 6.195
VOA: 15.21 9.760 6.040 5.995

The crime rate is low and there is little inequality between men and women, hence few problems should be encountered.

RAIL: There is an extensive rail system. The network is more frequent in the South where there are more people. 'Scanrail' cards etc can be purchased. ROAD: Sweden's roads are well maintained and relatively uncrowded. BUS: Cheap and efficient services are available to all towns. TAXI: Available in all towns and airports. CAR HIRE: Available in most towns and cities.

Normal social courtesies should be observed. Casual dress is acceptable for social occasions. Sweden is regarded as one of the safest countries in the world and crimes against foreigners are rare.

Switzerland

CAPITAL: Bern

 GMT + 1 (GMT + 2 during the summer).

 FROM UK: 41   IDD: Y
OUTGOING CODE: 00

 Ambulance : 144, Police : 117, Fire : 118.

 Embassy of the Swiss Confederation, 16–18 Montagu Place, London W1H 2BQ. Tel: (0171) 723 0701 or (0891) 331 313 (recorded visa information).
British Embassy, Minerva Strasse 117, 8032 Zurich. Tel: (1) 383 6560. Fax: (1) 383 6561.

 Switzerland Tourism, Swiss Centre, Swiss Court, London W1V 8EE. Tel: (0171) 734 1921. Fax: (0171) 437 4577.
National Tourist Office, Bellariastrasse 38, CH-8027 Zürich, Switzerland. Tel: (1) 288 1111. Fax: (1) 288 1205.

 Return Ticket required. Requirements may be subject to change at short notice. Contact the relevant authority before travelling.
VALID PASSPORT REQUIRED: Valid for 6 months after intended period of stay.

 Visa not required by Nationals of EU countries.

 All meat products.

 Sfr15, inclusive of ticket price.

 Swiss Franc (Sfr) = 100 rappen or centimes. Exch: Eurocheques are accepted. Major credit cards are accepted. Traveller's cheques are accepted at airports, railway stations and banks. Cheques in Swiss francs are preferred.
ATM AVAILABILITY: Over 4,000 locations.

 MONEYGRAM: 0 800 89 5973.
WESTERN UNION: 0512 22 33 58.

 AMEX: +44 1273 696933
DINERS CLUB: (41) (1) 8333738
MASTERCARD: 0800 89 7092
VISA: 0800 89 6046

 AMEX: 155 0100
THOMAS COOK: 0800 55 0130
VISA: 0800 55 7262

 0830–1630 Mon to Fri.

 Relatively expensive. Prices vary according to popularity of the resort.

 Mostly German in Central and Eastern parts. French in the West, some Italian in the South. Raeto-Romansch is spoken in the Southeast by 1%. English is spoken by many.

 Climate varies throughout Switzerland. In the Alpine regions the temperatures tend to be low. The lower land of the Northern areas has higher temperatures and warmer summers.

 Roman Catholic and Protestant.

 1998: Jan 1, 2, 6; Feb 23, 24; Mar 1, 2, 4, 19; Apr 10, 13, 20; May 1, 21; June 1, 11, 23; Aug 1, 15; Nov 1; Dec 8, 24, 25, 26, 31.
1999: Jan 1, 2, 6; Feb 23, 24; Mar 1, 2, 4, 19; Apr 2, 5, 20; May 1, 20, 31; June 10, 23; Aug 1, 15; Nov 1; Dec 8, 24, 25, 26, 31.

 220 volts AC 50 Hz.

 3 days. Poste Restante facilities available at post offices.

 BBC: 15.07 12.09 6.195 3.955
VOA: 15.20 11.96 9.760 6.040

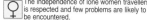 The independence of lone women travellers is respected and few problems are likely to be encountered.

ROAD: Many mountain roads are closed during the winter because of poor driving conditions. Road quality is generally good but mountain roads can be narrow and winding.
RAIL: Often more efficient than driving. Excellent services provided. Cheap fares are available through the 'Swiss Pass' and leaflets and timetables are available from the railway company. BUS: Postal motor coaches provide services to even the remotest villages but few long distance coaches are permitted to operate. TAXI: All taxis are metered although it is advisable to agree the fare in advance. CAR HIRE: All the major companies are present. DOCUMENTATION: A national driving licence is sufficient. 'Green card' is recommended.

 This is a very law abiding nation. Dropping litter can cause offence. Don't give Chrysanthemums or white Asters to a host, as they are considered to be funeral flowers. Many cultures overlap in Switzerland.

Syrian Arab Republic

CAPITAL: Damascus

GMT + 2 (GMT + 3 during the summer).

FROM UK: 963   IDD: Y
OUTGOING CODE: 00

Contact hotel operator.

Embassy of the Syrian Arab Republic, 8 Belgrave Square, London SW1X 8PH. Tel: (0171) 245 9012. Fax: (0171) 235 4621.
British Embassy, PO Box 37, Quarter Malki, 11 rue Mohammad Kurd Ali, Immeuble Kotob, Damascus, Syria. Tel: (11) 3712 561/2/3. Fax: (11) 373 1600. Consulate in Aleppo.

Not present.

Ministry of Tourism, rue Victoria, Damascus, Syria. Tel: (11) 221 5816. Fax: (11) 224 2636.

Requirements may be subject to short-term change. Contact the relevant authority before departure.
VALID PASSPORT REQUIRED

Visa required.

All gold jewellery must be declared on arrival.

S£ 200, payable in local currency. Transit passengers are exempt.

Holders of passports containing a visa (valid or expired) for Israel and those holding a stamp indicating an Israel-Jordan border crossing.

MALARIA: Exists in the vivax variety in tiny pockets of the Northern border areas May–Oct. YELLOW FEVER: A vaccination certificate is required from passengers arriving from infected areas. OTHER: Bilharzia, Visceral leishmaniasis and Hepatitis A and B.

W2

Syrian Pound (S£) = 100 piastres. NOTE: The export of local currency is prohibited. Amex and Diners Club are the most commonly accepted. Some hotels accept MasterCard and Visa. Traveller's cheques are accepted but can not always be exchangeable at Damascus airport.
ATM AVAILABILITY: Unavailable.

MONEYGRAM: Unavailable.
WESTERN UNION: Unavailable.

AMEX: +44 1273 696933
DINERS CLUB: No local number.
MASTERCARD: 1 314 542 7111
VISA: (1) 410 581 9091
AMEX: (973) 256 834
THOMAS COOK: +44 1733 318950
VISA: +44 1733 318949

0800–1400 Sat and Thur (banks tend to close early on Thursday).

Can be expensive in the high season, especially in Damascus. Savings can be made by purchasing local food from the markets.

Arabic. French and English may also be spoken.

Summers are hot and dry whilst nights are often cool. Winter is cold.

Mostly Muslim. Christian (mainly Greek Orthodox and Greek Catholic).

1998: Jan 1, 30*; Mar 8, 21; Apr 7, 12, 17, 19, 28; May 6*; July 6*; Oct 6; Dec 25.
1999: Jan 1, 30*; Mar 8, 21; Apr 4, 7, 17, 19, 28; May 6*; July 6*; Oct 6; Dec 25.

220 volts AC, 50 Hz.

Airmail to Western Europe takes up to 1 week. Parcels sent from Syria should be packed at the post office.

BBC: 15.07 12.09 11.76 9.410
VOA: 15.20 11.90 9.700 7.205.

Muslim customs apply. Modest dress is recommended at all times. Wearing a wedding ring will make one appear more respectable. If rude remarks are made it is advisable to ignore them and make no eye contact.
ROAD: Well over half the roads are tarred. Those that aren't are unsuitable for the wet season. BUS: Orange and white air-conditioned buses serve terminals in city centres. Seats must be booked in advance. TAXIS: Shared taxis operate and are available to all parts of the country. DOCUMENTATION: IDP required. Insurance is required by law and a customs certificate is needed.

Syria is one of the safest places to travel in and most people are friendly and hospitable. Beach-wear should not be worn away from the pool or beach. Conservative casual clothes are suitable. PHOTOGRAPHY: Ensure you do not photograph anything connected with the military.

CAPITAL: Papeete

 Ranges from -9 to -10 depending on the particular island.

 FROM UK: 689   IDD: Y
OUTGOING CODE: 00 (Operator's assistance may be required.)

 Dial Operator.

 Refer to French Embassy.

 Honorary British Consulate, BP 1064, Polynésie Car Sarl, rue Charles Vienot, Papeete, Tahiti. Tel: 428 457 or 424 355. Fax: 410 847.

 Tahiti Tourism Promotion Board, c/o maison de France, 178 Piccadilly, London W1V 0AL. Tel: (0171) 629 2869 or (0891) 244 123 (information line).

 Tahiti Tourisme BP 65, Fare Manihini, boulevard Pomare, Papeete, Tahiti. Tel: 505 700 or 505 703. Fax: 436 619.

 See France.
VALID PASSPORT REQUIRED:See France.

 See France

 Plants, cats, dogs and dangerous goods. Baggage from Brazil, Samoa and Fiji will be fumigated, allow for at least 2 hours.

 CFP Fr 920, payable in local currency.

 See France.

 POLIO, TYPHOID: R.
YELLOW FEVER: A vaccination certificate is required for those over 1 year of age arriving from infected areas.

 W2

 French Pacific Franc (CFP Fr) = 100 centimes. Exchange facilities are available at the airport, major banks and authorised hotels and shops. Amex is the most widely accepted credit card, while others have only limited acceptance. Traveller's cheques are accepted, in any international currency.
ATM AVAILABILITY: 11 locations.

 MONEYGRAM: Unavailable.
WESTERN UNION: Unavailable.

 AMEX: +44 1273 696933
DINERS CLUB: No local number.
MASTERCARD: 1 314 542 7111
VISA: (1) 410 581 9091

 AMEX: (61) 2 886 0689
THOMAS COOK: 44 1733 318950
VISA: 44 1733 318949

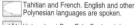 0745–1530 Mon to Fri.

 Caters for all types of budgets. Accommodation ranges from hotels to thatched-roof bungalows.

 Tahitian and French. English and other Polynesian languages are spoken.

 Hot and wet Dec–Feb. Cool and dry Mar–Nov.

 Protestant and Roman Catholic.

 1998: Jan 1; Mar 5; Apr 10, 13; May 1, 21; June 1, 29; July 14; Aug 15; Nov 1, 11; Dec 25.
1999: Jan 1; Mar 5; Apr 2, 5, 10; May 1, 21, 31; June 29; July 14; Aug 15; Nov 1, 11; Dec 25.

 110/220 Volts AC, 50 Hz.

 Up to 2 weeks by airmail to Western Europe.

BBC: 17.83 15.34 11.95 9.740
VOA: 15.18 11.72 9.525 5.985

 Local women wear traditional dress in bright pareos, reflecting the country's history.

FLIGHTS: Domestic flights connect Tahiti with neighbouring islands, which make up French Polynesia. SEA: Daily connections to neighbouring islands can be made. ROAD: BUS: Basic buses offer an inexpensive service, no schedule is operated. CAR HIRE: Major and local agencies rent cars in the main islands. DOCUMENTATION: National driving licence will be sufficient.

French Polynesia comprises of 130 islands divided into 5 archipelajos, Tahiti being the most popular. Tipping is not practised.

Taiwan

CAPITAL: Taipei

GMT + 8

FROM UK: 886   IDD: Y
OUTGOING CODE: 002

Police: 110 (Chinese only)

No Embassy in the UK.

Taipei Representative Office in the UK, 50 Grosvenor Gardens, London SW1 0EB. Tel: (0171) 396 9152. Fax: (0171) 396 9143.

Refer to representative office above.

Taiwan Visitors Association, 5th Floor, 9 Minchuan East Road, Section 2, Taipei, Taiwan. Tel: (2) 701 2671. Fax: (2) 754 2107.

Return Ticket Required. Requirements may change at short notice. Contact the embassy before departure.
VALID PASSPORT REQUIRED: valid for 6 months.

Visa not required by UK nationals if their stay does not exceed 14 days, they are holding a passport valid for at least 6 months and are of previous good character. If staying for more than 14 days a visa is required.

No-canned meat products. Toy pistols and gambling articles.

NT$300 is levied on international departures, payable in local currency. Children under 2 years and transit passengers are exempt.

Passengers holding passports issued by the People's Republic of China.

POLIO, TYPHOID: R.
YELLOW FEVER: A vaccination certificate is required if arriving from an infected area.
OTHER: Cholera, Rabies.

W1

New Taiwan Dollar (NT$) = 100 cents.
NOTE: Import and export of local currency is limited to NT$ 40,000. All exchange receipts must be retained. Export of foreign currency is limited to the equivalent of US$ 5000 for passengers leaving within 6 months of arrival. Credit cards and traveller's cheques are accepted in most hotels, shops and restaurants. US dollars are the preferred currency. ATM AVAILABILITY: Over 1400 locations.

MONEYGRAM: 0080 10 3678.
WESTERN UNION: Unavailable.

AMEX: +44 1273 696933
DINERS CLUB: (886) (2) 5211717
MASTERCARD: 0080 10 3400
VISA: 0080 89 6046

AMEX: (852) 885 9331
THOMAS COOK: +44 1733 318950
VISA: +44 1733 318949

0900–1530 Mon to Fri, 0900–1230 Sat.

It is possible to live relatively cheaply by shopping at markets. Good quality, cheap, accommodation may be more difficult to find.

Mandarin (Chinese), English and Japanese.

Subtropical climate with moderate temperatures in the North where there is a winter season. June–Oct is the typhoon season.

Buddhism, Taoism, Christianity, (Roman Catholic and Protestant) and Muslim.

1998: Jan 1, 3, 27–30; Apr 5, 6; May 30; July 1; Oct 5, 10; Nov 12.
1999: Jan 1, 3, 27–30; Apr 5, 6; May 30; July 1; Oct 5, 10; Nov 12.

110 Volts Ac 60 Hz.

Up to 10 days.

BBC: 15.36 11.95 9.740 7.110
VOA: 17.74 15.29 11.76 6.110

A patriarchal culture prevails. Women play a traditional role in society.

ROAD: There is an adequate road system joining all major cities. DOCUMENTATION: IDP is required. BUS: Local and long distance bus services operate. TAXI: There are numerous taxis which are inexpensive – but beware of drivers. RAIL: Air-conditioned, electric trains run hourly.

Taiwan is sensitive to political discussions regarding neighbouring China, but is still heavily influenced by Chinese culture. However as a major economic force in the Pacific it has adopted western free-market practices.

CAPITAL: Dushanbe

 GMT + 5.

 FROM UK: 7 (then 3772 for Dushanbe).
IDD: Y, but services are unreliable.
OUTGOING CODE: International calls have
to go through the operator.

 Not present.

 No representation

 No representation

 Intourist, Intourist House, 219 Marsh Wall,
Isle of Dogs, London E14 9PD. Tel: (0171)
538 8600. Fax: (0171) 538 5967.

 Intourist Tajikistan, c/o Hotel Tajikistan, ulitsa
Shotemur 22, Dushanbe 734001, Tajikistan.
Tel: (3772) 274 973. Fax: (3772) 275 155.

 Return Ticket required. Requirements may be
subject to short-term change. Contact the relevant authority before departure.
VALID PASSPORT REQUIRED: 10-year
passport valid for at least 6 months prior to
departure.

 Visa required.

 All valuable items and foreign currency
should be declared on arrival.

 US$10 is levied on all foreign travellers.

 POLIO, TYPHOID: R.
MALARIA: Reports have indicated there may
be a risk of malaria near the Southern border
in the vivax variety.
OTHER: There is a Diphtheria epidemic.
Cholera and Rabies also exist. NOTE:
Medical advice should be sought before travelling bearing in mind the potential medical
risk when travelling in Tajikistan.

 W1

 Rouble. Exch: The preferred hard currency is
the US Dollar although others are acceptable.
All bills are usually settled in cash. NOTE:
Import of local currency is prohibited. Visa
has limited acceptance in some hotels in the
capital. Traveller's cheques are not accepted.
ATM AVAILABILITY: Unavailable.

MONEYGRAM: Unavailable.
WESTERN UNION: Unavailable.

 AMEX: No local number
DINERS CLUB: No local number
MASTERCARD: No local number
VISA: (1) 410 581 9091
AMEX: No local number
THOMAS COOK: No local number
VISA: No local number

 0900–1730 Mon to Fri. Closed Sat.

 High inflation has resulted in lower prices.

 Tajik. Russian and English (by those
involved in tourism) are also spoken.

 Temperatures vary between 12ºC min in the
winter to 45ºC max in the summer.

 Mainly Sunni Muslim with a large Ishmaeli
minority and a smaller Russian Orthodox
minority.

 1998: Jan 1, 30*; Mar 21*; Sept 9; Nov 6.
1999: Jan 1, 18*; Mar 21*; Sept 9; Nov 5.

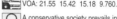 220 volts AC, 50 Hz.

 Mail can take anything between two weeks
and two months to reach Western Europe or
the USA.
BBC: 17.79 15.31 11.76 9.740
VOA: 21.55 15.42 15.18 9.760.

 A conservative society prevails in accordance with religious beliefs.

 ROAD: In poor weather conditions the roads
are mainly impassable. During winter the
roads from the capital are often closed
because of snow. TAXI: Agree the fare in
advance and use the old and new street
names, which have been created since independence. Officially marked taxis are safe
but avoid sharing with strangers. BUS: There
are services between the major towns when
the roads are open. DOCUMENTATION: IDP
and insurance are required.

 NOTE: The FCO advises against all travel to
Tajikistan. Outbursts of fighting continue and
the potential for terrorist incidents, targeted
against the Russian military, continue to
exist. There is no British mission in
Tajikistan. Travellers are advised to check
local conditions with the German or US
Embassies. Do not travel alone or on foot
after dark. Be vigilant and dress down.
Shorts are rarely seen and if worn by
females are likely to create unwanted attention from local men. Do not travel out of
Dushanbe or Khojand unless with persons
from an international organisation.

CAPITAL: Dodoma

 GMT + 3

 FROM UK: 255   IDD: Y
OUTGOING CODE: International Calls must
go through the operator.

 Not present.

 High Commission for the United Republic of
Tanzania, 43 Hertford Street, London, W1Y
8DB. Tel (0171) 499 8951. Fax: (0171) 499
8954/491 9321.

 British High Commission, PO Box 9200,
Hifadhi House, Samor Avenue, dar es
Salaam, Tanzania. Tel: (51) 46300/4 or
29601. Fax: (51) 46301.

 Refer to the High Commission.

Tanzania Tourist Board, PO Box 2485, Dar
es Salaam, Tanzania. Tel: (51) 27672. Fax:
(51) 46780.

 Return Ticket Required. Requirements may
change at short notice. Contact the embassy
before departure.
VALID PASSPORT REQUIRED

 Visa required.

 Narcotics.

 Tsh1000, US$45, Sterling £18. Transit pas-
sengers and those under two years of age
are exempt.

 POLIO, TYPHOID: R.
MALARIA: Exists all year round throughout
the country in the Falciparum variety. High
resistance to chloroquine has been reported.
YELLOW FEVER: A vaccination certificate is
required for all travellers over 1 year of age
travelling from infected countries.
OTHER: Bilharzia, Rabies.

 W1

Tanzanian Shilling (Tsc) = 100 cents. Exch:
Authorised dealers or bureaux de change
NOTE: The import and export of local currency is prohibited. Mastercard and Visa have
only limited acceptance. Traveller's cheques
can be cashed at authorised exchange
bureaux, such as Forex. US dollars are the
preferred currency.
ATM AVAILABILITY: Unavailable.

 MONEYGRAM: Unavailable.
WESTERN UNION: 51 382 12.

 AMEX: No local number
DINERS CLUB: No local number
MASTERCARD: 1 314 542 7111
VISA: (1) 410 581 9091

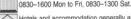 AMEX: +44 1273 571 600
THOMAS COOK: +44 1733 318950
VISA: +44 1733 318949

 0830–1600 Mon to Fri, 0830–1300 Sat.

 Hotels and accommodation generally are
expensive.

 Swahili and English. Other languages are
also spoken.

 Tropical climate. The rainy season is Mar–
May along the coast. Highlands rainy season
is from Nov–Dec and Feb–May. Cooler season: June–May.

 Muslim, Hindu, Christian, and traditional
beliefs.

 1998: Jan 1, 12, 30*; Apr 7, 10, 13, 26; May
1; July 6, 7*; Aug 8; Dec 9, 25, 26.
1999: Jan 1, 12, 30*; Apr 2, 5, 7, 26; May 1;
July 6, 7*; Aug 8; Dec 9, 25, 26.

 240 Volts AC 50 Hz. Plugs may be round or
square 3 pin, fused or unfused.

 5 days by airmail to Europe.

 BBC: 21.47 17.88 15.42 6.135
VOA: 21.49 15.60 9.525 6.035

 Formal dress is recommended.

FLIGHTS: Air Tanzania runs regular flights
between the main towns. RAIL: Regular
trains run between the main cities. ROADS:
The road network is good, although the rainy
season makes minor roads impassable. It is
inadvisable to drive at night because of the
wild animals. There are often petrol shortages and a lack of spare parts. CAR HIRE:
Companies operate but are extremely
expensive. DOCUMENTATION: IDP is recommended.

Travellers should avoid border areas. Visitors
should register with the High Commission.
Petty crime is common.

CAPITAL: Bangkok

 GMT + 7.

 FROM UK: 66   IDD: Y
OUTGOING CODE: 001

 Not present.

Royal Thai Embassy, 1/3 Yorkshire House, Grosvenor Crescent, London SW1X 7ET. Tel: (0171) 371 7621 or 259 5005 (visa section) or 0891 600 150 (recorded message). Fax: (0171) 235 9808.

British Embassy, Wireless Road, Bangkok 10330, Thailand. Tel: (2) 253 0191. Fax (2) 255 8619 or 255 6051.

Tourism Authority of Thailand, 49 Albermarle Street, London W1X 3FE. Tel: (0171) 499 7679. Fax: (0171) 629 5519.

Tourism Authority of Thailand, 372 Bamrung Muang Road, Bangkok 10100, Thailand. Tel: (2) 226 0060. Fax (2) 224 6221.

Return Ticket Required. Requirements may change at short notice. Contact the embassy before departure.
VALID PASSPORT REQUIRED

Due to frequent changes to visa requirements it is advisable to check current regulations with your consulate prior to travel.

Images of Buddha can not be exported in addition to articles of historical value.

Bt250, payable in local currency, for all passengers above 2 years of age and not in immediate transit.

POLIO, TYPHOID :R. MALARIA: Exists in the Falciparum variety in rural areas throughout the year. Resistance to chloroquine has been reported. YELLOW FEVER: A vaccination certificate is required to those over 1 year of age arriving from infected areas. OTHER: Cholera, Japanese Encephalitis, Rabies Dengue Fever, Dysentery, Hepatitis A and E.

W1

Baht (Bt) = 100 satang. NOTE: Export of local currency is limited to Bt 50,000. All credit cards are accepted. Traveller's cheques, preferably in US dollars or Pound sterling, are accepted in large hotels and shops.
ATM AVAILABILITY: Over 2,300 locations.
MONEYGRAM: 001 800 12 066 0542.
WESTERN UNION: (02) 254 9121.
AMEX:+44 1273 696933
DINERS CLUB: (66) (2) 2335775 6
MASTERCARD: 001 800 11 887 0663
VISA: 001 800 11 481 0664

 AMEX: 088 227312
THOMAS COOK: +44 1733 318950
VISA: +44 1733 318949

 0830–1530 Mon to Fri.

Relatively inexpensive. especially outside of Bangkok.
Thai. English, Malay and Chinese are also spoken.

 Generally hot particularly mid Feb–June. The monsoon season = mid May to Oct when the climate is hot with torrential rain. The most comfortable time for travelling is Nov to Feb.

 Buddhism. Muslim and Christian Minorities.

1998: Jan 1, 30; Feb 11; Apr 6, 13–16; May 1, 5, 11; July 1, 9; Aug 12, Oct 23; Dec 7, 10, 31.
1999: Jan 1, 30; Feb 11; Apr 6, 13–16; May 1, 5, 11; July 1, 9; Aug 12, Oct 23; Dec 7, 10, 31.

 220 Volts AC, 50 Hz. A variety of plugs are used.

Up to 1 week.

BBC: 15.36 11.95 9.740 6.195
VOA: 15.20 11.95 9.760 6.040.

Thai culture is the result of historical interchange between India, China and recently the west. Subsequently the culture appears at times confusing and exploitative of women and children. In recent years there has been a steady migration, including young women, from rural areas to the cities, resulting in overcrowding, poverty and forced labour. Be vigilant if travelling alone. It may be advisable to travel around Thailand with a companion.

FLIGHTS: There are services between main towns. ROAD: A reasonable network – all the major roads are paved. DOCUMENTATION: IDP required. BUS: Very cheap but very crowded. Privately owned buses are more comfortable and moderately priced. When taking the bus in the city leave the back seat free for the Saffron-robed monks. BOAT: Good services. Get a good map as finding your way around can be confusing.

 Thai laws on the use and transportation of narcotics are stringent. Tourists should be vigilant of any packages or gifts given. The monarchy and religion are sacred. Insults to either, such as climbing on statues of Buddha, will not be tolerated. Beach-wear should be confined to the beach/pool side. Shoes should be removed before entering houses. Discretion should be used and permission obtained before taking photos.

Togo

CAPITAL: Lomé

 GMT

 FROM UK: 228   IDD:Y to main cities
OUTGOING CODE: 00

 Not present.

No embassy in the UK. EUROPE: Embassy of the Republic of Togo, 8 rue Alfred Roll, 75017 Paris, France. Tel: (1) 43 80 12 13. Fax: (1) 43 80 90 71.

British Honorary Consulate, BP 20050, British School of Lomé, Lomé, Togo. Tel: 214 606. Fax: 214 989.

Not present.

Direction des Professions Touristiques, BP 1289, Lomé, Togo. Tel 215 662. Fax: 218 927.

 Return Ticket Required. Requirements may change at short notice. Contact the embassy before departure.
VALID PASSPORT REQUIRED: Not required by nationals of Great Britain.

 Visa not required by nationals of Great Britain.

 Narcotics.

 POLIO, TYPHOID: R.
MALARIA: Exists throughout the year in the Falciparum variety reported to be highly resistant to chloroquine.
YELLOW FEVER: A vaccination certificate is required for all passengers arriving over one year of age.

OTHER: Bilharzia, Cholera, Meningitis, Rabies.

 W1

CFA Franc (CFA Fr) = 100 Centimes. Amex is widely accepted, but all other credit cards are unacceptable. Traveller's cheques are only accepted in the capital city, The preferred currency is French francs.
ATM AVAILABILITY: Unavailable.

 MONEYGRAM: Unavailable.
WESTERN UNION: (228) 21 6411.

 AMEX:+44 1273 696933
DINERS CLUB: No local number
MASTERCARD: No local number
VISA: No local number

 AMEX: +44 1273 571 600
THOMAS COOK: +44 1733 318950
VISA: +44 1733 318949

 0800–1600 Mon to Fri.

 Hotels are of international standard, but accommodation in general is in short supply. Consequently prices are high.

 French and local African languages. English is spoken very little.

 Rainy season: Apr–June. Hottest months: Feb–Mar. Short rains: Oct–Nov.

 Mainly Animist, Christian and Muslim.

 1998: Jan 1, 13, 30*; Apr 7*, 13, 27; May 1, 21; June 1, 21; Aug 15; Dec 25.
1999: Jan 1, 13, 30*; Apr 7*, 5, 27; May 1, 20, 31; June 21; Aug 15; Dec 25.

 220 Volts AC 50Hz single phase. Plugs are square or round 2 pin.

 Up to 2 weeks by airmail to Europe. Postal facilities are limited to the main towns. Post Restante is available and very reliable

 BBC: 17.83 15.40 15.07 7.160
VOA: 21.49 15.41 9.575 6.035

 FLIGHTS: Air Togo runs flights to the main cities. ROAD: Are generally impassable during the rainy season. RAIL: Services operate between Lomé and main cities. BUS/TAXI: Most are efficient and cheap. CAR HIRE: Available in Lomé. DOCUMENTATION: IDP is required.

 Beachwear to be worn at the pool/beach side. Voodoo is still practised in some areas, which also serve the tourist industry. Visitors should stop at all checkpoints upon request.

CAPITAL: Nuku'alofa

 GMT + 13

 FROM UK: 676   IDD: Y
OUTGOING CODE: 0

 All services: 911.

Tonga High Commission, 36 Molyneux Street, London, W1H 6AB. Tel: (0171) 724828. Fax: (0171) 723 9074.

British High Commission, PO Box 56, Vuna Road, Nuku'alofa, Tonga. Tel: 21020/1. Fax: 24109.

Refer to High Commission.

Tonga Visitor's Bureau, PO Box 37, Vuna Road, Nuku'alofa, Tonga. Tel: 21733. Fax: 22129.

 Return Ticket Required. Regulations may be subject to change at short notice. Contact the embassy before departure.
VALID PASSPORT REQUIRED

 Visa issued on arrival to nationals of all countries.

 Arms, ammunition and pornography are prohibited. Birds, animals, fruit and plants are subject to quarantine regulations. Valuable artefacts and certain flora and fauna can not be exported.

 T$15, payable in local currency. Infants are exempt.

 Visitors must have proof of adequate funds for duration of stay and posses onward or return tickets.

 POLIO, TYPHOID: R.
YELLOW FEVER: A vaccination certificate is required from passengers over 1 year of age arriving from infected areas.

 W2

 Pa'anga (T$) = 100 seniti. Credit cards have limited use. Traveller's cheques are accepted at some hotels and tourist shops. Australian dollar cheques are preferred.
ATM AVAILABILITY: Unavailable.

 MONEYGRAM: Unavailable.
WESTERN UNION: 24345.

 AMEX: +44 1273 696933
DINERS CLUB: No local number.
MASTERCARD: 1 314 542 7111
VISA: (1) 410 581 9091

 AMEX: (61) 2 886 0689
THOMAS COOK: +44 1733 318950
VISA: +44 1733 318949

 0930–1530 Mon to Fri. 0830–1130 Sat.

 Relatively cheap.

 Tongan and English.

 Marginally cooler than most tropical areas. The best time is May to November. Heavy rains occur between Dec and Mar.

 Wesleyan Church, Roman Catholic, Anglican.

 1998: Jan 1; Apr 10, 13, 25; May 4; June 4; July 4; Nov 4; Dec 4, 25, 26.
1999: Jan 1; Apr 2, 5, 25; May 4; June 4; July 4; Nov 4; Dec 4, 25, 26.

 240 Volts Ac 50 Hz.

 10 days.

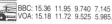 BBC: 15.36 11.95 9.740 7.145
VOA: 15.18 11.72 9.525 5.985.

 Generally considered safe for women travellers, although the islanders may think it strange if a woman is travelling alone. Single women should avoid deserted beaches in the evenings. Women are often required to wear long dresses for evening functions

FLIGHTS: Royal Tongan Airlines operate regular flights between the main cities. SEA: Ferries sail between all the island groups. Schedules are subject to change according to demand and the weather. ROAD: A good network of metalled roads exists. Horses are often used. CAR HIRE: May be arranged through a number of agencies. DOCUMENTATION: A local licence is required from the police traffic department on production of a valid international or national driving licence, the fee and a passport. Minimum driving age is 18.

 Shorts are not acceptable in towns. Visitors are not expected to tip.

Trinidad and Tobago

CAPITAL: Port of Spain

GMT – 4

FROM UK: 1 809
OUTGOING CODE: 01
IDD: Y

Police: 9, Ambulance/Fire: 990

High Commission for the Republic of Trinidad and Tobago, 42 Belgrave Square, London SW1X 8NT. Tel: (0171) 245 9351. Fax: (0171) 823 1065.
British High Commission, PO Box 778, 19 St Clair Avenue, St Clair, Port of Spain, Trinidad. Tel: 622 2748. Fax: 622 4555.
Trinidad and Tobago Tourist Office, TIDCO's UK representatives, Morris-Kevan International, International House, 47 Chase Side, Enfield, Middlesex EN2 6NB. Tel: (0181) 367 3752. Fax: (0181) 367 9949.
Tourism and Industry Development Corporation of Trinidad and Tobago (TIDCO), 10–14 Phillip Street, Port of Spain, Trinidad. Tel: 624 2953. Fax 623 4056.

Return Ticket required. Requirements may be subject to short-term change. Contact embassy before departure.
VALID PASSPORT REQUIRED

Visa not required by Nationals of EU countries for stays not exceeding 3 months.

Forms of declaration of items must be completed on arrival.

TT$75, payable in local currency, is levied. Children under 5 years of age and passengers in transit are exempt.

Visitors must have sufficient funds to cover their stay.

POLIO, TYPHOID: R.
YELLOW FEVER: A vaccination certificate is required from travellers over 1 year of age coming from infected areas.
OTHER: Rabies.

W2

Trinidad & Tobago Dollar (TT$) = 100 cents. Exch: Foreign currency can be exchanged at authorised banks only and some hotels. The export of local currency is limited to the amount declared on arrival. Both credit cards and traveller's cheques are widely accepted. Any international currency is acceptable. ATM AVAILABILITY: Over 100 locations.

MONEYGRAM: 1 800 543 4080.
WESTERN UNION: 623 6000.

AMEX: +44 1273 696933
DINERS CLUB: No local number.
MASTERCARD: 1 800 307 7309
VISA: (1) 410 581 9091
AMEX: (1) 801 964 6665
THOMAS COOK: 1 800 223 7373
VISA: 1 800 732 1322

0900–1400 Mon to Thur, 0900–1200 and 1500–1700 Fri.

Caters for all types of traveller whatever their budget.

English. French, Spanish, Hindi and Chinese are also spoken.

Tropical climate with cooling trade winds. Hottest June–Oct.

Roman Catholic, Hindu, Anglican, Muslim and Christian denomination minorities.

1998: Jan 1; Feb 23; Mar 30; Apr 10, 13; May 30; June 11, 19; Aug 1, 31; Dec 25, 26.
1999: Jan 1; Feb 22; Mar 30; Apr 2, 5; May 30; June 11, 19; Aug 1, 31; Dec 25, 26.

115-220 volts Ac 60 Hz. Continental 2 pin plugs are standard but variations may occur.

Up to 2 weeks

BBC: 17.82 11.86 9.640 5.975
VOA: 15.21 11.70 6.130 5.995.

Women are influenced by a mixture of Calypso and Latin culture.
SEA: A regular passenger service operates between Port of Spain and Tobago. ROAD: The network of roads between major towns is good but traffic around Port of Spain can be difficult. BUS: Services operate in most towns. They are cheap but can become crowded. TAXI: Official Taxis can be identified by 'H' symbol. Not all taxi fares are fixed rate, so it is advisable to find out the price before undertaking the journey. CAR HIRE: Available from the city or hotels. DOCUMENTATION: National driving licences are valid for 3 months. NOTE: Travel documents stating date of entrance to Tobago should be carried when driving.

Attacks on travellers, especially in Trinidad around the Port of Spain, have risen over recent years. Tobago, the smaller of the two islands, enjoys a relatively crime-free existence.

Tunisia

CAPITAL: Tunis

 GMT + 1

 FROM UK: 216   IDD: Y
OUTGOING CODE: 00

 Not present.

Embassy of the Republic of Tunisia, 29 Prince's Gate, London SW7 1QG. Tel: (0171) 584 8117. Fax: (0171) 225 2884.

British Embassy, 5 Place de la Victiore, Tunis, Tunisia. Tel: (1) 340 239. Fax: (1) 354 877.

Tunisian National Tourist Office, 77a Wigmore Street, London W1H 9LJ. Tel: (0171) 224 5561. Fax: (0171) 224 4053.

Office National du Tourism Tunisien, 1 Avenue Mohamed V, 1002 Tunis, Tunisia. Tel: (1) 341 077. Fax: (1) 350 997.

 Return Ticket Required. Requirements may change at short notice. Contact the embassy before departure.
VALID PASSPORT REQUIRED

 Visa required.

 Obscene material and any material which may be regarded as dangerous to public security, health, morality etc.

 POLIO, TYPHOID: R.
YELLOW FEVER: A vaccination certificate is required for visitors over one year of age travelling from infected areas.
OTHER: Rabies.

 W1

 Tunisian Dinar (TD) = 1000 millimes. Exch: All banks and most 3 star and above hotels. NOTE: Import and export of local currency is prohibited. All major credit cards are widely accepted. Traveller's cheques are accepted in major international currencies.
ATM AVAILABILITY: Over 35 locations.

 MONEYGRAM: Unavailable.
WESTERN UNION: 1 34 07 33.

 AMEX: +44 1273 696933
DINERS CLUB: No local number.
MASTERCARD: 1 314 542 7111
VISA: (1) 410 581 9091

 AMEX: +44 1273 571 600
THOMAS COOK: +44 1733 318950
VISA: +44 1733 318949

 0830–1200 and 1300–1700 Mon to Fri.

 Tourists can expect to pay more then locals but bargains can be found at the Souks. Traditionally Tunisia has been considered inexpensive, but large hotels are now comparable with Southern Mediterranean prices.

 Arabic, English and French are widely spoken.

 Warm climate throughout the year with higher temperatures inland which can be very hot. Winter has the highest rainfall.

 Islam with Roman Catholic and Protestant minority.

 1998: Jan 1, 30*; Mar 20, 21; Apr 7*, 9; May 1; July 6*, 25; Aug 13; Nov 7.
1999: Jan 1, 30*; Mar 20, 21; Apr 7*, 9; May 1; July 6*, 25; Aug 13; Nov 7.

 220 Volts AC 50Hz. Plugs: 2 pin continental.

 3–5 days airmail to Europe. Poste Restante operates in the main cities.

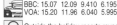 BBC: 15.07 12.09 9.410 6.195
VOA: 15.20 11.96 6.040 5.995

 Outside the holiday resorts revealing beach wear should not be worn.

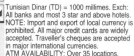 FLIGHTS: Regular daily domestic flights operate. ROAD: Extensive road network. The Garde Nationale will assist breakdowns free of charge. It is forbidden to drive in the Sahara without first contacting the Garde Nationale. DOCUMENTATION: log books, valid national driving licence and green cards are required. RAIL: Regular trains operate between Tunis and the major cities. Tickets must be purchased before the journey or double far will be charged.

 Dress can be informal but Islam conventions must be respected when visiting religious monuments. PHOTOGRAPHY: Do not take photos of military installations.

Turkey

CAPITAL: Ankara

GMT + 2 (GMT + 3 during the summer).

FROM UK: 90   IDD: Y
OUTGOING CODE: 00

Ambulance: 112, Fire: 111, Police: 155.

Embassy of the Republic of Turkey, Belgrave Square, London SW1X 8PA. Tel: (0171) 393 0202 or 235 6968 (press office). Fax: (0171) 393 0066. Turkish Consulate General, Rutland Lodge, Rutland Gardens, London SW7 1BW. Tel: (0171) 589 0360 or 589 0949 or (0891) 600 130 (recorded visa information). Fax: (0171) 584 6235.

British Embassy, Ersan Caddesi 46A, Cankaya, Ankara, Turkey. Tel: (312) 468 6230. Fax: (312) 468 6230.

Turkish Tourist Office, First Floor, 170 – 173 Piccadilly, London W1V 9DD. Tel: (0171) 629 771. Fax: (0171) 491 0773.

Ministry of Tourism, Ismet Inönü Bulvar 5, Bahçelievler, Ankara, Turkey. Tel: (312) 212 5070. Fax: (312) 212 3529.

Return Ticket Required. Requirements may be subject to change at short notice. Contact the relevant authority before travelling. VALID PASSPORT REQUIRED.

Visa required. Tourists from Ireland and the UK can obtain their visas on arrival for a fee for visits not exceeding 3 months.

Export of souvenirs such as carpets are subject to regulations. Export of antiques is forbidden. More than two sets of playing cards. Breaking the customs regulations carries very serious penalties.

US$ 12 payable on all international departures.

POLIO, TYPHOID: R. MALARIA: Potential risk in the vivax form exists during period throughout the year in various areas.
OTHER: Cholera incidents have not been evident over recent years but simple precautions when eating and drinking are advised. Rabies is present.

W2

Turkish Lira (TL). Exch: Certificates of exchange must be retained to prove that legally exchanged currency was used. Money can be exchanged at all PTT branches. Major credit cards are accepted. Traveller's cheques in US dollars can be easily exchanged.
ATM AVAILABILITY: Over 5, 000 locations.

MONEYGRAM: 00800 13 293 0909.
WESTERN UNION: Unavailable.
AMEX: +44 1273 696933
DINERS CLUB: (90) (1) 1750510
MASTERCARD: 00 800 13 887 0903
VISA: (1) 410 581 9091
AMEX: 00 800 44 91 4820
THOMAS COOK: 00 800 44 91 4895
VISA: 00 800 44 91 4899

0830–1200 and 1300–1700 Mon to Fri.

Relatively inexpensive.

Turkish, Kurdish. French, German and English are also spoken.

The coasts have a hot Mediterranean climate with hot summers and mild winters.

Muslim and Christianity.

1998: Jan 1, 30; Apr 7, 23; May 19; Aug 30; Oct 29.
1999: Jan 1, 30; Apr 7, 23; May 19; Aug 30; Oct 29.

220 Volts AC, 50 Hz.

Airmail to Europe takes 3 days.

BBC: 17.64 12.10 6.180 1.323
VOA: 9.760 6,040 1.197 0,792.

Muslim laws and cultures apply. However Turkey does not discriminate against non-Muslim beliefs. Women may receive harassment from some local men.

ROAD: An extensive road development and maintenance programme. Care must be taken if driving as accidents can lead to serious complications and delay your travels.
RAIL: Fares are comparatively cheap. BUS: Many companies provide services between major cities. CAR HIRE: Available in all main towns. DOCUMENTATION: IDP is required for visits over 3 months.

Although the PKK (Kurdistan Workers Party) has kept a low profile recently, this may alter at any time. Respect the Islamic customs. Informal wear is accepted but confine beachwear to the beach/pool. Drunkenness is not really tolerated. PHOTOGRAPHY: Do not take photographs of anything connected with the military.
There are terrorism risks. Avoid all travel to Eastern Turkey. Do not try to climb Mt Ararat in Eastern Turkey.

Turkmenistan

CAPITAL: Ashgabat

 GMT + 5.

 FROM UK: 7 (3632 for Ashgabat).
IDD: Not available from Ashgabat, but calls can be made through the international operator who speaks English.
OUTGOING CODE: 00

 All services: 03

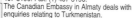 No Embassy in the UK. EUROPE: Embassy of Turkmenistan, Friedrich Schmidtplatz 3, 1080, Vienna, Austria. Tel: (1) 407 3188 or 407 3190. Fax: (1) 407 3190.

The Canadian Embassy in Almaty deals with enquiries relating to Turkmenistan.

Intourist, 219 Marsh Wall, Isle of Dogs, London E14 9PD. Tel: (0171) 538 8600. Fax: (0171) 538 5967.

Turkmenintour, U1. Makhtumkhuli 74, Ashgabat, Turkmenistan. Tel: (1) 225 6932 or 225 5191. Fax: (1) 229 3169.

 Requirements may be subject to short-term change. Contact the relevant authority before departure.
VALID PASSPORT REQUIRED

 Visa required. Visitors are usually asked to produce hotel bookings or a letter of invitation if on business.

 Loose pearls, pornography, anything carried for a third party. A complete list will be available from Intourist. NOTE: A customs declaration form must be completed on arrival and retained until departure. Customs inspection can be detailed, it is advisable to ask for a certificate from shops when purchases have been made which state that goods have been paid for in hard currency.

 Tax is variable and must be paid in hard currency, preferably US dollars.

 POLIO, TYPHOID: R.   MALARIA: R.
OTHER: Cholera is a particular risk, medical advice is recommended. Diphtheria and Rabies are also potential dangers.

 W1

 1 Manat = 100 tenge. Exch: The preferred hard currency is US Dollars, visitors may find it hard to change other currencies. A cash only economy exists. NOTE: Import of local currency is prohibited. Credit cards are not accepted. Only traveller's cheques drawn on banks with special arrangements with the Turkmen National Bank are accepted.
ATM AVAILABILITY: Unavailable.

 MONEYGRAM: Unavailable.
WESTERN UNION: Available.

 AMEX: No local number
DINERS CLUB: No local number
MASTERCARD: No local number
VISA: No local number

 AMEX: +44 1273 696933
THOMAS COOK: +44 1733 318950
VISA: +44 1733 318949

 0900–1300 Mon to Fri. Closed on Sat.

 Exploitative for the traveller.

 Turkmen. Russian is also spoken.

 Extreme Continental climate. Summers are very hot and dry and winters are very cold.

 Mainly Sunni Muslim with a small Russian Orthodox minority.

 1998: Jan 1, 12, 30*; Feb 16; Mar 8, 21; Apr 7; May 9, Oct 18.
1999: Jan 1, 12, 18*; Feb 16; Mar 0, 21; Apr 7; May 9, Oct 18.

 20 volts AC, 50 Hz. Plugs are usually the round 2 pin type.

 Mail to the USA and Western Europe can take anything from two weeks to two months.

BBC: 15.58 12.09 9.410 6.195
VOA: 9.760 6.040 1.197 0.792.

 Usual precautions should be taken. Conservative clothing should be worn in accordance with religious beliefs.

BUS: Services are available to all major towns. TAXI: They can be found I all major towns. Many are unlicensed and fares should be agreed in advance. As many of the street names have changed since independence it is advisable to use both old and new names. DOCUMENTATION: When car hire is available an IDP will be required.

Bread should never be placed upside down. Shoes must be removed on entering someone's home. Shorts are rarely seen – if worn by women they may attract unwelcome attention.

CAPITAL: Cockburn Town

 GMT − 5 (GMT −4 from first Sunday in Apr to Saturday before the last Sunday in Oct).

 FROM UK: 1 809   IDD: Y
OUTGOING CODE: 01

 All services: 911

 Commonwealth Information Centre, Commonwealth Institute, 230 Kensington High Street, London, W8 6NQ. Tel: (0171) 603 4535, ext. 210 (information). Fax: (0171) 602 7374.

 No British Embassy is present.

 Turks and Caicos Tourist Information Office, International House, 47 Chase Side, Enfield, EN2 6NB. Tel: (0181) 364 45188. Fax: (0181) 367 9949.

 Turks and Caicos Islands Tourist Board, PO Box 128, Pond Street, Grand Turk, Turks and Caicos Islands. Tel: 946 2321. Fax: 946 7233.

 Return Ticket required. Requirements may be subject to short term change. Contact embassy before departure.
VALID PASSPORT REQUIRED

 Visa not required by Nationals of Great Britain.

 Firearms and spear-guns.

 US$10. Children under 12 years of age are exempt.

 POLIO, TYPHOID: R.

 W1

 US Dollar (US$) = 100 cents. All major credit cards are accepted. Traveller's cheques are widely accepted, preferably in US dollars. ATM AVAILABILITY: Unavailable.

 MONEYGRAM: Unavailable.
WESTERN UNION: 941 3702.

 AMEX: +44 1273 696933
DINERS CLUB: No local number.
MASTERCARD: 1 800 307 7309
VISA: (1) 410 581 9091

 AMEX: (1) 801 964 6665
THOMAS COOK: 1 800 223 7373
VISA: 1 800 732 1322

 0830–1430 Mon to Thur, 0830–1230 and 1430–1630 Fri (Barclays Bank), 0830–1430 Mon to Thur and 0830–1630 Fri (Scotia Bank).

 Extremely expensive. Hotels range from standard to 2 luxury and 2 deluxe, with private beaches and moorings.

 English.

 Tropical climate with cool winds. Nights are cool with rain in the winter.

 Roman Catholic, Anglican, Methodist, Baptists, Seventh Day Adventist and Pentecostal minorities.

 1998: Jan 1; Mar 10; Apr 10, 13; May 25; June 13, 14; Aug 1, 3; Sept 28; Oct 12, 24, 26; Dec 25, 26.
1999: Jan 1; Mar 10; Apr 2, 5; May 25; June 13, 14; Aug 1, 3; Sept 28; Oct 12, 24, 26; Dec 25, 26.

 110 volts AC

 5 days.

 BBC: 17.84 15.22 6.195 5.975
VOA: 15.21 11.58 9.590 6.130

 Influenced by British Colonialism, variants depending on island.

ROAD: Less than a quarter of the roads are tarred. TAXI: Available at the airport but may be scarce meaning they may have to be shared. CAR HIRE: Limited selection available from local firms. DOCUMENTATION: A local licence is obtainable on presentation of a national or IDP licence.

The islands consist of 30 in total, forming the southern eastern Bahamas chain. Access is primarily by boat, although the larger islands have airports.

CAPITAL: Funafuti

 GMT + 12

 FROM UK: 688　　　　　IDD: Y
OUTGOING CODE: Calls must be made through the international operator.

 Not present.

 No embassy in the UK. EUROPE: Honorary Consulate of Tuvalu, Klovensteenweg 115 A, 22559 Hamburg, Germany. Tel (40) 810 580. Fax: (40) 811 016.

 British Embassy, PO Box 1355, Victoria House, 47 Gladstone Road, Suva, Fiji. Tel: 311033. Fax: 301 406.

 Refer to the Honorary Consulate.

 Ministry of Commerce and Natural Resources, Vaiaku, Funafuti, Tuvalu. Tel/Fax: 20182.

 Return Ticket Required. Regulations may be subject to change at short notice. Contact the Embassy before departure.
VALID PASSPORT REQUIRED

 Visa not required by nationals of the UK provided they have sufficient proof of onward travel and funds to finance stays of up to 1 month.

 Pornography, pure alcohol, narcotics, arms and ammunition are prohibited imports. Animal and plant materials are subject to quarantine. Export of artefact and certain flora and fauna is restricted.

 AS$ 10 is levied on all international departures.

 POLIO, TYPHOID: R.

 Australian Dollar is used for transactions over one dollar but Tuvaluan (Dollar) currency may also be used. Credit cards are not accepted although Mastercard is accepted by the national bank. Traveller's cheques in Australian dollars can be cashed at the national bank only.
ATM AVAILABILITY: Unavailable.

 MONEYGRAM: Unavailable.
WESTERN UNION: Unavailable.

 AMEX: No local number
DINERS CLUB: No local number
MASTERCARD: 1 314 542 7111
VISA: No local number

 AMEX: (61) 2 886 0689
THOMAS COOK: +44 1733 318950
VISA: +44 1733 318949

 0930–1300 Mon to Thur, 0830–1200 Fri.

 There is only one main hotel which offers moderate facilities, whilst other guest houses offer basic accommodation. All are inexpensive. Commodities are scarce due an undeveloped tourist industry.

 Tuvaluan and English are the main languages.

 Hot and Humid with little variation throughout the year. Mar to Oct tends to be slightly cooler and therefore more pleasant. Nov – Feb is the wet season when the climate may be uncomfortable.

 Mainly Protestant.

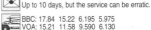 1998: Jan 1; Mar 2; Apr 10, 13; June 14; Aug 4; Oct 1–2; Nov 14; Dec 25–26.
1999: Jan 1; Mar 2; Apr 2, 5; June 14; Aug 4; Oct 1–2; Nov 14; Dec 25–26.

 110 volts AC

 Up to 10 days, but the service can be erratic.

BBC: 17.84　15.22　6.195　5.975
VOA: 15.21　11.58　9.590　6.130

 Culture and tradition play a strong part in Tuvaluan life. Religious holidays are taken very seriously. Women are conservative in behaviour.

SEA: The islands are served by passenger and cargo-vessels. ROAD: Mainly dirt tracks TAXIS: Limited. BIKES: Push and motor bikes can be hired hotels.

Men must wear shirts in public places. Sunday is regarded as a sacred day and should be respected along with local customs.

Uganda

CAPITAL: Kampala

 GMT + 3

 FROM UK: 256   IDD:Y to main towns.
OUTGOING CODE: International calls must go through the operator.

 Not present.

 High Commission of the Republic of Uganda, Uganda House, 58–59 Trafalgar Square, London, WC2N 5DX. Tel: (0171) 839 5783. Fax: (0171) 839 8925.

 British High Commission, PO Box 7070, 101–12 Parliament Avenue, Kampala, Uganda. Tel: (41) 257 301/4 or 257 054/9.

 Refer to the High Commission.

 Uganda Tourist Board, PO Box 7211, Parliament Avenue, Kampala, Uganda. Tel: (41) 242 196. Fax: (41) 242 188.

 Return Ticket required. Requirements may change at short notice. Contact the embassy before departure.
VALID PASSPORT REQUIRED

 Visa required.

 Import of foreign currency must be declared.

 US$20 is levied on international departures. Transit and passengers under 2 years of age are exempt.

 Passengers not holding sufficient funds.

 POLIO, TYPHOID: R.
MALARIA: Exists all year throughout the country. Resistance to chloroquine has been reported.
YELLOW FEVER: Vaccination is strongly recommended to all passengers and a vaccination certificate is required by passengers arriving from infected areas.
OTHER: Bilharzia, Meningitis, Rabies.

W1

Uganda Shilling (Ush) = 100 cents. Exch: central bank, commercial banks and exchange bureaux. NOTE: Import and export of local currency is prohibited. Visa is widely accepted, but other credit cards have limited acceptance. Traveller's cheques, preferably in US dollars are accepted.
ATM AVAILABILITY: Unavailable.

 MONEYGRAM: Unavailable.
WESTERN UNION: 41 234 570

 AMEX: +44 1273 696933
DINERS CLUB: No local number.
MASTERCARD: 1 314 542 7111
VISA: (1) 410 581 9091

 AMEX: +44 1273 571 600
THOMAS COOK: +44 1733 318950
VISA: +44 1733 318949

 0830–1400 Mon to Fri.

 Since a new privatisation programme was introduced in the last few years, the cost of living has risen.

 English and Luganda and Kiswahili is also widely spoken.

 The higher altitudes can be quite cool. There is heavy rain: Mar–May, Oct–Nov.

 Majority Christian, with Animist and Muslim.

 1998: Jan 1, 26, 30*; Mar 8; Apr 7*, 10, 13; June 3, 9; Oct 9; Dec 25, 26.
1999: Jan 1, 26, 30*; Mar 8; Apr 2, 5, 7*; June 3, 9; Oct 9; Dec 25, 26.

 240 Volts Ac 50 Hz

 Airmail to Europe can take 3 days to several weeks.

 BBC: 17.88 15.42 9.630 6.135
VOA: 21.49 11.58 9.575 6.035

 Usual precautions should be taken.

 FLIGHTS: Domestic flights operate regularly between major cities. ROAD: Vary in quality and are sparse in the North. DOCUMENTATION: A national driving licence or IDP is required. RAIL: Passenger facilities are limited and timetables can be erratic although regular services operate. BUS: Services are often overcrowded and unreliable.

 Consult the Embassy before travelling. The South and West are considered safe to travel but safety can not be guaranteed in the North and Northeast. Risk remains elsewhere of armed robbery and car-jackings. Do not travel after dark. Taking photos of anything connected to the military is prohibited.

Ukraine

CAPITAL: Kyiv

 GMT + 2 (GMT+ 3 during British summer time).

 FROM UK: 380
IDD: Available in most cities.
OUTGOING CODE: 810

 Embassy of Ukraine, 78 Kensington Park Road, London W11 2PL. Tel: (0171) 727 6312 or 0891 515 919 (recorded information).

 British Embassy, vul. Desyatinna 9, 252025 Kyiv, Ukraine. Tel +44 462 0011/2. Fax: +44 462 0013.

 Intourist, 219 Marsh Wall, Isle of Dogs, London E14 9PD. Tel: 0171 538 8600 or 538 5902.

 Ministry of Foreign Affairs, vul. Mykhailoivska pl. 1, 252018 Kyiv, Ukraine. Tel: +44 226 3379. Fax +44 226 3169.

 Regulations may change at short notice and you are advised to contact the relevant consular authority before finalising travel arrangements.
VALID PASSPORT REQUIRED

 Visa required.

 Contact the consular authority for up to date information.

 Cholera and Diphtheria

 W2

 Currency: Hryvnya. Banks and currency offices will exchange money. Credit cards are not widely accepted. The preferred currency for traveller's cheques is US dollars. ATM AVAILABILITY: only a handful.

 MONEYGRAM: 8 then 100 11
WESTERN UNION: (044) 295 2552

AMEX: +44 1273 696933
DINERS CLUB: no local number
MASTERCARD: (1) 314 542 7111
VISA: (1) 410 581 9091

 AMEX: +44 1273 571 600
THOMAS COOK: +44 1733 318950
VISA: +44 171 937 8091

 0900–1600

 Less expensive than Western Europe.

 Ukrainian is the official state language. Russian is also widely spoken.

 Temperate with warm summers, crisp sunny autumns and cold, snowy winters

 Ukrainian Orthodox. A type of Catholicism is exists in the Western part of the country.

 1998: Jan 1, 7; Mar 8; May 2, 9; Nov 7.
1999: Jan 1, 7; Mar 8; May 2, 9; Nov 7.

 220 volts Ac 50 Hz

 Services are erratic. Letters to Western Europe can take up to 2 weeks.

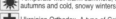 BBC: 15.58 12.10 9.410 6.180
VOA: 9.760 6.040 1.197 0.792

 Usual common sense precautions should be taken.

 FLIGHTS: not recommended as flights are far from comfortable and buying tickets is extremely difficult. RAIL: as buying tickets is difficult it is advisable to pre book through Intourist in London. ROAD: Buses exist but are not recommended, taxis are available and fares should be agreed in advance.

! A room in a private home is an excellent accommodation option in the Ukraine as the people are friendly and hospitable.

United Arab Emirates

CAPITAL: Abu Dhabi

GMT + 4

FROM UK: 971   IDD: Y
OUTGOING CODE: 00

All services: 344 663 (only Abu Dhabi)

Embassy of the United Arab Emirates, 30 Prince's Gate, London SW7 1PT. Tel: (0171) 581 1281. Fax: (0171) 581 9616. Consulate of the United Arab Emirates, 48 Prince's Gate, London SW7 1PT. Tel: (0171) 589 3434.
British Embassy, PO Box 248, Abu Dhabi, UAE. Tel (2) 326 600 or 321 364. Fax: (2) 341 744 or 318 138, and PO Box 65, Dubai, UAE. Tel: (4) 521 070. Fax: (4) 525 750.

Refer to Consulate.

Federal Ministry of Tourism and Culture, PO Box 5053, Dubai, UAE. Tel: (4) 615 500. Fax: (4) 615 648.
Return Ticket required. Requirements may be subject to short-term change. Contact the relevant authority before departure.
VALID PASSPORT REQUIRED: valid for at least 6 months from date of arrival.
Visa not required by Nationals of the UK with the endorsement 'British Subject Citizen of the UK and Colonies' or 'British Citizen' for a maximum of 30 days.

Loose Pearls.

POLIO, TYPHOID: R. MALARIA: A risk exists in the valleys and the lower slopes of mountainous areas of the Northern States.
OTHER: Cholera, Rabies.

W2

UAE Dirham (UAE Dh) = 100 fils. Exch: Most hotels. All credit cards are accepted.
Traveller's cheques, preferably in US dollars, can be easily exchanged.
ATM AVAILABILITY: Over 280 locations.

MONEYGRAM: 800 121 then 800 592 3688.
WESTERN UNION: 0800 2344.

AMEX: +44 1273 696933
DINERS CLUB: (971) (4) 255 400
MASTERCARD: 1 314 542 7111
VISA: (1) 410 581 9091

AMEX: (973) 256 834
THOMAS COOK: +44 1733 318950
VISA: +44 1733 318949

0800–1200 Sat to Wed and 0800–1100 Thur.

Relatively expensive although the budget traveller will be able to find cheaper hotels and food, away from the main tourist areas. Prices are constant throughout the year.

Arabic. English is widely spoken.

June–Sept is the hottest period with little rainfall. Oct–May is more comfortable to visit.

Mostly Sunni Muslim.

1998: Jan 1, 30*; Apr 7, 16, 28; July 6*; Aug 6; Nov 17; Dec 2, 3.
1999: Jan 1, 30*; Apr 7, 16, 28; July 6*; Aug 6; Nov 17; Dec 2, 3.
220/240 volts AC, 50 Hz. Square 3 pin plugs are widespread.

Airmail takes about 5 days to reach Western Europe.

BBC: 15.57 12.10 11.76 9.410
VOA: 15.21 9.740 1.548 1.260.

In general this is one of the more liberal Muslim countries in the Middle East incorporating many western traditions. Foreign female travellers should be vigilant especially when looking for cheaper accommodation in the cities.
SEA: Passenger services serve all coastal ports. ROAD: There are good roads running along the West Coast. BUS: A limited service links most towns. However most hotels run their own scheduled service to the airport, city centre and beach. TAXI: Most travellers find taxis to be the most convenient and quickest method of transport. Taxis are metered and there is a surcharge for air-conditioned taxis. CAR HIRE: Most international companies have agencies at the airport and hotels. DOCUMENTATION: Renters must produce 2 photographs, passports and either a valid international or national licence. IDP is recommended.

This is one of the most liberal countries in the Gulf, although it is still very conservative by Western standards. Respect Muslim traditions. It is illegal to smoke or drink in public places during Ramadam. Western entertainment is available in the form of cocktail bars, public houses and cinemas.

United Kingdom

CAPITAL: London

 GMT (+1 during the summer time).

 FROM UK: 44   IDD: Y
OUTGOING CODE: 00

 Police, Ambulance, Fire: 999

 British Tourist Authority and British Tourist Board, Thames Tower, Black's Road, Hammersmith, London W6 9EL. Tel (0181) 846 9000. Fax: (0181) 563 0302.

 Requirements may be subject to change at short notice. Contact the relevant authority before travelling.
VALID PASSPORT REQUIRED: Required by all except: Nationals of EU countries with a valid ID card for tourist visits not exceeding 3 months. Nationals of Iceland Liechtenstein, Monaco, Norway and Switzerland with valid ID cards for tourist/social visits of not less than 6 months and in possession of a British Visitor's guide available from travel agencies.

 Visa not required by EU nationals and citizens of Australia, Canada, USA and Japan.

 All cats and dogs must spend 6 months in quarantine on arrival in the country. An import licence is required for all pets.

 £20 is payable on all departures.

 Pound (£) = 100 pence. Banks, Thomas Cook offices, exchange bureaux and many hotels will exchange currency. All major credit cards are accepted. Traveller's cheques are widely accepted, preferably in Pound sterling.
ATM AVAILABILITY: Over 22, 000 locations.

 MONEYGRAM: 800 66639472.
WESTERN UNION: 800 833 833.

 AMEX: +44 1273 696933
DINERS CLUB: +44 (252) 375252
MASTERCARD: 0800 96 4767
VISA: 0800 96 3833

 AMEX: 0800 521313
THOMAS COOK: 0800 622101
VISA: 0800 515884

 0900–1730 Mon to Fri. Main branches are open on Saturday mornings.

 London and major tourist centres can be especially expensive.

 English. Welsh is spoken in areas of Wales. Gaelic is spoken in parts of Scotland and N. Ireland. French and Norman French are spoken in the Channel Islands. There are a variety of ethnic minorities (Hindi, Urdu, Turkish, Greek, Cantonese and Mandarin).

 The climate is temperate with warm, wet summers and mild, wet winters. It is variable throughout the year and the country as a whole.

 Protestant (Church of England), Roman Catholic, Church of Scotland, Evangelical, Non-Conformist, Baptist, Jewish, Muslim and Hindu minorities.

 1998: Jan 1, 2 (Scotland only); March 17 (Ireland only); Apr 10, 13; May 4, 25; July 12 (Northern Ireland only), 13; Aug 3 (Scotland only), 31 (not Scotland); Dec 25–26, 28.
1999: Jan 1, 2 (Scotland only); March 17 (Ireland only); Apr 2, 5; May 3, 24; July 12 (Northern Ireland only), 13; Aug 2 (Scotland only), 30 (not Scotland); Dec 25–26, 28.

 240 volts AC, 50 Hz. Square 3 pin plugs are used.

 Post destined for outside Europe should be sent airmail.

 BBC: 12.10 9.410 6.195 0.648
VOA: 9.760 6.040 1.197 0.792

 British society is deemed equal, incorporating punitive measures for sexism and racism.

 There is a comprehensive nationwide rail and bus network.

 Although a cease-fire is currently in place in Northern Ireland, sectarian violence still persists. If visiting avoid discussions on religion and politics. Normal social courtesies apply.

CAPITAL: Washington DC

USA has 6 time zones ranging from GMT -5 on the East coast to -10 in Hawaii.

FROM UK: 1   IDD: Y
OUTGOING CODE: 001

911

Embassy of the United States of America, 24–31, Grosvenor Square, London, W1A 1AE. Tel: (0171) 499 9000.

British Embassy, 3100 Massachusetts, NW, Washington DC, 20008. Tel: (202) 462 1340. Fax: (202) 898 4255. Consulates in major cities.

United Sates Travel and Tourism Administration, 14th Constitutional Avenue, NW, Washington DC. Tel: (202) 482 3811 or 482 2000. Fax (202) 482 2887.

Return Ticket required. Requirements may change at short notice. Contact the embassy before departure.
VALID PASSPORT REQUIRED

Visa not required by nationals of EU countries if not exceeding 90 days and with a valid passport.

Some seeds, fruits and plants, pornography, switchblade knives, narcotic drugs unless with prescription, knives and hazardous items.

US$10 is levied on all foreign travellers.

Anyone with communicable diseases, a criminal record, narcotic addicts and drug traffickers and anyone who has been deported or denied admission within the previous 5 years.

Rabies

US Dollar (US$) = 100 cents. Exch: Most hotels do not exchange foreign currency and only a few major banks are willing to do so. It is advisable to take US$. Credit cards and traveller's cheques are widely accepted, preferably in US dollars.
ATM AVAILABILITY: Over 135,000 locations.

MONEYGRAM: 1 800 926 9400.
WESTERN UNION: 800 325 6000.

AMEX: +44 1273 696933
DINERS CLUB: 1 800 525 9040
MASTERCARD: 1 800 307 7309
VISA: 1 800 847 2399

AMEX: 1 800 221 7282
THOMAS COOK: 1 800 223 7373
VISA: 1 800 732 1322

Variable but generally 0900–1500 Mon to Fri.

Food, accommodation and petrol are cheaper than Western Europe allowing budget travel to be a possibility.

English. Many other languages are also spoken.

Varies considerably with region.

Protestant. Roman Catholic, Jewish and many minorities.

1998: Jan 1, 19; Feb 16; Apr 10, 13; May 25; July 3, 4; Sept 7; Oct 12; Nov 11, 26; Dec 25.
1999: Jan 1, 19; Feb 16; Apr 2, 5; May 24; July 3, 4; Sept 7; Oct 12; Nov 11, 26; Dec 25.

110/220 Volts 60 HZ. Plugs are of the flat 2-pin type.

Up to 1 week.

BBC: 17.84 15.26 9.590 5.975.

Society is founded on equality for both sexes, however women's roles are dependent upon the cultural, social, and legislative heritage of each individual state.

A variety of convenient modes of transport exist. When driving IDP is recommended.

A wide variety of cultures and customs are prevalent which co-exist within a diverse topography. Crime rates vary from state to state.

US Virgin Islands

CAPITAL: Charlotte Amalie

GMT – 4

FROM UK: 1 809   IDD: Y
OUTGOING CODE: 011

All services – 911

The US Virgin Islands are represented abroad by US Embassies. See USA Entry.

No British Embassy is present.

US Virgin Islands Division of Tourism, 2 Cinnamon Row, Plantation Wharf, York Place, London SW11 3TW. Tel: (0171) 978 5262. Fax: (0171) 924 3171.

US Virgin Islands Division of Tourism, PO Box 6400, Charlotte Amalie, St Thomas, VI 00804-6400. Tel: 774 8784. Fax: 774 4390.

See the USA entry.
VALID PASSPORT REQUIRED: See the USA entry.

See the USA entry.

See USA entry.

US$ 10 is levied on all foreign nationals.

See the USA entry.

POLIO, TYPHOID: R.

US Dollar (US$) = 100 cents. All major credit cards and traveller's cheques, preferably in US dollars are accepted.
ATM AVAILABILITY: 10 locations approximately.

MONEYGRAM: Single location.
WESTERN UNION: Unavailable.

AMEX: +44 1273 696933
DINERS CLUB: No local number.
MASTERCARD: 1 800 307 7309
VISA: 1 800 847 2399

AMEX: 1 800 221 7282
THOMAS COOK: 1 800 223 7373
VISA: 1 800 732 1322

0900–1430 Mon to Thur, 0900–1400 and 1530–1700 Fri.

Expensive, especially in the tourist centres. However, luxury items up to $1200 are cheaper, as they are duty-free.

English, Spanish, Creole is widely spoken.

Hot climate with cool winds. Aug–Oct is the wettest period.

Christian, mainly Protestant.

1998: Jan 1, 6, 19; Feb 16; Mar 31; Apr 9, 10, 13, 24; May 25; June 15; July 3, 4, 27; Sept 7; Oct 12, 19; Nov 1, 2, 3, 11, 26; Dec 25, 26.
1999: Jan 1, 6, 19; Feb 16; Mar 31; Apr 1, 2, 5, 24; May 25; June 15; July 3, 4, 27; Sept 7; Oct 12, 19; Nov 1, 2, 3, 11, 26; Dec 25, 26.

120 volts AC, 60 Hz.

Up to 1 week.

BBC: 17.84 15.22 6.195 5.975
VOA: 15.21 11.70 6.130 0.930

Usual precautions should be followed.

SEA: Ferries operate services between islands. ROAD: Well-maintained roads connect all main towns but not much else. TAXI: Available on all the islands. They follow set routes and their prices are published. CAR HIRE: There are international agencies operating at the airport and in the main towns. DOCUMENTATION: A national licence is acceptable.

The islands have more hotels, per square mile than any other in the Caribbean.

Uruguay

CAPITAL: Montevideo

 GMT – 3

 FROM UK: 598
IDD: Y, although difficulties may be encountered.
OUTGOING CODE: 00

 All services: 999 (Police: 109, Ambulance: 105, Fire: 104, in Montevideo only)

 Embassy of the Oriental Republic of Uruguay, 2nd Floor, 140 Brompton Road, London, SW3 1HY. Tel: (0171) 584 8192 or 589 8735 (visa section). Fax: (0171) 581 9585.

British Embassy, PO Box 16024, Calle Marco Bruto 1073, 11300 Montevideo, Uruguay. Tel: (2) 622 3630/36/50. Fax: (2) 622 7815.

 Refer to the Embassy.

 Dirección Nacionale de Turismo, Agraciado 1409, 4º, 5º y 6º, Montevideo, Uruguay. Tel: (2) 904 148.

 Return Ticket required. Requirements may change at short notice. Contact the embassy before departure.
VALID PASSPORT REQUIRED

 Visa not required by Nationals of Great Britain for stays not exceeding 3 months.

 Imported duty free goods are not to exceed US$30, and exported goods are not to exceed US$150.

 US$12 is levied on international departures. Children under 2 years of age are exempt.

 Recommended for Typhoid, incidents of Polio have not been reported.
OTHER: Rabies

 W2

 Uruguan Peso = 100 centesimos. Foreign exchange: Hotels not recommended as they tend to give unfavourable rates – use gambios and banks. NOTE: Inflation tends to lead to wide fluctuations in exchange rates. All credit cards are accepted. Traveller's cheques in US dollars are acceptable.
ATM AVAILABILITY: Over 60 locations.

 MONEYGRAM: 000 413 598 2083.
WESTERN UNION: 0800 2024/2036.
AMEX: +44 1273 696933
DINERS CLUB: (598) (2) 920207
MASTERCARD: 1 314 542 7111
VISA: (1) 410 581 9091

 AMEX: (1) 801 964 6665
THOMAS COOK: 1 800 223 7373
VISA: 1 800 732 1322

 1330–1730 Mon to Fri (summer).
1300–1700 Mon to Fri (winter).

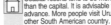 Coastal resorts tend to be more expensive than the capital. It is advisable to book well in advance. More people visit Uruguay than any other South American country.

 Spanish. English may also be spoken.

 Mild summers and winters. Summer is Dec–Mar and the most pleasant time. Nights are often cool.

 Roman Catholic.

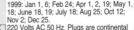 1998: Jan 1, 6; Feb 24; Apr 9, 10, 19; May 1, 18; June 18, 19; July18; Aug 25; Oct 12; Nov 2; Dec 25.
1999: Jan 1, 6; Feb 24; Apr 1, 2, 19; May 1, 18; June 18, 19; July18; Aug 25; Oct 12; Nov 2; Dec 25.

 220 Volts AC 50 Hz. Plugs are continental flat 3 pin or round 2 pin.

 Airmail to Europe takes 3–5 days. Postal rates are reasonable but the service can be unreliable. It is recommended that important items are sent by registered mail.

 BBC: 15.19 11.75 9.915 5.970
VOA: 15.12 11.58 9.590 5.995

 Inequality between men and women prevails. This is mostly seen in the over populated capital city.

 FLIGHTS: Domestic flights are operated between major centres but can be very expensive compared to other modes of transport. RAIL: Services operate between the capital and the major towns. Buffet service is available, air conditioning isn't. ROAD: 80% of roads are suitable for all weather. BUS: Services connect all the main towns and border points. CAR HIRE: Available in Montevideo. DOCUMENTATION: IDP is recommended but not required. A temporary driving licence must be obtained from the town hall.

 Uruguayans are very hospitable and like to entertain at home as well as in restaurants. Shaking hands is the usual social greeting. Normal social courtesies should be applied.

CAPITAL: Tashkent

GMT + 5

FROM UK: 7 (3712 for Tashkent).
IDD: Y   OUTGOING CODE:00

All services: 03

Embassy of the Republic of Uzbekistan, 41 Holland Park, London W11 3RP. Tel: (0171) 229 7679. Fax: (0171) 229 7029.
British Embassy, 67 Gogolya Street, Tashkent, Uzbekistan. Tel: (3712) 133 9847/8313/8416. Fax: (873) 406 549.
Uzbektourism, 13 Marylebone Lane, London W1. Tel: (0171) 935 1899. Fax: (0171) 935 9554.
Ministry of Tourism, 47 Khorezmakaya Street, Tashkent 700047, Uzbekistan. Tel: (3172) 336 475. Fax: (3712) 391 517.

Requirements may be subject to short-term change. Contact the relevant authority before departure.
VALID PASSPORT REQUIRED: Passports must be valid for 6 months prior to departure date.

Visa required. All visitors are advised to contact the relevant authority for a full list of regulations.

Items over 100 years old or anything of cultural importance can not be exported.

US$10 is levied on all foreign travellers.

POLIO, TYPHOID: R.
MALARIA: Risk exists near the Afghan border.
OTHER: Diphtheria is endemic. Rabies and Cholera are also health risks. Vaccinations for Hepatitis are also recommended.

W1

The Som is now the official currency, which was introduced in 1994. Cash is the only real form of currency; US Dollars are the preferred foreign currency. Exchange: use banks and official bureaux de change. NOTE: The import and export of local currency is prohibited. Credit cards and traveller's cheques are not accepted.
ATM AVAILABILITY: Unavailable.

MONEYGRAM: Unavailable.
WESTERN UNION: Unavailable.

AMEX: No local number
DINERS CLUB: No local number
MASTERCARD: No local number
VISA: No local number
AMEX: No local number
THOMAS COOK: No local number
VISA: No local number

0900–1700 Mon to Fri.

The limited variety of goods that are available are extremely inexpensive.

Uzbek. Russian, Tajik, Kazakh and English are also spoken.
Continental Climate. South is the warmest. Summer temperatures can be very hot. The most comfortable time to visit is during the spring or Autumn.

Mainly Sunni Muslim with; Shia, Russian Orthodox and Jewish minorities.

1998: Jan 1, 2; Mar 8, 21; Sept 1; Dec 8.
1999: Jan 1, 2; Mar 8, 21; Sept 1; Dec 8.

220 volts AC, 50 Hz. Round 2 pin continental plugs are standard.

Letters to Western Europe and the USA take between two weeks and two months.

BBC: 15.58 12.10 9.410 6.195
VOA: 9.670 6.045 5.990 1.143.

Conservative dress should be worn in accordance with religious beliefs. Usual precautions should be taken and maintaining a low profile is advised.

ROAD: A reasonable road network exists.
BUS: Services connect the major towns and cities. TAXIS: Can be found in all major centres. Many licences are unlicensed which should be avoided. Travellers are advised to agree the fare in advance and not share with strangers. Use the old and new (since independence) street names when asking for directions. DOCUMENTATION: IDP will be required when car hire is introduced.

Keep valuables out of sight. Long distance travel by train should be avoided. Do not leave the compartment unattended and lock the door. It is not recommended to use local airlines as they are not always regularly maintained. Shorts are rarely worn and women should be prepared for unwelcome attention from the local male population if they wear them.

Vanuatu

CAPITAL: Port Vila

 GMT + 12

 FROM UK: 678   IDD: Y
OUTGOING CODE: Calls must be made through the International operator.

 Police: 22 222, Ambulance: 22 100, Fire: 22 333, Doctor: 22 826.

Not present.

British High Commission, PO Box 567, KPMG House, rue Pasteur, Port Vila, Vanuatu. Tel: 23100. Fax: 23651.

Tourism Council of the South Pacific, 375 Upper Richmond Road West, London SW14 7NX. Tel: (0181) 392 1838.

Vanuatu National Tourism Office, PO Box 209. Kumul Highway, Port Vila, Vanuatu. Tel: 22515 or 22685 or 22813. Fax: 23889.

 Return Ticket Required. Regulations may be subject to change at short notice. Contact the embassy before departure.
VALID PASSPORT REQUIRED: valid for at least 4 months beyond period of stay.
Visa not required for Nationals of Great Britain for visits up to 30 days, providing they are bona fide tourists in possession of confirmed onward travel documents.

 Pornography. All plant and animal material must be declared.

V2500, payable in local currency, is levied on all international departures.

 Persons of dubious morality and persons who may become a public charge.
POLIO, TYPHOID: R.
MALARIA: Exists in the Falciparum variety in most parts of the country, throughout the year, which has been reported as being highly resistant to chloroquine.

W2

Vatu (V) = 100 centimes. Exch: Facilities are available at the airport and trade banks. Credit cards and traveller's cheques are widely accepted. Australian dollars are the preferred currency in traveller's cheques.
ATM AVAILABILITY: Unavailable.

 MONEYGRAM: Unavailable.
WESTERN UNION: Available.

 AMEX: +44 1273 696933
DINERS CLUB: No local number.
MASTERCARD: 1 314 542 7111
VISA: (1) 410 581 9091
AMEX: (61) 2 886 0689
THOMAS COOK: +44 1733 318950
VISA: +44 1733 318949

Generally 0830–1500 Mon to Fri.

 There are three international standard resorts, which are expensive, as well as smaller resorts and conventional hotel-style accommodation, which are affordable. Moderately priced self-contained apartments and bungalows are available around Port Vila on the main island. Usual services are inexpensive.

Bislama (Pidgin English). French and English are widely spoken. There are many (local) dialects totally well over 100).

 Hot and Humid. Wet season: Nov–Feb.

 Presbyterian, Anglican, Roman Catholic, Seventh Day Adventists, Apostolic Church and Church of Christ.

 1998: Jan 1; Mar 1; Apr 10, 13; May 1; July 24, 30; Aug 15; Oct 5; Nov 29; Dec 25, 26;
1999: Jan 1; Mar 1; Apr 2, 5; May 1; July 24, 30; Aug 15; Oct 5; Nov 29; Dec 25, 26.

 220 volts AC 50 Hz. Australian type flat 3 pin plugs are used.

 7 days.

 BBC: 17.83 15.34 11.95 9.740
VOA: 18.82 15.18 9.525 1.735

 Western influences are tolerated in and around tourist areas, but customs and traditions on remote islands and in rural areas remain unchanged. Women in remote areas still rely on a communal feudal village system, where appliances, tools and clothing are handmade.

FLIGHTS: The government's airline operates domestic flights, as do private airlines. SEA: Inter Island ferries operate from Port Vila and Espiritu Santo to the northern and southern islands. BUS: Limited bus service. CAR HIRE: Major car hire operators have offices in Port Vila. DOCUMENTATION: A national driving licence is acceptable.

 Traditional customs should be respected. Beachwear should be confined to the pool/beach side. Consumption of alcohol is not permitted outside licensed premises.

Vatican City

CAPITAL: Vatican City

GMT + 1 (GMT + 2 during the summer)

FROM UK: As for Rome, (6) plus 698, followed by a 5 digit number.
IDD: Y   OUTGOING CODE: 00

Police: 112, Ambulance: 113, Fire: 115

 Aspotolic Nunicature, 54 Parkside, Wimbledon, London SW19 5NE. Tel: (0891) 946 1410. Fax: (0181) 947 2494.

 British Embassy, Via Condotti 91, 00187 Rome, Italy. Tel (6) 678 9462 or 679 7479. Fax: (6) 994 0684.

 Italian State Tourist Office can provide information. See Italian entry.

 There are no formalities required to enter the Vatican city, but entry will be via Rome and Italian visa/passport requirements have to be met.
VALID PASSPORT REQUIRED: See Italy.

 See Italy.

 See Italy.

 See Italy.

See Italian entry for Health Recommendations.

 See Italian entry.

 Vatican coins are smaller in size, value and denomination to those of Italy. The monetary system is different from that in Italy, however Italian Lira is legal tender there. See Italian entry. Limited acceptance of credit cards and traveller's cheques.
ATM AVAILABILITY: Unavailable.

 MONEYGRAM: Unavailable.
WESTERN UNION: Unavailable.

AMEX: +44 1273 696933
DINERS CLUB: 39 6 3213841
MASTERCARD: 1678 70866
VISA: 1678 75617

AMEX: 1678 72000
THOMAS COOK: 1678 72050
VISA: 1678 70987

 Not present.

 There are no taxes and no customs/excise duties in the Vatican City. Accommodation is unavailable to the public.

 Italian.

 See Italy.

 Roman Catholic.

 1998: As for Italy.
1999: As for Italy.

 220 volts, 50 Hz.

 Stamps issued in the Vatican City are valid only within its boundaries.

 BBC: As for Italy.
VOA: As for Italy.

Revealing clothing should not be worn.

 RAIL: Vatican City has its own railway station. The trains are reasonably priced and offer discounts. There is a speed limit of 30 kph in the Vatican City. For travel in Rome see the entry for Italy.

Arms, shoulders and legs should be covered out of respect when visiting religious buildings. Beware of pickpockets and other thieves.

CAPITAL: Caracas

GMT – 4

FROM UK: 58   IDD: Y
OUTGOING CODE: 00

Doctor: 02 483 7021, Ambulance: 02 545 4545.

Embassy of the Republic of Venezuela, 1 Cromwell Road, London SW7 2HW. Tel: (0171) 584 4206/7. Fax: (0171) 589 8887.

British Embassy, Apartado 1246, Edificio Torre Las Mercedes 3º, Avenida la Estancia, Chuao, Caracas 1060, Venezuela. Tel: (2) 993 4111. Fax: (2) 993 9989.

Refer to the Venezuelan Consulate, 56 Grafton Way, London W1P 5LB. Tel: (0171) 387 6727. Fax: (0171) 383 3253.

Torre Oeste Piso 35, Parque Centrale, Caracas, Venezuela. Tel: (2) 507 8815/16. Fax: (2) 573 8983.

Return Ticket Required. Requirements may change at short notice. Contact the embassy before departure.
VALID PASSPORT REQUIRED: must be valid for at least 6 months.
Visa not required by Nationals of EU countries.

All organic substances.

B5400 is levied on all international departures. Children less than 2 years and transit passengers are exempt.

POLIO, TYPHOID: R.
MALARIA: Exists in the Falciparum variety which has been reported as being highly resistant to chloroquine.
YELLOW FEVER: A vaccination certificate is not required as a condition of entry but is recommended to all visitors who plan to travel out side of the urban areas.
OTHER: Bilharzia.

W2

Bolívar (B) = 100 centimos. Visa, Mastercard and Amex are widely accepted. Traveller's cheques in US dollars are easily exchanged. ATM AVAILABILITY: Over 1,500 locations.

 MONEYGRAM: 800 11 120 then 800 592 3888.
WESTERN UNION: (2) 242 1742.

 AMEX: +44 1273 696933
DINERS CLUB: (58) (2) 5071440
MASTERCARD: 8001 2902
VISA: 8001 3355

AMEX: (1) 801 964 6665
THOMAS COOK: 1 800 223 7373
VISA: 1 800 732 1322

0830–1130 and 1400–1630 Mon to Fri.

Caters for all travellers and budgets.

Spanish. English, French, German and Portuguese.

Most pleasant time is from Jan–Apr. Rainy season is May–Dec.

Roman Catholic.

 1998: Jan 1; Feb 24; Mar 19; Apr 9–10, 19; May 1; June 24; July 5, 24; Oct 12; Nov 1; Dec 8, 25.
1999: Jan 1; Feb 24; Mar 19; Apr 1–2, 19; May 1; June 24; July 5, 24; Oct 12; Nov 1; Dec 8, 25.

 110 Volts AC 60 Hz American 2 pin type plugs are used.

 3–7 days to Europe. Internal mail can often take longer and surface mail to Europe may take up to one month.

 BBC: 15.90 11.75 11.74 7.325
VOA: 15.21 11.58 9.775 5.995

 Culture is a mixture of Latin, Caribbean and Spanish, all co-existing. In the interior traditional tribal rituals persist.

FLIGHTS: Connects all major centres and is regarded as the most convenient form of internal transport. NOTE: The services are in heavy demand and may be overbooked. Passengers are advised to confirm seats well in advance. ROAD: Between main cities are of a high standard. CAR HIRE: Available at the airport and in major cities but is expensive. DOCUMENTATION: IDP is required.

 Relatively safe when compared to neighbouring countries but theft is increasing. Caracas is by far the most dangerous place in the country. Care must be taken at night, avoid less busy areas. Use taxis where possible. There are several check-points so keep documents ready. Beach wear should be kept for the beach and pool side.

CAPITAL: Hanoi

GMT + 7

FROM UK: 84
IDD: Y to Hanoi and Ho Chi Min City.
OUTGOING CODE: International calls must be made though the operator.

Police: 13, Fire: 14, Ambulance: 15.

Embassy of the Socialist Republic of Vietnam, 12–14 Victoria Road, London W8 5RD. Tel: (0171) 937 1912. Fax: (0171) 937 6108.

British Embassy, 16 Pho Ly Thuong Kiet, Hanoi, Vietnam. Tel: (4) 261 151. Fax (4) 265 762.

Not present.

Vietnam Tourism, Ho Chi Minh City, Vietnam. Tel: (4) 829 4253.

Return Ticket Required. Requirements may change at short notice. Contact the embassy before departure.
VALID PASSPORT REQUIRED

Visa required.

Non prescribed drugs and pornography.

US$ 8 is levied on all foreign nationals.

POLIO, TYPHOID: R.
MALARIA: Exists in certain areas in the Falciparum variety, which has been reported being highly resistant to chloroquine.
YELLOW FEVER: A vaccination certificate is required for travellers arriving from infected areas.
OTHER: Bilharzia, Cholera, Japanese encephalitis, Plague, Rabies, TB.

W1

New Dong (D) = 100 hao. Exch: US$ is the most favoured currency. Limited acceptance of MasterCard and Visa. American Express and Thomas Cook traveller's cheques are accepted at hotels and banks. US dollars are the preferred currency.
ATM AVAILABILITY: 3 locations.

MONEYGRAM: Available in all major cities.
WESTERN UNION: Available.

AMEX: +44 1273 696933
DINERS CLUB: No local number.
MASTERCARD: 1 314 542 7111
VISA: (1) 410 581 9091

AMEX: (852) 885 9331
THOMAS COOK: +44 1733 318950
VISA: +44 1733 318949

0800–1630 Mon to Fri.

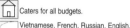
Caters for all budgets.

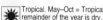
Vietnamese, French, Russian, English, Chinese.

Tropical. May–Oct = Tropical Monsoons. The remainder of the year is dry.

Buddhist, Taoist, Confucian, Hoa Hao, Caodist, Christian (mainly Roman Catholic.)

1998: Jan 1, 27–31; Apr 30; May 1; Sept 2.
1999: Jan 1, 27–31; Apr 30; May 1; Sept 2.

110/220 Volts AC 50 Hz.

Very slow usually taking up to 3 weeks Correspondence should be taken to the Post office individually, to minimise theft and tampering.

BBC: 15.36 11.95 9.740 6.195
VOA: 17.74 15.43 11.76 6.110.

Due to Vietnam's turbulent history, women's role varies from region to region.

FLIGHTS: Regular services operate between the main cities. RAIL: Longer distance trains are more reliable than shorter routes. ROAD: Reasonable road network but driving can be hair raising. DOCUMENTATION: An IDP and test taken in Vietnam is required. BUS: Services are poor and over crowded.

Some parts of the country are closed to visitors. Exercise caution if travelling in border areas.
Avoid wearing shorts. Footwear should be removed when entering Buddhist Pagodas. Vietnamese people should not be touched on the head. PHOTOGRAPHY: Restrictions apply at ports, airports and harbours. Be vigilant for street theft particularly of spectacles it is advisable to keep them on a cord around the neck..

CAPITAL: Sana'a

 GMT + 3.

 FROM UK: 967
IDD: Available in parts of the country.
OUTGOING CODE: 00

Not applicable.

Embassy of the Republic of Yemen, 57 Cromwell Road, London SW7 2ED. Tel: (0171) 584 6607. Fax: (0171) 589 3350.
British Embassy, PO Box 1287, 129 Haddah Road, Sana'a, Republic Of Yemen. Tel: (1) 264 081. Fax: (1) 263 059.

Not applicable.

 Yemen Tourist Company, PO Box 1526, Sana'a, Republic of Yemen. Tel: (1) 330 039.
Return Ticket required. Requirements may be subject to short-term change. Contact the relevant authority before departure.
VALID PASSPORT REQUIRED

 Visa required.

 Obscene literature and all products of Israeli origin.

US$10 on international departures.

 Holders of passports with Israeli visa stamps, valid or expired will be refused entry.

 POLIO, TYPHOID: R. MALARIA: Exists in the falciparum form throughout the year. Resistance to chloroquine has been reported. YELLOW FEVER: A vaccination certificate is required if coming from infected areas.
OTHER: Cholera, Bilharzia, Rabies.

 W1

 Yemeni Riyal is preferred (YR) = 100 fils, Yemeni Dinar is also in circulation. Import and export of local currency is limited to YAR 5000 or equivalent. Diners Club and Amex are widely accepted. Traveller's cheques can be exchanged in most banks and hotels. US dollars are the preferred currency.
ATM AVAILABILITY: Unavailable.

 MONEYGRAM: Single location in capital city.
WESTERN UNION: Unavailable.
AMEX: +44 1273 696933
DINERS CLUB: No longer number.
MASTERCARD: No local number
VISA: No local number

AMEX: (973) 256 834
THOMAS COOK: +44 1733 318950
VISA: +44 1733 318949

 0800–1200 Sat to Wed, 0800–1100 Thur.

 If you conform to traditional Yemeni lifestyle you can live relatively cheaply, but western food and en-suite facilities are expensive. Book all accommodation in advance.

Arabic and English.

 Climate varies according to altitude. Highland is warmer in summer. During winter (Oct–Mar) nights can be very cold in the mountains. Temperatures in the summer can be very high. The best time to visit is Oct–Apr.

 Sunni Muslim (especially in the North). Shia Muslim and small Christian communities.

 1998: Jan 30*; Apr 7, 28; May 1, 22; July 6, 7*; Sept 26; Oct 14; Nov 17, 30.
1999: Jan 30*; Apr 7, 28; May 1, 22; July 6, 7*; Sept 26; Oct 14; Nov 17, 30.

 220/230 volts AC, 50 Hz.

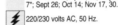 Airmail to Western Europe from Sana'a takes about 4 days, mail to and from other towns may take longer.

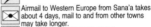 BBC: 15.57 15.07 12.09 9.410
VOA: 15.44 11.96 9.700 6.060

 Women are veiled and cannot visit Yemen without a male companion. Dress modestly and do not look or smile at local men.

 SEA: Local ferries connect ports. ROAD: The network is mainly limited to desert track. Use of 4-wheel drive vehicles with a guide is recommended. BUS: Regular intercity bus services. TAXI: Sharing taxis is the cheapest transport between cities. Negotiate fares beforehand. CAR HIRE: Available in main towns. DOCUMENTATION: IDP is required.

NOTE: The security situation in Yemen is improving though there remains the potential for instability. The risk of random kidnapping remains. All British travellers to Yemen should register with the British Embassy. Beachwear and shorts should be confined to the beach/pool. Smoking is forbidden in public during Ramadam. Where possible travel in organised groups with well-established tour agents. Armed theft of vehicles is common. There remains some danger from mines laid during the civil war in the Southern and Eastern Governances. Off-road travel is not recommended. Respect local sensitivities regarding religious sites.

CAPITAL: Belgrade

 GMT +1 (GMT + 2 during the summer).

 FROM UK: 381
IDD: Still available as part of the former Yugoslav federation.
OUTGOING CODE: 00

 Police: 92, Fire: 93, Ambulance: 94.

 Embassy of the Federal Republic of Yugoslavia, 5–7 Lexham Gardens, London W8 5JJ. Tel: (0171) 370 6105. Fax: (0171) 370 3838. Visa information: (0891) 600 279.
British Embassy, General Zdanova 46, 11000 Belgrade, Yugoslavia. Tel: (11) 235 1434 or 235 1465 or 235 1483. Fax: (11) 659 651.

 Currently not present in the UK.

Ministry of Commerce and Tourism, Nemanjina 22, 11000 Belgrade, Yugoslavia. Tel: (11) 658 755. Fax (11) 642 148.

 Return Ticket required. NOTE: Due to the current political situation, requirements may be subject to short-term change. Contact the relevant authority for up to date information.
VALID PASSPORT REQUIRED

 Visa required.

 Narcotics.

 YuD80 is payable on international departures.

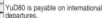 POLIO, TYPHOID: R.
OTHER: Rabies.

 W2

 New Yugoslav Dinar (Yu D) = 100 paras. German DM and US Dollars are the only currencies of value in the ex-Yugoslav Republics. Traveller's cheques and credit cards are not accepted.
ATM AVAILABILITY: Unavailable.

MONEYGRAM: Unavailable.
WESTERN UNION: Unavailable.

 AMEX: No local number
DINERS CLUB: No local number
MASTERCARD: No local number
VISA: No local number

 AMEX: No local number
THOMAS COOK: No local number
VISA: No local number

 0700–1500 Mon to Fri. Some branches are open on Sat for payment and withdrawals.

 Relatively cheap when compared with Western Europe. Limited commodities available outside Belgrade. Accommodation is sparce as a consequence of the civil war.

 Serbo-Croat. Albanian and Hungarian are also spoken in the autonomous regions of Kosovo and Vojvodina respectively.

 Serbia has a continental climate with cold winters and warm summers. Montenegro is mainly the same but with Alpine conditions in the mountains.

 Mostly Eastern Orthodox Serbs with a large Muslim ethnic Albanian minority (especially in the province of Kosovo) and a small Roman Catholic ethnic Hungarian minority (mainly located in the province of Vojvodina).

 1998: Jan 1, 2, 7; Mar 28; Apr 20, 27; May 1; July 7, 13; Nov 30; Dec 1.
1999: Jan 1, 2, 7; Mar 28; Apr 27; May 1; July 7, 13; Nov 30; Dec 1.

 220 volts AC, 50 Hz.

 Postal services between the former Yugoslav republics have been suspended. Postal services within Serbia are resonable.
BBC: 15.57 12.09 9.410 6.180
VOA: 9.760 6.040 1.197 0.792.

 Since Yugoslavia has divided, women have suffered all kinds of atrocities during the war and current xenophobia.

 RAIL: Internal rail services are generally poor, often overbooked and unreliable. ROAD: NOTE: Petrol stations may suffer shortages of fuel although the offer of hard currency may make otherwise rationed fuel available. Spare parts are difficult to obtain. COACH: Good, efficient services connect towns. DOCUMENTATION: Full national driving licence. Insurance and 'green card' also necessary.

HIGH RISK. Avoid travel to the border areas between Northwest Serbia and Croatia. Register with your Embassy when you arrive and inform them of any change of address. Contact the FCO Travel Advice Unit before finalising travel arrangements. Violent crime has increased and places all visitors in danger. Theft of cars is becoming a growing problem and personal theft is particularly common on trains. All currency brought into the country must be declared on arrival. Failure to do so can risk a fine and confiscation of all remaining cash on departure.

Zaire

CAPITAL: Kinshasa

 Kinshasa and Mbanaka GMT + 1. Haut Zaïre, Kasai, Kivu and Shaba GMT + 2

 FROM UK: 243   IDD: Y
OUTGOING CODE: 00

 Not present.

 Embassy of the Republic of Zaïre, 26 Chesham Place, London, SW1X 8TH. Tel: (0171) 235 6137. Fax: (0171) 235 9048.

 British Embassy, BP 8049, avenue de trois 'Z', Kinshasa-Gombe, Zaïre. Tel: (12) 34775/8. Consulates in Lubumbasi, Goma, Kisangani.

 Refer to the Embassy.

 Office Nationale du Tourisme, BP 9502, 2a/2b avenue des Orangers, Kinshasa-Gombe, Zaïre. Tel: (12) 30070.

 Return Ticket required. Requirements may change at short notice. Contact the embassy before departure.
VALID PASSPORT REQUIRED

 Visa required. Obtain prior to travel.

 Arms and ammunition require an import licence.

 Presently none, although this may change at short notice.

 POLIO, TYPHOID: R.
MALARIA: Exists all year round in the Falciparum variety throughout the country. Reported to be highly resistant to chloroquine.
YELLOW FEVER: A vaccination certificate is required for travellers over one year of age.
OTHER: Bilharzia, Cholera, Plague, Rabies.

 W1

 Zaïre (Z) = 100 makuta. Exch: There is a large market for exchanging money but this is illegal. NOTE: Import and export of local currency is prohibited. The purchase of airline tickets can only be made with officially exchanged money. All major credit cards are accepted on a limited basis in Kinshasa, only. Traveller's cheques are accepted in large towns and cities. US dollars are the preferred currency.
ATM AVAILABILITY: Unavailable.

 MONEYGRAM: Unavailable.
WESTERN UNION: Unavailable.

 AMEX: +44 1273 696933
DINERS CLUB: No longer number.
MASTERCARD: 1 314 542 7111
VISA: (1) 410 581 9091

 AMEX: +44 1273 571 600
THOMAS COOK: +44 1733 318950
VISA: +44 1733 318949

 0800–1130 Mon to Fri.

 All travellers are considered extremely wealthy by local people and will be charged accordingly.

 French and many local dialects.

 North: Dry season is Dec–Mar. South: Dry season is May–Oct. It can be humid throughout the year.

 Mainly Roman Catholic with Protestant and Animist minorities.

 1998: Jan 1, 4; May 1; June 24, 30; Aug 1; Oct 14, 27; Nov 17; Dec 25.
1999: Jan 1, 4; May 1; June 24, 30; Aug 1; Oct 14, 27; Nov 17; Dec 25.

 220 Volts AC 50 Hz.

 Post takes 4–18 days to reach Europe.

 BBC: 32.55 17.8 15.24 6.190
VOA: 21.49 15.60 9.55 6.035

 Due to the civil war and unrest women have been left as sole earners within the family unit.

 There are indefinite restrictions on tourist travel within Zaïre. Overland journeys by local public transport or foreign vehicle are forbidden. Nothing runs on time. Don't take any roads marked on a map as anything other than a possibility. ROADS: These are amongst the worst in Africa. DOCUMENTATION: IDP is recommended. RIVER: This is one of the best ways to travel, although can be unreliable due to river shortages.

 Eastern Zaire should be considered a war zone. Tourists, if they must to travel to Zaire should restrict themselves to the capital city. A permit is required to take photos on Zaïrean river boats.

CAPITAL: Lusaka

GMT + 2

FROM UK: 260   IDD: Y
OUTGOING CODE: 00

All services: 1 2 25067/254798.

High Commission for the Republic of Zambia.
2 Palace Gate, London W8 5NG. Tel: (0171)
589 6655. Fax: (0171) 581 1353.

British High Commission, PO Box 50050,
Independence Avenue 15101 Ridgeway,
Lusaka, Zambia. Tel: (1) 251 133. Fax: (1)
253 798.

Refer to the High Commission.

Zambia National Tourist Board, PO Box
30017, Century House, Cairo Road, Lusaka,
Zambia. Tel: (1) 229 087.

Return Ticket required. Requirements may
change at short notice. Contact the embassy
before departure.
VALID PASSPORT REQUIRED

Visa not required by Nationals of Ireland and
the UK.

US$20. Transit passengers are exempt.

POLIO, TYPHOID: R.
MALARIA: Exists in the Falciparum variety
throughout the whole country al year.
Resistance to chloroquine has been reported.
YELLOW FEVER: Vaccination is strongly
recommended to all travellers. Those arriving
from infected areas will require a vaccination
certificate.
OTHER: Bilharzia, Cholera and Rabies.

W1

Kwacha (K) = 100 ngwee. Exch: only at
authorised banks and bureaux de changes.
NOTE: Import and export of local currency is
limited to K100. Currency exchange forms
must be shown if purchasing airline tickets in
Zambia. American Express is widely accepted, with other credit cards less so.Traveller's
cheques are widely accepted. US dollars are
the preferred currency.
ATM AVAILABILITY: Unavailable.

MONEYGRAM: Unavailable.
WESTERN UNION: Unavailable.

AMEX: +44 1273 696933
DINERS CLUB: No local number
MASTERCARD: No local number
VISA: No local number

AMEX: +44 1273 571 600
THOMAS COOK: +44 1733 318950
VISA: +44 1733 318949

0815–1430 Mon to Fri.

High inflation means that prices for tourists
tend to be expensive.

English and over 73 local dialects.

High altitudes prevents the temperatures
becoming too hot. The winter is cool and dry
from May–Sept. The weather is hot and dry
from Oct–Nov and the hot rainy season is
Dec–Apr.

Mainly Christian with Animist, Muslim and
Hindu minority.

1998: Jan 1; Mar 12; Apr, 10. 11, 13; May 1,
25; July 6, 7; Aug 3; Oct 24; Dec 25.
1999: Jan 1; Mar 12; Apr, 2, 4, 5; May 1, 25;
July 6, 7; Aug 3; Oct 24; Dec 25.

220 Volts, AC, 50 Hz.

7–14 days to Europe.

BBC: 17.88 15.42 11.94 3.255
VOA: 21.49 15.60 9.525 6.035

Patriarchal society prevails.

FLIGHTS: There are over 127 airstrips in the
country and several charter companies operate domestic flights. ROADS: A good network exists but they ban be dangerous in the
rainy season. DOCUMENTATION: IDP is
recommended. BUS: Services are often
unreliable and can be very overcrowded.
RAIL: Trains serve Lusaka, Ndola, Kitwe and
Mulobezi. Local services are limited.

Travellers to remote area will be met with
curiosity. Particular care should be taken in
these areas. African culture and traditions
dominate. Traditional dancing is popular
throughout the country and many colourful
annual ceremonies take place.

Zimbabwe

CAPITAL: Harare

 GMT + 2

 FROM UK: 263   IDD: Y
OUTGOING CODE: 110

 Police: 995, Ambulance: 994, Fire: 993,
General emergencies: 999.

 High Commission for the Republic of
Zimbabwe, Zimbabwe House, 429 Strand,
London WC2R 0SA. Tel: (0171) 836 7755.
Fax: (0171) 379 1167.

 British High Commission, PO Box 4490,
Stanley House, Jason Moyo Avenue, Harare,
Zimbabwe. Tel: (4) 793 781. Fax (4) 728 380.

 Address as High Commission.

 Zimbabwe Tourist Development Corporation
(ZTDC), PO Box 8052, corner of Jason Moyo
Avenue and Fourth Street, Causeway,
Harare, Zimbabwe. Tel: (4) 793 666. Fax: (4)
793 669.

 Return Ticket required. Requirements may
change at short notice. Contact the embassy
before departure.
VALID PASSPORT REQUIRED BY ALL:
with at least 6 months from date of entry.

 Visa not required by Nationals of EU
countries

 Indecent film and publications, various food
products, various agricultural products, birds
and bee keeping equipment.
Departure tax of US$ 20 for non-residents, or
Z$ 20 for residents.

 POLIO, TYPHOID: R. MALARIA: Exists in
certain areas throughout the year in the
Falciparum variety. Resistance to chloroquine
has been reported. YELLOW FEVER: A vaccination certificate is required for travellers
arriving from infected areas. OTHER:
Bilharzia, Cholera and Rabies.

W1

Zimbabwe Dollar (Z$) = 100 cents. Exch:
Major currencies at hotels and banks.. Import
and export of local currency is limited to
Z$250. American Express, Diners Club and
Visa are widely accepted. Banks and major
hotels will exchange Traveller's cheques.US
dollars are the preferred form of currency.
ATM AVAILABILITY: Over 75 locations.

 MONEYGRAM: Unavailable
WESTERN UNION: Available.

 AMEX: +44 1273 696933
DINERS CLUB: No longer number.
MASTERCARD: No local number
VISA: (1) 410 581 9091

 AMEX: +44 1273 571 600
THOMAS COOK: +44 1733 318950
VISA: +44 1733 318949

 0800–1500 Mon, Tues, Thur and Fri.
0800–1300 Wed and 0800–1130 Sat.

 Lower prices can be found away from the
tourist centres if you are willing to live simply.

 English, Shona and Ndebele.

 Sept–Oct is hot, dry season. Rainy season is
Nov to Mar. Best time to visit is Apr–May and
Aug–Sept.

 Christianity, Hindu and Muslim minorities.
Traditional beliefs in rural areas.

 1998: Jan 1; Apr 10, 11, 13, 18; May 1, 25;
Aug 11, 12; Dec 22, 25, 26.
1999: Jan 1; Apr 2, 3, 5, 18; May 1, 25; Aug
11, 12; Dec 22, 25, 26.

 220/240 Volts AC, 50 Hz.

 Up to 1 week to Europe by airmail.

 BBC: 17.88 11.94 6.190 3.255
VOA: 11.97 9.670 6.040 5.995

 Although apartheid has ceased in, some
racism still persists in Zimbabwe.

 FLIGHTS: Domestic flights run between the
main cities. ROADS: Excellent road network.
DOCUMENTATION: IDP and vehicle identification required. BUS: Services in most parts
of the country. NOTE: If you are white and
use the bus you may provoke attention.
RAIL: Daily between the main cities.

Urban culture in Zimbabwe is greatly influenced by Western culture and education, but
in rural areas traditional values continue.
Casual dress is suitable for daytime, but
jackets and ties are expected in smart hotels
and restaurants.
Petty crime is prevalent in Harare.
Backpackers are at risk in the main tourist
areas.

DISTANCES (approx. conversions)

1 kilometre (km) = 1000 metres (m) 1 metre = 100 centimetres (cm)

Metric	Imperial/US	Metric	Imperial/US	Metric	Imperial/US	Metric	Imperial/US
m	ft in	km	miles	km	miles	km	miles
0.01 (1cm)	3/8	0.75	0.50	20	12.43	200	124.27
0.50 (50cm)	1 8	1	0.62	30	18.64	300	186.41
1	3 3	2	1.24	40	24.85	400	248.45
2	6 6	3	1.86	50	31.07	500	310.69
3	10 0	4	2.49	60	37.28	600	372.82
4	13 0	5	3.10	70	43.50	700	434.96
5	16 6	6	3.73	80	49.71	800	497.10
7	23 0	7	4.35	90	55.92	900	559.23
9	29 0	8	4.97	100	62.14	1000	621.37
10 (11yd)	33 0	9	5.59	125	77.67	1100	683.54
20 (22yd)	66 0	10	6.21	150	93.21	1200	745.68
50 (54yd)	164 0	15	9.32	175	108.74	1300	807.82
100 (110yd)	330 0					1400	869.96
200 (220yd)	660 0					1500	932.10
300 (330yd)	984 0					2000	1242.74
500 (550yd)	1640 0					3000	1864.11

1 kilometre = 0.6214 miles
1 mile = 1.609 kilometres

LADIES' CLOTHES

UK	France	Italy	Rest of Europe	US
10	36	38	34	8
12	38	40	36	10
14	40	42	38	12
16	42	44	40	14
18	44	46	42	16
20	46	48	44	18

TEMPERATURE

°C	°F	°C	°F	°C	°F	°C	°F
-20	-4	-5	23	10	50	25	77
-15	5	0	32	15	59	30	86
-10	14	5	41	20	68	35	95

FLUID MEASURES

Litres	Imp.gal.	US gal.	Litres	Imp.gal.	US gal.
5	1.1	1.3	30	6.6	7.8
10	2.2	2.6	35	7.7	9.1
15	3.3	3.9	40	8.8	10.4
20	4.4	5.2	45	9.9	11.7
25	5.5	6.5	50	11.0	13.0

MENS' CLOTHES

UK	Europe	US
36	46	36
38	48	38
40	50	40
42	52	42
44	54	44
46	56	46

MENS' SHIRTS

UK	Europe	US
14	36	14
15	38	15
15½	39	15½
16	41	16
16½	42	16½
17	43	17

WEIGHT

Kg	lbs	Kg	lbs	Kg	lbs
1	2¼	5	11	25	55
2	4½	10	22	50	11
3	6½	15	33	75	165
4	9	20	45	100	220

MENS' SHOES

UK	Europe	US
6	40	7
7	41	8
8	42	9
9	43	10
10	44	11
11	45	12

LADIES' SHOES

UK	Europe	US
3	36	4½
4	37	5½
5	38	6½
6	39	7½
7	40	8½
8	41	9½

24 HOUR CLOCK

0000	=	Midnight	1415	=	2.15 pm
0600	=	6.00 am	1645	=	4.45 pm
0715	=	7.15 am	1800	=	6.00 pm
0930	=	9.30 am	2000	=	8.00 pm
1200	=	Noon	2110	=	9.10 pm
1300	=	1.00 pm	2345	=	11.45 pm

This index details the subjects covered in this book. As the Directory section lists countries in alphabetical order, these have not been included. However, a few countries may be more familiar by another name or might be difficult to find, so these are given below for ease of reference.

Country

Your Feedback . . .

Please return comments to:

The Project Editor, World Wise
Thomas Cook Publishing, PO Box 227
Thorpe Wood, Peterborough PE3 6PU, United Kingdom

Your Feedback . . .

Country

Your Feedback . . .

Please return comments to:

The Project Editor, World Wise
Thomas Cook Publishing, PO Box 227
Thorpe Wood, Peterborough PE3 6PU, United Kingdom

Country

Your Feedback . . .

Please return comments to:

The Project Editor, World Wise
Thomas Cook Publishing, PO Box 227
Thorpe Wood, Peterborough PE3 6PU, United Kingdom

Your Feedback . . .

Country

Your Feedback . . .

Please return comments to:

The Project Editor, World Wise
Thomas Cook Publishing, PO Box 227
Thorpe Wood, Peterborough PE3 6PU, United Kingdom

Your Feedback . . .

Country

Your Feedback . . .

Country

Your Feedback . . .

Please return comments to:

The Project Editor, World Wise
Thomas Cook Publishing, PO Box 227
Thorpe Wood, Peterborough PE3 6PU, United Kingdom

Your Feedback . . .

Country

Your Feedback . . .

Please return comments to:

The Project Editor, World Wise
Thomas Cook Publishing, PO Box 227
Thorpe Wood, Peterborough PE3 6PU, United Kingdom

Your Feedback . . .

Country

Your Feedback . . .

Please return comments to:

The Project Editor, World Wise
Thomas Cook Publishing, PO Box 227
Thorpe Wood, Peterborough PE3 6PU, United Kingdom

Your Feedback . . .